D1483327

CONTEMPORARY RESEARCH IN PHILOSOPHICAL LOGIC
AND LINGUISTIC SEMANTICS

THE UNIVERSITY OF WESTERN ONTARIO
SERIES IN PHILOSOPHY OF SCIENCE

A SERIES OF BOOKS

ON PHILOSOPHY OF SCIENCE, METHODOLOGY,

AND EPISTEMOLOGY

PUBLISHED IN CONNECTION WITH

THE UNIVERSITY OF WESTERN ONTARIO

PHILOSOPHY OF SCIENCE PROGRAMME

VOLUME 4

CONTEMPORARY RESEARCH
IN PHILOSOPHICAL LOGIC
AND LINGUISTIC SEMANTICS

PROCEEDINGS OF A CONFERENCE
HELD AT THE UNIVERSITY OF WESTERN ONTARIO,
LONDON, CANADA

Edited by

D. HOCKNEY, W. HARPER, AND B. FREED

D. REIDEL PUBLISHING COMPANY

DORDRECHT-HOLLAND / BOSTON-U.S.A.

Library of Congress Cataloging in Publication Data

Main entry under title:

Contemporary research in philosophical logic and linguistic semantics.

(The University of Western Ontario series in philosophy of science ;
    v. 4)
    Includes bibliographies.
    1. Semantics—Congresses. 2. Generative grammar—
Congresses. 3. Logic—Congresses. I. Hockney, D. J., ed.
II. Harper, William, ed. III. Freed, B., ed. IV. Series: London,
Ont. University of Western Ontario. Series in philosophy of science ;
v. 4.
P39.C65   1975   415   74–34079
ISBN 90–277–0511–9
ISBN 90–277–0512–7 pbk.

Published by D. Reidel Publishing Company,
P.O. Box 17, Dordrecht, Holland

Sold and distributed in the U.S.A., Canada, and Mexico
by D. Reidel Publishing Company, Inc.
306 Dartmouth Street, Boston,
Mass. 02116, U.S.A.

TABLE OF CONTENTS

59187

PREFACE

In 1973 a workshop was held at The University of Western Ontario on topics of common interest to philosophers and linguists. This volume contains most of the papers presented at the workshop. Also included are previously unpublished essays by R. Dougherty and H. Lasnik as well as a comment on G. Lakoff's paper by B. van Fraassen. K. Donnellan's paper was presented at the workshop and subsequently appeared in *The Philosophical Review*. We thank the editors of this journal for permission to publish the paper here. The papers by D. Lewis, R. Stalnaker, G. Lakoff, B. Partee and H. Herzberger appeared earlier in *Journal of Philosophical Logic* by arrangement of the editors with B. van Fraassen and D. Reidel Publishing Company.

The editors thank the officers of The University of Western Ontario for making the workshop possible and Pauline Campbell for making the workshop work.

THE EDITORS

DAVID LEWIS

COUNTERFACTUALS AND COMPARATIVE POSSIBILITY*

In the last dozen years or so, our understanding of modality has been much improved by means of possible-world semantics: the project of analyzing modal language by systematically specifying the conditions under which a modal sentence is true at a possible world. I hope to do the same for counterfactual conditionals. I write $A \square \rightarrow C$ for the counterfactual conditional with antecedent A and consequent C. It may be read as 'If it were the case that A, then it would be the case that C' or some more idiomatic paraphrase thereof.

1. ANALYSES

I shall lead up by steps to an analysis I believe to be satisfactory.

ANALYSIS 0. $A \square \rightarrow C$ *is true at world i iff C holds at every A-world such that* —. 'A-world', of course, means 'world where A holds'.

The blank is to be filled in with some sort of condition restricting the A-worlds to be considered. The condition may depend on i but not on A. For instance, we might consider only those A-worlds that agree with i in certain specified respects. On this analysis, the counterfactual is some fixed strict conditional.

No matter what condition we put into the blank, Analysis 0 cannot be correct. For it says that if $A \square \rightarrow \bar{B}$ is true at i, $\bar{B}$ holds at every A-world such that —. In other words, there are no AB-worlds such that —. Then $AB \square \rightarrow \bar{C}$ and $AB \square \rightarrow C$ are alike vacuously true, and $-(AB \square \rightarrow C)$ and $-(AB \square \rightarrow \bar{C})$ are alike false, for any C whatever. On the contrary: it can perfectly well happen that $A \square \rightarrow \bar{B}$ is true, yet $AB \square \rightarrow \bar{C}$ is non-vacuous, and $AB \square \rightarrow C$ is false. In fact, we can have an arbitrarily long sequence like this of non-vacuously true counterfactuals and true denials of their opposites:

$$A \square \rightarrow \bar{B} \quad \text{and} \quad -(A \square \rightarrow B),$$
$$AB \square \rightarrow \bar{C} \quad \text{and} \quad -(AB \square \rightarrow C),$$

Hockney et al. (eds.), Contemporary Research in Philosophical Logic and Linguistic Semantics, 1–29. *All Rights Reserved*

$$ABC \,\square\!\!\rightarrow \bar{D} \quad \text{and} \quad -(ABC \,\square\!\!\rightarrow D),$$
etc.

Example: if Albert had come to the party, he would not have brought Betty; for, as he knows, if he had come and had brought Betty, Carl would not have stayed; for, as Carl knows, if Albert had come and had brought Betty and Carl had stayed, Daisy would not have danced with him; ... Each step of the sequence is a counterexample to Analysis 0. The counterfactual is not any strict conditional whatever.

Analysis 0 also says that $A\,\square\!\!\rightarrow C$ implies $AB\,\square\!\!\rightarrow C$. If C holds at every A-world such that —, then C holds at such of those worlds as are B-worlds. On the contrary: we can have an arbitrarily long sequence like this of non-vacuously true counterfactuals and true denials of their opposites:

$$A \,\square\!\!\rightarrow \bar{Z} \quad \text{and} \quad -(A \,\square\!\!\rightarrow Z),$$
$$AB \,\square\!\!\rightarrow Z \quad \text{and} \quad -(AB \,\square\!\!\rightarrow \bar{Z}),$$
$$ABC \,\square\!\!\rightarrow \bar{Z} \quad \text{and} \quad -(ABC \,\square\!\!\rightarrow Z),$$
etc.

Example: if I had shirked my duty, no harm would have ensued; but if I had and you had too, harm would have ensued; but if I had and you had too and a third person had done far more than his duty, no harm would have ensued... For this reason also the counterfactual is not any strict conditional whatever.

More precisely, it is not any one, fixed strict conditional. But this much of Analysis 0 is correct: (1) to assess the truth of a counterfactual we must consider whether the consequent holds at certain antecedent-worlds; (2) we should not consider all antecedent-worlds, but only some of them. We may ignore antecedent-worlds that are gratuitously remote from actuality.

Rather than any fixed strict conditional, we need a *variably strict conditional*. Given a far-fetched antecedent, we look perforce at antecedent-worlds remote from actuality. There are no others to look at. But given a less far-fetched antecedent, we can afford to be more fastidious and ignore the very same worlds. In considering the supposition 'if I had just let go of my pen...' I will go wrong if I consider bizarre worlds where the law of gravity is otherwise than it actually is; whereas in considering the supposition 'if the planets traveled in spirals...' I will go just as wrong if I ignore such worlds.

It is this variable strictness that accounts for our counter-example sequences. It may happen that we can find an A-world that meets some stringent restriction; before we can find any AB-world we must relax the restriction; before we can find any ABC-world we must relax it still more; and so on. If so a counterexample sequence of the first kind definitely will appear, and one of the second kind will appear also if there is a suitable Z.

We dream of considering a world where the antecedent holds but everything else is just as it actually is, the truth of the antecedent being the one difference between that world and ours. No hope. Differences never come singly, but in infinite multitudes. Take, if you can, a world that differs from ours *only* in that Caesar did not cross the Rubicon. Are his predicament and ambitions there just as they actually are? The regularities of his character? The psychological laws exemplified by his decision? The orders of the day in his camp? The preparation of the boats? The sound of splashing oars? Hold *everything* else fixed after making one change, and you will not have a possible world at all.

If we cannot have an antecedent-world that is otherwise just like our world, what can we have? This, perhaps: an antecedent-world that does not differ gratuitously from ours; one that differs only as much as it must to permit the antecedent to hold; one that is closer to our world in similarity, all things considered, than any other antecedent world. Here is a first analysis of the counterfactual as a variably strict conditional.

ANALYSIS 1. *$A \square \!\!\rightarrow C$ is true at i iff C holds at the closest (accessible) A-world to i, if there is one.* This is Robert Stalnaker's proposal in 'A Theory of Conditionals', *Studies in Logical Theory* (*A.P.Q.* supplementary monograph series, 1968), and elsewhere.

It may be objected that Analysis 1 is founded on comparative similarity – 'closeness' – of worlds, and that comparative similarity is hopelessly imprecise unless some definite respect of comparison has been specified. Imprecise it may be; but that is all to the good. Counterfactuals are imprecise too. Two imprecise concepts may be rigidly fastened to one another, swaying together rather than separately, and we can hope to be precise about their connection. Imprecise though comparative similarity may be, we *do* judge the comparative similarity of complicated things like cities or people or philosophies – and we do it often without benefit of any definite respect of comparison stated in advance. We balance off various similarities and dissimilarities according to the importances we attach to various respects of comparison and according to the degrees of similarity in the various respects. Conversational context, of course, greatly affects our weighting of respects of comparison, and even in a fixed context we have plenty of latitude. Still, not anything goes. We have concordant mutual expectations, mutual expectations of expectations, etc., about the relative importances we will attach to respects of comparison. Often these are definite and accurate and firm enough to resolve the imprecision of comparative similarity to the point where we can converse without misunderstanding. Such imprecision we can live with. Still, I grant that a counterfactual based on comparative similarity has no place in the language of the exact sciences.

I imposed a restriction to A-worlds 'accessible' from i. In this I follow Stalnaker, who in turn is following the common practice in modal logic. We might think that there are some worlds so very remote from i that they should always be ignored (at i) even if some of them happen to be A-worlds and there are no closer A-worlds. If so, we have the wherewithal to ignore them by deeming them *inaccessible* from i. I can think of no very convincing cases, but I prefer to remain neutral on the point. If we have no need for accessibility restrictions, we can easily drop them by stipulating that all worlds are mutually interaccessible.

Unfortunately, Analysis 1 depends on a thoroughly implausible assumption: that there will never be more than one closest A-world. So fine are the gradations of comparative similarity that despite the infinite number and variety of worlds every tie is broken.

Example: A is 'Bizet and Verdi are compatriots', F is 'Bizet and Verdi are French', I is 'Bizet and Verdi are Italian'. Grant for the sake of argument that we have the closest F-world and the closest I-world; that these are distinct (dual citizenships would be a gratuitous difference from actuality); and that these are the two finalists in the competition for closest A-world. It might be that something favors one over the other – for all I know, Verdi narrowly escaped settling in France and Bizet did not narrowly escape settling in Italy. But we can count on no such luck. The case may be perfectly balanced between respects of comparison that favor the F-world and respects that favor the I-world. It is out of the question, on

Analysis 1, to leave the tie unbroken. That means there is no such thing as *the* closest *A*-world. Then anything you like holds at the closest *A*-world if there is one, because there isn't one. If Bizet and Verdi had been compatriots they would have been Ukranian.

ANALYSIS 2. *$A \square \rightarrow C$ is true at i iff C holds at every closest (accessible) A-world to i, if there are any.* This is the obvious revision of Stalnaker's analysis to permit a tie in comparative similarity between several equally close closest *A*-worlds.

Under Analysis 2 unbreakable ties are no problem. The case of Bizet and Verdi comes out as follows. $A \square \rightarrow F$, $A \square \rightarrow \bar{F}$, $A \square \rightarrow I$, and $A \square \rightarrow \bar{I}$ are all false. $A \square \rightarrow (F \vee I)$ and $A \square \rightarrow (\bar{F} \vee \bar{I})$ are both true. $A \square \rightarrow FI$ and $A \square \rightarrow \bar{F}\bar{I}$ are both false. These conclusions seem reasonable enough.

This reasonable settlement, however, does not sound so good in words. $A \square \rightarrow F$ and $A \square \rightarrow \bar{F}$ are both false, so we want to assert their negations. But negate their English readings in any straightforward and natural way, and we do not get $-(A \square \rightarrow F)$ and $-(A \square \rightarrow \bar{F})$ as desired. Rather the negation moves in and attaches only to the consequent, and we get sentences that seem to mean $A \square \rightarrow \bar{F}$ and $A \square \rightarrow \bar{\bar{F}}$ – a pair of falsehoods, together implying the further falsehood that Bizet and Verdi could not have been compatriots; and exactly the opposite of what we meant to say.

Why is it so hard to negate a whole counterfactual, as opposed to negating the consequent? The defender of Analysis 1 is ready with an explanation. Except when *A* is impossible, he says, there is a unique closest *A*-world. Either *C* is false there, making $-(A \square \rightarrow C)$ and $A \square \rightarrow \bar{C}$ alike true, or *C* is true there, making them alike false. Either way, the two agree. We have no need of a way to say $-(A \square \rightarrow C)$ because we might as well say $A \square \rightarrow \bar{C}$ instead (except when *A* is impossible, in which case we have no need of a way to say $-(A \square \rightarrow C)$ because it is false).

There is some appeal to the view that $-(A \square \rightarrow C)$ and $A \square \rightarrow \bar{C}$ are equivalent (except when *A* is impossible) and we might be tempted thereby to return to Analysis 1. We might do better to return only part way, using Bas van Fraassen's method of supervaluations to construct a compromise between Analyses 1 and 2.

ANALYSIS 1½. *$A \square \rightarrow C$ is true at i iff C holds at a certain arbitrarily chosen one of the closest (accessible) A-worlds to i, if there are any. A sen-*

tence is super-true iff it is true no matter how the arbitrary choices are made, super-false iff false no matter how the arbitrary choices are made. Otherwise it has no super-truth value. Unless a particular arbitrary choice is under discussion, we abbreviate 'super-true' as 'true', and so on. Something of this kind is mentioned at the end of Richmond Thomason, 'A Fitch-Style Formulation of Conditional Logic', *Logique et Analyse* 1970.

Analysis $1\frac{1}{2}$ agrees with Analysis 1 about the equivalence (except when A is impossible) of $-(A \square \rightarrow C)$ and $A \square \rightarrow \bar{C}$. If there are accessible A-worlds, the two agree in truth (i.e. super-truth) value, and further their biconditional is (super-)true. On the other hand, Analysis $1\frac{1}{2}$ tolerates ties in comparative similarity as happily as Analysis 2. Indeed a counterfactual is (super-)true under Analysis $1\frac{1}{2}$ iff it is true under Analysis 2. On the other hand, a counterfactual false under Analysis 2 may either be false or have no (super-)truth under Analysis $1\frac{1}{2}$. The case of Bizet and -Verdi comes out as follows: $A \square \rightarrow F, A \square \rightarrow \bar{F}, A \square \rightarrow I, A \square \rightarrow \bar{I}$, and their negations have no truth value. $A \square \rightarrow (F \vee I)$ and $A \square \rightarrow (\bar{F} \vee \bar{I})$ are (super-)true. $A \square \rightarrow FI$ and $A \square \rightarrow \bar{F}\bar{I}$ are (super-)false.

This seems good enough. For all I have said yet, Analysis $1\frac{1}{2}$ solves the problem of ties as well as Analysis 2, provided we're not too averse to (super-) truth value gaps. But now look again at the question how to deny a counterfactual. We have a way after all: to deny a 'would' counterfactual, use a 'might' counterfactual with the same antecedent and negated consequent. In reverse likewise: to deny a 'might' counterfactual, use a 'would' counterfactual with the same antecedent and negated consequent. Writing $A \diamond \rightarrow C$ for 'If it were the case that A, then it might be the case that C' or some more idiomatic paraphrase, we have these valid-sounding equivalences:

(1) $- (A \square \rightarrow C)$ is equivalent to $A \diamond \rightarrow \bar{C}$,
(2) $- (A \diamond \rightarrow C)$ is equivalent to $A \square \rightarrow \bar{C}$.

The two equivalences yield an explicit definition of 'might' from 'would' counterfactuals:

$$A \diamond \rightarrow C =^{df} - (A \square \rightarrow \bar{C});$$

or, if we prefer, the dual definition of 'would' from 'might'. According to this definition and Analysis 2, $A \diamond \rightarrow C$ is true at i iff C holds at some closest (accessible) A-world to i. In the case of Bizet and Verdi, $A \diamond \rightarrow F$,

$A\Diamond\!\!\rightarrow\!\bar{F}$, $A\Diamond\!\!\rightarrow\!I$, $A\Diamond\!\!\rightarrow\!\bar{I}$ are all true; so are $A\Diamond\!\!\rightarrow\!(F\vee I)$ and $A\Diamond\!\!\rightarrow\!(\bar{F}\vee\bar{I})$; but $A\Diamond\!\!\rightarrow\!FI$ and $A\Diamond\!\!\rightarrow\!\bar{F}\bar{I}$ are false.

According to the definition and Analysis 1 or $1\frac{1}{2}$, on the other hand, $A\Diamond\!\!\rightarrow\!C$ and $A\Box\!\!\rightarrow\!C$ are equivalent except when A is impossible. That should put the defender of those analyses in an uncomfortable spot. He cannot very well claim that 'would' and 'might' counterfactuals do not differ except when the antecedent is impossible. He must therefore reject my definition of the 'might' counterfactual; and with it, the equivalences (1) and (2), uncontroversial though they sound. He then owes us some other account of the 'might' counterfactual, which I do not think he can easily find. Finally, once we see that we do have a way to negate a whole counterfactual, we no longer appreciate his explanation of why we don't need one. I conclude that he would be better off moving at least to Analysis 2.

Unfortunately, Analysis 2 is not yet satisfactory. Like Analysis 1, it depends on an implausible assumption. Given that some A-world is accessible from i, we no longer assume that there must be *exactly* one closest A-world to i; but we still assume that there must be *at least* one. I call this the *Limit Assumption*. It is the assumption that as we proceed to closer and closer A-worlds we eventually hit a limit and can go no farther. But why couldn't it happen that there are closer and closer A-worlds without end – for each one, another even closer to i? Example: A is 'I am over 7 feet tall'. If there are closest A-worlds to ours, pick one of them: how tall am I there? I must be $7+\varepsilon$ feet tall, for some positive ε, else it would not be an A-world. But there are A-worlds where I am only $7+\varepsilon/2$ feet tall. Since that is closer to my actual height, why isn't one of these worlds closer to ours than the purportedly closest A-world where I am $7+\varepsilon$ feet tall? And why isn't a suitable world where I am only $7+\varepsilon/4$ feet even closer to ours, and so ad infinitum? (In special cases, but not in general, there may be a good reason why not. Perhaps $7+\varepsilon$ could have been produced by a difference in one gene, whereas any height below that but still above 7 would have taken differences in many genes.) If there are A-worlds closer and closer to i without end, then any consequent you like holds at every closest A-world to i, because there aren't any. If I were over 7 feet tall I would bump my head on the sky.

ANALYSIS 3. $A\Box\!\!\rightarrow\!C$ *is true at i iff some (accessible) AC-world is closer* *to i than any $A\bar{C}$-world, if there are any (accessible) A-worlds*. This is my final analysis.

Analysis 3 looks different from Analysis 1 or 2, but it is similar in principle. Whenever there are closest (accessible) A-worlds to a given world, Analyses 2 and 3 agree on the truth value there of $A\,\square\!\!\rightarrow C$. They agree also, of course, when there are no (accessible) A-worlds. When there are closer and closer A-worlds without end, $A\,\square\!\!\rightarrow C$ is true iff, as we proceed to closer and closer A-worlds, we eventually leave all the $A\bar{C}$-worlds behind and find only AC-worlds.

Using the definition of $A\,\Diamond\!\!\rightarrow C$ as $-(A\,\square\!\!\rightarrow \bar{C})$, we have this derived truth condition for the 'might' counterfactual: $A\,\Diamond\!\!\rightarrow C$ is true at i iff for every (accessible) $A\bar{C}$-world there is some AC-world at least as close to i, and there are (accessible) A-worlds.

We have discarded two assumptions about comparative similarity in going from Analysis 1 to Analysis 3: first Stalnaker's assumption of uniqueness, then the Limit Assumption. What assumptions remain?

First, the *Ordering Assumption*: that for each world i, comparative similarity to i yields a *weak ordering* of the worlds accessible from i. That is, writing $j\leqslant_i k$ to mean that k is not closer to i than j, each $\leqslant_i$ is *connected* and *transitive*. Whenever j and k are accessible from i either $j\leqslant_i k$ or $k\leqslant_i j$; whenever $h\leqslant_i j$ and $j\leqslant_i k$, then $h\leqslant_i k$. It is convenient, if somewhat artificial, to extend the comparative similarity orderings to encompass also the inaccessible worlds, if any: we stipulate that each $\leqslant_i$ is to be a weak ordering of *all* the worlds, and that j is closer to i than k whenever j is accessible from i and k is not. (Equivalently: whenever $j\leqslant_i k$, then if k is accessible from i so is j.)

Second, the *Centering Assumption*: that each world i is accessible from itself, and closer to itself than any other world is to it.

2. REFORMULATIONS

Analysis 3 can be given several superficially different, but equivalent, reformulations.

2.1. *Comparative Possibility*

Introduce a connective $\prec$. $A\prec B$ is read as 'It is less remote from actuality that A than that B' or 'It is more possible that A than that B' and is true at a world i iff some (accessible) A-world is closer to i than is any B-world. First a pair of modalities and then the counterfactual can be defined from this new connective of comparative possibility, as follows. (Let $\perp$ be a sentential constant false at every world, or an arbitrarily chosen contradiction; later, let $\top =^{df} - \perp$.)

$$\Diamond A =^{df} A \prec \perp; \quad \Box A =^{df} - \Diamond - A;$$
$$A \;\Box\!\!\rightarrow\; C =^{df} \Diamond A \supset (AC \prec A\bar{C}).$$

The modalities so defined are interpreted by means of accessibility in the usual way. $\Diamond A$ is true at i iff some A-world is accessible from i, and $\Box A$ is true at i iff A holds throughout all the worlds accessible from i. If accessibility restrictions are discarded, so that all worlds are mutually interaccessible, they became the ordinary 'logical' modalities. (We might rather have defined the two modalities and comparative possibility from the counterfactual.

$$\Box A =^{df} \bar{A} \;\Box\!\!\rightarrow\; \perp; \quad \Diamond A =^{df} - \Box - A;$$
$$A \prec B =^{df} \Diamond A \,\&\, ((A \vee B) \;\Box\!\!\rightarrow\; A\bar{B}).$$

Either order of definitions is correct according to the given truth conditions.)

Not only is comparative possibility technically convenient as a primitive; it is of philosophical interest for its own sake. It sometimes seems true to say: It is possible that A but not that B, it is possible that B but not that C, C but not that D, etc. Example: A is 'I speak English', B is 'I speak German' (a language I know), C is 'I speak Finnish', D is 'A dog speaks Finnish', E is 'A stone speaks Finnish', F is 'A number speaks Finnish'. Perhaps if I say all these things, as I would like to, I am equivocating – shifting to weaker and weaker noncomparative senses of 'possible' from clause to clause. It is by no means clear that there are enough distinct senses to go around. As an alternative hypothesis, perhaps the clauses are compatible comparsions of possibility without equivocation: $A \prec B \prec C \prec D \prec E \prec F$. (Here and elsewhere, I compress conjunctions in the obvious way.)

2.2. Cotenability

Call B *cotenable* at i with the supposition that A iff some A-world accessible from i is closer to i than any $\bar{B}$-world, or if there are no A-worlds accessible from i. In other words: iff, at i, the supposition that A is either more possible than the falsity of B, or else impossible. Then $A \mathbin{\Box\!\!\rightarrow} C$ is true at i iff C follows from A together with auxiliary premises B_1, ..., each true at i and cotenable at i with the supposition that A.

There is less to this definition than meets the eye. A conjunction is cotenable with a supposition iff its conjuncts all are; so we need only consider the case of a single auxiliary premise B. That single premise may always be taken either as $\bar{A}$ (if A is impossible) or as $A \supset C$ (otherwise); so 'follows' may be glossed as 'follows by truth-functional logic'.

Common opinion has it that laws of nature are cotenable with any supposition unless they are downright inconsistent with it. What can we make of this? Whatever else laws may be, they are generalizations that we deem especially important. If so, then conformity to the prevailing laws of a world i should weigh heavily in the similarity of other worlds to i. Laws should therefore tend to be cotenable, unless inconsistent, with counterfactual suppositions. Yet I think this tendency may be overridden when conformity to laws carries too high a cost in differences of particular fact. Suppose, for instance, that i is a world governed (in all respects of the slightest interest to us) by deterministic laws. Let A pertain to matters of particular fact at time t; let A be false at i, and determined at all previous times to be false. There are some A-worlds where the laws of i are never violated; all of these differ from i in matters of particular fact at all times before t. (Nor can we count on the difference approaching zero as we go back in time.) There are other A-worlds exactly like i until very shortly before t when a small, local, temporary, imperceptible suspension of the laws permits A to come true. I find it highly plausible that one of the latter resembles i on balance more than any of the former.

2.3. *Degrees of Similarity*

Roughly, $A \mathbin{\Box\!\!\rightarrow} C$ is true at i iff either (1) there is some degree of similarity to i within which there are A-worlds and C holds at all of them, or (2) there are no A-worlds within any degree of similarity to i. To avoid the questionable assumption that similarity of worlds admits somehow of numerical measurement, it seems best to identify each 'degree of similarity to i' with a set of worlds regarded as the set of all worlds within that degree mof siilarity to i. Call a set S of worlds a *sphere* around i iff every S-world is accessible from i and is closer to i than is any $\bar{S}$-world. Call a sphere *A-permitting* iff it contains some A-world. Letting spheres represent degrees of similarity, we have this reformulation: $A \,\square\!\!\rightarrow C$ is true at i iff $A \supset C$ holds throughout some A-permitting sphere around i, if such there be.

To review our other operators: $A \Diamond\!\!\rightarrow C$ is true at i iff AC holds somewhere in every A-permitting sphere around i, and there are such. $\square A$ is true at i iff A holds throughout every sphere around i. $\Diamond A$ is true at i iff A holds somewhere in some sphere around i. $A \prec B$ is true at i iff some sphere around i permits A but not B. Finally, B is cotenable at i with the supposition that A iff B holds throughout some A-permitting sphere around i, if such there be.

Restated in terms of spheres, the Limit Assumption says that if there is any A-permitting sphere around i, then there is a smallest one – the Intersection of all A-permitting spheres is then itself an A-permitting sphere. We can therefore reformulate Analysis 2 as: $A \,\square\!\!\rightarrow C$ is true at i iff $A \supset C$ holds throughout the smallest A-permitting sphere around i, if such there be.

These systems of spheres may remind one of neighborhood systems in topology, but that would be a mistake. The topological concept of closeness captured by means of neighborhoods is purely local and qualitative, not comparative: adjacent vs. separated, no more. Neighborhoods do not capture comparative closeness to a point because arbitrary supersets of neighborhoods of the point are themselves neighborhoods of a point. The spheres around a world, on the other hand, are nested, wherefore they capture comparative closeness: j is closer to i than k is (according to the definition of spheres and the Ordering Assumption) iff some sphere around i includes j but excludes k.

2.4. *Higher-Order Quantification*

The formulation just given as a metalinguistic truth condition can also be stated, with the help of auxiliary apparatus, as an explicit definition in the object language.

$$A \,\square\!\!\rightarrow C =^{\mathrm{df}} \Diamond A \supset \exists S (\varPhi S \;\&\; \Diamond SA \;\&\; \square (SA \supset C)).$$

Here the modalities are as before; 'S' is an object-language variable over propositions; and $\varPhi$ is a higher-order predicate satisfied at a world i by a proposition iff the set of all worlds where that proposition holds is a sphere around i. I have assumed that every set of worlds is the truth-set of some – perhaps inexpressible – proposition.

We could even quantify over modalities, these being understood as certain properties of propositions. Call a modality *spherical* iff for every world i there is a sphere around i such that the modality belongs at i to all and only those propositions that hold throughout that sphere. Letting ■ be a variable over all spherical modalities, and letting ◆ abbreviate –■–, we have

$$A \,\square\!\!\rightarrow C =^{df} \Diamond A \supset \exists \blacksquare (\blacklozenge A \,\&\, \blacksquare (A \supset C)).$$

This definition captures explicitly the idea that the counterfactual is a variably strict conditional.

To speak of variable strictness, we should be able to compare the strictness of different spherical modalities. Call one modality *(locally) stricter* than another at a world i iff the second but not the first belongs to some proposition at i. Call two modalities *comparable* iff it does not happen that one is stricter at one world and the other at another. Call one modality *stricter* than another iff they are comparable and the first is stricter at some world. Call one *uniformly stricter* than another iff it is stricter at every world. Comparative strictness is only a partial ordering of the spherical modalities: some pairs are incomparable. However, we can without loss restrict the range of our variable ■ to a suitable subset of the spherical modalities on which comparative strictness is a linear ordering. (Perhaps – iff the inclusion orderings of spheres around worlds all have the same order type – we can do better still, and use a subset linearly ordered by uniform comparative strictness.) Unfortunately, these linear sets are not uniquely determined.

Example: suppose that comparative similarity has only a few gradations. Suppose, for instance, that there are only five different (nonempty) spheres around each world. Let $\square_1 A$ be true at i iff A holds throughout the innermost (nonempty) sphere around i: let $\square_2 A$ be true at i iff A holds throughout the innermost-but-one; and likewise for $\square_3$, $\square_4$, and $\square_5$. Then the five spherical modalities expressed by these operators are a suitable linear set. Since we have only a finite range, we can replace quantification by disjunction:

$$A \:\square\!\!\rightarrow C =^{\mathrm{df}} \Diamond A \supset . (\Diamond_1 A \:\&\: \square_1 (A \supset C))$$
$$\vee \cdots \vee (\Diamond_5 A \:\&\: \square_5 (A \supset C))$$

See Louis Goble, 'Grades of Modality', *Logique et Analyse* 1970.

2.5. *Impossible Limit-Worlds*

We were driven from Analysis 2 to Analysis 3 because we had reason to doubt the Limit Assumption. It seemed that sometimes there were closer and closer A-worlds to i without limit – that is, without any closest A-worlds. None, at least, among the *possible* worlds. But we can find the closest A-worlds instead among certain *impossible* worlds, if we are willing to look there. If we count these impossible worlds among the worlds to be considered, the Limit Assumption is rescued and we can safely return to Analysis 2.

There are various ways to introduce the impossible limits we need. The following method is simplest, but others can be made to seem a little less *ad hoc*. Suppose there are closer and closer (accessible, possible) A-worlds to i without limit; and suppose Σ is any maximal set of sentences such that, for any finite conjunction C of sentences in Σ, $A \Diamond\!\!\rightarrow C$ holds at i according to Analysis 3. (We can think of such a Σ as a full description of one – possible or impossible – way things might be if it were that A, from the standpoint of i.) Then we must posit an impossible limit-world where all of Σ holds. It should be accessible from i alone; it should be closer to i than all the possible A-worlds; but it should be no closer to i than any possible world that is itself clossr than all the possible A-worlds. (Accessibility from, and comparative similarity to, the impossible limit-worlds is undefined. Truth of sentences there is determined by the way in which these worlds were introduced as limits, not according to the ordinary truth conditions.) Obviously the Limit Assumption is satisfied once these impossible worlds have been added to the worlds under consideration. It is easy to verify that the truth values of counterfactuals at possible worlds afterwards according to Analyses 2 and 3 alike agrees with their original truth values according to Analysis 3.

The impossible worlds just posited are impossible in the least objectionable way. The sentences true there may be *incompatible*, in that not all of them hold together at any possible world; but there is no (correct) way to derive any contradiction from them. For a derivation proceeds from finitely many premises; and any finite subset of the sentences true at one of the limit-worlds *is* true together at some possible world. Example: recall the failure of the Limit Assumption among possible worlds when *A* is 'I am over 7 feet tall'. Our limit-worlds will be impossible worlds where *A* is true but all of 'I am at least 7.1 feet tall', 'I am at least 7.01 feet tall', 'I am at least 7.001 feet tall' etc. are false. (Do not confuse these with possible worlds where I am infinitesimally more than 7 feet tall. For all I know, there are such; but worlds where physical magnitudes can take 'non-standard' values differing infinitesimally from a real number presumably differ from ours in a very fundamental way, making them far more remote from actuality than some of the standard worlds where I am, say, 7.1 feet tall. If so, 'Physical magnitudes never take non-standard values' is false at any possible world where I am infinitesimally more than 7 feet tall, but true at the impossible closest *A*-worlds to ours.)

How bad is it to believe in these impossible limit-worlds? Very bad, I think; but there is no reason not to reduce them to something less objectionable, such as sets of propositions or even sentences. I do not like a parallel reduction of possible worlds, chiefly because it is incredible in the case of the possible world *we* happen to live in, and other possible worlds do not differ in kind from ours. But this objection does not carry over to the impossible worlds. We do not live in one of those, and possible and impossible worlds do differ in kind.

2.6. *Selection Functions*

Analysis 2, vindicated either by trafficking in impossible worlds or by faith in the Limit Assumption even for possible worlds, may conveniently be reformulated by introducing a function *f* that selects, for any antecedent *A* and possible world *i*, the set of all closest (accessible) *A*-worlds to *i* (the empty set if there are none). $A \square \rightarrow C$ is true at a possible world *i* iff *C* holds throughout the selected set $f(A, i)$. Stalnaker formulates Analysis 1 this way, except that his $f(A, i)$ is the unique member of the selected set, if such there be, instead of the set itself.

If we like, we can put the selection function into the object language; but to do this without forgetting that counterfactuals are in general contingent, we must have recourse to *double indexing*. That is, we must think of some special sentences as being true or false at a world *i* not absolutely, but in relation to a world *j*. An ordinary sentence is true or false at *i*, as the case may be, in relation to any j; it will be enough to deal with ordinary counterfactuals compounded out of ordinary sentences. Let fA (where A is ordinary) be a special sentence true at j in relation to i iff j belongs to $f(A, i)$. Then $fA \supset C$ (where C is ordinary) is true at j in relation to i iff, if j belongs to $f(A, i)$, C holds at j. Then $\square(fA \supset C)$ is true at j in relation to i iff C holds at every world in $f(A, i)$ that is accessible from j. It is therefore true at i in relation to i itself iff C holds throughout (fA, i) – that is, iff $A \square\!\!\rightarrow C$ holds at i. Introducing an operator $\dagger$ such that $\dagger B$ is true at i in relation to j iff B is true at i in relation to i itself, we can define the counterfactual:

$$A \square\!\!\rightarrow C = ^{df} \dagger\square (fA \supset C).$$

An f-operator without double indexing is discussed in Lennart Åqvist, 'Modal Logic with Subjunctive Conditionals and Dispositional Predicates', *Filosofiska Studier* (Uppsala) 1971; the $\dagger$ operator was introduced in Frank Vlach, ' "Now" and "Then" '(in preparation).

2.7. *Ternary Accessibility*

If we like, we can reparse counterfactuals as $[A \square\!\!\rightarrow]C$, regarding $\square\!\!\rightarrow$ now not as a two-place operator but rather as taking one sentence A to make a one-place operator $[A \square\!\!\rightarrow]$. If we have closest A-worlds – possible or impossible – whenever A is possible, then each $[A \square\!\!\rightarrow]$ is a necessity operator interpretable in the normal way by means of an accessibility relation. Call j *A-accessible* from i (or *accessible from i relative to A*) iff j is a closest (accessible) A-world from i; then $[A \square\!\!\rightarrow]C$ is true at i iff C holds at every world A-accessible from i. See Brian F. Chellas, 'Basic Conditional Logic' (in preparation).

3. FALLACIES

Some familiar argument-forms, valid for certain other conditionals, are invalid for my counterfactuals.

Transitivity	Contraposition	Strengthening	Importation
$A \square\!\!\rightarrow B$			
$B \square\!\!\rightarrow C$	$A \square\!\!\rightarrow C$	$A \square\!\!\rightarrow C$	$A \square\!\!\rightarrow (B \supset C)$
$A \square\!\!\rightarrow C$	$\bar{C} \square\!\!\rightarrow \bar{A}$	$AB \square\!\!\rightarrow C$	$AB \square\!\!\rightarrow C$

However, there are related valid argument-forms that may often serve as substitutes for these.

$A \Box\!\!\rightarrow B$	$\bar{C}$	$A \diamondsuit\!\!\rightarrow B$	$A \diamondsuit\!\!\rightarrow B$
$AB \Box\!\!\rightarrow C$	$A \Box\!\!\rightarrow C$	$A \Box\!\!\rightarrow C$	$A \Box\!\!\rightarrow (B \supset C)$
$A \Box\!\!\rightarrow C$	$\bar{C} \Box\!\!\rightarrow \bar{A}$	$AB \Box\!\!\rightarrow C$	$AB \Box\!\!\rightarrow C$

Further valid substitutes for transitivity are these.

	$B \Box\!\!\rightarrow A$	$B \diamondsuit\!\!\rightarrow A$
$A \Box\!\!\rightarrow B$	$A \Box\!\!\rightarrow B$	$A \Box\!\!\rightarrow B$
$\Box (B \supset C)$	$B \Box\!\!\rightarrow C$	$B \Box\!\!\rightarrow C$
$A \Box\!\!\rightarrow C$	$A \Box\!\!\rightarrow C$	$A \Box\!\!\rightarrow C$

4. TRUE ANTECEDENTS

On my analysis, a counterfactual is so called because it is suitable for non-trivial use when the antecedent is presumed false; not because it implies the falsity of the antecedent. It is conversationally inappropriate, of course, to use the counterfactual construction unless one supposes the antecedent false; but this defect is not a matter of truth conditions. Rather, it turns out that a counterfactual with a true antecedent is true iff the consequent is true, as if it were a material conditional. In other words, these two arguments are valid.

$$(-)\frac{A, \quad \bar{C}}{-(A \Box\!\!\rightarrow C)} \quad (+)\frac{A, \; C}{A \Box\!\!\rightarrow C}.$$

It is hard to study the truth conditions of counterfactuals with true antecedents. Their inappropriateness eclipses the question whether they are true. However, suppose that someone has unwittingly asserted a counterfactual $A \Box\!\!\rightarrow C$ with (what you take to be) a true antecedent A. Either of these replies would, I think, sound cogent.

(−) Wrong, since in fact A and yet not C.

(+) Right, since in fact A and indeed C.

The two replies depend for their cogency – for the appropriateness of the word 'since' – on the validity of the corresponding arguments.

I confess that the case for (−) seems more compelling than the case for (+). One who wants to invalidate (+) while keeping (−) can do so if he is prepared to imagine that another world may sometimes be just as similar to a given world as that world is to itself. He thereby weakens the Centering Assumption to this: each world is self-accessible, and at least as close to itself as any other world is to it. Making that change and keeping everything else the same, $(-)$ is valid but $(+)$ is not.

5. COUNTERPOSSIBLES

If A is impossible, $A \square\!\!\rightarrow C$ is vacuously true regardless of the consequent C. Clearly some counterfactuals with impossible antecedents are asserted with confidence, and should therefore come out true: 'If there were a decision procedure for logic, there would be one for the halting problem'. Others are not asserted by reason of the irrelevance of antecedent to consequent: 'If there were a decision procedure for logic, there would be a sixth regular solid' or '... the war would be over by now'. But would these be confidently *denied*? I think not; so I am content to let all of them alike be true. Relevance is welcome in the theory of conversation (which I leave to others) but not in the theory of truth conditions.

If you do insist on making discriminations of truth value among counterfactuals with impossible antecedents, you might try to do this by extending the comparative similarity orderings of possible worlds to encompass also certain impossible worlds where not-too-blatantly impossible antecedents come true. (These are worse than the impossible limit-worlds already considered, where impossible but consistent infinite combinations of possibly true sentences come true.) See recent work on impossible-world semantics for doxastic logic and for relevant implication; especially Richard Routley, 'Ultra-Modal Propositional Functors' (in preparation).

6. POTENTIALITIES

'Had the Emperor not crossed the Rubicon, he would never have become Emperor' does *not* mean that the closest worlds to ours where there is a unique emperor and he did not cross the Rubicon are worlds where there is a unique emperor and he never became Emperor. Rather, it is *de re* with respect to 'the Emperor', and means that he who actually is (or was at the time under discussion) Emperor has a counterfactual property, or *potentiality,* expressed by the formula: 'if x had not crossed the Rubicon, x

would never have become Emperor'. We speak of what would have befallen the actual Emperor, not of what would have befallen whoever would have been Emperor. Such potentialities may also appear when we quantify into counterfactuals: 'Any Emperor who would never have become Emperor had he not crossed the Rubicon ends up wishing he hadn't done it' or 'Any of these matches would light if it were scratched'. We need to know what it is for something to have a potentiality – that is, to satisfy a counterfactual formula $A(x)\,\square\!\!\rightarrow C(x)$.

As a first approximation, we might say that something x satisfies the formula $A(x)\,\square\!\!\rightarrow C(x)$ at a world i iff some (accessible) world where x satisfies $A(x)$ and $C(x)$ is closer to i than any world where x satisfies $A(x)$ and $\bar{C}(x)$, if there are (accessible) worlds where x satisfies $A(x)$.

The trouble is that this depends on the assumption that one and the same thing can exist – can be available to satisfy formulas – at various worlds. I reject this assumption, except in the case of certain abstract entities that inhabit no particular world, and think it better to say that concrete things are confined each to its own single world. He who actually is Emperor belongs to our world alone, and is not available to cross the Rubicon or not, become Emperor or not, or do anything else at any other world. But although he himself is not present elsewhere, he may have *counterparts* elsewhere: inhabitants of other worlds who resemble him closely, and more closely than do the other inhabitants of the same world. What he cannot do in person at other worlds he may do vicariously, through his counterparts there. So, for instance, I might have been a Republican not because I myself am a Republican at some other world than this – I am not – but because I have Republican counterparts at some worlds. See my 'Counterpart Theory and Quantified Modal Logic', *Journal of Philosophy* 1968.

Using the method of counterparts, we may say that something x satisfies the formula $A(x)\,\square\!\!\rightarrow C(x)$ at a world i iff some (accessible) world where some counterpart of x satisfies $A(x)$ and $C(x)$ is closer to i than any world where any counterpart of x satisfies $A(x)$ and $\bar{C}(x)$, if there are (accessible) worlds where a counterpart of x satisfies $A(x)$. This works also for abstract entities that inhabit no particular world but exist equally at all, if we say that for these things the counterpart relation is simply identity.

A complication: it seems that when we deal with relations expressed by counterfactual formulas with more than one free variable, we may need to mix different counterpart relations. 'It I were you I'd give up' seems to mean that some world where a character-counterpart of me is a predicament-counterpart of you and gives up is closer than any where a character-counterpart of me is a predicament-counterpart of you and does not give up. (I omit provision for vacuity and for accessibility restrictions.) The difference between Goodman's sentences

> (1)   If New York City were in Georgia, New York City would be in the South.
>
> (2)   If Georgia included New York City, Georgia would not be entirely in the South.

may be explained by the hypothesis that both are *de re* with respect to both 'New York City' and 'Georgia', and that a less stringent counterpart relation is used for the subject terms 'New York City' in (1) and 'Georgia' in (2) than for the object terms 'Georgia' in (1) and 'New York City' in (2). I cannot say in general how grammar and context control which counterpart relation is used where.

An independent complication: since closeness of worlds and counterpart relations among their inhabitants are alike matters of comparative similarity, the two are interdependent. At a world close to ours, the inhabitants of our world will mostly have close counterparts; at a world very different from ours, nothing can be a very close counterpart of anything at our world. We might therefore wish to fuse closeness of worlds and closeness of counterparts, allowing these to balance off. Working with comparative similarity among *pairs* of a concrete thing and the world it inhabits (and ignoring provision for vacuity and for accessibility restrictions), we could say that an inhabitant x of a world i satisfies $A(x) \square\!\!\rightarrow C(x)$ at i iff some such thing-world pair $\langle y, j \rangle$ such that y satisfies $A(x)$ and $C(x)$ at j is more similar to the pair $\langle x, i \rangle$ than is any pair $\langle z, k \rangle$ such that z satisfies $A(x)$ and $\bar{C}(x)$ at k. To combine this complication and the previous one seems laborious but routine.

7. COUNTERCOMPARATIVES

'If my yacht were longer than it is, I would be happier than I am' might be handled by quantifying into a counterfactual formula: $\exists x, y$ (my yacht is

x feet long & I enjoy y hedons & (my yacht is more than x feet long $\square\!\!\rightarrow$ I enjoy more than y hedons)). But sometimes, perhaps in this very example, comparison makes sense when numerical measurement does not. An alternative treatment of countercomparatives is available using double indexing. (Double indexing has already been mentioned in connection with the f-operator; but if we wanted it both for that purpose and for this, we would need triple indexing.) Let A be true at j in relation to i iff my yacht is longer at j than at i (more precisely: if my counterpart at j has a longer yacht than my counterpart at i (to be still more precise, decide what to do when there are multiple counterparts or multiple yachts)); let C be true at j in relation to i iff I am happier at j than at i (more precisely: if my counterpart...). Then $A\,\square\!\!\rightarrow C$ is true at j in relation to i iff some world (accessible from j) where A and C both hold in relation to i is closer to j than any world where A and $\bar{C}$ both hold in relation to i. So far, the relativity to i just tags along. Our countercomparative is therefore true at i (in relation to any world) iff $A\,\square\!\!\rightarrow C$ is true at i in relation to i itself. It is therefore $\dagger(A\,\square\!\!\rightarrow C)$.

8. Counterfactual Probability

'The probability that C, if it were the case that A, would be r' cannot be understood to mean any of:

(1)   Prob $(A\,\square\!\!\rightarrow C) = r$,
(2)   Prob $(C \mid A) = r$, or
(3) $A\,\square\!\!\rightarrow$ Prob$(C) = r$.

Rather, it is true at a world i (with respect to a given probability measure) iff for any positive ε there exists an A-permitting sphere T around i such that for any A-permitting sphere S around i within T, Prob$(C \mid AS)$, unless undefined, is within ε of r.

Example. A is 'The sample contained abracadabrene', C is 'The test for abracadabrene was positive', Prob is my present subjective probability measure after watching the test come out negative and tentatively concluding that abracadabrene was absent. I consider that the probability of a positive result, had abracadabrene been present, would have been 97%. (1) I know that false negatives occur because of the inherently indeterministic character of the radioactive decay of the tracer used in the test, so I am convinced that no matter what the actual conditions were, there might have been a false negative even if abracadabrene had been present. $\text{Prob}(A \diamondsuit \rightarrow \bar{C}) \approx 1$; $\text{Prob}(A \square \rightarrow C) \approx 0$. (2) Having seen that the test was negative, I disbelieve C much more strongly than I disbelieve A; $\text{Prob}(AC)$ is much less than $\text{Prob}(A)$; $\text{Prob}(C \mid A) \approx 0$. (3) Unknown to me, the sample was from my own blood, and abracadabrene is a powerful hallucinogen that makes white things look purple. Positive tests are white, negatives are purple. So had abracadabrene been present, I would have strongly disbelieved C no matter what the outcome of the test really was. $A \square \rightarrow \text{Prob}(C) \approx 0$. (Taking (3) *de re* with respect to 'Prob' is just as bad: since actually $\text{Prob}(C) \approx 0$, $A \square \rightarrow \text{Prob}(C) \approx 0$ also.) My suggested definition seems to work, however, provided that the outcome of the test at a close A-world does not influence the closeness of that world to ours.

9. ANALOGIES

The counterfactual as I have analyzed it is parallel in its semantics to operators in other branches of intensional logic, based on other comparative relations. There is one difference: in the case of these analogous operators, it seems best to omit the provision for vacuous truth. They correspond to a doctored counterfactual $\square \Rightarrow$ that is automatically false instead of automatically true when the antecedent is impossible: $A \square \Rightarrow C =^{\text{df}} \diamondsuit A \,\&\, (A \square \rightarrow C)$.

Deontic: We have the operator $A \square \Rightarrow_d C$, read as 'Given that A, it ought to be that C', true at a world i iff some AC-world evaluable from the standpoint of i is better, from the standpoint of i, than any $A\bar{C}$-world. Roughly (under a Limit Assumption), iff C holds at the best A-worlds. See the operator of 'conditional obligation' discussed in Bengt Hansson, 'An Analysis of Some Deontic Logics', *Noûs* 1969.

Temporal: We have $A \square \Rightarrow_f C$, read as 'When next A, it will be that C', true at a time t iff some AC-time after t comes sooner after t than any $A\bar{C}$-time; roughly, iff C holds at the next A-time. We have also the past mirror image: $A \square \Rightarrow_p C$, read as 'When last A, it was that C'.

Egocentric (in the sense of A. N. Prior, 'Egocentric Logic', *Noûs* 1968): We have $A \square \Rightarrow_e C$, read as 'The A is C', true for a thing x iff some AC-thing in x's ken is more salient to x than any $A\bar{C}$-thing; roughly, iff the most salient A-thing is C.

To motivate the given truth conditions, we may note that these operators all permit sequences of truths of the two forms:

$$A \,\square\!\Rightarrow \bar{B}, \qquad A \,\square\!\Rightarrow Z,$$
$$AB \,\square\!\Rightarrow \bar{C}, \quad \text{and} \quad AB \,\square\!\Rightarrow Z,$$
$$ABC \,\square\!\Rightarrow \bar{D}, \qquad ABC \,\square\!\Rightarrow Z,$$
$$\text{etc.;} \qquad\qquad \text{etc.}$$

It is such sequences that led us to treat the counterfactual as a variably strict conditional. The analogous operators here are likewise variably strict conditionals. Each is based on a binary relation and a family of comparative relations in just the way that the (doctored) counterfactual is based on accessibility and the family of comparative similarity orderings. In each case, the Ordering Assumption holds. The Centering Assumption, however, holds only in the counterfactual case. New assumptions hold in some of the other cases.

In the deontic case, we may or may not have different comparative orderings from the standpoint of different worlds. If we evaluate worlds according to their conformity to the edicts of the god who reigns at a given world, then we will get different orderings; and no worlds will be evaluable from the standpoint of a godless world. If rather we evaluate worlds according to their total yield of hedons, then evaluability and comparative goodness of worlds will be absolute.

In the temporal case, both the binary relation and the families of comparative relations, both for 'when next' and for 'when last', are based on the single underlying linear order of time.

The sentence $(A \vee \bar{B})\,\square\!\Rightarrow_f AB$ is true at time t iff some A-time after t precedes any $\bar{B}$-time after t. It thus approximates the sentence 'Until A, B', understood as being true at t iff some A-time after t is not preceded by any $\bar{B}$-time after t. Likewise $(A \vee \bar{B})\,\square\!\Rightarrow_p AB$ approximates 'Since A, B', with 'since' understood as the past mirror image of 'until'. Hans Kamp has shown that 'since' and 'until' suffice to define all possible tense operators, provided that the order of time is a complete linear order; see his *Tense Logic and the Theory of Order* (U.C.L.A. dissertation, 1968). Do my approximations have the same power? No; consider 'Until $\top$, $\bot$', true at t iff there is a next moment after t. This sentence cannot be translated using my operators. For if the order of time is a complete linear order with discrete stretches and dense stretches, then the given sentence will vary in truth value; but if in addition there is no beginning or end of time, and if there are no atomic sentences that vary in truth value, then no sentences that vary in truth value can be built up by means of truth-functional connectives, $\square\Rightarrow_f$, and $\square\Rightarrow_p$.

Starting from any of our various $\square\Rightarrow$-operators, we can introduce one-place operators I shall call the *inner modalities*:

$$\boxdot A =^{df} \top \square\Rightarrow A,$$
$$\Diamond A =^{df} -\boxdot-A,$$

and likewise in the analogous cases. The inner modalities in the counter-factual case are of no interest (unless Centering is weakened), since $\boxdot A$ and $\Diamond A$ are both equivalent to A itself. Nor are they anything noteworthy in the egocentric case. In the deontic case, however, they turn out to be slightly improved versions of the usual so-called obligation and permission operators. $\boxdot_d A$ is true at i iff some (evaluable) A-world is better, from the standpoint of i, than any $\bar{A}$-world; that is, iff either (1) there are best (evaluable) worlds, and A holds throughout them, or (2) there are better and better (evaluable) worlds without end, and A holds throughout all sufficiently good ones. In the temporal case, $\boxdot_f A$ is true at t iff some A-time after t comes sooner than any $\bar{A}$-time; that is, iff either (1) there is a next moment, and A holds then, or (2) there is no next moment, and A holds throughout some interval beginning immediately and extending into the future. $\boxdot_f A$ may thus be read 'Immediately, A'; as may $\Diamond_f A$, but in a somewhat different sense.

If no worlds are evaluable from the standpoint of a given world – say, because no god reigns there – it turns out that $\boxdot_d A$ is false and $\Diamond_d A$ is true for any A whatever. Nothing is obligatory, everything is permitted. Similarly for $\boxdot_f A$ and $\Diamond_f A$ at the end of time, if such there be; and for $\boxdot_p A$ and $\Diamond_p A$ at its beginning. Modalities that behave in this way are called *abnormal*, and it is interesting to find these moderately natural examples of abnormality.

10. AXIOMATICS

The set of all sentences valid under my analysis may be axiomatised taking the counterfactual connective as primitive. One such axiom system – not the neatest – is the system **C1** of my paper 'Completeness and Decidability of Three Logics of Counterfactual Conditionals', *Theoria* 1971, essentially as follows.

Rules:

> If A and $A \supset B$ are theorems, so is B.
> If $(B_1 \ \& \ \cdots) \supset C$ is a theorem, so is
> $$((A \ \square\!\!\rightarrow B_1) \ \& \ \cdots) \supset (A \ \square\!\!\rightarrow C).$$

Axioms:

> All truth-functional tautologies are axioms.
> $A \ \square\!\!\rightarrow A$
> $(A \ \square\!\!\rightarrow B) \ \& \ (B \ \square\!\!\rightarrow A) . \supset . (A \ \square\!\!\rightarrow C) \equiv (B \ \square\!\!\rightarrow C)$
> $((A \vee B) \ \square\!\!\rightarrow A) \vee ((A \vee B) \ \square\!\!\rightarrow B) \vee (((A \vee B) \ \square\!\!\rightarrow C) \equiv$
> $$(A \ \square\!\!\rightarrow C) \ \& \ (B \ \square\!\!\rightarrow C))$$
> $A \ \square\!\!\rightarrow B . \supset . A \supset B$
> $AB \supset . A \ \square\!\!\rightarrow B$

(Rules and axioms here and henceforth should be taken as schematic.) Recall that modalities and comparative possibility may be introduced via the following definitions: $\square A =^{\mathrm{df}} \bar{A} \square\!\!\rightarrow \perp$; $\diamond A =^{\mathrm{df}} - \square - A$; $A \prec B =^{\mathrm{df}} \diamond A \ \& \ ((A \vee B) \square\!\!\rightarrow A\bar{B})$.

A more intuitive axiom system, called **VC**, is obtained if we take comparative possibility instead of the counterfactual as primitive. Let $A \preccurlyeq B =^{\mathrm{df}} - (B \prec A)$.

Rules:

> If A and $A \supset B$ are theorems, so is B.
> If $A \supset B$ is a theorem, so is $B \preccurlyeq A$.

Basic Axioms:

> All truth-functional tautologies are basic axioms.
> $A \preccurlyeq B \preccurlyeq C . \supset . A \preccurlyeq C$
> $A \preccurlyeq B . \vee . B \preccurlyeq A$
> $A \preccurlyeq (A \vee B) . \vee . B \preccurlyeq (A \vee B)$

Axiom **C**:

> $A\bar{B} \supset . A \prec B$

Recall that modalities and the counterfactual may be introduced via the following definitions: $\Diamond A =^{\mathrm{df}} A \prec \bot$; $\Box A =^{\mathrm{df}} - \Diamond - A$; $A \Box \to C =^{\mathrm{df}}$ $\Diamond A \supset (AC \prec A\bar{C})$.

VC and **C1** turn out to be definitionally equivalent. That is, their respective definitional extensions (via the indicated definitions) yield exactly the same theorems. It may now be verified that these theorems are exactly the ones we ought to have. Since the definitions are correct (under my truth conditions) it is sufficient to consider sentences in the primitive notation of **VC**.

In general, we may define a *model* as any quadruple $\langle I, R, \leqslant, [\![\ ]\!] \rangle$ such that

(1) I is a nonempty set (regarded as playing the role of the set of worlds);

(2) R is a binary relation over I (regarded as the accessibility relation);

(3) $\leqslant$ assigns to each i in I a weak ordering $\leqslant_i$ of I (regarded as the comparative similarity ordering of worlds from the standpoint of i) such that whenever $j \leqslant_i k$, if iRk then iRj;

(4) $[\![\ ]\!]$ assigns to each sentence A a subset $[\![A]\!]$ of I (regarded as the set of worlds where A is true);

(5) $[\![-A]\!]$ is $I - [\![A]\!]$, $[\![A \ \& \ B]\!]$ is $[\![A]\!] \cap [\![B]\!]$, and so on;

(6) $[\![A \prec B]\!]$ is $\{i \varepsilon I$: for some j in $[\![A]\!]$ such that iRj, there is no k in $[\![B]\!]$ such that $k \leqslant_i j\}$.

The *intended models*, for the counterfactual case, are those in which I, R, $\leqslant$, and $[\![\ ]\!]$ really are what we regarded them as being: the set of worlds, some reasonable accessibility relation, some reasonable family of comparative similarity orderings, and an appropriate assignment to sentences of truth sets. The Ordering Assumption has been written into the very definition of a model (clause 3) since it is common to the counterfactual case and the analogous cases as well. As for the Centering Assumption, we must impose it on the intended models as a further condition:

(C) R is reflexive on I: and $j \leqslant_i i$ only if $j = i$.

It seems impossible to impose other purely mathematical conditions on the intended models (with the possible exception of (U), discussed below). We therefore hope that **VC** yields as theorems exactly the sentences valid – true at all worlds – in all models that meet condition (C). This is the case.

VC is sound for models meeting (C); for the basic axioms are valid, and the rules preserve validity, in all models; and Axiom **C** is valid in any model meeting (C).

VC is complete for models meeting (C): for there is a certain such model in which only theorems of **VC** are valid. This model is called the *canonical model* for **VC**, and is as follows:

(1)   *I* is the set of all maximal **VC**-consistent sets of sentences;
(2)   *iRj* iff, for every sentence *A* in *j*, $\Diamond A$ is in *i*;
(3) $j \leqslant_i k$ iff there is no set Σ of sentences that overlaps *j* but not *k*, such that whenever $A \leqslant B$ is in *i* and *A* is in Σ then *B* also is in Σ;
(4)   *i* is in $[\![A]\!]$ iff *A* is in *i*.

In the same way, we can prove that the system consisting of the rules, the basic axioms, and *any* combination of the axioms listed below is sound and complete for models meeting the corresponding combination of conditions. Nomenclature: the system generated by the rules, the basic axioms, and the listed axioms — is called **V—**. (Note that the conditions are not independent. (C) implies (W), which implies (T), which implies (N). (S) implies (L). (A—) implies (U—). (W) and (S) together imply (C). (C) and (A—) together imply (S) by implying the stronger, trivializing condition that no world is accessible from any other. Accordingly, many combinations of the listed axioms are redundant.)

Axioms

N: $\Box^\top$
T: $\Box A \supset A$
W: $AB \supset . \Diamond A \,\&\, A \leqslant B$
C: $A\bar{B} \supset A \prec B$
L: (no further axiom, or some tautology)
S: $A \,\Box\!\!\rightarrow C . \vee . A \,\Box\!\!\rightarrow \bar{C}$
U: $\Box A \supset \Box\Box A$ and $\Diamond A \supset \Box \Diamond A$
A: $A \leqslant B \supset \Box(A \leqslant B)$ and $A \prec B \supset \Box(A \prec B)$.

Conditions

(N)   (normality): For any *i* in *I* there is some *j* in *i* such that *iRj*.
(T)   (total reflexivity): *R* is reflexive on *I*.

(W) (weak centering): R is reflexive on I; for any i and j in I, $i \leqslant_i j$.

(C) (centering): R is reflexive on I; and $j \leqslant_i i$ only if $j = i$.

(L) (Limit Assumption): Whenever iRj for some j in $[\![A]\!]$, $[\![A]\!]$ has at least one $\leqslant_i$-minimal element.

(S) (Stalnaker's Assumption): Whenever iRj for some j in $[\![A]\!]$, $[\![A]\!]$ has exactly one $\leqslant_i$-minimal element.

(U−) (local uniformity): If iRj, then jRk iff iRk.

(A−) (local absoluteness): If iRj, then jRk iff iRk and $h \leqslant_j k$ iff $h \leqslant_i k$.

The Limit Assumption (L) corresponds to no special axiom. Any one of our systems is sound and complete both for a combination of conditions without (L) and for that combination plus (L). The reason is that our canonical models always are rich enough to satisfy the Limit Assumption, but our axioms are sound without it. (Except **S**, for which the issue does not arise because (S) implies (L).) Moral: the Limit Assumption is irrelevant to the logical properties of the counterfactual. Had our interest been confined to logic, we might as well have stopped with Analysis 2.

Omitting redundant combinations of axioms, we have the 26 distinct systems shown in the diagram.

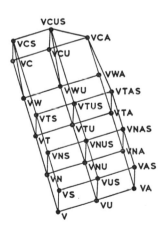

The general soundness and completeness result still holds if we replace the local conditions (U−) and (A−) by the stronger global conditions (U) and (A).

(U)   (uniformity): For any i, j, k in I, jRk iff iRk.

(A)   (absoluteness): For any h, i, j, k in I, jRk iff iRk and $h \leqslant_j k$ iff $h \leqslant_i k$.

Any model meeting $(U-)$ or $(A-)$ can be divided up into models meeting (U) or (A). The other listed conditions hold in the models produced by the division if they held in the original model. Therefore a sentence is valid under a combination of conditions including (U) or (A) iff it is valid under the combination that results from weakening (U) to $(U-)$, or (A) to $(A-)$.

In the presence of (C), (W), or (T), condition (U) is equivalent to the condition: for any i and j in I, iRj. **VCU** is thus the correct system to use if we want to drop accessibility restrictions. **VW**, or perhaps **VWU**, is the correct system for anyone who wants to invalidate the implication from A and C to $A \square \rightarrow C$ by allowing that another world might be just as close to a given world as that world is to itself. **VCS**, or **VCUS** if we drop accessibility restrictions, is the system corresponding to Analysis 1 or $1\frac{1}{2}$. **VCS** is definitionally equivalent to Stalnaker's system **C2**.

The systems given by various combinations of **N**, **T**, **U**, and **A** apply, under various assumptions, to the deontic case. **VN** is definitionally equivalent to a system **CD** given by Bas van Fraassen in 'The Logic of Conditional Obligation' (forthcoming), and shown there to be sound and complete for the class of what we may call *multi-positional models* meeting (N). These differ from models in my sense in that a world may occur at more than one position in an ordering $\leqslant_i$. (Motivation: different positions may be assigned to one world *qua* realizer of different kinds of value.) Technically, we no longer have a direct ordering of the worlds themselves; rather, we have for each i in I a linear ordering of some set V_i and an assignment to each world j such that iRj of one or more members of V_i, regarded as giving the positions of j in the ordering from the standpoint of i. $A \prec B$ is true at i iff some position assigned to some A-world j (such that iRj) is better according to the given ordering than any position assigned to any B-world. My models are essentially the same as those multi-positional models in which no world does have more than one assigned position in any of the orderings. Hence **CO** is at least as strong as **VN**; but no stronger, since **VN** is already sound for all multi-positional models meeting (N).

All the systems are decidable. To decide whether a given sentence A is a theorem of a given system, it is enough to decide whether the validity of A under the corresponding combination of conditions can be refuted by a *small* countermodel – one with at most 2^n worlds, where n is the number of subsentences of A. (Take (U) and (A), rather than (U−) and (A−), as the conditions corresponding to U and A.) That can be decided by examining finitely many cases, since it is unnecessary to consider two models separately if they are isomorphic, or if they have the same I, R, $\leqslant$, and the same $[\![P]\!]$ whenever P is a sentence letter of A. If A is a theorem, then by soundness there is no countermodel and *a fortiori* no small counter-model. If A is not a theorem, then by completeness there is a counter-model $\langle I, R, \leqslant, [\![\ ]\!] \rangle$. We derive thence a small countermodel, called a *filtration* of the original countermodel, as follows. Let D_i, for each i in I, be the conjunction in some definite arbitrary order of all the subsentences of A that are true at i in the original countermodel, together with the negations of all the subsentences of A that are false at i in the original countermodel. Now let $\langle I^*, R^*, \leqslant^*, [\![\ ]\!]^* \rangle$ be as follows:

(1) I^* is a subset of I containing exactly one member of each nonempty $[\![D_i]\!]$;
(2)   for any i and j in I^*, iR^*j iff i is in $[\![\Diamond D_j]\!]$;
(3)   for any i, j, k in I^*, $j \leqslant^*_i k$ iff i is in $[\![D_j \leqslant D_k]\!]$;
(4)   for any sentence letter P, $[\![P]\!]^*$ is $[\![P]\!] \cap I^*$; for any compound sentence B, $[\![B]\!]^*$ is such that $\langle I^*, R^*, \leqslant^*, [\![\ ]\!]^* \rangle$ meets conditions (5) and (6) in the definition of a model.

Then it may easily be shown that $\langle I^*, R^*, \leqslant^*, [\![\ ]\!]^* \rangle$ is a small counter-model to the validity of A under the appropriate combination of conditions, and thereby to the theoremhood of A in the given system.

Princeton University

NOTE

* The theory presented in this paper is discussed more fully in my book *Counterfactuals* (Blackwell and Harvard University Press). My research on counterfactuals was supported by a fellowship from the American Council of Learned Societies.

ROBERT STALNAKER

PRESUPPOSITIONS

My aim is to sketch a general abstract account of the notion of presupposition, and to argue that the presupposition relation which linguists talk about should be explained in terms of this general account. The notion I will discuss is a *pragmatic* notion, as opposed to a purely *semantic* one. This means that the presupposition relation cannot be explained solely in terms of the meaning or content of sentences, but must be explained partly in terms of facts about the users of sentences: their beliefs, intentions and expectations. My notion will thus contrast with the standard account of presupposition which has been given by philosophers and linguists. According to this standard account, one sentence presupposes another just in case the latter must be true in order that the former have a truth value at all. This definition was given by Strawson[1], and has been developed formally by van Fraassen[2]. Generative semanticists such as G. Lakoff, Horn, and Karttunen[3] have used or assumed this kind of semantic definition.

According to the contrasting idea that I will focus on, the basic presupposition relation is not between propositions or sentences, but between a person and a proposition. A person's presuppositions are the propositions whose truth he takes for granted, often unconsciously, in a conversation, an inquiry, or a deliberation. They are the background assumptions that may be used without being spoken – sometimes without being noticed – for example as suppressed premises in an enthymematic argument, or as implicit directions about how a request should be fulfilled or a piece of advice taken. I will argue that it is in terms of this intuitive idea of presupposition, or a refinement of it, that the linguistic phenomenon of presupposition should be explained.

The treatment of presupposition by linguists begins not with an abstract account, but with some paradigm cases of a presumed relation between sentences. For example, sentences with factive verbs like 'know' and 'regret' presuppose the truth of the proposition expressed by the nominalized sentence which is the complement of the verb. Past tense sub-

*Hockney et al. (eds.), Contemporary Research in Philosophical Logic
and Linguistic Semantics*, 31–41. *All Rights Reserved*
Copyright © 1975 by *D. Reidel Publishing Company, Dordrecht-Holland*

junctive conditional statements presuppose the falsity of the antecedent, and perhaps also of the consequent. A diverse collection of words like few, even, only, again, stop, accuse, refuse, admit, confess, pretend, continue, resume, before, and after each gives rise to characteristic presuppositions in sentences in which it occurs. What unites these cases is just the intuitive idea of presupposition, together with a few rough generalizations like the following: generally, if a statement *A* has a particular presupposition, then so does the denial of *A*, as well as the statement that says that it *might* be that *A*. So that if 'Ted is the only man who could have won' presupposes that Ted could have won, then so does 'Ted is not the only man who could have won', as well as 'Ted might be the only man who could have won'.

Although a great many interesting facts have been turned up by linguists exploring this phenomenon, so far as I know, little has been said by them about the general nature of the presupposition relation that the examples they have discovered are examples of. They usually assume that the account of presupposition as a semantic relation defined in terms of truth values is the correct theoretical analysis. But I believe that their substantive claims about the phenomenon rarely depend on this assumption. The examples and generalizations can be more adequately explained, and some puzzles avoided, if we define the linguistic notion of presupposition in terms of a development of the pragmatic account of presupposition as a propositional attitude. From the point of view of this alternative account, the technical semantic relation of presupposition will be just one reason among others why a statement may require a presupposition in the pragmatic sense.

I will start my defense of this claim with a sketch of the pragmatic notion. Statements and requests are made, questions asked, proclamations and commands issued, against a background of common knowledge, or at least what is represented as common knowledge. This background of knowledge or beliefs purportedly shared by the speaker and his audience constitute the presuppositions which define the context. A rough definition might go something like this: *A speaker presupposes that P at a given moment in a conversation just in case he is disposed to act, in his linguistic behavior, as if he takes the truth of P for granted, and as if he assumes that his audience recognizes that he is doing so.* I will comment on some of the qualifying phrases of this rough and tentative definition.

First on acting as if: the speaker need not really be taking the truth of

P for granted. He and his audience might be accepting a known falsehood, or a proposition whose truth value is in doubt, in order to further the purpose of the conversation. In such a case, the behavior may involve transparent pretense, but nevertheless, it may be essential to understanding and interpreting the conversation to recognize that the participants are acting as if they had certain common beliefs. In the same way, the speaker need not *really* be assuming that his audience recognizes in advance that he is taking something for granted. In some cases, the central purpose of making a statement may be to communicate a presupposition which is required by that statement. For example, someone asks of my daughter, 'how old is he?' I answer, '*she* is ten months old'. Or, *a* says, of the new secretary, 'Jennifer is certainly an attractive woman'. *b* replies, 'Yes, her husband thinks so too'. In these cases, the speaker represents himself as assuming that certain propositions are part of the background of common knowledge. The representation is again a transparent pretense, but it is nevertheless by means of the representation that communication is accomplished.

Second, on being disposed: I may be presupposing something, according to this definition, even if nothing I say or do indicates that I am. For example, you ask, 'Who do you think will win the next presidential election?' I answer, 'George McGovern'. Now as a matter of fact in this conversation, we both presuppose from the beginning that Richard Nixon will be one of the candidates, even though neither your question nor my answer *requires* that presupposition. We presuppose it because it is obviously true, and we each recognize that the other knows that it is obviously true. Although neither of us does in fact *act* in any way that indicates that we take it for granted that Nixon will be a candidate, we are each *disposed* to so act, should the occasion arise. This means that if I wanted to express a proposition which could most easily be expressed with a sentence whose use required that presupposition, I would use that sentence. So, for example, I might say, 'Harry doesn't even realize that Nixon is going to run again'. Or, if I wanted to argue to a conclusion that required the premiss that Nixon was a candidate, I would not feel obliged to make that premiss explicit. So for example, I might argue, 'McGovern is going to win, so Nixon will lose'. Because I *would* act, in my linguistic behavior, as if I take the truth of that proposition for granted in these ways, I *do* in fact presuppose it.

I do not want to pretend that the notion of being disposed to act, in one's linguistic behavior, as if he takes the truth of some proposition for granted is clear, nor am I confident that some other qualifying phrase is not required to get the definition right. But what I want to get out of the definition does not depend on its details. There are two things I want to use the definition to justify: first, some claims about the formal structure of the concept of presupposition; second, some general conversational rules involving the notion of presupposition.

First, whatever the details of the definition, it is clear that presupposition is a propositional attitude. More specifically, it is an attitude of accepting something to be true. Hence it is reasonable to require, as at least a rational ideal, that the set of all presuppositions made at any given moment be consistent and deductively closed. If the set of all presuppositions in force at a given moment meets these conditions, then we can characterize it in terms of a set of possible states of affairs or courses of events – possible worlds if you like. Given the presuppositions, this set of possible worlds is defined as containing just those in which all the presuppositions are true. Given the set of possible worlds, the set of presuppositions is defined as containing just those which are true in all the possible worlds in the set. Intuitively, this set of possible worlds, which I will call the presupposition set, contains just the alternative possibilities which the speaker considers to be relevant to the purposes of the participants in the conversation, or just the alternative possibilities among which the participants are expected to have some reason to distinguish with the propositions they might express.

Second, I want the definition to provide justification for some general rules of conversation. The kind of justification that I want is an argument that shows the rules to be, not just arbitrary stipulations or conventions, but maxims which derive from general principles of rational cooperative behavior. If we have such a justification for certain maxims, and can use the maxims to explain some of the linguistic facts about presuppositions that have been noted, then we will be able to show that there is no need to postulate specific syntactic or semantic rules in order to explain the facts.[4]

What is important for justifying such rules or maxims is just the fact that a presupposition is *like* an item of presumed common knowledge, or what is taken to be a shared belief. Whatever the details of the definition, it implies that in typical, naive, straightforward uses of language, the presuppositions will coincide with what is taken by the speaker to be the beliefs shared by him and his audience. The only reason that the definition of presupposition cannot stop with this is that as soon as there are established and mutually recognized rules relating what is said to the presumed common beliefs, it becomes possible to exploit those rules by acting as if the shared beliefs were different than they in fact are known to be. The existence and mutual recognition of the rules is what makes it possible to communicate such a pretense, and thus to use the pretense to communicate. Since we want to say that the presuppositions are present even when such rules are being exploited in this way, we cannot simply identify presupposition with what is actually taken to be common knowledge.[5]

Now as linguists use the term, it is *sentences* that have presuppositions. Although according to the notion I have sketched it is persons, and not sentences, that have presuppositions in the primary sense, we may say that a sentence has a presupposition in a derivative sense just in case the use of that sentence would *for some reason* normally be inappropriate unless the speaker presupposed a particular proposition. In such a case, I will say that a sentence *requires* a presupposition. This notion of presupposition *requirement* will be the explication of the linguists' notion of presupposition.

It should be noted that if, in a normal context, a speaker uses a sentence which requires a presupposition in this sense, then by that very act, he does make the required presupposition. Whatever his actual beliefs and assumptions, he does *act as if* he takes the truth of the proposition for granted, and as if he assumes that his audience recognizes that he is doing so. Thus the act of *making* a presupposition, like the act of meaning something, is not a mental act which can be separated by an act of will from overt linguistic behavior.

If this notion of presupposition requirement is a roughly correct account of what it is for a *sentence* to have a presupposition, then the question whether a presupposition relation holds is independent of questions about what happens to the truth value of a statement when its presuppositions are false. It may be that in many, even most, cases, a statement will fail to have a truth value when one of its presuppositions is false, but if so, this will be a substantive generalization, and not something true by definition. If, however, the simplest and otherwise most plausible semantical theory requires that some statements have truth values even when

some of their presuppositions are false, we will not be prevented, by definition, from accepting this theory.

The relation between the semantic notion of presupposition and the
pragmatic notion of presupposition requirement is not, of course, just
accidental. Among the reasons that a pragmatic presupposition might
be required by the use of a sentence, by far the most obvious and compelling reason would be that the semantical rules for the sentence failed to
determine a truth value for the sentence in possible worlds in which the
required presupposition is false. Since the whole point of expressing a
proposition is to divide the relevant set of alternative possible situations –
the presupposition set – into two parts, to distinguish those in which the
proposition is true from those in which the proposition is false, it would
obviously be inappropriate to use a sentence which failed to do this. Thus,
that a proposition is presupposed by a sentence in the technical semantic
sense provides a reason for requiring that it be presupposed in the pragmatic sense whenever the sentence is used. This explains where the semantic notion gets its name, and why linguists and philosophers have
been tempted to identify presupposition in general with this semantic
relation.

Why do I think it is important *not* to make this identification? Because
it obscures the diversity of the sources of presupposition requirements,
and the different kinds of inappropriateness which may be responsible for
presupposition requirements. Because it may needlessly complicate the
semantical rules determining truth values for sentences. More generally,
because it obscures the explanation of the central role of presuppositions
in a general account of communication.

I will give – or at least point to – three arguments in support of this way
of accounting for the linguistic phenomenon of presupposition. First, I
will give two examples of sources of presupposition requirements which
seem to be independent of what happens to truth values when the required
presupposition fails. In such cases, it is at least not necessary to say that
statements lack a truth value when their presuppositions are false. Second,
I will argue that if we regard the presupposition relation as the relation of
pragmatic presupposition requirement, then this relation can be seen as a
special case of a more general kind of constraint on language. The more
general notion is the notion of a constraint imposed by the proper use of
a sentence on a pragmatic presupposition set. Other specific cases of the

more general notion may be useful for the explanation of linguistic phenomena. Third, I shall argue that this approach to presupposition is likely to yield a more natural solution to what has been called the projection problem, or the compositional problem for presuppositions.

First, two examples of different explanations of presupposition requirements: (a) Normally, any proposition expressed, whether as the content of an assertion, a supposition, a conjecture, a request, or whatever, must be compatible with what is taken for granted by the speaker to be true. As I understand it, one role of the subjunctive mood in English is to indicate that this normal expectation is suspended. If this is right, then there will usually be a reason to use the subjunctive, say to make a conditional statement, or a claim that something is possible, only when the antecedent of the conditional, or the proposition said to be possible, is presupposed to be false. Since one normally has reason to use the subjunctive only when this presupposition is present, one suggests that it is present by using the subjunctive. It would therefore normally be inappropriate to use the subjunctive when the presupposition is not made. Hence, it is required in the sense defined. But there is no reason to conclude from this fact that a subjunctive conditional lacks a truth value when its antecedent is true. There is no connection between this explanation of the presupposition requirement and the truth value of the conditional when the presupposition fails.

(b) According to a recent analysis of the role of the word 'even', the insertion of this word in a sentence makes no contribution to what is asserted, but only affects what is presupposed.[6] If I say 'Even George Lakoff might be the Democratic nominee for President this year', I assert exactly what I would assert if I dropped the 'even'. What is added are the presuppositions that other people also might be the Democratic nominee, and that it is somehow unexpected that Lakoff might be the nominee. If this account is right, then the simplest way to give truth conditions for the original statement would be to ignore the 'even' altogether. Its role is to indicate, and thus to require, pragmatic presuppositions; it would be a gratuitous complication to add that it also may turn an otherwise true statement into one that is neither true nor false.

I should emphasize that I do not want to rest any part of my argument on intuitive judgments that statements like 'Even Gödel could prove that theorem', 'If Nixon were President we'd be in a hell of a mess', and 'All of

Lyndon Johnson's sons are bastards' in fact *have* truth values. I do not think any of us have very clear intuitions about the truth values of statements which have false presuppositions, and so I do not think that the truth value, or lack of it, of such statements can be data against which to test competing generalizations. My point is that there *need* be no essential connection between presupposition requirements and truth value gaps. Where we have an independent explanation for the presupposition requirement, then we are free to accept the consequences of what is otherwise the simplest and most plausible semantical account, even if it assigns truth values to sentences when their presuppositions are false.

Second, on general constraints on the presupposition set: If presupposition requirements are defined in terms of pragmatic presupposition sets as I have suggested, then they may be seen as one kind of constraint among others which the use of a sentence imposes on the presumed background assumptions of the context of use of that sentence. I will mention two other related types of constraints. (a) It may be that the use of a sentence requires that some proposition *not* be presupposed. The simplest example is that it is in general required that the proposition which is expressed by the use of a sentence in a context *not* be presupposed in that context. Obviously, by asserting something, a person acts as if he does *not* take it for granted. This principle helps explain the oddity of sentences like 'John's aardvark is sleeping, and John has an aardvark'. It is not that the sentence requires contradictory presuppositions, but that it requires that one and the same proposition both be presupposed and also not be presupposed. (b) Some sentences may require that a proposition of a certain kind be presupposed without requiring that any particular one of them be presupposed. This is true in general of sentences using demonstratives and personal pronouns. If I say 'he is a linguist', there must be a particular male (the referent of 'he') who is presupposed to exist, but there is no single male whose existence is required by every use of that sentence. In different uses of the sentence, the existence presupposition will be different. In terms of the notion of presupposition as a semantic relation, we cannot give an adequate account of these constraints on the use and interpretation of sentences, which are closely related to those imposed by presupposition requirements.

Third, on the projection or compositional problem. This is the problem of how the presuppositions required by a complex sentence relate to the presuppositions required by its component clauses. If presupposition is regarded as a semantic relation, then this problem, say for sentences of the form 'A and B', will be a problem of determining the truth value of a sentence of that form when one or another of the conjuncts lacks a truth value. Examples discussed by Morgan and Karttunen[7] show that the proper account of the matter would be complicated, and would have some surprising consequences – for example that conjunction is not in general symmetric; the inference from 'A and B' to 'B and A' does not always preserve truth. On the other hand, if we regard presupposition from the perspective I am suggesting, the problem looks quite different; it concerns the way that pragmatic presuppositions, or background assumptions, change in the course of a conversation. Here is one obvious principle about how pragmatic presuppositions change: after some proposition has been asserted, then the speaker may reasonably presuppose it in subsequent conversation until it is denied, challenged, retracted or forgotten. If one asserts a proposition using a conjunctive sentence, then according to this simple and obvious principle, the presuppositions will change in the middle of the assertion. The first conjunct will be added to the initial presuppositions before the second conjunct is asserted.

Now the following generalization about the presuppositions *required* by conjunctive sentences follows from, and is explained by, the simple pragmatic principle given above: a conjunctive assertion requires all the presuppositions required by the first conjunct, and also all the presuppositions required by the second conjunct *except those (if any) entailed by the first conjunct*.[8] Thus 'John has children and all of his children are asleep' does not require the presupposition that John has children, even though the second conjunct does require this presupposition. This is exactly the generalization proposed by Karttunen on the basis of examples. The pragmatic account of presupposition gives a natural intuitive explanation for a rule which, on the semantic account, looks *ad hoc*. More important than this, the pragmatic account separates the semantic question of the truth value of a conjunction from the pragmatic question of the presuppositions it requires. Because we have made this separation, we can reconcile the semantical symmetry of the conjunction operation with the asymmetry of conjunctive assertions with respect to the presuppositions they require. 'A and B' says exactly the same thing as 'B and A', but the first way of saying it may require different presuppositions than the second. The analogous problem for disjunctive and conditional statements is not quite so straightforward, but I expect that a reasonably natural explanation for the facts can be given using plausible assumptions about the way background assumptions change in the course of a conversation.

Let me conclude by summarizing what I have tried to do. First, I gave a tentative definition of the concept of pragmatic presupposition and explained the notion of a sentence requiring a presupposition in terms of it. Then I gave reasons for thinking that this notion would yield explanations of linguistic phenomena which were more plausible than those that might be given in terms of the usual account of presupposition as a semantic relation. If we separate the problem of presupposition from the problem of truth value, I suggested, then it is likely that simpler accounts of the semantic relations among sentences can be given. By tying presupposition phenomena to a concept that should be central to a general account of rational communication, we might get explanations of the phenomena which are deeper and intuitively more natural. All of what I have said is very programmatic, but I hope I have convinced someone that the program is worth pursuing.

Cornell University

NOTES

[1] P. F. Strawson, *Introduction to Logical Theory* (London, 1952), pp. 175ff.
[2] Bas van Fraassen, 'Singular Terms, Truth Value Gaps and Free Logic', *Journal of Philosophy* **63** (1966), 481–95, and 'Presupposition, Implication and Self-Reference', *Journal of Philosophy* **65** (1968), 136–52.
[3] George Lakoff, 'Generative Semantics', in Danny Steinberg and Leon Jakobovits, *Semantics: an Interdisciplinary Reader in Philosophy, Linguistics and Psychology* (Cambridge, 1971), Laurence Horn, "A Presuppositional Analysis of 'Only' and 'Even'," in *Papers from the Fifth Regional Meeting of the Chicago Linguistics Society* (Chicago, 1969), Lauri Karttunen, 'Plugs, Filters, and Holes: The Projection Problem for Presuppositions'. (Paper presented at the Second Annual Meeting of the Northeastern Linguistic Society, October 24, 1971, in Montreal, Quebec.)
[4] The influence of H. P. Grice on these remarks will be clear to anyone who knows his work. The influence comes to me (by way of the grapevine) mainly from his as yet unpublished *Logic and Conversation*.
[5] There are perhaps two notions of presupposition which are relevant here: the first would be the notion I am trying to define; the other would be the simpler notion of presumed common knowledge. The distinction roughly parallels a distinction that Grice has emphasized between what is *said* and what is *meant*. In the naive, straightforward

uses of language, what is said coincides with what is meant (or at least coincides with part of what is meant), just as what is presupposed in the first sense coincides with what is presupposed in the second. And the rules which relate what is *said* to what is presupposed in the sense I am trying to define are the same rules which relate what is *meant* to what is presupposed in the simpler sense.

⁶ Horn, *op. cit.*

⁷ Karttunen, *op. cit.*, Jerry Morgan, 'On the Treatment of Presupposition in Transformational Grammar', in *Papers from the Fifth Regional Meeting of the Chicago Linguistics Society* (Chicago, 1969).

⁸ This is an oversimplification. Any presupposition required by the second conjunct, but entailed by the first conjunct *conjoined with any other initial presupposition* is not required by the sentence as a whole. But this qualification is included in Karttunen's account, as well as explained by the pragmatic account.

BAS C. VAN FRAASSEN

INCOMPLETE ASSERTION
AND BELNAP CONNECTIVES*

When a theory is confronted by new phenomena, should every effort be made to give an account of these phenomena within the confines of that theory, or should the theory be amended so as to provide an account? Philosophy of science used to answer that the criterion of success of a theory is that it need not be amended to provide an account for new phenomena. But in a science's growing stages, the practice is to amend theories as fast as new phenomena can be found.

If this is correct, semantics is growing healthily, and its proponents are laudably undogmatic about its extant theories. For we seem to be as happy to find new linguistic phenomena that do not fit out old semantic analyses as we are to see demonstrations of the wide applicability of these analyses. If there is a generation after us, it may enter what Kuhn calls a 'normal' stage.

In his 1970 paper on various strange connectives, Belnap generalized the usual semantics of modal logic simultaneously in two ways.[1] It is now clear that both generalizations can be motivated also by other developments in the field. However, it was probably not realized by Belnap that his connectives do not require, in principle, the full realization of the potentialities of his newly generalized framework.

Section I of this paper will outline the generalizations of older frameworks for semantic analysis that seem to have become imperative. In Section II I shall study Belnap connectives piecemeal, by superimposing them individually on more classical background languages. Section III will forego the advantages of retaining such a classical backdrop, and will show how a rudimentary quantum logic also belongs to the rctinue oj languages with Belnap connectives.

I. LIBERALIZATION OF SEMANTICS

1. *First Movement: Modalities*

The semantic analysis of logic consists in exhibiting logical relations

Hockney et al. (eds.), Contemporary Research in Philosophical Logic and Linguistic Semantics, 43–70. *All Rights Reserved*

among expressions as a pale reflection of relations among (extra-linguistic) entities associated with those expressions. The weasel word 'associated' is crucial here; some familiar terminology may give a sense of understanding: a noun is associated with its referent, a sentence with its truth-value. Perhaps nouns are further associated with senses, and sentences with meanings or propositions; clearly, a semantic theory must begin by spelling out this association between expressions and entities which it considers significant. The theory will be somewhat general about this, say, associating 'Pierre Trudeau' with a man, but not stipulating *which* man. A stipulation that removes the generality of the association is an *interpretation* countenanced (ruled admissible) by the semantic theory.

The simplest, if not the oldest, interpretation of sentences is the assignment to each sentence of its actual truth-value. And the simplest, if not the oldest, general theory for which this is an admissible interpretation is the theory that says: what the actual truth-value of a sentence is, depends on what is the case, i.e. what is the actual (total) state of affairs; there is a set H of possible states of affairs (or worlds) of which the actual is one; so each interpretation is a function which maps sentences plus states of affairs into truth-values.

Using terminology of Thomason's I shall call the elements of H *semantic determinants*. Note that this theory says that if you have a sentence A and are specified a semantic determinant x, then you know the truth-value of the sentence; let us call that $|A|_x$. An example of how this semantic theory explains logical relations is this: The argument with premise A and conclusion B is *valid* (or, A *semantically entails* B) exactly if for every x in H, if $|A|_x = T$ then $|B|_x = T$.

The first liberalization came with the semantic analysis of alethic modalities. 'It is possible that Pisarro pegasizes' is true in state of affairs x exactly if there is a state of affairs y which is possible relative to x, and in which 'Pisarro pegasizes' is true. What is needed then is a specification of the set $K(x)$ of elements y of H which are possible relative to x. The function K is also a semantic determinant. Now the theory says that if you have a sentence A and are specified both some element x of H and some function K of this sort (i.e. all the semantic determinants) then you have a truth-value; let us call that value $|A|^K_x$. Semantic entailment of B by A now means that, for all x in H and all relevant functions K, $|B|^K_x = T$ if $|A|^K_x = T$.

There is a clear sense in which the notion of semantic entailment has not changed. For an interpretation is specified exactly when all semantic determinants are specified. Hence we can give the general definition, fitting both semantic theories, that A semantically entails B if B is true on every interpretation on which A is true.

What I want to describe next is not a liberalization or amendment, but a change in point of view. What the actual state of affairs is, is logically irrelevant. So let us say that the interpretans $[A]$ of sentence A is what is specified when we are given all semantic determinants except the actual state of affairs. Clearly, in the second case we know $[A]$ as soon as we know the function K. And we can reify entity $[A]$ in one of two ways in this case:

(a) $[A]$ maps H into $\{T, F\}$ by the equation $[A](x) = |A|^K_x$

(b) $[A]$ is a subset of H, namely $\{x \in H: |A|^K_x = T\}$

Both reifications are found in the literature; in both cases the interpretans of A is called the *proposition expressed* by A. And the slogan formulation of this is: the truth-value of a sentence varies from one state of affairs to another (from world to world); it is jointly determined by which proposition the sentence expresses and by what is the case.

The first signs of a new generalization came in Hans Kamp's work on tense logic. [2] The above scheme fitting 'ordinary' modal logic also fitted 'ordinary' tense-logic. For example, the sentence 'Pisarro will pegasize' is true at x if there is a state of affairs y later than x such that 'Pisarro (now) pegasizes' is true at y. All that is needed then is a specification of K: $K(x) =$ (the set of elements y of H that are later than x), and the proposition ['Pisarro will pegasize'] can be determined. In the interpretation, 'now' is taken to refer to the state of affairs at which the sentence is being evaluated. Recalcitrant examples are those in which a second temporal reference occurs:

It is sunny now, but it was raining then.

If we evaluate that sentence at x, we take x as the referent of 'now' (I am assuming a one-one correspondence between times and states of affairs for simplicity), but we need also a referent for 'then'.

One response is to introduce as further semantic determinant the referent of 'then' and denote the truth-value of A as $|A|^K_{x,y}$; But what is the case *then* is logically speaking no less arbitrary then what is the case *now*. So it seems less natural to say that the proposition expressed by A is

$$[A]: [A] (x) = |A|^K_{x,y}$$

than that it is the proposition expressed by A at x. And it seems less natural to say that $|A|^K_{x,y}$ is the truth-value of A at x than that it is the truth-value of A at x *with respect to y*.

What I have just described is the second main liberalization to appear: it typifies not only Kamp's work in tense-logic but also Kaplan's theory of demonstratives, Segerberg's general theory of *two-dimensional* modal logic, and some work by Vlach and Lewis.[3] We can sloganize it in one of two equivalent ways: we can say that truth at a world has been generalized to truth at one world with respect to another, *or* we can say that the proposition expressed by a sentence now varies from world to world.

This generalization is one of the two generalizations of the semantics of ordinary modal logic in Belnap's 1970 paper. I shall need a bit of a detour to explain the other.

2. *Second Movement: Value-Gaps*

Suppose we say that a sentence must have associated with it a *proposition*, and that logical relations among sentences must be explained in terms of relations among propositions. Suppose in addition that we insist in addition that any logically relevant relation or distinction among sentences must be explainable in terms of truth-values. Then how many propositions are there? Two of course, the Tru and the False. And then, to say that a sentence's truth-value changes from one state of affairs or world to another, is to say that the proposition it expresses varies from world to world.

Looked at this way, the many-valued logicians may be regarded either as saying that there are more than two truth-values, or that there are more than two propositions. If they are regarded as saying the latter, it is necessary to ask which of those propositions are true – but this they can be regarded as answering, because they singled out certain values as *designated*, and they typically regarded as valid any argument that led from designated values only to designated values. However, it is not perfectly clear whether 'designated' corresponds simply to 'true' or to 'necessarily true'. If the latter, a full interpretation must specify among the non-designated values those propositions which happen to be true in the actual world.

What I have just said would presumably have been anathema to those who actually developed many-valued logic. They argued that really, some sentences are neither true nor false. However, the modal logicians could 'understand' work in many-valued logic by looking at it in some such way as I have described. There was however, a basic difference that would remain: modal logicians tend to regard *any* map of the set of worlds as a proposition, that is, as something that an interpretation can associate with a sentence. This is unrealistic if we assume some background specification of the meaning of the expressions of which sentences are built up. But many-valued logicians went to the other extreme: they regarded the set of propositions that can be expressed by sentences as exactly delimited, and normally finite. For example, Łukasiewicz first argued for a three-valued logic, and later for a four-valued logic.

But just the sort of motive that had led to the rejection of a two-valued (two propositions) account of logical relations would plague any finite-valued account. For suppose there are exactly m propositions. Then there are exactly $n = m^2$ couples of propositions and hence 2^n binary relations among propositions. So if we manage to distinguish more than 2^n logical relations among sentences, we cannot explain them all semantically within an m-valued logic. Modal logicians were playing with hypotheses according to which no upper bound could be set on the number of distinguishable propositions.

Now this gave a way of regarding modal logic as a generalization of many-valued logic: either by allowing infinite-valued matrices, or by regarding as valid only arguments valid in each of an infinite family of ever larger matrices. And some of the first truly semantic work in modal logic consisted in such assimilations to many-valued logic.

But as I said, none of this is in keeping with the original philosophical motivations for many-valued logic. For the idea was that some sentences are neither true nor false, and more generally that there are *value-gaps*: whereas ordinarily an expression has an associated (extra-linguistic) entity, sometimes it does not.

This philosophical stance was strongly articulated anew by Strawson in the early fifties. 4 He argued that, for example, such a sentence as

The (present) king of France is bald

has as *presupposition*

The (present) king of France exists

and *unless that presupposition is true*, the term 'The (present) king of France' has no referent and the sentence 'The (present) king of France is bald' has no truth-value. He also argued that nevertheless ordinary logic is sound (classically valid arguments are really valid and classical tautologies are always true), and that due regard to presuppositions leads to new and viable theories of definite descriptions and of categorical statements. In the fulness of time he has been shown essentially right about all this, notwithstanding the almost universal first impression of the logical community that he was contradicting himself. (His intuitions about the relations among categorical statements proved the most recalcitrant, but I feel that they are essentially vindicated by that 1970 paper of Belnap, though Belnap looked at this matter in a very different way.)

Because I intend to use these notions below, I shall here explain *presupposition* and *supervaluation*. 5

1.   *A presupposes B if and only if (on any interpretation) A is true or false only if B is true.*

If presupposition is not to be a trivial relation, there must then be truth-value gaps, that is interpretations on which a sentence may be neither true nor false.

2.   *s is a supervaluation if and only if there is a set V of interpretations such that, for any sentence A, $s(A) = T$ exactly if A is true on all members of V and $s(A) = F$ exactly if A is false on all members of V.*

Two things are obvious when stated: that $s(A)$ may be neither T nor F, namely if some elements of V differ with respect to the truth-value of A; *and* that if A semantically entails B (within the given set of original interpretations) and $s(A) = T$, then $s(B) = T$ also. These two features of supervaluations suit them to the job of representing Strawson's intuitions that first, there are truth-value gaps, and second, that arguments valid by ordinary criteria are really valid.

Supervaluations were combined with modal logic semantics in Thomason's work on indeterminism and tense logic. [6] If, in such a combination, we try to define the proposition expressed by a sentence we get something gappy: a partially defined mapping into truth-values. Were we now to introduce the second important generalization of semantics described in the preceding section, we would get another gappy mapping, this time into propositions of the old sort (=fully defined mappings into truth-values). This is how I shall approach Belnap connectives.

3. Third Movement: Belnap Connectives

In a strict sense, I shall identify as Belnap connectives only those connectives actually described in Belnap's 1970 paper. This allows one to speak unambiguously of a Belnap conditional, Belnap negation, Belnap conjunction, and Belnap disjunction. However, in a wider sense it is sometimes useful to identify as a Belnap connective any connective introduced by a schema of the general form employed by Belnap (and described below). What I call a *quasi Belnap conditional* observing the narrow sense, I shall call a *Belnap quasi-conditional* in the wide sense; and henceforth, I shall leave it to the reader to make narrow/wide sense distinctions.

In Belnap's scheme, if a sentence expresses something, that something is a proposition of the old (ordinary modal logic) sense. That is, what a sentence expresses can be reified either as a map of the states of affairs or worlds into truth-values. But what a sentence expresses is not the same in all worlds (in which it expresses something). In this way, Belnap has followed the second generalization, the one that has led to two-dimensional modal logic and such. But finally, in Belnap's scheme, a sentence need not express anything in a given world (be *non-assertive*, in his terminology). There are value gaps.

So to give all semantic information about a sentence A requires two steps

(1)   Specification of the conditions under which A is assertive.
(2)   Specification of what A expresses when it is assertive.

Similarly then, to introduce a connective ϕ semantically, it is necessary to specify when $\phi(A_1,..., A_n)$ is assertive (given total semantic information about $A_1,..., A_n$), and then for those cases in which it is assertive, to specify the proposition expressed by $\phi(A_1,..., A_n)$ in terms of the semantic information about $A_1,..., A_n$.

What is now an interesting question not considered by Belnap is: what connectives are such that they *require* such a generalized semantic framework? One way to answer this question is to axiomatize the logic and look at the completeness proof. The connectives explicitly introduced by Belnap do not fare well here; Dunn gave a completeness proof which utilizes a three-valued matrix. [7] In addition, in Sections II and III I shall treat Belnap connectives using sets of possible worlds; in the completeness proofs that set has only one member. However in Section III I shall also construct a rudimentary quantum logic following Belnap's scheme; it is essential to the completeness proof there that the set of possible worlds is a large one. However, there we find that, although a sentence does not express a proposition in each world, it does express the same proposition in all the worlds in which it is assertive. What is needed to fulfill all the potentialities of Belnap's scheme is connectives which require large sets of possible worlds, and by which sentences are composed which are not always assertive, and when assertive, do not always express the same propositions. Perhaps a theory of demonstratives with presuppositions, or a Kampian Tense-logic for Thomason's indeterministic time, would be of this sort.

II. BELNAP CONNECTIVES WITH CLASSICAL BACKGROUND

In this section I shall introduce Belnap connectives one by one into languages which have a conjunction (&) and a negation ($\sim$) for which classical logic is sound. This superimposition is by means of supervaluations.

1. *Conditionals and Quasi-Conditionals*

Belnap gives roughly the following account of conditionals. Sentences *may* express propositions; if they do, they are *assertive*. The conditional (A/B) – read as 'if A then B' – is assertive exactly if A is either true or non-assertive (briefly: non-false), and B is assertive. If assertive, (A/B) expresses the same proposition as B.

That conditional I shall call the *Belnap conditional*; I take the above account to identify it independently of other features of the languages in which it occurs. The *quasi-Belnap conditional*, also symbolized here as (A/B), is similar but simpler: $|(A/B)| = |B|$ if $|A|$ is (defined and) true and $|B|$ defined; otherwise $|(A/B)|$ is undefined. The only difference is that we have replaced the condition that A be non-false by the stronger condition that A be true.

Belnap negation is what elsewhere I call choice negation: $\sim A$ is assertive exactly if A is assertive, and $\sim A$ expresses the denial (complement) of what A expresses.

I have been convinced that there are probably no statements of form (A/B) in English. Of course, now that we know what Belnap's '/' amounts to, we can exercise our free will and begin to use sentences like 'If it rains, John will not go' to mean 'It rains/John will not go', and we may find this very useful and convenient. But whether or not the use of Belnap conditionals becomes common practice, they are interesting. The reason for their interest lies in the subject of wishes, promises, commands and requests. As is well-known each of these acts have conditional forms; consider:

(a)   If I lose an arm, let it be my left.
(b)   If you bring me a horse, I (promise that I) shall give you my kingdom.
(c)   If it rains, don't (you) go.
(d)   If you are a policeman, will you please come?

I would like to suggest that these acts are *fulfilled* if the following are true, *violated* if they are false, and *terminated* (adapting Rescher's terminology) if they are not false:[8]

(a′)   (I lose an arm/I lose my left arm)
(b′)   (You bring me a horse/I give you my kingdom)
(c′)   (It rains/you do not go)
(d′)   (You are a policeman/you come)

I won't speculate further on whether these should be Belnap conditionals or quasi-conditionals. Work dealing with subjects related to these examples has been done by Ruth Manor.[9]

Belnap introduced his conditional by reference to a passage in Quine: the main idea was that if someone were to utter (A/B), and B was false, then it would be as if he had said (asserted) nothing. But is it possible to say (utter) something and assert nothing? Not only Belnap but Strawson seems to have thought so; Strawson holds that if someone uses a sentence, and circumstances are not propitious, then he does not succeed in 'making a statement' at all.

The argument to the contrary is that in saying anything one implies (tacitly or contextually) that what one says is true, and hence that all relevant presuppositions hold. If what one says is not true, then one has *a fortiori* asserted something false, namely, that what one said is true. Such arguments were used by some medievals to attempt to disarm the liar paradox. Reminiscent of such arguments is also Russell's defence against Strawson: if I deceive someone by inducing him to believe A and A is neither true nor false, can I defend myself by arguing that I wasn't saying nothin' at all, guv'nor?

I think these arguments are spurious, because they fudge the distinction between stating and presupposing too much. What one asserts on a given occasion is not what is semantically entailed by what one says, but (a) nothing if what one says is neither true nor false, (b) what is semantically entailed by what one says if that is true or false. What one presupposes is of course the same whether what one says is true or false: it is exactly what must be the case for what one says to be true or false. And whether one is guilty of deception depends not so much on whether what one says is true or false (it is perfectly possible to deceive by making true statements) but on how and when one says it. [10]

2. *The Quasi-Belnap Conditional*

The relation of semantic entailment between A and B (under any admissible valuation of the language in question, if A is true then B is true) I symbolize as $\Vdash$. While Belnap considers various implicative relationships, I shall restrict myself to this one. The following relations all hold for both the quasi and the genuine:

$$A, (A/B) \Vdash B$$
$$\sim (A/B) \Vdash (A/\sim B)$$
$$(A/\sim B) \Vdash \sim (A/B)$$
$$(A/B) \Vdash B$$
$$A, B \Vdash (A/B)$$

but the following holds for neither

$$(A/B) \Vdash (\sim B/ \sim A)$$

and the next holds only for the quasi-conditional:

$$(A/B) \Vdash A$$

Some of these may look curious, but it must be kept clearly in mind that if someone asserts (A/B), and A is not true (or false, in the genuine Belnap conditional case), then it is as if he had said nothing. So if he did say something true, then A must be true (respectively, non-false). And in that case, *what he said* is exactly that B; so then B must be true.

Suppose that what he said was false, in which case $\sim (A/B)$ is true. Then he said something (nothing would not be true or false), so A must be true (respectively, non-false). And the false thing he said must then exactly be that B; hence $(A/\sim B)$ would have made exactly the same assertion as $\sim (A/B)$.

If anything is confusing here, it is the innate or learned inclination to assume that if $A \Vdash B$ and $B \Vdash A$ then A and B are alike in all semantic respects.

Let the syntax be as usual, with sentential variables and connectives $\sim$, $/$, &. For semantics, define a *model structure* to be a non-empty set K ('worlds') plus a non-empty set Val of maps of sentences times worlds into subsets of K ('propositions'). The elements of Val are called *proto-valuations*. Val is subject to the conditions:

2.1 $\quad V_\alpha(\sim A) = K - V_\alpha(A);$

2.2 $\quad V_\alpha(A \,\&\, B) = V_\alpha(A) \cap V_\alpha(B);$

2.3 $\quad V_\alpha(A/B) = V_\alpha(B)$ if $\alpha \in V_\alpha(A);$

2.4 $\quad$ if $V_\alpha(A) \neq V'_\alpha(A)$ there is a V'' in Val such that
$\qquad V''_\alpha(A) = \Lambda;$

2.5 $\quad$ If $\alpha \notin V_\alpha(A)$ there are V' and V'' in Val such that
$\qquad V'_\alpha(A/B) \neq V''_\alpha(A/B);$

for all V, V' in Val.

What a sentence expresses is not given by any proto-valuation, but by the *valuation* $V^\alpha(A)$ which is defined to be $V_\alpha(A)$ if for all V' in Val, $V'_\alpha(A) = V_\alpha(A)$, and which is undefined otherwise. In earlier terminology, V^α is a 'super-valuation'. [11]

That at least one model structure $\langle K, \text{Val} \rangle$ exists, is shown as part of the completeness proof below.

Semantic results

LEMMA 1. If X implies A in propositional logic, then $X \Vdash A$.

This is proved from clauses 2.1, 2.2, and 2.4, and can be proved similarly for other languages constructed below in this section.

Note that if $B_1, \ldots, B_n$ are all true at α then $B_1 \& \ldots \& B_n$ is true at α. Suppose that $B_1, \ldots, B_n$ imply A in propositional logic, and $B_1, \ldots, B_n$ are true at α. Then $\alpha \in V^\alpha(B_1 \& \ldots \& B_n)$ and $(B_1 \& \ldots \& B_n) \supset A$ is a theorem of that logic, so by 2.1 and 2.2, $V^\alpha((B_1 \& \ldots \& B_n) \supset A) = K$. So specifically, $\alpha \in V'_\alpha(B_1 \& \ldots \& B_n)$ and $\alpha \in V'_\alpha((B_1 \& \ldots \& B_n) \supset A)$ so $\alpha \in V'_\alpha(A)$, for each V' in Val. In that case, $V'_\alpha(A) \neq \Lambda$ for any V' in Val, so by 2.4, $V^\alpha(A)$ is defined. Since $\alpha \in V_\alpha(A)$, $\alpha \in V^\alpha(A)$.

LEMMA 2. If A is true at α then $V^\alpha(A/B) = V^\alpha(B)$ iff B is assertive at α.

Suppose A is true at α (that is, $\alpha \in V^\alpha(A)$). Then for all $V' \in \text{Val}$, $\alpha \in V'_\alpha(A)$. Hence for all V' in Val, $V'_\alpha(A/B) = V'_\alpha(B)$. But then, if B is assertive, $V^\alpha(B)$ exists and equals $V'_\alpha(B)$ for all V' in Val. Hence, in that case $V^\alpha(A/B)$ exists, and equals $V^\alpha(B)$.

On the other hand, if B is not assertive, then there are V, V' in Val such that $V_\alpha(B) \neq V'_\alpha(B)$; so then $V_\alpha(A/B) = V_\alpha(B) \neq V'_\alpha(B) = V'_\alpha(A/B)$; therefore (A/B) is not assertive. (Throughout we shall take an equation $t = s$ to be true only if t and s both exist.)

LEMMA 3. If A is not true at α, then (A/B) is not assertive at α.

If for some V in Val, $\alpha \notin V_\alpha(A)$, then (A/B) is not assertive, by clause 2.5. But if A is not true at α, then either A is false at α (in which case $\alpha \notin V_\alpha(A)$ for any V in Val $\neq \Lambda$) or A is not assertive at α, and then there is a V'' such that $\alpha \notin V''_\alpha(A)$ by clause 2.4.

Note that the effect of 2.4 is to make A non-true if and only if there is some V in Val such that $\alpha \notin V_\alpha(A)$.

3. *Logic of Quasi-Conditionals.*

Each logical system described in this paper will be characterized by mean- of its consequence operator: for any set X, $\text{Cn}(X)$ will be the set of sens tences deductively implied by X, and the single turnstile ⊢ will be used such that $\text{Cn}(X) = \{A : X \vdash A\}$. As a preliminary, we define:

An operation Cn on sets of sentences is a *logical closure operator* iff, for all sets of sentences X and Y:

(a) $X \subseteq \text{Cn}(X)$

(b) $\text{Cn}(\text{Cn}(X)) \subseteq \text{Cn}(X)$

(c)   if $X \subseteq Y$ then $\text{Cn}(X) \subseteq \text{Cn}(Y)$

Each consequence operator will be a logical closure operator, and will in addition be *finitary* (i.e. if $A \in \text{Cn}(X)$ then X has a finite subset Y such that $A \in \text{Cn}(Y)$).

The system QBC has as its consequence operator the smallest logical closure operator Cn such that:

3.1   if X implies A by propositional logic then $A \in \text{Cn}(X)$

3.2 $[A \supset (A/B) \equiv B] \in \text{Cn}(\Lambda)$

3.3 $(A \ \& \ B) \in \text{Cn}(\{(A/B)\})$

3.4 $\text{Cn}(\{\sim(A/B)\}) = \text{Cn}(\{(A/\sim B)\})$

Both modus ponens and $A, B \vdash (A/B)$ follow from 3.2 and 3.1. Note that there is no implication from $X \cup \{A\} \vdash B$ to $X \vdash (A/B)$ – that is, no deduction theorem for the quasi-conditional. Even (A/A) is not a theorem (and is semantically invalid).

The clue to the completeness proof is the fact that the constructed language has a 'radical presuppositional' sub-language; I shall give the proof directly however.

That the logical system is sound means that $X \Vdash A$ if $A \in \text{Cn}(X)$; and that this is so follows quite easily from our semantic lemmas above. Completeness is the converse property: $A \in \text{Cn}(X)$ if $X \Vdash A$. For the present case, this follows from a much stronger result: for any set Y, the set $\text{Cn}(Y)$ is such that, in a certain model structure, *all and only* the sentences in $\text{Cn}(Y)$ are true.

Let $X = \text{Cn}(X)$. Then let $K = \{\alpha\}$ and let Val be such that $\{V_\alpha : V \in \text{Val}\}$ is the set of all 'classical' valuations that satisfy X. (A *classical valuation* is any map of the sentences into $\{T, F\}$ which follows the truth-tables for & and $\sim$; there are no restrictions on what these assign to conditionals.) Identify K with T and Λ with F. It needs to be shown that conditions 2.1–2.5 hold for Val; if that is so V^α will satisfy X, but no sentence outside X, and thus show that not $X \vdash A$ if not $X \Vdash A$.

That conditions 2.1 and 2.2 hold follows from the definition of Val. Concerning 2.4: if $V_\alpha(A) \neq V'_\alpha(A)$ then one equals Λ, and α is not in that.

The set X contains $A \supset ((A/B) \equiv B)$. Therefore, if $V_\alpha(A) = T$, then $V_\alpha((A/B) \equiv B) = T$, by 3.2, so $V_\alpha(A/B) = V_\alpha(B)$; thus clause 2.3 holds. If $V_\alpha(A) \neq T$ then A cannot belong to X. But then X cannot contain either (A/B) or $(A/\sim B)$, by 3.3, hence neither (A/B) nor $\sim (A/B)$, by 3.4. But then, there are two classical valuations satisfying X which assign different values to (A/B) – see 3.1 – so clause 2.5 holds. This ends the confirmation that $\langle K, \text{Val} \rangle$ is a model structure of the language.

4. *The Belnap Conditional*

The quasi-Belnap conditional semantically implies, and is so implied, by the conjunction of its antecedent and consequent. The Belnap conditional (A/B) must be similarly semantically equivalent to $I(A)$ & B, where $I(A)$ is a sentence tantamount to: A is not false.

This sentence $I(A)$ can be formulated by means of the conditional itself. There is a sentence T which is always true, namely $\sim (A \& \sim A)$. Now (A/T) is true if and only if A is not false and T is true, hence if and only if A is not false.

As model structures, couples $\langle K, \text{Val} \rangle$ are chosen such that K ('worlds') is a non-empty set, and *Val* ('proto-valuations') is a set of maps of sentences times worlds into subsets of K ('propositions') subject to:

4.1 $V_\alpha(\sim A) = K - V_\alpha(A)$

4.2 $V_\alpha(A \& B) = V_\alpha(A) \cap V_\alpha(B)$

4.3 $V_\alpha(A/B) = V_\alpha(B)$ if for some V' in Val, $\alpha \in V'_\alpha(A)$

4.4   if for some V', V'' in Val, $V'_\alpha(A) \neq V''_\alpha(A)$ then there is a V in Val such that $\alpha \in V_\alpha(A)$ and also a V' in Val such that $V'_\alpha(A) = \Lambda$.

4.5   if for all V' in Val, $\alpha \notin V'_\alpha(A)$ then there are V, V'' in Val such that $V_\alpha(A/B) \neq V''_\alpha(A/B)$

Again, the *valuation* on $\langle K, \text{Val} \rangle$ is the map V defined by: $V^\alpha(A) = V_\alpha(A)$ if for all V' in Val, $V'_\alpha(A) = V_\alpha(A)$; otherwise $V^\alpha(A)$ is undefined.

Semantic results

Let us say that A is *non-false* at α if either $V^\alpha(A)$ is defined and $\alpha \in V^\alpha(A)$ – 'A is true at α' – or $V^\alpha(A)$ is undefined.

LEMMA 1. A is non-false at α iff there is a $V \in$ Val such that $\alpha \in V_\alpha(A)$.

This is so because if A is true at α then $\alpha \in V_\alpha(A)$ for all V in Val; if $V^\alpha(A)$ is undefined, then for some V and V' in Val, $V_\alpha(A) \neq V'_\alpha(A)$; hence by clause 4.4, there is a V in Val such that $\alpha \in V_\alpha(A)$. Conversely, if $\alpha \in V_\alpha(A)$ for some V in Val, then, if $V^\alpha(A)$ is defined, $\alpha \in V^\alpha(A)$.

LEMMA 2. If A is non-false at α, and $V^\alpha(B)$ is defined, then $V^\alpha(A/B) = = V^\alpha(B)$.

If A is non-false at α, then, by Lemma 1, there is a V' in Val such that $\alpha \in V'_\alpha(A)$. Hence $V_\alpha(A/B) = V_\alpha(B)$ for each V in Val. If $V^\alpha(B)$ is defined, then $V_\alpha(B) = V'_\alpha(B)$ for all V, V' in Val. Hence in that case, $V_\alpha(A/B = = V'_\alpha(A/B) = V_\alpha(B)$ for each V, V' in Val, so $V^\alpha(A/B)$ is defined, and equals $V^\alpha(B)$.

LEMMA 3. If A is false at α, then $V^\alpha(A/B)$ is not defined. For if A is false at α, then $\alpha \notin V'_\alpha(A)$ for any V' in Val; in that case, by 4.5, $V^\alpha(A/B)$ is not defined.

LEMMA 4. Let $I(A)$ be $(A/A \supset A)$. Then $I(A)$ is assertive at α (i.e. $V^\alpha(IA)$ is defined) if and only if A is non-false at α, and $I(A)$ is true at α if and only if $I(A)$ is assertive at α.

If A is non-false then (Lemma 2), $(A/A \supset A)$ is assertive, and $V^\alpha(A/A \subseteq A) = V^\alpha(A \supset A) = K$; so in addition, $I(A)$ is then true at α.

If A is false then (Lemma 3), $I(A)$ is not assertive.

These are the only two possible cases.

LEMMA 5. $A \supset (B \equiv (A/B))$ is valid.

This is so because for all α in K, all V in Val, $\alpha \in V_\alpha(A \supset (B \equiv (A/B)))$. For suppose $\alpha \in V_\alpha(A)$. Then for some V' in Val, $\alpha \in V'_\alpha(A)$; hence $V_\alpha(B) = V_\alpha(A/B)$. But $\supset$ and $\equiv$ are classical in this context: $V_\alpha(C \equiv D) = = K$ if $V_\alpha(C) = V_\alpha(D)$ and $V_\alpha(C \supset D) = (K - V_\alpha(C)) \cup V_\alpha(D)$. So we have: either $\alpha \notin V_\alpha(A)$ or $\alpha \in V_\alpha(B \equiv (A/B))$; hence $\alpha \in V_\alpha(A \supset (B \equiv (A/B)))$.

LEMMA 6. Either A is false at α or $[C \equiv (A/C)]$ is true at α.

If A is not false at α then there is (Lemma 1) a member V' of Val such that $\alpha \in V'_\alpha(A)$. But then, for each V in Val, $V_\alpha(C) = V_\alpha(A/C)$. So, for each V in Val, $V_\alpha(C \equiv (A/C)) = K$. Thus $V^\alpha(C \equiv (A/C)) = K$.

LEMMA 7. $I(\sim A)$ is true at α iff A is not true at α.

By Lemma 4, $I(\sim A)$ is true at α iff $\sim A$ is not false at α. But $\sim A$ is false at α iff A is true at α. Hence $I(\sim A)$ is true at α iff A is not true at α.

LEMMA 8. If $\Vdash A \equiv B$ then $I(A) \Vdash I(B)$.

If $A \equiv B$ is true at α, then $V^\alpha(A \equiv B)$ is defined, and for all V' in Val, $\alpha \in V'_\alpha(A \equiv B)$. But $V'_\alpha(A \equiv B) = V'_\alpha(A \,\&\, B) \cup V'_\alpha(\sim A \,\&\, \sim B)$. Hence $\alpha \in V'_\alpha(A)$ iff $\alpha \in V'_\alpha(B)$ in this case. Now suppose $\alpha \in V^\alpha(I(A))$. Then there is a V' such that $\alpha \in V'_\alpha(A)$, and hence $\alpha \in V'_\alpha(B)$. So, if A is non-false at α, then B is non-false at α. (Note from Lemmas 1 and 4 that $I(A)$ is true at α iff there is a V' such that $\alpha \in V'_\alpha(A)$.)

5. Logic of Belnap Conditionals

As logical system – call it BC – I offer: let Cn be the smallest logical closure operator such that:

5.1	if X implies A by propositional logic, then $A \in \mathrm{Cn}(X)$
5.2	$[A \supset (B \equiv (A/B))] \in \mathrm{Cn}(A)$
5.3	$B \in \mathrm{Cn}(\{A, I(\sim A)\})$
5.4	if $A \equiv B \in \mathrm{Cn}(A)$ then $I(A) \in \mathrm{Cn}(\{I(B)\})$
5.5	$\mathrm{Cn}(X \cup \{A\}) \cap \mathrm{Cn}(X \cup \{I(\sim A)\}) \subseteq \mathrm{Cn}(X)$
5.6	$\mathrm{Cn}(\{(A/B)\}) = \mathrm{Cn}(\{I(A), B\})$
5.7	$\mathrm{Cn}(\{\sim(A/B)\}) = \mathrm{Cn}(\{(A/\sim B)\})$
5.8	$\mathrm{Cn}(X \cup \{C \equiv (A/C)\}) \cap \mathrm{Cn}(X \cup \{\sim A\}) \subseteq \mathrm{Cn}(X)$

Consistency can be shown at once by interpreting $I(A)$ as A and (A/B) as $(A \,\&\, B)$. Soundness follows from the lemmas in the preceding section.

Completeness. The clue to completeness is that this language has a 'conservative presuppositional' sublanguage, but as for QBC, I shall give the proof directly.

The strategy is slightly different from last time. Suppose $A \notin \mathrm{Cn}(Y)$. In that case, either $Y \cup \{\sim A\}$ or $Y \cup \{I(\sim A)\}$ is consistent, because of 5.5. But a consistent set can be extended into a maximal consistent set because Cn is finitary. So there is a maximal consistent set X which has Y as a subset and either $\sim A$ or $I(\sim A)$ as a member. If we can now show that there is a model structure in which all the members of X are true (at a certain world), it will follow that Y does not semantically entail A, since A can certainly not be true there.

Let X be a maximal consistent set of BC. Then X is also a deductively closed consistent set of propositional logic, and there is at least one classical valuation (see Section III) which satisfies X. Choose $K=\{\alpha\}$, identify T with K and F with Λ, and let Val be such that $\{V_\alpha : V \in \text{Val}\}$ is the set of classical valuations which satisfy X.

$\langle K, \text{Val}\rangle$, as defined, needs to be a model structure. That clauses 4.1 and 4.2 hold is obvious. If $\alpha \in V'_\alpha(A)$ for some V' in Val, then $\sim A \notin X$. Since X is maximal, it follows that $C \equiv (A/C) \in X$ for all C. (For if inconsistency followed equally from the addition of $\sim A$ or of $C \equiv (A/C)$ to X, for any C, then by 5.8, X would already be inconsistent.) Hence for each $V \in \text{Val}$: $V_\alpha(C \equiv (A/C)) = T$, hence $V_\alpha(C) = V_\alpha(A/C)$. So clause 4.3 holds.

If Val contains V', V'' such that $V'_\alpha(A) \neq V''_\alpha(A)$, then either $\alpha \in V'_\alpha(A)$ or $\alpha \in V''_\alpha(A)$, for one equals K, the other Λ. So 4.4 holds.

If for all V' in Val, $\alpha \notin V'_\alpha(A)$, then all V'_α satisfy $\sim A$, so $\sim A \in X$. But then neither (A/B) nor $(A/\sim B)$ is in X, for each deductively implies $I(A)$, by 5.6; and $\{\sim A, I(A)\}$ is inconsistent by 5.3 and 5.4. But then neither (A/B) nor $\sim (A/B)$ is in X, for the latter implies $(A/\sim B)$, by 5.7. Therefore there are classical valuations satisfying X which differ with respect to (A/B), by the completeness of propositional logic. So if for all V' in Val, $\alpha \notin V'_\alpha(A)$, then there are V, V'' in Val such that $V_\alpha(A) \neq V''_\alpha(A)$. Thus 4.5 holds also.

This ends the proof.

6. Belnap Disjunction and Conjunction

Disjunction and conjunction were introduced by Belnap in a parallel way, which could be adapted to any commutative set operation: in any world α, the proposition expressed by $\Phi(A, B)$ is

> $|\Phi(A, B)|$ is (a) $\Phi(|A|, |B|)$ if A, B are both assertive
> (b) $|A|$ if A only is assertive
> (c) $|B|$ if B only is assertive
> (d) undefined if neither A nor B is assertive

Here Φ could be, for example, $\cup$, $\cap$, or $+$. As example I shall take Belnap disjunction, which I symbolize as $\lor$.

A model structure is a couple $\langle K, \text{Val}\rangle$ as before, but the conditions on elements of Val are now:

6.1 $V_\alpha(\sim A) = K - V_\alpha(A)$

6.2 $V_\alpha(A \,\&\, B) = V_\alpha(A) \cap V_\alpha(B)$

6.3 $V_\alpha(A \lor B) =$ (a) $V_\alpha(A) \cup V_\alpha(B)$ if $As(\alpha, A)$ and $As(\alpha, B)$
  (b) $V_\alpha(A)$ if $As(\alpha, A)$ and not $As(\alpha, B)$
  (c) $V_\alpha(B)$ if $As(\alpha, B)$ and not $As(\alpha, A)$

6.4 If neither $As(\alpha, A)$ nor $As(\alpha, B)$, then there are V and V' in Val such that $V_\alpha(A \lor B) \ne V'_\alpha(A \lor B)$.

6.5 If not $As(\alpha, A)$ then there is a V' in Val such that $V'_\alpha(A) = \Lambda$.

These conditions are to hold for all V in Val; '$As(\alpha, A)$' abbreviates '$V'_\alpha(A) = V_\alpha(A)$ for all V, V' in Val'.

Finally, the valuation V^α on $\langle K, Val \rangle$ is defined as usual.

Semantic results. $V^\alpha(A \,\&\sim A)$ is always defined and equals Λ. So $V_\alpha(A \lor (A \,\&\sim A))$ is $V^\alpha(A)$ if that is defined, and is Λ otherwise. Hence also, $V_\alpha(\sim(A \lor (A \,\&\sim A))$ is $K - V^\alpha(A)$ if that is defined, and K otherwise. Thus there are two possibilities, if we define $\approx A$ as $\sim(A \lor (A \,\&\sim A))$:

LEMMA 1. $\approx A$ is always assertive, and is true if and only if A is non-true.

For suppose A is non-true. Then A is either false or not assertive. If A is false, $V^\alpha(A)$ is defined and $V^\alpha(\approx A) = K - V^\alpha(A) = V^\alpha(\sim A)$, and $\alpha \in V^\alpha(\sim A)$ and hence $\alpha \in V^\alpha(\approx A)$. If A is not assertive, then $V^\alpha(\approx A) = K$, and $\alpha \in V^\alpha(\approx A)$.

Suppose conversely that $\alpha \in V^\alpha(\approx A)$. Then if A were true, $V^\alpha(A)$ would be defined, and α would belong to $V^\alpha(A)$ and to $K - V^\alpha(A)$ which is impossible.

LEMMA 2. A is not assertive if and only if $\approx A$ and $\approx(\sim A)$ are both true.

If A is not assertive, both A and $\sim A$ are non-true, and so $\approx A$ and $\approx(\sim A)$ are true. If $\approx A$ and $\approx(\sim A)$ are true, then A and $\sim A$ are both non-true, so A is not assertive.

LEMMA 3. $A \Vdash A \lor B$; $B \Vdash A \lor B$; if $X \cup \{A\} \Vdash C$ and $X \cup \{B\} \Vdash C$ then $X \cup \{A \lor B\} \Vdash C$.

If A is true it is assertive, so then $V^\alpha(A \lor B)$ is either $V^\alpha(A)$ or $V^\alpha(A) \cup V^\alpha(B)$; hence if $\alpha \in V^\alpha(A)$ then $\alpha \in V^\alpha(A \lor B)$.

If any valuation V is such that $\alpha \in V^\alpha(A \lor B)$, then either $V^\alpha(A)$ is defined or $V^\alpha(B)$ is defined, and in addition, either $\alpha \in V^\alpha(A)$ or $\alpha \in V^\alpha(B)$, since $V^\alpha(A \lor B)$ equals either $V^\alpha(A)$ or $V^\alpha(B)$ or $V^\alpha(A \cup B)$. This suffices to prove the lemma.

It follows from Lemmas 1 and 3 that $A \lor \approx A$ is valid, and that $\sim A \Vdash \approx A$.

LEMMA 4. $\{\sim A, \approx B\} \Vdash \sim (A \lor B)$

$\qquad\qquad \{\approx A, \sim B\} \Vdash \sim (A \lor B)$

If A is false and B is not true, there are two possibilities: B is false, and $V^\alpha(A \lor B) = V^\alpha(A) \cup V^\alpha(B)$; B is not assertive, and $V^\alpha(A \lor B) = V^\alpha(A)$. In either case, $A \lor B$ is assertive and not true; hence false.

LEMMA 5. $\approx (\sim A), \approx (\sim B) \Vdash \approx (\sim (A \lor B))$

Suppose $A \lor B$ were false. Then either A or B is assertive, and neither can be true (because of Lemma 3). Hence either $\sim A$ or $\sim B$ is true. But then $\approx (\sim A)$ and $\approx (\sim B)$ cannot both be true, by Lemma 1.

7. *Logic of Belnap Disjunction*

The logical system *BD* has as consequence operator the least logical closure operator Cn such that

7.1   if X implies A by propositional logic, $A \in \text{Cn}(X)$.

7.2 $A \lor B \in \text{Cn}(A) \cap \text{Cn}(B)$

7.3 $\text{Cn}(X \cup \{A\}) \cap \text{Cn}(X \cup \{B\}) \subseteq \text{Cn}(X \cup \{A \lor B\})$

7.4 $\text{Cn}(X \cup \{A\}) \cap \text{Cn}(X \cup \{\approx A\}) \subseteq \text{Cn}(X)$

7.5 $\sim (A \lor B) \in \text{Cn}(\{\sim A, \approx B\}) \cap \text{Cn}(\{\approx A, \sim B\})$

7.6 $\approx (\sim (A \lor B)) \in \text{Cn}(\{\approx (\sim A), \approx (\sim B)\})$

The soundness of *BD* follows from the lemmas in the preceding section. For convenience we prove some theorems about *BD*.

Proof-theoretic results

T.1 $\sim B \Vdash \approx B$. For $\sim B, B \vdash \approx B$; $\sim B, \approx B \Vdash \approx B$; and 7.4

T.2 $\sim A, \sim B \vdash \sim (A \lor B)$. By T1. and 7.5

T.3 $\approx A, A \vdash B$. For $\approx A \vdash \sim (A \lor (A \,\&\, \sim A))$ by def; while $A \vdash A \lor (A \,\&\, \sim A)$ by 7.2.

T.4 $\approx A, A \lor B \vdash B$; $\approx A, A \vdash B$ (T.3) and $\approx A, B \vdash B$; and 7.3

T.5 $A \lor B \vdash B \lor A$. By 7.3 also.

T.6 $\vdash A \lor \approx A$. By 7.4
T.7   if $X, A \vdash (A \mathbin{\&} \sim A)$ then $X \mathbin{x} \approx A$.

For then $X, A \mathbin{x} \approx A$ and $X, \approx \mathbin{x} \approx A$; use 7.4

T.8 $\approx A, \approx B \vdash \approx (A \lor B)$. From T.7 via 7.3.

Completeness If $A \notin Cn(Y)$ then $Y \cup \{\approx A\}$ is consistent (see 7.4) and can be extended into a maximal consistent set which does not contain A (see T.3).

Let X be a maximal consistent set of BD, and Val, $K = \{\alpha\}$ be such that $\{V_\alpha : V \in \text{Val}\}$ is the set of classical valuations that satisfy X, where $T = K$ and $F = \Lambda$. As before, it will do to show that $\langle K, \text{Val} \rangle$ is a model structure.

Clauses 6.1, 6.2, 6.5 hold of course. If $As(\alpha, A)$ and $As(\alpha, B)$ then either A or $\sim A$, and either B or $\sim B$ are in X. In the first three cases $A \lor B \in X$ by 7.2; in the last case $\sim (A \lor B)$ by T2. In each case $V^\alpha(A \lor B) = V^\alpha(A) \cup \cup V^\alpha(B)$. If $As(\alpha, A)$ and not $As(\alpha, B)$ then neither B nor $\sim B$ is in X, but A and $\approx B$ are, or $\sim A$ and $\approx B$ are. In the first case $A \lor B$ by 7.2, and in the second case $\sim (A \lor B)$ by 7.5 belongs to X. So $A \lor B$ is assertive and expresses the same proposition as A. So clause 6.3 holds.

To show that 6.4 holds, suppose that not $As(\alpha, A)$ and not $As(\alpha, B)$. Then $A, \sim A, B, \sim B$ are not members of X, but $\approx A, \approx (\sim A), \approx B, \approx (\sim B)$ are. Therefore, $\approx (A \lor B)$ is in X by T8, and $\approx (\sim (A \lor B))$ is in X by 7.6. Because of T3 it follows that $(A \lor B)$ and $\sim (A \lor B)$ are both absent from X. So by the completeness of propositional logic, Val has members V and V' which differ on $(A \lor B)$. This ends the proof.

III. BELNAP CONNECTIVES AND QUANTUM LOGIC

In this section I will not superimpose connectives on a classical background language, as I did in Section II. Apart from that I have two rather disparate objectives: the first, to examine a language whose *only* connectives are Belnap negation, Belnap disjunction, and the quasi Belnap conditional; the second, to develop a rudimentary quantum logic within Belnap's scheme.[12]

1. *A Minimal Logical Base*

Belnap negation is the best behaved of his connectives; it is exactly the choice negation that I have studied in various other contexts. Hence I can follow my earlier method of construction to the extent of superimposing the other connectives on a language with classical negation. The absence of classical conjunction (or other suitably chosen truth-functional connectives) is what creates the difficulties. (Even with a constant true or constant false sentence in the language, there would be no real departure from Section II in the completeness proof here. Therefore I will not assume the existence of such a sentence in this context.)

Let L_0 be a language whose set of sentences is closed under unary connective $\sim$; other aspects of its grammar I leave indeterminate for now. The admissible valuations of L_0 are the maps v of its sentences into $\{T, F\}$ such that $v(\sim A) = T$ if and only if $v(A) = F$. The logic SC_0 has as consequence the least logical consequence operator Cn such that

1.1 $B \in \mathrm{Cn}(\{A, \sim A\})$

1.2 $\mathrm{Cn}(X \cup \{A\}) \cap \mathrm{Cn}(X \cup \{\sim A\}) \subseteq \mathrm{Cn}(X)$

As before, Cn is finitary. I shall abbreviate "$\{A, B\}$" and "$X \cup \{A\}$" to "A, B" and "X, A", and so on, when convenient.

The soundness and completeness proofs for SC_0 with respect to L_0 are very simple. Note specifically that $X \Vdash A$ exactly if $\{X, \sim A\}$ cannot be satisfied, and that a maximal consistent set (*vis à vis* SC_0) contains exactly one of A and $\sim A$, for each sentence A. (Because of 1.2 if X is consistent, so is either $X \cup \{A\}$ or $X \cup \{\sim A\}$, so that A or $\sim A$ belongs to X if X is a maximal consistent set; maximal consistent sets exist because Cn is finitary.)

2. Combination of the Quasi Belnap Conditional, Negation, and Disjunction

The syntax of L_0 and of L is the same now: a set of sentences closed under unary connective $\sim$ and binary connectives $\lor$ and $/$. For the semantics of L, an m.s. is a couple $\langle K, \mathrm{Val} \rangle$, with K a non-empty set, and Val a set of proto-valuations (maps of K times sentences into $P(K)$) such that

2.1 $V_\alpha(\sim A) = K - V_\alpha(A)$

2.2 $V_\alpha(A/B) = V_\alpha(B)$ if A is true at α and B assertive at α.

2.3 $V_\alpha(A \lor B) = V_\alpha(A) \cup V_\alpha(B)$ if A and B are both assertive at α; $V_\alpha(A)$ if A but not B is assertive at α; and $V_\alpha(B)$ if B but not A is assertive at α.

2.4   (a) if $V_\alpha(A) \neq V'_\alpha(A)$ there is a V'' in Val such that $V''_\alpha(A) = \Lambda$.

          (b) if $\alpha \notin V_\alpha(A)$ there are V', V'' in Val such that $V'_\alpha(A/B) \neq$
            $\neq V''_\alpha(A/B)$

          (c) if neither A nor B is assertive at α there are V, V' in Val
            such that $V_\alpha(A \lor B) \neq V'_\alpha(A \lor B)$.

LEMMA 1. A is not true at α iff for some V in Val, $\alpha \notin V_\alpha(A)$.

Proof. If A is false at α, $\alpha \notin V^\alpha(A) = V_\alpha(A)$. If A is neither true nor false at α then by 2.4(a) there is a V'' such that $V''_\alpha(A) = \Lambda$ and $\alpha \notin \Lambda$.

LEMMA 2. If $X \Vdash A$ in L_0 then $X \Vdash A$ in L.

Proof. Suppose $V^\alpha(B)$ to be defined for all B in X, and $\alpha \in V^\alpha(B)$ for such B; and also A not true at α. Then by Lemma 1, there is a V' in Val such that $\alpha \notin V'_\alpha(A)$. But clearly $\alpha \in V'_\alpha(B)$ for all B in X. For V'_α, define the map v: $v(C) = \begin{cases} T \text{ if } \alpha \in V'_\alpha(C) \\ F \text{ otherwise} \end{cases}$ for all sentences C. By clause 2.1, v is an admissible valuation of L_0; it satisfies X but not A. Hence if not $X \Vdash A$ in L then not $X \Vdash A$ in L_0.

LEMMA 3. If A is false, then either B or $\sim (A \lor B)$ is true. In the latter case, so are $\sim (B \lor A)$ and $(\sim A \lor \sim B)$.

The logical system I shall call QBND; its consequence is the least logical consequence operator such that:

q1.   If $X \vdash A$ in SC_0 then $A \in Cn(X)$

q2. $Cn(A/B) = Cn(\{A, B\})$

q3. $Cn(\sim (A/B) = Cn(A/\sim B)$

q4. $A \lor B \in Cn(A) \cap Cn(B)$

q5. $Cn(X, A) \cap Cn(X, B) \subseteq Cn(X, A \lor B)$

q6. $\sim (A \lor B) \in Cn(\{\sim A, \sim B\})$

q7. $(\sim A \lor \sim B) \in Cn(\sim (A \lor B))$
        and $Cn(\sim (A \lor B)) = Cn(\sim (B \lor A))$

q8. $Cn(X, B) \cap Cn(X, \sim (A \lor B)) \subseteq Cn(X, \sim A)$

The soundness of these consequence conditions can be demonstrated as for similar conditions in Section II.

For the completeness proof, *prime* theories (a notion to be defined presently) will play the role that maximal consistent theories played before. Let X be a set such that $A \notin Cn(X)$. Call a theory *prime* if it is consistent, and contains B or C if it contains $B \lor C$. Then there is a prime theory Y containing

X but not A. We construct Y as follows: let $A_1, \ldots, A_k, \ldots$ be all the sentences.

$$X_0 \quad = X$$
$$X_{i+1} = \quad\quad X_i \cup \{A_i\} \text{ if that does not imply } A; \text{ otherwise}$$
$$X_i \cup \{\sim A_i\} \text{ if that does not imply } A; \text{ otherwise}$$
$$X_{i+1} = X_i$$
$$Y \quad = \bigcup_{i=0}^{\infty} X_i.$$

First, Y contains X, and Y does not imply A because none of its finite subsets do. Secondly, if $Y \vdash A_i$, then $X_i \cup \{A_i\}$ does not imply A; hence X_{i+1} and so also Y, contains A_i if $Y \vdash A_i$. Thirdly, if $(A_i \lor A_k)$ is in Y, then either $Y \cup \{A_i\}$ or $Y \cup \{A_k\}$ does not imply A (see q5) so $X_i \cup \{A_i\}$ *or* $X_k \cup \{A_k\}$ does not imply A; therefore A_i or A_k belongs to Y.

Fourthly, if $\sim A_i$ is in Y, and A_j is not, then $A_l = \sim (A_i \lor A_j)$ is in Y. For suppose that $X_j \cup \{A_j\}$ and $X_l \cup \{A_l\}$ implied A. Then $Y, A_j \vdash A$ and $Y, A_l \vdash A$; so by q8, $Y, \sim A_i \vdash A$, which cannot be if $\sim A_i$ is in Y.

It will suffice therefore to show that any prime theory Y can be satisfied while not satisfying any sentence not in Y. Let Y be a prime theory, $\alpha = Y$, $K = \{\alpha\}$, $T = K$ and $\Lambda = F$, and Val such that $\{V_\alpha : V \in \text{Val}\}$ is the set of L_0 valuations that satisfy Y. Then we need to verify that $\langle K, \text{Val} \rangle$ is an m.s. for L and V^α satisfies only Y.

LEMMA $V^\alpha(A) = T$ if $A \in Y$ and $V^\alpha(A) = F$ if $\sim A \in Y$; A is not assertive otherwise.

Most of this is obvious. If neither A nor $\sim A$ belongs to Y, we note that Y is closed under Cn, and hence under SC_0 deduction (ql); therefore Y is an SC_0 theory, and does not imply A or $\sim A$. But then $Y \cup \{A\}$ and $Y \cup \{\sim A\}$ are SC_0 consistent, and so satisfied by distinct L_0 valuations V_α, V'_α. Therefore, in such a case, A is not assertive at α.

LEMMA $\langle K, \text{Val} \rangle$ is an m.s. for L.

The set Val is not empty because Y is a consistent SC_0 theory $V_\alpha(\sim A) = K - V_\alpha(A)$ by the definition of Val and L_0-valuation.

If A is true then $A \in Y$ by the preceding lemma; so by q2, (A/B) is in Y iff B is in Y. So then, if B is assertive, so is (A/B), and $V^\alpha(B) = V^\alpha(A/B)$ in that case.

Clause 2.3 is a bit more complicated. If A or B is in Y then so is $A \lor B$;

and if $A \lor B$ is in Y so is A or B (q4). Hence $A \lor B$ is true exactly if at least one of A and B is true. If $\sim A$ and $\sim B$ are in Y, so is $\sim (A \lor B)$ by q6; so if A and B are false, so is $A \lor B$. If $\sim A$ is in Y, and B is not then $\sim (A \lor B)$ and $\sim (B \lor A)$ are in Y, so if A is false and B not assertive, or conversely, then $A \lor B$ is false. Finally, if $\sim (A \lor B)$ is in Y then so is $(\sim A \lor \sim B)$ by q7, hence also either $\sim A$ or $\sim B$; and neither A nor B by q1, q4, q7. Therefore, $A \lor B$ is false exactly if either A or B is false and the other not true.

2.4(a) is immediate because $V_\alpha(A) \in \{K, \Lambda\}$. Clause 2.4(b) also gives little difficulty: if $\alpha \notin V_\alpha(A)$ then A is not true, so $A \notin Y$, so (A/B) and $(A/\sim B)$ are not in Y. Hence by q3, (A/B) and $\sim (A/B)$ are outside Y. There are then, for reasons indicated already, L_0 valuations V_α and V'_α respectively satisfying $Y \cup \{(A/B)\}$ and $Y \cup \{\sim (A/B)\}$. Finally, the third clause of 2.4 is essentially established above: if $(A \lor B)$ or $\sim (A \lor B)$ is in Y, then either A or B, or either $\sim A$ or $\sim B$ is in Y. So if neither A nor B is assertive, then neither $(A \lor B)$ nor $\sim (A \lor B)$ are in Y, and there are L_0 valuations V_α, V'_α each satisfying Y but disagreeing on $(A \lor B)$.

Therefore, $\langle K, \text{Val} \rangle$ is an L-m.s.

3. Empirically Testable Propositions

In each of the preceding completeness proofs, the set K was a unit set. Hence the modal character of the connectives is minimal. I will now describe a language with Belnap connectives in which the completeness proof requires a set K of large cardinality. This could have been done by introducing a Belnap necessity or strict conditional, say, but in fact it derives from an idea due to Professor C. Hooker, who pointed out that quantum-logical propositions might be said to have presuppositions, in our technical sense, concerning what measurements can in principle be performed. What I shall report now is a small part of the work he and I are presently doing together.

In quantum logic and related endeavors, the possible worlds are construed as possible states of a given physical system. The 'logic' of such a system is a family **P** of propositions which are generated as follows: there is a set O of observables, and a family B (a field of sets of real numbers) and for each m in O and E in B we can ask the question: *if a measurement of m is made on a system in state α, will the result found be in E*? Much of the empirically testable content of the physical theory is reflected in its answers to these questions. If $Q(\alpha)$ is such a question, then the following two sets are *empirical propositions*:

$$p = \{\alpha \in K: \text{the answer to } Q(\alpha) \text{ is } yes\}$$
$$p' = \{\alpha \in K: \text{the answer to } Q(\alpha) \text{ is } no\}$$

For many α in K, the question $Q(\alpha)$ is not answered (by the theory). Minimal assumptions about the character of a physical theory make it possible to impose on **P** the condition that it be orthocomplemented. Precisely:

$\langle \mathbf{P}, \subseteq, ', K \rangle$ is an *orthocomposet*:
(a) $\subseteq$ partially orders $P \subseteq P(K)$
(b) ', as introduced above, is an orthocomplement:
$p'' = p$
if $p \subseteq q$ then $q' \subseteq p'$
$p \cap p' = \Lambda$
$p \uplus p' = (p' \cap p'')' = K$
(c) Λ and K are (the zero and unit) elements of **P**.

Now let us have as language a set of sentences closed under $\sim$ and &, and containing a special absurd sentence f. Then we can assign propositions to these sentences in an obvious way:
The m.s. is $\langle K, \mathbf{P}, ', s \rangle$ where s maps sentences into **P** as follows:

3.0 $s(f) = \Lambda$.
3.1   if $s(A)$ is defined it is in **P**
3.2 $s(\sim A) = s(A)'$ if $s(A)$ is defined
3.3 $s(A \& B) = s(A) \cap s(B)$ if $s(A)$ and
$s(B)$ are defined and
$s(A) \cap s(B) \in \mathbf{P}$.
3.4 A is true at α in K iff $s(A)$ is defined and $\alpha \in s(A)$ – false if $s(A)$ is defined and $\alpha \in s(A)'$

We can construe these as Belnap connectives, but as the special case in which, as in ordinary 'one-dimensional modal logic' the intension of a sentence is the same from world to world when defined. We can also regard this as having gaps caused by presuppositions: A presupposes that $s(A)$ is defined.

The only well-behaved sentence is f; it is always false, its negation is always true. Negation is fairly well-behaved, $\sim A$ being true (false) iff A

is false (true), and otherwise valueless, as always. But even here, we have
to worry a bit. We know that if $p\subseteq q$ then $q'\subseteq p'$; but while $A \& B \Vdash A$
must hold, the truth of $\sim A$ cannot guarantee that $A \& B$ has a truth-value.
Hence we cannot simply transpose the algebraic equations into rules of
logical consequence.

The great simplifying factor is that $s(A)$ is defined exactly if (at any α),
the sentence $f\supset A$ – i.e. $\sim(f \& \sim A)$ – is true. Nevertheless, the resulting
logical system OCPS is not neat: it has the least logical consequence Cn
such that, if we define $X\vdash A$ to mean $A\in\text{Cn}(X)$, the following hold:

DEFINITION. X^0 is the set of elements of X which have form $(f\supset A)$.

al. $B\in\text{Cn}(f)$
a2. $\sim f, (f\supset f)\in\text{Cn}(\Lambda)$
a3. $f\in\text{Cn}(A, \sim A)$
a4. $\text{Cn}(A) = \text{Cn}(\sim\sim A)$
a5. $(f\supset A)\in\text{Cn}(A)$
a6. $(f\supset\sim A)\in\text{Cn}(f\supset A)$
a7. $(f\supset B)\in\text{Cn}(f\supset A)$ if B is a subformula of A
a8.   If $f\supset A, f\supset B\in\text{Cn}(X)$ and $B\in\text{Cn}(X^0, A)$ then $\sim A\in\text{Cn}(X, \sim B)$
a9. $A, B\in\text{Cn}(A \& B)$
a10. $A \& B\in\text{Cn}(A, B, f\supset(A \& B))$
a11.   If $f\supset A, f\supset B, f\supset C\in\text{Cn}(X)$ and $C\in\text{Cn}(X^0, A, B)$ and $A, B\in\text{Cn}(X^0, C)$ then $f\supset(A \& B)\in\text{Cn}(X)$.

The soundess lemmas are fairly straightforward and I shall only give a
few.

LEMMA 1. f is always false, and A is assertive if and only if $(f\supset A)$ is
true.

Clause 3.0 yields the first part; if A is assertive, i.e. $s(A)$ is defined, then
$\sim A$ is assertive and $s(f \& \sim A)=s(f)\cap s(\sim A)$ if that is in **P**. But it
equals Λ, hence is in **P**. So $\sim(f \& \sim A)$, which is $f\supset A$, is also assertive,
and $s(f\supset A)=K$. On the other hand, if $s(f\supset A)$ is defined then by clause
3.3, $s(\sim A)$, and hence $s(A)$ must also be defined.

LEMMA 2. If $X\Vdash f\supset A$ and $X\Vdash f\supset B$ and $X^0, A\Vdash B$ then $X, \sim B\Vdash\sim A$.

Let all the antecedent hold, and suppose that all of X is true at α in K,
and also $\sim B$. Then because $X\Vdash f\supset A$, A is assertive at α, so A is true or

false. If it were true, then because $X^0, A \Vdash B$, B would be true at α. But B is false at α, so A is false at α: $\sim A$ is true at α.

LEMMA 3. If $X \Vdash f \supset A$, $X \Vdash f \supset B$, and $X \Vdash f \supset C$ and $X^0, A, B \Vdash C$, X^0, $C \Vdash A$ and X^0, $C \Vdash B$, then $X \Vdash f \supset (A \ \& \ B)$.

Suppose that all the antecedent is true and all of X is true at α in K. Then A, B, and C are assertive. Also, because X^0 is true throughout, $s(C) \subseteq s(A)$, $s(C) \subseteq s(B)$, and $s(A) \cap s(B) \subseteq s(C)$. So $s(C) = s(A) \cap s(B)$. Hence $s(A) \cap s(B)$ is in $\mathbf{P}$. But then all conditions of 3.3 are fulfilled so $s(A \ \& \ B)$ is defined. Hence by Lemma 1, $f \supset (A \ \& \ B)$ is true at α.

Strong completeness can be proved as follows: if X is a consistent OCPS theory, then there is a way to satisfy all and only those sentences that belong to X.

Let X be such a theory, and Σ the set of all consistent OCPS theories Y such that $X^0 \subseteq Y^0$. Define $|A| = \{\alpha \in \Sigma : A \in \alpha\}$ and $\mathbf{P} = \{|A| : f \supset A \in X^0\}$.

LEMMA 4. For all sentences A, B, $|A| \subseteq |B|$ iff X^0, $A \vdash B$.

X^0 is part of every member of Σ. Hence if $X^0, A \vdash B$, then $|A| \subseteq |B|$. On the other hand, if it is not the case that $X^0, A \vdash B$, then $B \notin \alpha = \text{Cn}(X^0 \cup \cup \{A\}) \in \Sigma$. So $\alpha \in |A| - |B|$.

LEMMA 5. If $f \supset A \in X^0$ and $f \supset B \in X^0$, and $|A| = |B|$ then $|\sim A| = |\sim B|$.

If $f \supset A$ and $f \supset B$ belong to X^0 and $|A| = |B|$, then $f \supset \sim A$ and $f \supset \sim B$ belong to X^0 (see a6) and X^0, $A \vdash B$ and X^0, $B \vdash A$ by Lemma 4. Hence, by a8, X^0, $\sim B \vdash \sim A$ and X^0, $\sim A \vdash \sim B$. So by Lemma 4 again, $|\sim A| = |\sim B|$.

DEFINITION. If $p \in \mathbf{P}$, then $p' = |\sim A|$ where A is any sentence such that $p = |A|$ and $f \supset A \in X^\circ$.

The m.s. $M = \langle \Sigma, \mathbf{P}, ', s \rangle$, where s is the map: $s(A) = |A|$, defined if and only if $f \supset A \in X^0$, is now such that $X \in s(A)$ iff $A \in X$, and hence as required. The following lemmas establish that M is indeed an m.s.

LEMMA 6. $\mathbf{P}$ is an orthocomposet.

If p is in $\mathbf{P}$, we can discuss it with reference to a representative $|A|$ such that $p = |A|$ and $(f \supset A) \in X^0$. If we have, for such representatives, $|A| \subseteq |B|$ then (Lemma 4), X^0, $A \vdash B$, and $f \supset A$, $f \supset B \in X^0$. So by a6 and a8, X^0, $\sim B \vdash \sim A$; hence $|\sim B| \subseteq |\sim A|$ by Lemma 4. Also, by a4, $|\sim \sim A| = |A|$, and by a3 $|A| \cap |\sim A| = \Lambda$. Now $\Lambda \in \mathbf{P}$ because it is $|f|$ and

$(f \supset f) \in X^0$; hence $p \cap p' = \Lambda \in \mathbf{P}$. And $(p \cap p')' = \Lambda' = |\sim f| = \Sigma \in \mathbf{P}$ because $(f \supset f)$, and hence $(f \supset \sim f) \in X^0$, by a2 and a6. So $\mathbf{P}$ is orthocomplemented.

LEMMA 7. Map s fulfils clauses 3.0–3.3.

By a2, $s(f)$ is defined, and by a1, it equals Λ. By a6 and a7 $s(A)$ is defined iff $s(\sim A)$ is defined, and by definition and Lemma 4, the latter equals $s(A)'$. Finally, suppose $s(A \& B)$ is defined. Then X^0, A, $B \vdash A \& B$ and X^0, $A \& B \vdash A$ and X^0, $A \& B \vdash B$, so $s(A \& B) = s(A) \cap s(B)$. Suppose on the other hand that $s(A)$, $s(B)$ are defined and $s(A) \cap s(B) \in \mathbf{P}$. Then it must be $|C| = s(C)$ for some sentence C such that $(f \supset C) \in X^0$. But then X^0, A, $B \vdash C$ and X^0, $C \vdash A$ and X^0, $C \vdash B$; so by a.11, $X^0 \vdash f \supset (A \& B)$. Hence $s(A \& B)$ is then defined.

This ends the proof.

University of Toronto

NOTES

* Research for this paper was supported by Canada Council grant S71-0546.
[1] N. D. Belnap Jr., 'Conditional Assertion and Restricted Quantification', *Nous* **4** (1970), 1–12.
[2] H. Kamp, 'Formal Properties of 'Now' ', *Theoria* **37** (1971), 227–273.
[3] K. Segerberg, 'Two-Dimensional Modal Logic', *Journal of Philosophical Logic* (forthcoming); D. Lewis, 'Anselm and Actuality', *Nous* **4** (1970), 175–188; D. Kaplan, 'The Logic of Demonstratives', mimeographed UCLA 1971. Credit for priority must reportedly be given to the doctoral dissertation (UCLA, 1972) of F. Vlach.
[4] P. F. Strawson, *Introduction to Logical Theory*, Methuen, London, 1952.
[5] Cf. B. van Fraassen, *Formal Semantics and Logic*, Macmillan Co., New York, 1971, Ch. V, Section 3.
[6] R. H. Thomason, 'Indeterminist Time and Truth-Value Gaps', *Theoria* **36** (1970), 264–281.
[7] J. M. Dunn, 'Comments on N. D. Belnap, Jr.'s 'Conditional Assertion and Restricted Quantification' ', *American Philosophical Association, Western Division Annual Meeting*, St. Louis, May 1970.
[8] N. Rescher, *The Logic of Commands*, Routledge and Kegan Paul, London, 1966.
[9] R. Manor, 'Conditional Forms: Assertion, Necessity, Obligation and Commands', Doctoral dissertation, University of Pittsburgh, 1971.
[10] B. van Fraassen, *loc. cit.* (note 5); or B. van Fraassen, 'Presuppositions, Supervaluations, and Free Logic', in K. Lambert (ed.), *The Logical Way of Doing Things*, pp. 67–91, Yale University Press, New Haven, 1969.
[11] See notes 5 and 10.
[12] For an introduction, see Sections I and II of B. van Fraassen, 'Semantic Analysis of Quantum Logic', in C. A. Hooker (ed.), *Contemporary Research in the Foundation and Philosophy of Quantum Theory*, D. Reidel Publ. Co., Dordrecht, 1973.

HANS G. HERZBERGER

DIMENSIONS OF TRUTH*

I

The following dialogue is drawn from Plato's *Cratylus*.
Socrates is the questioner, and Hermogenes the respondent.

How about truth, then? You would acknowledge that there is in words a true and a
false? *Certainly*. And there are true and false propositions? *To be sure*. And a true
proposition says that which is, and a false proposition says that which is not? *Yes;
what other answer is possible?* [385b]

Evidently, Hermogenes was conceptually unprepared for any challenge
to a certain conception of truth. Perhaps for him, no other answer was
possible.[1]

Logic, we are told, is founded in truth. And who would dare to deny it?
Logic in its broadest conception is the theory of truth. And who among
us would care to deny it? Long ago one tradition bold enough to challenge
these doctrines flourished for a century or so, and then vanished from
sight. Perhaps the first to follow this way was the scholastic master of
paradox John Buridan. He came upon it through consideration of the
dimensions of truth.

What are the dimensions of truth? First above all comes correspondence with reality – a notion as tricky to formulate as it is simple to grasp.
Socrates called it 'saying that which is'. In mediaeval times it was 'how-
soever it signifies, so it is in things signified'.[2] Other traditions have grap-
pled with this notion, each in its own favored mode of expression. According to the fifth century Hindu logician Vatsyayana, it is the *sadbhavam*
of the *sataha*, and the *asadbhavam* of the *asataha* – which translates as 'the
positivity of the positive and the negativity of the negative'.[3] Or, in the no
less impenetrable peripatatetic formula, 'to say of what is that it is' (the
positivity of the positive) and 'to say of what is not that it is not' (the
negativity of the negative).[4] These formulas have been adapted from
various expressions of the correspondence theory of truth, according to

*Hockney et al. (eds.), Contemporary Research in Philosophical Logic
and Linguistic Semantics, 71–92. All Rights Reserved*
Copyright © 1975 by D. Reidel Publishing Company, Dordrecht-Holland

which articulation of the concept of truth terminates upon the dimension of correspondence.

It's a good theory of truth, in much the same sense that Newtonian mechanics is a good theory of motion. Schematically, the main idea can be given by the equation:

$$T = C$$

which has its modern formulation for example in Leibniz, who writes: 'These coincide: the proposition L and the proposition L *is true*'.[5] This equation has penetrated so deeply into our logic and our ways of thought as to seem downright trivial – especially when viewed in the light of examples which the tradition has laid down as watchwords for itself. Tarski's particular formulation of the correspondence equation in his 'Convention T' appears so bland that denials of it seem, in his words, 'somewhat paradoxical'. And indeed they do; for who among us would rush to endorse equivalences like the one which Tarski offers to his antagonist:[6]

'*Snow is white*' *is true iff Snow is not white.*

And the tradition reaches back almost all the way to the beginnings of Western thought, to Hermogenes' ingenuous response: 'Yes; what other answer is possible?' And so, the correspondence equation has rooted itself very firmly in our intuitions.

Therefore, it was a great liberating act on Buridan's part[7] to argue that in certain cases another answer might be required, to illustrate how it might be implemented, and to draw out some of its fundamental consequences. I believe that the semantic framework arising from this tradition may find some application as an instrument of study for the semantics of natural languages. Not only does it set the logic free from presuppositions, it disengages the two sufficiently to set the presupposition-theory at the same time free from pure logic. It accommodates both a classical consequence relation and a theory of bivalence which in the relevant sense could be bivalence-functional: in this way it appears likely to prove useful for the investigation of presuppositions and semantic categories. It offers a viable alternative to the powerful method of supervaluations. There is even a sense in which it may support a general theory of presuppositional languages, within which languages based on supervaluations could be represented as a restricted case.[8] Of more practical importance, however, is that it provides principles for constructing a rich and diverse class of novel formal languages which can be brought to bear on natural semantic structures.

My plan will be to introduce the fundamental ideas in their historical context, and then to sketch out some contemporary applications. I consider this an appropriate procedure, but the reader must be cautioned to distinguish sharply between historical motivations and contemporary applications. Buridan's ideas on truth, like those of Russell and Tarski after him, were forged in the heat of the Liar paradox. What emerged – in each of these cases, I believe – were some formidable semantic instruments with all sorts of applications. After all these years the Liar is still among us, and many of us still yearn, unrequited, for a semantically closed language. But, while paradox may be the driving force in the theory of truth, paradox is not all – even for philosophers! And the first applications of Buridan's semantic framework probably will be found in areas closer to home than his original esoteric concerns.

II

Buridan's philosophy holds truth to be composed of several parts or factors. It views pure logic as the projection onto one coordinate of a multidimensional semantic space. It promises to render the complexities of truth into more orderly individual components – with a major division between the logical dimension on the one hand, and auxiliary dimensions on the other. Some clue to the division to be drawn can be obtained from our common intuitive division between the 'assertive' and the 'presuppositional' content of a sentence. The notion of 'assertive content' bears closely upon Buridan's notion of correspondence.

Turning to the details of Buridan's theory of truth, we are to consider now amending the correspondence equation by the addition of at least one more factor, one more dimension of truth:

$$T = C + X$$

Buridan's discussion of the auxiliary factor X turns on a phenomenon which I will call *semantic incompetence*. For various reasons it may happen that a sentence becomes disqualified from asserting a proposition it is grammatically constituted to express. Some interference between content and mode of expression may prevent a sentence from being true even though it might somehow be seen to 'hold' from the perspective of an external standpoint. Buridan drew upon two cases of this phenomenon, around which he constructed two doctrines of the auxiliary factor X. These particular efforts on Buridan's part are hardly adequate; but they do illuminate the way.

Buridan's initial example of semantic incompetence was the sentence *No sentence is negative,* which he took to be self-refuting – for it stands as a counterexample to its own claim. As he puts it in Chapter 8 of his *Sophisms,* 'God could destroy all negatives, leaving the affirmatives'.[9] If so, our sentence would correspond with reality, but it would not exist and so, Buridan reasons, it would not be true. He concludes that correspondence is not sufficient for truth:[10]

Those propositions are indeed in conflict with regard to being true, but they are not in conflict with regard to the case being as they signify.

The case depends on the existence of sentences – within Buridans' nominalistic semantics upon spoken or written realizations of them. The first part of Buridan's doctrine then adjoins to correspondence a condition of realization:

Truth = Correspondence + Realization

In Benson Mates' language this initial doctrine analyzes the notion of being *true-in* a possible world into being *true-of* that world plus being *in* that world. The cogency of the particular example is problematic, and the position founded on it, equally so; but for centuries it was received doctrine, and it still manages to command some assent today.[11]

Much more telling is Buridan's second example of semantic incompetence, for which he draws upon the Liar paradox. Let there be written on a certain board:

| *The sentence on the board is not true* |

Now it is elementary that no sentence can truly deny its own truth, affirm its own falsity, and the like. So any sentence in undertaking to do this seals its own incompetence: things will be as it signifies, that is, it will not be true. And so it will correspond and yet not be true. Buridan's diagnosis of this case follows a certain 'vicious-circle' principle, which he applies in the course of stipulating truth-conditions for categorical propositions:[12]

Because of reflection of that proposition on itself, it follows from it, together with the circumstance of its assertion, that it is false.

An exact account of what Buridan may have in mind here involves several difficulties.[13] Without getting tangled in them let us simply call 'virtuous in the sense of Buridan' any sentence free from that sort of vicious circle. This produces the articulated equation:

$$Truth \ = \ Correspondence \ + \ Semantic \ Competence$$
$$Realization \qquad Semantic \ Virtue$$

It seems clear that some many-valued semantics would be appropriate for implementing this articulation of the concept of truth. We might for example have one valuation-function for correspondence, another to assign realization-values, and a third to award virtue or vice marks according to association in the wrong kinds of semantic circles. Each sentence then would be evaluated thrice on separate dimensions of the semantic space; these values would be aggregated, and we might see what sort of logic – possibly a six-valued logic – would come out. Buridan heroically tried to enfold the whole semantics at once into a two-valued framework, without great success. Many-valued logics can sometimes be so enfolded into bivalent semantics,[14] but they tend to be easier to develop and study initially on their own. In any event determining the exact number of values appropriate to Buridan's articulation of truth is far less crucial than grasping the principle upon which he proceeds.

Any rejection of the correspondence equation calls for a positive theory of correspondence, that is a recursive definition of some function C to evaluate sentences according to whether things are or are not as they signify. A definite theory of correspondence can I believe be culled from Buridan's discussion of truth-conditions, modalities, and the consequence relation.

III

Buridan not only denies the correspondence equation, he does so in a very particular way, offering a full reconstruction of classical intuitions by way of a *conceptual transposition*, under which correspondence comes, in all major logical points, to play the role formerly allotted to truth. This manoeuvre is nontrivial to precisely the extent that not all semantic points are logical ones. And so it will be important later on to sharpen the notion of purely logical conceptions and operations.

Buridan's transposition can be seen at work throughout his treatment of the foundations of logic. What we normally think of as truth-conditions, according to Buridan, should have 'exceptions' to allow for cases of semantic incompetence. Thus:[15]

... for the truth of an indefinite or particular categorical affirmative, it is required and it suffices that the subject and predicate stand for the same, unless because of the reflection of that proposition on itself, it follows from it, together with the circumstances of its assertion, that it is false.

Such rules themselves reflect a division of the semantics into two factors. Firstly there are the normal conditions which normally suffice for truth: in Scholastic terms, that the subject and predicate should 'stand for the same'. Translating this condition into contemporary language, it requires for any monadic atomic sentence that the denotation of its subject-term belong to the extension of its predicate-term. I regard this as a condition of correspondence, and the so-called 'exception' as a condition of semantic competence. Rules of correspondence for molecular sentences and for sentences of more complex logical structure can be obtained through consideration of Buridan's theory of modality and consequence.

The major concepts of a logical theory can often be explained in terms of the notion of the logical range of a sentence. According to Wittgenstein this is 'the room (Spielraum) which is left to facts by the proposition'.[16] Classically the range of a sentence is the totality of models in which it is true. Then the logically valid sentences are taken to be those with a universal range, the contravalid sentences to be those with an empty range, and logical consequence is taken as range-inclusion. The generic concept of range can for present purposes be specialized to two notions: let the *truth-range* of a sentence be the totality of all models under which it is true, and its *correspondence-range* be the totality of all models under which it 'corresponds with reality'. Now Buridan argued in these terms that the logical range of a sentence must be wider than its truth-range, and must be precisely its correspondence-range. In the first place he argued that *No sentence is negative* is possible although it has an empty truth-range. As he puts it:[17]

And so it is manifest that a proposition is not called possible because it can be true, nor impossible because it cannot be true. But it is called possible because *as it signifies, so it can be...*

so that truth-ranges do not, on his account, adequately capture modal status. Nor, as he argued, can they do justice to the consequence relation. Going strictly by truth-ranges, *No sentence is negative* would imply *A stick is in the corner*; for the truth-range of the antecedent, being empty, is included in the truth-range of the consequent. For the consequence-relation to hold, more is required than preservation of truth. Preservation of truth, by this example, is not sufficient for logical consequence, and by other examples is not necessary either.[18] What is required on Buridan's formulation is precisely that:[19]

It is not possible for it to be as the first signifies, unless it is as the second signifies.

In present terms, Buridan's consequence relation is inclusion of corre-spondence-ranges rather than inclusion of truth-ranges.

Buridan's focus on correspondence-ranges fixes his notion of corre-spondence in its most general features, and determines the general out-lines of his model theory. Of particular significance is the two-dimensional character of this model theory: pure logic, which depends only on corre-spondence-values, is in effect confined to one dimension of the semantic space, and thereby isolated from various complications arising from the vagaries of the expressive mechanism.

Before proceeding further, it will be convenient now to cut loose from particular scholastic doctrines of semantic competence, and at least temporarily from the whole phenomenon and problems of semantic closure. One of the beauties of two-dimensional semantics lies in the freedom it affords for discriminating and isolating different factors for separate consideration. And now we may try replacing Buridan's two-fold articulation of the auxiliary factor X by a more familiar covering term, giving us a new equation for a fresh start:

$$Truth = Correspondence + Bivalence$$

Having arrived thus far, we shall be able to hold the correspondence factor fixed, and experiment with alternative theories of bivalence. The method to be followed will be that of product-logics in the sense of Jaskowski.[20]

Imagine now a four-valued semantics, based on two separate valuation-
functions – one for correspondence and one for bivalence – applied to a
molecular language. For any model, each sentence will have an ordered
pair of values, one on each semantic dimension. The four possible combinations of values can be named *Truth* and *Falsity* (with capital initials)
and *truth-manqué* and *falsity-manqué* (with lower-case initials). These
values occupy corners of a unit-square in the two-dimensional semantic
space:

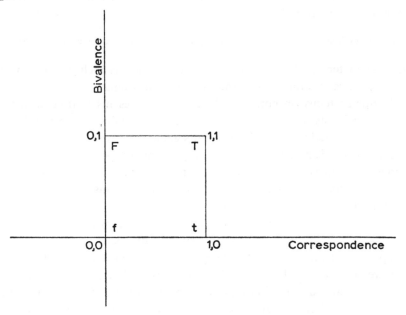

Fig. 1. Semantic Values in Two Dimensions.

We turn our attention first to the 'correspondence' dimension of this
semantic space, within which pure logic is to be confined. The general
features of this dimension will be tied down by translating various historical themes into contemporary terms.

From the outset, there is something in Buridan's theory of consequence
that will be familiar to students of many-valued logic: correspondence
within Buridan's logic plays much the same role as a technically impor-

tant but philosophically rather neglected notion from many-valued logic:
the notion of designation. The parallel is worth drawing out, inasmuch
as it could clarify each of the concepts it brings together.

In many-valued logics, it is customary to superimpose over the primary
many-valued structure, a secondary two-valued structure which determines the notions of logical range, validity and consequence. Some of the
logical values – normally including the value *True* – are picked out as
'designated', and the rest are called 'undesignated'. The logical range of
any sentence is specified as the totality of admissible valuations under
which the sentence assumes a designated value; and validity and consequence are defined in terms of logical range in the usual way. In these
terms it seems right to attribute to Buridan the principle that *designation
equals correspondence*; so that a sentence 'corresponds' if and only if it
has a designated value. This principle assigns a novel interpretation to the
concept of designation, and thereby becomes double-edged. Those who
feel uncomfortable with the scholastic notion of correspondence, are now
free to translate part of the doctrine into more familiar and philosophically less charged terms. On the other hand, those who always wondered at
the intuitive content of the device of designated values, should feel no
less free to make their translation run in the other direction.

Two varieties of many-valued logic might now be distinguished:
'restricted' theories which designate exactly the single value *Truth*, and
'extended' theories which designate certain other values along with
Truth. This division among many-valued logics seems to do some justice
to the distinction between logics adhering to the correspondence equation, and logics like Buridan's which depart from it.

The principle equating designation and correspondence uniquely
determines the designated values of our product-logic: that is all and only
those composite values having the value 1 in their first coordinate. If the
semantic space has two dimensions, as in Figure 1, then the designated
values on this principle will be T and t (numerically $\langle 1, 1 \rangle$ and $\langle 1, 0 \rangle$).

Now if the notions of validity and consequence are to be classical, an
overall view of the correspondence dimension emerges. When we project
the semantic space onto the correspondence dimension, everything is to
have a classical appearance. And this is just the result to be expected
from Buridan's policy of conceptual transposition: all the elementary
logical operators which classically are truth-functional, within this theory

will be *correspondence-functional*. For example, let the classical matrix for
the negation operator be written in terms of the abstract values 1 and 0:

P	$\sim P$
1	0
0	1

Instead of reading these values as True and False, we read them now as
defining a correspondence-function with values 1 for *corresponds* and 0
for *anticorresponds*. The same can be done with all of the classical connectives, establishing the molecular part of the pure logic, on the dimension of correspondence.

v

The next step is to sketch out a family of formal languages which incorporate these basic ideas. The heart of the matter lies in the most
elementary logical structure, that of molecular logic. It is on this level
that the family $\mathscr{C}$ of *classical two-dimensional languages* will be introduced. Languages in this family will concur in their purely logical structure, which will be classical; and they will differ on other aspects of their
semantics, particularly in their treatment of bivalence-conditions.

The syntax is that of propositional calculus augmented with one 'semantic operator'. Thus we have some atomic sentences, two purely
logical operators (negation [$\sim$] and disjunction [$\vee$]) and one auxiliary
singulary operator (the 'horizontal' operator [h]). Molecular sentences
are constructed in the usual way from these elements.

A model for any language in the family $\mathscr{C}$ will be a function m that
assigns to each atomic sentence one of the four values $\{T, F, t, f\}$. Each
language will incorporate semantic rules that determine for each model
m a valuation-function V_m which assigns to every sentence of the syntax
one of the four values $\{T, F, t, f\}$, subject to certain general conditions
which constitute the universal semantics of the family $\mathscr{C}$.

The first condition on valuations is that the valuation-function V_m
shall in each case be determined by two component valuation-functions
C_m, B_m, which specify 'correspondence-values' and 'bivalence-values'
(each in $\{1, 0\}$) for any sentence. The composite valuation is determined
by its components as follows, in accordance with the schematism of

Figure 1:

$$V_m(W) = \begin{cases} T & \text{iff} & C_m(W) = 1 & \text{and} & B_m(W) = 1 \\ F & \text{iff} & C_m(W) = 0 & \text{and} & B_m(W) = 1 \\ t & \text{iff} & C_m(W) = 1 & \text{and} & B_m(W) = 0 \\ f & \text{iff} & C_m(W) = 0 & \text{and} & B_m(W) = 0 \end{cases}.$$

That is, our four values are to be thought of as composite values, where the first coordinate registers correspondence-values and the second coordinate registers bivalence-values.

Now further conditions are set down on the component valuation-functions. These will in effect completely determine the structure of the correspondence-dimension of languages in $\mathscr{C}$, and will leave completely open the structure of the bivalence-dimension. The first rules govern correspondence-values for atomic sentences and for logical compounds:

RC1   The correspondence-value of any atomic sentence is the value of the first coordinate of its semantic value.
That is: $C_m(A) = 1 \equiv m(A) \in \{T, t\}$.

RC2   The correspondence-value of any negation is the opposite of the correspondence-value of the negated sentence.
That is: $C_m(\sim W) = 1 - C_m(W)$.

RC3   The correspondence-value of any disjunction is the maximum of the correspondence-values of its disjuncts.
That is: $C_m(W \vee Z) = \max \{C_m(W), C_m(Z)\}$.

These rules are equivalent to specifying two basic correspondence functions by the classical matrices:

W	Z	$W \vee Z$	$\sim W$
1	1	1	0
0	1	1	1
1	0	1	0
0	0	0	1

Correspondence Matrices
For the Logical Operators

Obviously we have here a logically complete basis: all possible correspondence-functions are definable in terms of the correspondence functions associated with disjunction and negation by RC2 and RC3. The proof is precisely the same as the standard proof for the functional completeness of the classical propositional calculus.

Now we set down a rule governing the 'horizontal' operator. This auxiliary connective is designed to endow languages of the family $\mathscr{C}$ with some modest degree of semantic closure. That is, for each sentence W there will be a pair of related sentences hW, $h\sim W$, which register the semantic status of W so far as classical values are concerned. In particular, hW will 'correspond' if and only if W is True, and $h\sim W$ will 'correspond' if and only if W is False:

RC4   The correspondence-value of hW is the logical product of the correspondence-value of W and the bivalence-value of W. That is: $C_m(hW) = \min\{C_m(W), B_m(W)\}$.

It will be evident that RC4 is a rule of a new 'transverse' kind, which determines the correspondence-value of one sentence as a function of something besides merely the correspondence-values of its parts. The matrix underlying this rule takes four values into two:

W	hW
T	1
F	0
t	0
f	0

Correspondence Matrix
For the Semantic Operator

The semantic operator h is not correspondence-functional, and this feature sharply distinguishes it from any purely logical operator. In this way a wedge is driven between pure logical structure and more general semantic structure. Such contrasts have important applications when one is concerned to distinguish between logical consequence and inference based on presuppositions.[21]

Finally, we leave quite open the semantics on the bivalence dimension, subject only to the general condition that each sentence W have a unique 'bivalence-value' $B_m(W)$ in $\{1, 0\}$ for each model m, and:

RB1   The bivalence-value of any atomic sentence is the value of the second coordinate of its semantic value. That is: $B_m(A) = 1 \equiv m(A) \in \{T, F\}$

Many different languages of the family $\mathscr{C}$ will result from alternative ways of specifying rules of bivalence. Some of these languages will be 'bivalence-functional', so that the interpretation of the connectives can be given by 'bivalence matrices'. These are the product-logics in the standard sense. In terms of immediate applications they may be the most interesting as well as the most intuitively accessible of the languages from the family $\mathscr{C}$. But some indication will also be given of languages incorporating theories of bivalence of more sophisticated and complex sorts. We turn now to three prototypical illustrations of this framework.

VI

Perhaps the simplest theory of bivalence adapts an idea from Frege's semantics, the idea that a logical compound is bivalent if and only if each of its parts is bivalent. This rudimentary idea has some intuitive backing in application to limited regions of natural language. But all efforts to incorporate it into a logical system have so far encountered serious complications. Appropriate three-valued matrices can readily be set down, but they inevitably yield nonstandard consequence relations. On the molecular level, there are well-known three-valued implementations of the Fregean principle. Let the three logical values be *True, False*, and *Nonbivalent*: [22]

$\vee$	T	F	N	$\sim$
T	T	T	N	F
F	T	F	N	T
N	N	N	N	N

*Logical Basis for the
Kleene-Bochvar System*

The three-valued logic generated by this basis is Kleene's 'weak' (Bochvar's 'internal') system, which has been the starting-point for some recent linguistic research.[23] Independently of the issue of its merit as a doctrine of bivalence, it has notorious shortcomings in its logical aspects. No matter which values are designated, something goes wrong with the consequence relation. Two policies of designation are available, determining a restricted and an extended three-valued logic, in the sense of Section 4. On the restricted policy which designates the single value T, there would be no valid sentences at all, and such classical consequences as $P \Vdash P \vee Q$ and $P \Vdash Q \supset P$ would not hold.[24] The extended policy yields slightly better results. If both of the values $\{T, N\}$ are designated, then exactly the classical tautologies would be valid, but consequence relation still would be nonclassical. For example, $P \;\&\; {\sim}P \Vdash Q$ would not hold, nor would the law of simplification $P \;\&\; Q \Vdash P$. We can do much better than this in a two-dimensional semantics.

To obtain a language of the class $\mathscr{C}$ which incorporates the Fregean principle of bivalence, we set down the rule:

Bivalence-Rule for the Language L_1: The bivalence-value of any molecular sentence is the logical product of the bivalence-values of its parts.

In particular then we have:

(i)   The bivalence-value of any negation is the same as the bi-valence-value of the negated sentence.
That is: $B_m({\sim}W) = B_m(W)$.

(ii)   The bivalence-value of any disjunction is the minimum of the bivalence-values of its disjuncts.
That is: $B_m(W \vee Z) = \min\{B_m(W), B_m(Z)\}$.

(iii)   The bivalence-value of hW is the same as that of W.
That is: $B_m(hW) = B_m(W)$.

Superimposing our rules of correspondence with these rules of bi-valence, the whole semantics of this first language can be encapsulated in a four-valued matrix:

$\vee$	T	F	t	f	$\sim$	h
T	T	T	t	t	F	T
F	T	F	t	f	T	F
t	t	t	t	t	f	f
f	t	f	t	f	t	f

Four-Valued Basic Matrix for the Language L_1

Our principle equating correspondence and designation (Section 4) fixes the designated values of this language as the pair $\{T, t\}$, and this desig-nation is uniform for all languages in the family $\mathscr{C}$. From this it will be obvious that the consequence relation is perfectly classical in the sense of being a conservative extension of the classical consequence relation. That is, so far as sentences made up only with classical connectives $({\sim}, \vee)$ are concerned, the consequence relation for the language L_1 coincides with that for the classical propositional calculus. Thus even in this rather pedestrian application, the two-dimensional approach can solve problems which have resisted the best efforts of a number of advocates of three-valued logic.

VII

Our second illustration adds to the preceding account another idea due partly to Frege and more fully to Bochvar: the idea of an operator which systematically fills in truth-value gaps.[25] In the linguistic literature, this idea is more often put in terms of 'suspension' or 'cancellation' of presuppositions by means of certain special syntactic devices.

The language L_2 to be constructed now draws upon our distinction between logical and semantic operators, and treats them differentially with respect to conditions of bivalence:

Bivalence-Rule for the Language L_2: The bivalence-value of any purely logical compound is the logical product of the bivalence-values of its parts; but any semantic compound (of the form hW) is inherently bivalent.

This principle treats disjunction and negation exactly as they are treated in the language L_1. The horizontal operator now is such that any horizontalized sentence has a bivalence-value of 1 for any model m. That is: $B_m(hW) = 1$. Once again, superimposing our general rules of correspondence, the whole semantics of the second language can be presented in a four-valued matrix:

∨	T	F	t	f	~	h
T	T	T	t	t	F	T
F	T	F	t	f	T	F
t	t	t	t	t	f	F
f	t	f	t	f	t	F

Four-Valued Basic Matrix for the Language L_2

The resultant system is a four-valued analogue to Bochvar's extended three-valued logic:[26] but once again, it has an edge over its three-valued counterpart, in being fully classical in its logic (again, a conservative extension of classical propositional logic).

The two languages so far described are not only classical in their notions of validity and consequence, but they are thoroughly truth-functional as well. They are correspondence-functional in their pure logic, and bivalence-functional throughout. Taking 'presuppositions' to be conditions of bivalence, these languages are compositional in thier presuppositional structure. The presuppositions of each sentence are a function of the presuppositions of its parts. The compositional structures of L_1 and L_2 are of simple kinds, but they may serve to suggest the descriptive possibilities available within the two-dimensional framework. Previous treatment of the formal semantics of presuppositional languages do not seem to be compatible with compositionality of these kinds.

VIII

Thirdly I propose to outline a rather more exotic member of our general family $\mathscr{C}$ of languages, in order to further illustrate the scope and flexibility of the two-dimensional framework, and at the same time to open and engage more directly the question of its relation to supervaluational semantics.[27]

Let us remind ourselves that the universal semantics of the family $\mathscr{C}$ incorporates no substantive restrictions whatever on bivalence-valuations. So for possible languages in $\mathscr{C}$ certain connectives may behave classically on the dimension of correspondence and yet from a classical logical standpoint wildly misbehave on the dimension of bivalence. In particular they might also fail to be in any sense bivalence-functional. In fact each of Buridan's particular positions on semantic incompetence displays this character. A molecular sentence may 'exist' (be spoken) at some point of reference independently of whether its parts 'exist' at that point of reference. Likewise, a sentence might enter into a vicious semantic circle independently of whether its various compounds do so as well. Therefore within a two-dimensional semantics it is possible for the logic to be a classical matrix logic while the semantics is in no sense 'truth-functional' overall. Let me illustrate this possibility with a classical two-dimensional language that simulates the supervaluation principle on its bivalence-dimension.

Languages in the family $\mathscr{C}$ have four-valued models. For any such model m, some atomic sentences will have 'classical' values (in $\{T, F\}$) and the rest will have 'nonclassical' values (in $\{t, f\}$); we can think of the latter as constituting 'truth-value gaps'. Now let a *classical refinement* of any such model m be any model m' whose values are all in $\{T, F\}$, and which concurs with m over all atomic sentences whose values under m are classical. From the standpoint of any given model, its classical refinements convert nonclassical values into classical ones, and leave classical values alone. That is:

> A model m' is a classical refinement of a model m iff for each atomic sentence A: $m'(A) \in \{T, F\}$; and $m'(A) = m(A)$ provided that $m(A) \in \{T, F\}$.

All classical refinements of a given model are classical models, and, using the standard truth-tables, any logically compound sentence can be classically evaluated in the usual way, for any such model. To simplify our account, let the following development be confined to the narrowly logical part of our syntax, ignoring the semantic operator h. Thus what follows concerns only sentences constructed out of atomic sentences using disjunction and negation. Now let us say that a sentence from this narrow syntax is *classically stable* under a given four-valued model, provided its classical valuation is invariant under all classical refinements of that model:

> A sentence S is classically stable under a model m iff for any two classical refinements m', m'' of the given model, the classical value of S under m'' is identical with the classical value of S under m''.

Now we can provide the bivalence-principle appropriate to our third language. This principle identifies bivalence with classical stability:

Bivalence-Rule for the Language L_3: Any sentence of the narrowly logical syntax is bivalent under a model iff it is classically stable under that model. That is: $B_m(W) = 1$ iff W is classically stable under m.

Typical characteristics of supervaluational languages have exact counterparts in the language L_3. For example, in this language validity is logical truth and contravalidity is logical falsehood. That is, not only do the logically valid sentences all 'correspond', but the bivalence-rule guarantees they will also be bivalent and so thereby will actually be True. In other words, logically valid (and contravalid) sentences in L_3 are all 'exempt' from material presuppositions.

As promised, the overall semantics is not truth-functional in the ordinary sense, and yet the pure logic, on the correspondence-dimension, is the standard matrix logic. All the nonstandard features of this particular language are isolated upon the bivalence-dimension, and result from the stability principle. The two-dimensional framework here figures as an instrument of analysis, providing a neat separation between an explicit logic on the one dimension and an explicit account of bivalence structure on the other.

IX

In closing, I want to remark on some directions in which these elementary languages can be extended. In general it is to be expected that further articulation of the dimension of bivalence will yield separate factors governed by distinct principles. Buridan allowed for two subdimensions of semantic incompetence: 'realization' and 'semantic virtue'. In shifting our focus from semantic incompetence to bivalence, we have in no way closed the investigation of semantic incompetence as a subdimension of bivalence. Without much doubt, the principles controlling self-reference are very different from those controlling denotational presuppositions and sortal restrictions. For one thing, the former govern a very special category of expressions, principally 'semantic' predicates like 'is true', 'satisfies', 'denotes', and the rest. Even in the absence of a definite theory of semantic incompetence, the recognition of this factor as running skew to more ordinary conditions of bivalence, can advance our investigation.

The full power of a two-dimensional semantics casts our theory of conceptual structure into an unfamiliar four-valued scheme:

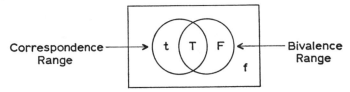

Fig. 2.   Schematism for Four-Valued Concepts.

Of the classes represented in this quadruplex schematism, two are exact counterparts of common notions, and two are strange. The truth-set (T) is just the *extension* of the concept, and the falsity-set (F) is just its *counterextension*; and the two jointly comprise its *sortal range*, the 'semantic interior' of the concept. Of the two additional classes (labelled t and f), it might be said that since physical theory has its strange particles, logical theory is entitled to a couple of strange semantic values. Should they turn out to be not only strange but also wonderful, we might gradually learn to assimilate them, as in the case of physical theory. The comparison is fanciful but nonetheless may be instructive. Our two strange values are rather akin to mirror-image modes of nonbivalence: perhaps they could be thought of as right-handed and left-handed truth-value gaps. The differences between them are important but subtl eand commonly negligible. Expanding on this the meit may be possible, as we learn to work with them, to dispel at least part of their strangeness.

Now the four logical values at our disposal do not after all require full employment everywhere throughout the semantics. We are in no way compelled to represent ordinary concepts as being quadruplex in the sense of dividing the logical space into four compartments. On the contrary, many of our intuitions about concepts may be best served by triplex representations. Accordingly, consider as a working hypothesis the principle that for ordinary concepts like the concept of redness, *the correspondence-range coincides with the extension*. This appears to have some initial plausibility, and it affords a schematization of concepts much closer to our customary three-valued paradigm:

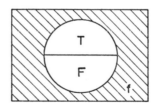

Fig. 3.   Schematism for the Concept of Redness.

The exterior of the concept (labelled with a small f) now consists of those things, including abstract entities, which have no color at all and thereby are outside the sortal range of the concept of redness. Consider a representative member of this class, say Cantor's Diagonal Theorem. Now to attribute redness to the Diagonal Theorem would be to make a claim which does not hold, although by hypothesis, it would not be false. In view of the account so far given of the nonclassical value f we seem to have so far an acceptable representation of these facts.

Our working hypothesis now needs sharpening: what is the scope of its application beyond the one case cited? One can hardly be precise here, but it seems to me that the hypothesis might be expected to apply to those non-semantic predicates that are logically primitive in the language under consideration, but not to all those that are logically definable. In particular, the logical contrary of any such concept is bound to fall under a different schematism:[28]

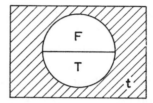

Fig. 4.   Schematism for the Logical Contrary of the Concept of Redness.

Here the extension and counterextension are interchanged as expected, and there is a correlative interchange in the exterior of the concept, where the orientation of the truth-value gap switches from 'left-handed' (f) to 'right-handed' (t). I believe that this interchange can be easily explained. The schematism represents the idea that attribution of the contrary of any concept is tantamount to denial of that concept. Now, to deny that the Diagonal Theorem is red would be to make a claim which in a sense would hold, although by hypothesis it would not be true. Therefore, it is fitting to assign it the value t.

The two nonclassical values thus behave as conjugate modes of non-bivalence, interchangeable through negation. The justification for postulating different modes of nonbivalence lies in the possibilities it opens for smoothly integrating while nonetheless sharply differentiating the factors of semantic complexity, by rendering them along separate dimensions of truth.

NOTES

* This paper derives from an earlier version entitled 'Buridan and Two-Dimensional Model Theory' delivered at Waterloo University in the Summer of 1969. Another version was given at Livingston College, Rutgers University in December 1971. My understanding of Buridan has been greatly helped by many discussions with Calvin Normore and Paul Spade. Recently John Martin has worked out some further develop-

ments in two-dimensional semantics, and I have benefitted from discussing this work with him.

[1] In N. Hanson's sense of 'conceptual possibility' described in his *Patterns of Discovery* (p. 84).

[2] *John Buridan: Sophisms on Meaning and Truth,* T. K. Scott, ed. (p. 83)

[3] *Nyaya Philosophy,* trans. by D. Chattopadhyaya and M. Gangopadhyaya, Indian Studies Publication, Calcutta, 1967.

[4] Aristotle, *Metaphysics,* Book Gamma, 1011b27.

[5] G. W. Leibniz, *General Inquiries About the Analysis of Concepts and of Truths,* §1 (1686). Reprinted in G. H. R. Parkinson, *Leibniz: Logical Papers.*

[6] A. Tarski, 'The Semantic Conception of Truth', §18.

[7] Or on the part of the author of the ideas which appear in his *Sophisms.* Apparently some of these ideas were considered if not adopted already at some earlier time. For example, a text falsely attributed to Duns Scotus discusses (and rejects) the consequence relation later advocated by Buridan. Cf. W. and M. Kneale, *The Development of Logic* (p. 287f).

[8] I expect that some results in these directions will be reported by John Martin in his forthcoming dissertation, 'Sortal Presuppositions'.

[9] Buridan, *Sophisms* (p. 181).

[10] Buridan, *Sophisms* (p. 183).

[11] On the first claim, see J. Ashworth, 'The Theory of Consequence in the Late Fifteenth and Early Sixteenth Centuries *Notre Dame Journal of Formal Logic* 14 (1973), 289–315. On the second claim see for example, B. Mates, 'Leibniz on Possible Worlds' in *Logic, Methodology and Philosophy of Science III,* 1968, B. van Rootselaar and F. Staal, eds.

[12] Buridan, *Sophisms* (p. 92).

[13] And possibly inconsistencies as well. See P. Spade, *The Mediaeval Liar,* Ph. D. dissertation, Toronto 1972.

[14] This is explained through the scholastic doctrine of *exponibilia* in my paper 'Setting Russell Free', mimeo Toronto 1971.

[15] Buridan, *Sophisms* (p. 92).

[16] L. Wittgenstein, *Tractatus Logico-Philosophicus* §4. 463.

[17] Buridan, *Sophisms* (p. 182). This doctrine was noted in E. Moody, *Truth and Consequence in Mediaeval Logic,* 1953, and has been discussed by others, notably A. Prior in 'The Possibly-True and the Possible', *Mind* 1970.

[18] One example Buridan offers is 'Every proposition is affirmative' implies 'No proposition is negative'; and yet, whenever the first is true, according to Buridan, the second is not true. See his *Sophisms* (p. 182).

[19] Buridan, *Sophisms* (p. 183).

[20] S. Jaskowski, 'Investigations into the System of Intuitionist Logic' 1936, reprinted in S. McCall, *Polish Logic.* A brief survey of product-logics can be found in Ch. 2 §16 of N. Rescher's *Many-Valued Logic.* Łukasiewicz advocated a particular four-valued product logic in his 'A System of Modal Logic', 1953, reprinted in *Jan Łukasiewicz: Selected Works,* L. Borkowski, ed. Other product logics in four values are given in A. Church, 'Non-Normal Truth-Tables for the Propositional Calculus', *Boletin de la Sociedad Matematica Mexicana,* 1953, and in A. Church, *Introduction to Mathematical Logic v.* 1, exercise §19.9.

[21] See Bas van Fraassen, 'Presupposition, Implication, and Self-Reference' *Journal of Philosophy,* 1968, and references cited therein.

[22] This matrix is given in the format of Łukasiewicz; it combines a table for disjunction

with one for negation. The value of any disjunction $(P \wedge Q)$ can be found at the intersection of the row headed by the value for P, with the column headed by the value for Q. The value of any negation $(\sim P)$ can be found in the rightmost column under the row headed by the value for P. The system is described in Rescher, *op.cit.* Ch. 2 §4–5.

[23] It is not uncommon to find the Fregean principle taken as an initial working hypothesis from which departures and exceptions are assessed. Cf. Laurence Horn, *On the Semantic Properties of Logical Operators in English*, Ph. D. dissertation, UCLA 1973; and also the work of Lauri Karttunen.

[24] Assuming of course that the standard connectives for the conditional and so forth are introduced through their usual definitions.

[25] Some historical remarks on this idea can be found in my paper, 'Truth and Modality in Semantically Closed Languages', in *The Paradox of The Liar*, Robert L. Martin, ed.

[26] This system includes Bochvar's 'internal' connectives, his 'external' connectives, and various 'mixed' operators as well. Thus it is *not* just the union of what Rescher calls B_3 and $B_3{}^E$ (Rescher, *op. cit.* Ch. 2 §4). For details see the appendix to my paper cited in Footnote 25.

[27] See Bas van Fraassen, *Formal Semantics and Logic,* Ch. III §6, Ch. V §3.

[28] Assuming that the logical contrary is formed by 'internal negation', that is by the negation operator of language L_1 of Section 6 above.

KEITH S. DONNELLAN

SPEAKING OF NOTHING*

Russell tells us in 'On Denoting' to test our logical theories by their 'ca-
pacity for dealing with puzzles'.[1] In this paper I raise the question of how
a theory of reference, one of recent origin, might handle one of the major
puzzles Russell mentioned. The theory of reference that I have in mind –
and one I subscribe to – I will call 'the historical explanation theory'.
(It, or ones similar to it in important respects, has also been called the
'causal theory'. For various reasons, I prefer a different title.[2])

Among a number of puzzles mentioned by Russell, two stand out as
more important than the others. One is the well-known problem of identity statements with which Frege begins his article, 'On Sense and Reference',[3] the question of how a statement of the form '*a* is identical to *b*',
when true, can differ in 'cognitive value' from a corresponding statement
of the apparently trivial form, '*a* is identical to *a*'. The second puzzle is the
topic of this paper. In a large number of situations speakers apparently
refer to the non-existent. The most obvious example of this is, perhaps,
the use of singular terms in negative existence statements, e.g., 'The
discoverer of the philosopher's stone does not exist' or 'Robin Hood did
not exist'. The problem is, of course, well-known and ancient in origin:
such statements seem to refer to something only to say about it that it
does not exist, How can one say something about what does not exist?
For a few philosophers, to be sure, these questions have led to attempts
to provide the referent. But in general such attempts have been met with
suspicion. Russell certainly thought it a merit of his theory of definite
descriptions (and his fully developed views on singular expressions) that
such apparent references to the non-existent were explained without
having to entertain the idea of referents of singular terms that are non-
existent.

Where the singular terms involved are definite descriptions, 'On Denoting' provided a solution to the two puzzles mentioned that was at once
a break-through in the treatment of these expressions and satisfying in
the coherent explanation it gave. Russell's fully developed theory of singu-

*Hockney et al. (eds.), Contemporary Research in Philosophical Logic
and Linguistic Semantics*, 93–118. *All Rights Reserved*
Copyright © 1975 *by The Philosophical Review*

lar terms, perhaps best represented in 'Lectures on Logical Atomism',[4] extends the proposed solution to ordinary proper names, for these turn out to be concealed definite descriptions. The view of 'On Denoting' now could be made to cover most of the uses of singular terms in language as we actually speak it and, moreover, seemed to meet the test of solving the various puzzles about reference. But the fully developed view also introduced a category of singular expressions that were acknowledged to be rarely, if ever, found in everyday speech, what Russell called names in 'the strict logical sense' or 'genuine' names.

Genuine names and the motivation for giving pride of place to such exotic singular terms have special interest for the historical explanation theory, because while its treatment of ordinary singular expressions is radically different from Russell's it has some similarities to his characterization of genuine names.

The question posed, then, is how the historical explanation theory of reference can handle the puzzle that Russell's view has no difficulty with, the problem of apparent reference to the non-existent.

I cannot in this paper plead the full case for the historical explanation theory, though I shall try to give its main features; so it may be best to consider it an exercise in the hypothetical: *if* the theory is correct what follows concerning apparent reference to the non-existent?[5]

1. THREE KINDS OF APPARENT REFERENCE TO THE NON-EXISTENT

We need to keep distinct three situations in which apparent reference to the non-existent occurs. The differences are important in their own right, but I need to call attention to them because one kind of situation will be excluded from consideration in this paper.

I will, in the first place, distinguish what I will call 'discourse about fiction' from 'discourse about actuality'; and, secondly, within the latter category, the use of 'predicative' statements from the use of 'existence' statements.[6] What is to be excluded from consideration here is an account of discourse about fiction. (This is not, of course, to say that such an account is not in the end needed.)

Under 'discourse about fiction' I mean to include those occasions on which it is a presupposition of the discourse that fictional, mythological, legendary, etc. persons, places or things are under discussion. I believe, for example, that said with the right intention, the following sentences would express true propositions: "The Green Hornet's car was called 'Black Beauty', 'Snow White lived with seven dwarves', and 'To reach the underworld, one must first cross the river Styx'." (By the 'right intention' I mean that the speaker wishes to be taken as talking about fiction, mythology, or legend.) At the same time I also believe it is true that neither the Green Hornet, his car, Snow White, nor the river Styx exists or ever has existed. These two beliefs, however, are entirely consistent. And therein lies the puzzle: how can there be true propositions that apparently involve predicating properties of what does not exist?

Discourse about actuality carries the presupposition that the speaker is talking about people, places or things that occur in the history of our world. A puzzle arises when the speaker is unfortunate enough to use a singular expression, intending to attribute a property to something, but fails, in his use of that expression, to refer to anything. This very likely occurred, for example, some years ago following the publication of *The Horn Papers*,[7] that purported to contain the diary of one Jacob Horn and that would, if genuine, have shed light on the colonial history of Washington County, Pennsylvania. Many people believed them to be genuine, but, on the evidence, it seems likely that they are not and that Jacob Horn did not exist. There must have been many believers, however, who made statements using the name 'Jacob Horn' with the intention of predicating various properties of a historical figure. For example, someone might well have said, "Jacob Horn wrote about Augusta Town and now we know where it was located." It would have been some sort of inconsistency – exactly what kind is another question – for such a speaker to then affirm the non-existence of Jacob Horn. This contrasts with discourse about fiction – there one can, for example, consistently deny the existence of Snow White while also stating that she enraptured a prince.[8]

The puzzle about predicative statements, as I shall call them, in discourse about actuality with a singular expression and no referent is more subtle philosophically then the puzzle about fictional discourse. There is not the same possibility of stating something true. Nor can the speaker with consistency acknowledge the non-existence of what he speaks about. To see how statements such as those made by believers in the authenticity of *The Horn Papers* can puzzle a philosopher requires the ability to see a difficulty in how one can even speak and be *understood* when using a singular expression with no referent.

The difference between discourse about fiction and discourse about reality, it is important to keep in mind, is a matter of presuppositions about the intent of the speech act. It is not that in the one fictional characters are involved and in the other real people, places and things. A not too well informed person might have taken (at least the first part of) the movie 'Doctor Strangelove' for a documentary. His statement, "Doctor Strangelove, the top military scientist in the United States, is a psychopath," would then be a bit of discourse about reality, even though Doctor Strangelove is, in fact, fictional. On the other hand, this very same sentence, used by someone having seen the whole movie would probably be a comment on the movie, a bit of discourse about fiction.

While I will need often to consider predicative statements about actuality, the problem I want to concentrate on concerns 'existence' statements – those that have either the form '*S* does not exist' or the form '*S* exists', where '*S*' is a singular expression. Negative existence statements, unlike predicative statements, are true when there is no referent for the singular expression. If I speak the truth in saying, 'Jacob Horn does not exist' I would be apparently referring to what does not exist. But even more paradoxically, the truth of what I say depends directly upon the non-existence of a referent for 'Jacob Horn'. Moreover, this is discourse about reality; I do not, clearly, intend to talk about a fictional character. Negative existence statements, of all those mentioned, bring apparent reference to the non-existent into sharpest focus.

It is of some importance to mention the difference between denying the existence of something altogether and denying its present existence or its existence at some point or during some period in time. To begin with we certainly want to distinguish between:

(1)   Napoleon no longer exists,

and

(2)   Napoleon does not and never did exist.

The first statement is both true and not an apparent reference to the non-existent in the sense we want. (1) contains a reference to Napoleon in the same way that 'Socrates was snub-nosed' contains a reference to Socrates. (1) should, it seems, be put into the class of predicative statements, despite the fact that existence is involved. On the other hand, (2) is a paradigm of the kind of statement that generates the problem of apparent reference to the non-existent.

What shall we say, however, about a statement such as,

(3)   Santa Claus does not exist?

Often, I believe, it expresses a statement of the same form as (2), an absolute denial of existence, not confined to any one period in time. But suppose, for example, that someone is unsure whether Jacob Horn ever did exist, but is certain that he does not now exist. He might express this by saying, 'Jacob Horn does not exist'. So, perhaps, sentences of the surface form of (3) are ambiguous. But what is the other meaning that they might have? The sentence given, in the imagined circumstances, seems to me to be equivalent to,

(4)   Jacob Horn does not now exist.

This is neither the absolute denial of Jacob Horn's existence nor the predicative assertion that Jacob Horn no longer exists. (4), I believe, amounts to the disjunction of the two: Either Jacob Horn does not and never did exist or he did exist and does no longer. In which case, the dichotomy illustrated by (1) and (2) is still maintained. In what follows, however, it is the absolute denial of existence that will be of concern and any examples of the form 'N does not exist', should be construed in that way.

2. A THEORY GONE WRONG WITH INTERESTING MOTIVES – RUSSELL

Russell's theory of singular terms holds interest for the historical explanation theory, not only because of obvious oppositions on some key issues – several more recent discussions would serve that purpose [9] – but also because certain problems and issues that evidently motivated features of Russell's theory that are nowadays generally ignored or thought obviously wrong are brought to the fore once again by the historical explanation theory. I believe that much of Russell's theory has been accepted by many philosophers with the thought that there was a certain excrescence that could be ignored. Russell's views on ordinary singular terms, definite descriptions, proper names in ordinary language, have wide acceptance;

his addition of 'genuine' names to the ranks has generally been ignored as so much metaphysical meandering. I think there is no doubt that 'genuine' names, as Russell characterised them, have no place in a correct theory of reference. But from the first, in 'On Denoting', Russell contrasted his account of those singular terms for which his theory provided a way out of puzzles about reference with another kind of singular term, a 'genuine' name, for which be seemed to feel there was a theoretical need. But, of course, 'genuine' names, if they were to be included in the general theory, could not reintroduce the same puzzles. This, I think, accounts for some of the peculiar properties attributes of 'genuine' names: for example, the distinction between 'knowledge by acquaintance' and 'knowledge by description' that gave the result that we could only genuinely name something we are acquainted with in a very strong sense seems to have been introduced in part to make it impossible to assert negative existence statements using 'genuine' names.

The reason this has interest for the historical explanation theory is that Russell's contrast, the radical difference between most singular terms in ordinary language and 'genuine' names is that the former have descriptive content and the latter do not. Given his view of singular terms with descriptive content, the puzzles about reference yield easily for them. He felt, however, some need to have singular expressions, nonetheless, that do not function in accord with his analysis of definite descriptions and ordinary proper names. The historical explanation theory denies that for at least many uses of ordinary singular expressions Russell's view is correct. In particular, it denies that ordinary proper names always have descriptive content. The question is, does this mean that perhaps ordinary singular expressions may fulfill the function that Russell thought only 'genuine' names, with all their peculiarities, could? And, if so, how can the historical explanation view deal with the puzzles about reference?

What was the motivation for introducing 'genuine' names? Russell often talks in ways that can seem nonsensical – that, for example, when a definite description such as 'the author of Waverly' is involved, the denotation of the definite description, Scott in this case, is not a 'constituent' of the proposition expressed. The implied contrast is that if 'Scott' is a genuine name and were there in place of the definite description, 'the author of Waverly', then Scott would be a constituent. But it certainly sounds queer at first glance to find a flesh and blood person in a proposition!

Russell's analysis of statements containing definite descriptions and, by extension, ordinary proper names, shows, he believed, that such statements are not really *about*, do not really *mention*, the denotation of the description or the referent of the name. Russell emphasizes this again and again. 'Genuine' names, on the other hand, can somehow perform the feat of really mentioning an individual particular. To try to put much weight on such terms as 'about' would lead us, I think, into a morass. What it is for a statement to be *about* an individual, if that requires any attempt to define *aboutness*, is a question better avoided if we are ever to get on with the problem. (After all, Russell himself recognized a well-defined relationship that a statement containing a definite description can have to some particular individual – its denotation. It would be a delicate task to show either that in no sense of 'about' is such a statement *about* the denotation of the definite description or that there is some clear sense of 'about' in which it is not.)

But I believe we can say something useful about the reasons Russell had for talking in this way. On this theory of definite descriptions the singular expression, the definite description, is really a device that introduces quantifiers and converts what might seem at first sight a simple proposition about an individual into a general proposition. 'The Φ is Ψ' expresses the same proposition as 'There is a Φ and there is at most one Φ and all Φ's are Ψ's'; and the latter clearly would express a general proposition about the world. Ordinary proper names, of course, function on his view in the same way, since they are in reality concealed definite descriptions. Now if we contrast these singular expressions with ones, if there are any, that do not introduce quantifiers, that when put as the subject of a simple subject-predicate sentence do not make the sentence express a general proposition, then I think there is a strong temptation to say that only the second kind of singular term can be used to really mention an individual.

Russell clearly believed that there must be the possibility, at least, of singular terms that do not introduce quantifiers; that seems in large part to be his reason for believing in 'genuine' names. Whether or not there is some argument that shows the necessity of such singular terms, I believe that prior to theory the natural view is that they occur often in ordinary speech. So if one says, e.g., 'Socrates is snub-nosed', the natural view seems to me to be that the singular expression 'Socrates' is simply a device used by the speaker to pick out what he wants to talk about while the rest of the sentence expresses what property he wishes to attribute to that individual. This can be made somewhat more precise by saying, first, that the natural view is that in using such simple sentences containing singular terms we are not saying something general about the world – that is, not saying something that would be correctly analyzed with the aid of quantifiers; and, second, that in such cases the speaker could, in all probability, have said the same thing, expressed the same proposition, with the aid of other and different singular expressions, so long as they are being used to refer to the same individual. To illustrate the latter point with a different example, if, at the same moment in time, one person were to say, 'Smith is happy', a second, 'You are happy', a third, 'My son is happy', and a fourth, 'I am happy', and if in each case the singular expression refers to the same person, then all four have expressed the same proposition, have agreed with each other.

What I see as the natural pre-theoretical view might be captured as a certain way of representing what proposition is expressed. For example, the sentence, 'Socrates is snub-nosed', might be represented as an ordered pair consisting of Socrates – the actual man, of course, not his name – and the predicate (or property, perhaps), being snub-nosed. (More complicated sentences, involving relations and more than one singular expression of this sort would be represented as ordered triplets, etc.) Now if someone were to say to Socrates, 'You are snub-nosed' or Socrates were to say about himself, 'I am snub-nosed', the proposition expressed would, in each case, be represented by the same ordered pair – propositional identity, given the same predicate, would be a function simply of what individual is referred to.

This way of representing propositions would, I think, meet with at least provisional approval by Russell, but only if it were restricted to those propositions expressed by statements containing 'genuine' names. We might even say that the manner of representation gives a respectable sense in which an individual might be a constituent of a proposition. But my examples of statements for which this representation was suggested would, on Russell's view, be incorrect just because they involve singular terms from ordinary language. For Russell, they would be examples of sentences that express complex general propositions and whetever our view of the nature of propositions, I do not think we would want proposi-

5९।८७

tional identity for general propositions to be a function of the individuals that happen to make the propositions true or false.

Russell pays the price, I believe, of giving up the natural view of many uses of ordinary singular terms, a price he is willing to pay – chiefly, perhaps, because he thus can dissolve puzzles about reference. The special properties of 'genuine' names, on the other hand, are supposed to rescue them. The 'natural' view, on the other hand, seems to generate Russell's budget of puzzles, in particular the one which is the concern of this paper. If I say, 'Socrates is snub-nosed', the proposition I express is represented as containing Socrates. If I say, instead, 'Jacob Horn does not exist', the 'natural' view seems to lead to the unwonted conclusion that even if what I say is true, Jacob Horn, though non-existent, must have some reality. Else what proposition am I expressing? The 'natural' view thus seems to land us with the Meinongian population explosion.

Russell, of course, avoids this problem easily. Since the proper name, 'Jacob Horn', would, for him, be a concealed definite description, to say, 'Jacob Horn does not exist', is not to refer to some individual in order to say something about him, but merely to assert that a particular class of things, perhaps the class of writers of diaries about certain events in early Pennsylvania history, is either empty or contains more than one member. (So a singular non-existence statement of this kind is on all fours with statements such as 'There are no flying horses' or 'There is more than one living ex-president'. It does not mention a particular individual any more than these do.)

The issue has importance for the historical explanation view because it denies that many singular terms in ordinary language, in particular proper names, are concealed descriptions of the sort that Russell had in mind. 'Homer', for example, is not a concealed description such as 'the author of the Homeric Poems', to use Russell's own example. The question is, does the historical explanation view, if correct, support what I have called the 'natural' view? In the next section this question will be considered.

3. THE HISTORICAL EXPLANATION VIEW: NEGATIVE ASPECT

I now want to begin to lay out the bare bones of the theory of reference I want to discuss. As I have said, I will not here argue for its correctness nor will I try to fill in all the gaps.

Russell and the majority of philosophers in contemporary times who have discussed (ordinary) proper names have held that by one mechanism or another they are surrogates for descriptions. For Russell, as I have mentioned, they are simply abbreviations for definite descriptions; for others, e.g., Searle,[10] they are correlated with a set of descriptions and what one is saying in, say, a simple subject-predicate sentence employing a proper name is that whatever best fits these descriptions has whatever property is designated by the predicate. The descriptions, both on Russell's view and on the looser view of Searle and others, which the proper name masks are thought of as obtained from the people who use them – roughly speaking, by what they would answer to the question, 'To whom (what) are your referring?' This view of ordinary proper names embodies what I have called the 'principle of identifiying descriptons'.[11] The theory of reference I am concerned with holds that the principle of identifying descriptions is false.

What this means, to give an example, is that supposing you could obtain from me a set of descriptions of who it is that I believe myself to refer to when I say, 'Socrates was snub-nosed', perhaps such things as, 'the mentor of Plato', "the inventor of the 'Socratic method'," 'the philosopher who drank the hemlock', etc., it is theoretically possible that I am referring to something about which no substantial number of these descriptions is true or that although there is something that fits these descriptions to whatever extent is required by the particular variation of the principle, that is not in fact the referent of the name I used.

On this theory, then, ordinary proper names are like Russell's 'genuine' names at least insofar as they do not conceal descriptions in the way he thought. This is, I think, a virtue of the theory. As David Kaplan has remarked, there was always something implausible about the idea that a referent of a proper name is determined by the currently associated descriptions.

4. THE HISTORICAL EXPLANATION THEORY: POSITIVE ASPECT

The first tenet of the theory of reference I've been describing was negative – the view that proper names must have a backing of descriptions that serves to pick out their referents is false. The second tenet is positive, but more tentative. How is the referent of a proper name, then, to be determined? On Russell's view and variants on it, the answer to this question would be simple: the referent is that which fits the associated descriptions best, where 'best' may be defined differently by different writers. As I see it, one of the main reasons a backing of descriptions for proper names is so attractive is that it furnishes a simple way of ascertaining what a speaker is saying, and of determining whether what he says is true or false (given that we are dealing only with assertions). We find, so to speak, that in the world which uniquely fits the descriptions and then see whether or not it has the properties ascribed to it. If proper names do not have a backing of descriptions, how do we decide whether or not when someone says, e.g., "Russell wrote 'On Denoting'," he has said something true or false?

Putting existence statemenst aside, when a speaker says something of the form, 'N is Φ', where 'N' is a name and 'Φ' a predicate, we can say that in general the truth conditions will have the following form: What the speaker has said will be true if and only if (a) there is some entity related in the appropriate way to his use of 'N' in this sentence, i.e., he has referred to some entity, and (b) that entity has the property designated by Φ. (I say 'in general' because there are difficulties for any theory of reference about uses of names for fictional characters, 'formal' objects, such as numbers, etc.) The question is, what is the 'appropriate relation' mentioned in condition (a)? How, that is, does an entity have to be related to the speaker's use of the name 'N' to be its referent? The principle of identifying descriptions, were it only true, has a simple answer to this: the entity must have (uniquely) the properties or some sufficient number of the properties designated by the 'backing of descriptions' for this use of the name 'N'. Roughly speaking, and on the most usual view, it will be the entity that answers to the descriptions the speaker would (ideally) give in answer to the question, 'To whom are you referring?'

But even without the arguments that, I believe, show the principle of identifying descriptions not only false, but implausible, putting the matter in this general way is somewhat liberating. It shows that what we need is *some* relation between the speech act involving the name 'N' and an object in the world – the right one, of course – but the relation supplied by the principle of identifying descriptions is now only a candidate for that office.

But if the principle of identifying descriptions is false, what then is the appropriate relation between an act of using a name and some object such that the name was used to refer to that object? The theory of reference I want to discuss has not as yet, so far as I know, been developed in such a way as to give a completely detailed answer. Yet there are positive things that can be said and enough I believe both to contrast it with the principle of identifying descriptions and to give us something like an answer to the original question, how will it handle apparent reference to the non-existent in such statements as, 'Santa Claus does not exist?'

The main idea is that when a speaker uses a name intending to refer to an individual and predicate something of it, successful reference will occur when there is an individual that enters into the historically correct explanation of who it is that the speaker intended to predicate something of. That individual will then be the referent and the statement made will be true or false depending upon whether it has the property designated by the predicate. This statement of the positive thesis leaves a lot to be desired in the way of precision, yet with some clarifying remarks I think it has more content than might at first sight be supposed.

Suppose someone says, 'Socrates was snub-nosed' and we ask to whom he was referring. The central idea is that this calls for an historical explanation; we search not for an individual who might best fit the speaker's descriptions of the individual whom he takes himself to be referring to (though his descriptions are usually important data), but rather for an individual historically related to his use of the name 'Socrates' on this occasion. It might be that an omniscient observer of history would see an individual related to an author of dialogues, that one of the central characters of these dialogues was modeled upon that individual, that these dialogues have been handed down and that the speaker has read translations of them, that the speaker's now predicatin gsnub-nosedness of something is explained by his having read those translations. This is the sort of account that I have in mind by a 'historical explanation'.

Several comments are in order here. First, it is not necessary, of course, that the individual in question be snub-nosed; obviously the speaker may have asserted something false about the referent of the name 'Socrates'. Secondly, if we take the set of descriptions the speaker could give were we to ask him to whom he was referring, the historical explanation as seen by our omniscient observer may pick out an individual as the referent of the name 'Socrates' even though that individual is not correctly described by the speaker's attempt at identification. For example, the speaker may believe that Socrates, i.e, the person he refers to, was a philosopher who invented the Socratic method. But it is clearly imaginable that our omniscient observer sees that while the author of the dialogues did intend one of the characters to be taken as a portrayal of a real person, he modestly attributed to him a method that was his own brain child. And, in general, it would be possible to have the historical connection with no end to mistaken descriptions in the head of the speaker. The descriptions the speaker gives, however, may play an important role, though not the one given to them by the principle of identifying descriptions. The omniscient observer may see, for example, that the reason the speaker believes himself to be referring to someone who invented a certain philosophical method is because his present use of the name 'Socrates' is connected with his having read certain translations of these dialogues. Or, to take a slightly different case, he may see that his descriptions come from a faulty memory of those dialogues, etc. The question for the omniscient observer is, 'What individual, if any, would the speaker describe in this way even if perhaps mistakenly?'

I have used the notion of an omniscient observer of history and, of course, we ordinary people cannot be expected to know in detail the history behind the uses of names by those with whom we converse. Nor do we often take the sort of historical enquiries which would reveal those details. We often assume, for example, that if another speakers' descriptions of the referent of a name he has used more or less jibe with descriptions we would give of a person, place or thing that we believe ourselves to know about, then he is referring to that. Also, for example, the context of the use of name may lead us to assume without question that the speaker refers to someone with whom we are both acquainted. But the historical explanation theory need not deny this or be troubled by it. All it needs to hold is that the *final* test for reference is the kind of historical connection I have described, that the customary assumptions and use of indicators are in the end dependent upon being fairly reliable guides to the existence of such a connection.

What the historical explanation theory must attempt to establish is that when there is an absence of historical connection between an individual and the use of a name by a speaker then, be the speaker's descriptions ever so correct about a certain individual, that individual is not the referent; and, on the other hand, that a certain historical connection between the use of a name and an individual can make the individual the referent even though the speaker's descriptions would not by themselves single out the individual. This job must be accomplished by building up examples in which these two points are made obvious. We might, for instance, try to show that the historical connection is necessary by constructing a situation in which, for instance, one person begins by assuming that another is referring to a friend of his, perhaps because the descriptions seem accurate, the context is appropriate, etc., and who then discovers that it is practically impossible for the speaker to have been acquainted with or otherwise related to his friend. In such an event surely confidence that the speaker was referring to the friend would be shaken despite the apparent accuracy of description or appropriateness of context. But, as I have said, I cannot here undertake the full defense of the historical explanation theory.

There are, however, two further points of clarification that ought to be mentioned here. It should be obvious that I have only provided an example of what counts as an historical explanation rather than a formula for obtaining the referent of a particular use of a name. Even in the illustration several individuals entered into the account, only one of which was the referent. Of the individuals who are in some way or other part of the historical explanation of a use of a name, which is the referent? What kind of theory is this if it does not give us the means to make this determination?

In defense against this charge that the theory is excessively vague, it is helpful, I think, to compare it with another philosophical theory about a quite different problem. The causal theory of perception can be taken as holding that an observer, O, perceives an object, M, only if M causes O to have sense impressions. The theory seems to me to have content and to be important, whether or not it is correct. For one thing, if true it means that certain other theories are mistaken. But the theory as stated does not, obviously, allow us to say which among the various causal factors involved in an observer having sense impressions is the thing he perceives; nor does it tell us which ways of causing sense impressions are relevant. Possibly no philosophical analysis can determine this, although in any particular case we may be able to say that this is or is not the right sort of causal connection. Analogously, the historical explanation theory lacks this sort of specificity. But for all that, if true, certain other theories, in particular the identifying descriptions theory, will be wrong and the theory does tell us something of importance.

Because there have sometimes been misunderstandings about this, I think I should point out that the history to which the historical explanation theory alludes is not the history of the use of a name. It is not the history of the use of, say, the name 'Socrates' that is important. Socrates may not have been, as far as theory goes, called 'Socrates'; corruption of names is just as possible as corruption of information. (The history of such a corruption, however, *might* enter into the historical explanation.) Nor, I think, should the theory be construed as holding that the historical connections end with some original 'dubbing' of the referent. It may be that people places and things usually receive names by some such cere- mony and that we generally use names (or corruptions of them) as a result of such a ceremony, but it is not a theoretical necessity that names enter our linguistic transactions in this way.[12]

What the historical explanation does, then, is to provide the relationship between the use of a referring expression and the referent which the prin- ciple of identifying descriptions presupposes could only be provided by some measure of correct descriptions of the referent known to the speaker. I think there are counterexamples to the principle of identifying descrip- tions [13] and, of course, if there *are* that defeats it straight off. Still a plausi- ble, if not clearly correct, alternative theory in this case also acts as an objection. For one of the principle reasons that many philosophers have for adopting the principle of identifying descriptions is that they cannot see how there *could* be an appropriate relation otherwise that would pick out the referent of (as the main example) a proper name.

I have, in describing this theory of reference, talked about an 'historical explanation'. I hope it is obvious that 'historical' is being used in the broadest sense possible; that all of what I have said could just as well be applied to cases in which one refers, by use of a name, say, to someone still extant, to someone who has just gone out of the room, or to someone presently in one's company. The 'historical explanation', in other words, can involve as brief an interval of time as one pleases.

5. A SOLUTION TO THE PUZZLE REJECTED

My problem, then, is to show how such a theory of reference can deal

with simple existence statements expressed by the use of a proper name.
The difficulty being that on this theory, proper names do not have a backing of descriptions and, in general, they function to refer *via* what I have
called an historical connection with some individual. But a true negative
existence statement expressed by using a name involves a name with no referent and the corresponding positive existence statement, if false, will
also. But in other contexts when a name is used and there is a failure of
reference then no proposition has been expressed – certainly no true
proposition. If a child says, 'Santa Claus will come tonight', he cannot
have spoken the truth, although, for various reasons, I think it better to
say that he has not even expressed a proposition.[14]

One apparently possible solution to the problem must be rejected.
Russell and others, as we have seen, thought of (ordinary) proper names
as concealed definite descriptions; he held a version, that is, of the principle
of identifying descriptions. Existential statements involving ordinary
proper names were therefore no problem for him – they were really
existential statements involving definite descriptions and could be analyzed in accordance with his theory of definite descriptions. The suggestion
I want to look at is that while our theory tells us that names in predicative
statements do no obey the principle of identifying descriptions and are
not concealed definite descriptions, existential statements may represent
a special case. Thus, so this suggestion would run, 'Santa Claus' in 'Santa
Claus will come tonight' is not a concealed definite description, but *is* one
in special context of 'Santa Claus does not exist' and 'Santa Claus exists'.
This would, of course, immediately solve our problem, but unfortunately
it is not a solution that our theory can accept. The difficulty is not that
names would be treated as functioning differently in different contexts;
in fact, as will become evident, my own view is that they do behave differently in existence statements. Rather, the trouble is that any theory
that rejects the principle of identifying descriptions for predicative statements must also reject it for existence statements.

To simplify matters, let us restrict ourselves to Russell's version of the
principle identifying descriptions in which a name simply stands in place
of some definite description. If we adopt the principle for existence statements involving names, this will come to saying that, for example, 'Socrates did not exist' means the same thing as (expresses the same proposition
as) some other sentence formed from this by replacing 'Socrates' by a def-

inite description, perhaps, say, the sentence, "The Greek philosopher who was convicted of corrupting the youth and drank hemlock did not exist." But, now, on any view we must, I think, accept the following:

(E)   That Socrates did not exist entails that it is not true
        that Socrates was snub-nosed.

Our theory tells us that the second occurrence of 'Socrates' in (E) is not a concealed definite description. But then neither can the first occurrence be one. For if we take some definite description such as the one suggested as what the first occurrence of 'Socrates' stands for, rejection of the principle of identifying descriptions for the second occurrence means that it *could* be true that Socrates was snub-nosed even though no unique individual existed who satisfied that description. That is to say, if 'Socrates' in 'Socrates did not exist' is a concealed definite description, but is not in 'Socrates was snub-nosed', then the antecedent of (E) could be true while the consequent is false. Since we want to accept the entailment expressed by (E) our theory cannot treat 'Socrates' as a concealed description in existential statements.

This solution not being open to us, we cannot on the other hand go to the opposite extreme and handle existential statements involving ordinary proper names in the way Russell did for what he called names 'in the strict logical sense'. There simply are no meaningful existential statements involving these 'genuine' names and so the problem does not arise about how to deal with them. But, of course, we cannot countenance this about ordinary proper names, for it does make sense to say, 'Homer existed' or 'Santa Claus does not exist'.

6. TRUTH CONDITIONS AND 'BLOCKS'

What we need to do first is to see what, on our theory of reference, the truth conditions are going to look like for existence statements involving names. In predicative statements, such as 'Homer was a great poet', if everything goes well, there will be some individual related to this use of 'Homer' 'historically', as I have put it, and the statement will be true if that individual had the property expressed by the predicate and false otherwise. This, of course, cannot be so for a negative existence statement such as 'Homer did not exist.' This statement would be true, in fact, just in case there is a failure of reference, not in the statement itself, but in other possible or actual predicative statements involving the name. That is, if there is no individual related historically in the right way to the use of 'Homer' in, say, the statement 'Homer was a great poet', no individual whose possession or non-possession of poetic genius makes this true or false, then we can truly state that Homer did not exist.

Initially then the question comes to this, 'What, on our theory, constitutes a failure of reference in a predicative statement involving a proper name?' (As we shall see there is more to the matter than just this.) Since the positive part of our theory, the part that attempts to say what successful reference to an individual consists in, has been, perhaps because of the nature of things, left more suggestive them in a rigorously formulated state, it cannot be hoped that we shall do much better with failure of reference. But we can say some things of a non-trivial nature.

Suppose a child who believed in Santa Claus now learns the truth, the truth which he expresses by saying, 'Santa Claus does not exist'. He comes to learn this, as usual, from cynical older children; what has he learned? Our account is that he has learned that when in the past he believed something, for example, which he would have expressed by saying, 'Santa Claus comes tonight', and would have thought himself in saying this to be referring to someone, the historical explanation of this belief does not involve any individual who could count as the referent of 'Santa Claus'; rather it ends in a story given to him by his parents, a story told to him as factual. I do not mean, of course, that the child would or could express the knowledge he has in his new state of disillusionment in this fashion – that would require him to know the correct account of reference. But if *we* are approaching the correct theory, then this is how we can state what he has discovered.

When the historical explanation of the use of a name (with the intention to refer) ends in this way with events that preclude any referent being identified, I will call it a 'block' in the history. In this example, the block is the introduction of the name into the child's speech via a fiction told to him as reality by his parents. Blocks occur in other ways. For example, children often invent imaginary companions whom they themselves come to speak of as actual. The block in such a case would occur at the point at which a name for the unreal companion gets introduced by the child himself via his mistaken belief that there is a companion to name. A somewhat different example would be this: Suppose the Homeric poems were not written by one person, but were a patchwork of the writings of many people, combined, perhaps, with fragments from an oral tradition. Suppose, further, that at some point in time an ancient scholar for whatever reasons – he might have seen a name attached to some written version of the poems and supposed it to be the name of the author – attributed the poems to a single person he called 'Homer'. If this were the historical explanation of our saying, e.g., 'Homer wrote the *Iliad*', then the block occurs at the point at which this scholar enters the picture.

On theories that subscribe to the principle of identifying descriptions examples of failure of reference such as occur in this last example would be treated as a failure to satisfy a uniqueness condition. The reason that Homer would not have existed given these circumstances is that no single individual satisfies the descriptions we associate with Homer (or satisfies a 'sufficient' number, according to certain views). But according to our theory this is not the reason for failure of reference; it is rather that the history of our use of the name, a history with which we may not be familiar, does not end in the right way. One way to see that the opposing account, though plausible, is wrong is to think of the possibility of someone existing who *does* satisfy the descriptions we might supply of the referent of a name we use, but who has no historical connection with us whatsoever. Suppose, for example, that contrary to what we adults believe we know, there is, in fact, a man with a long white beard and a belly like a bowl full of jolly who comes down chimneys on Christmas night to leave gifts (the ones whose labels are missing about which parents worry because they don't know to what aunt the child should write a thank-you note). We must, of course, imagine that it is absolutely fortuitous that our descriptions of Santa Claus happen to fit so accurately this jolly creature. In that case I do not think that he *is* Santa Claus. The fact that the story of Santa Claus, told to children as fact, is historically an invention constitutes a block even if the story happens to contain only descriptions that accurately fit some person.

7. A RULE FOR NEGATIVE EXISTENCE STATEMENTS

Using the technical, but admittedly not well-defined notion of a 'block', we can now sketch the way the historical explanation theory may treat negative existence statements involving names. A similar treatment could then be given for positive existence statements.

I will suggest a rule, using the notion of a block, that purports to give the truth-conditions for negative existence statements containing a name. This rule, however, does not provide an *analysis* of such statements; it does not tell us what such statements mean or what proposition they express. This means that in this case we are divorcing truth-conditions from meaning.

With the deletion of some qualifications that would be needed to make it strictly correct, the rule can be expressed as follows:

(R)   If N is a proper name that has been used in predicative state-
        ments with the intention to refer to some individual, then $\ulcorner N$
        does not exist$\urcorner$ is true if and only if the history of those uses
        ends in a block.

The rule as stated obviously requires some modifications. For one thing we would need some way of distinguishing, e.g., the denial of the existence of Aristotle, the philosopher, from Aristotle, the ship magnate. To accomplish this we must do two things: First, find a means of collecting together the uses of 'Aristotle' in predicative statements that were, so to speak, attempts to refer to the philosopher, separating them from a similar collection of uses of the name that were attempts to refer to the ship magnate, and do this without, of course, assuming that any of these uses succeeds in referring. Second, we must be able to relate a particular negative existence statement using the name 'Aristotle' to one such collection rather than any other.

The way of amending Rule (R) that seems to me in keeping with the historical explanation theory and to accomplish these tasks is this. Certain uses of the name 'Aristotle' in predicative statements will have similar histories, histories that will distinguish them from other uses of the name. Each use of the name will, of course, have its own historical explanation, but these may, at a certain point, join up. So, in tracing back several uses of the name 'Aristotle' by me and several uses by you, we may find a common root in certain ancient writings and documents. While other uses of the name by me or by you may have nothing in common with the history of the first set of uses. It is possible that the histories may join at what I have called a block. Another possibility, however, is that although different uses of the name end in different blocks, these blocks are themselves historically connected. This might occur, for example, for the use by different children of the name 'Santa Claus'. I have suggested that the block in this example occurs where the parents tell the children a fiction as if it were fact. The block, however, would be a different one for each child. Still the blocks themselves are historically related in an obvious way since the parents' deception is rooted in a common tradition.

Still another possible source of difficulty with Rule (R) as stated is that it makes use of prior instances of the name in predicative statements. Is it possible meaningfully to assert 'N does not exist' when N has never been used in predicative statements (about actuality)? If it is, then Rule (R) would have to be amended in some way, perhaps by talking of potential or possible uses. But at the moment I am not sure how this would go and I will not attempt it.

Even without worrying about the vagueness of the idea of a 'block', Rule (R) may look unexciting, but its consequences are interesting. In the first place its form is completely antithetical to the principle of identifying descriptions, for it has nothing to do with whether an individual of a certain description existed or not. Secondly it does not involve our theory of reference in any difficulties: there is the connection with the notion of historical explanation and so it ties in neatly with the positive aspects of the view, but it has no Meinongian implications, no overpopulation with entities whose existence is being denied. This result is bought, to be sure, at the price of making a name function differently in existence statements as opposed to predicative statements. But, as I have said, I think that this is not an unintuitive result.

While the above are important consequences of (R), what interests me about (R) is that it gives the truth-conditions for statements that assert that some *individual* does not exist in terms of a linguistic failure – the failure of a name to refer on account of a 'block'. And it should occur to one that there may be something wrong with this. How, it might be asked, can Homer's existence or non-existence be a matter of a fact about language, a fact about the name 'Homer'? One is reminded, at this point, of a similar problem connected with the other puzzle about reference mentioned at the beginning of this paper. In 'On Sense and Reference', immediately after propounding the puzzle about identity statements, Frege mentions a solution that he had formerly thought correct, but which he now repudiates just because it seems to involve turning identity statements, which apparently express facts about the world, into statements about a particular language.

Rule (R), insofar as it is supposed to express truth conditions for negative existence statements of a certain kind, seems objectionable for the same reasons. The crux of the problem in both cases seems to be this: We are inclined to say that the propositions expressed by us as 'The Evening Star is identical with the Morning Star' and 'Homer did not exist' can be the very same propositions that someone else may express using entirely different names. Therefore, how can we give a rule, such as (R), which makes the truth conditions of what we say depend upon facts about particular names?

The child who has become disillusioned expresses his new found knowledge by saying 'Santa Claus doesn't exist'. A French speaking child, with a similar history of being deceived by adults, might express his discovery by saying, 'Père Noël n'existe pas'. Although the names are different, I believe we should want to say that the two children have learned the same fact and, on that account, that they have expressed the same proposition. Yet if we apply Rule (R) to each case it seems that the truth conditions must be different; they involve a block in the history of the use of the name 'Santa Claus' for the English speaking child and a block for the French speaking child in the history of the use of the different name, 'Père Noël.'

Perhaps we can see the problem more clearly by looking for a moment at predicative statements. If we consider a simple (grammatically) subject-predicate statement, such as 'Socrates is bald', and think of this as divided into its referring element, 'Socrates' and its predicative element, 'is bald', then if a certain change in the predicative element, for example from 'is bald' to 'is short', results in a change in the truth conditions for the statement, we want to say that the result expresses a different proposition. In general only interchange of synonymous predicates will maintain the same truth conditions and the same proposition. If referring expressions, such as 'Socrates' *were* concealed descriptions, that is, introduced predicate elements into a statement, then the same could be said about them – substituting a different referring expression, unless it happened to conceal the same or synonymous descriptions as the one it is substituted for, would shift both the truth conditions and the proposition expressed.

(And, in fact, this is the heart of Frege's way of avoiding his puzzle about identity statements.)

But our theory of reference denies that referring expressions such as 'Socrates', conceal descriptions or introduce predicate elements. If we keep the predicative element the same and substitute a different referring expression, say 'Plato' for 'Socrates', then whether or not we have the same proposition expressed depends solely upon whether or not the same thing is referred to. And this in turn depends upon whether the historical explanation of the use of these two expressions traces back to the same individual. If you say 'Henry is bald' and I say 'George is bald' we express the same proposition if the person you referred to by using the name 'Henry' end I by using the name 'George' are the same person. But what you say is true if and only if the person you referred to, i.e., the person historically connected, when you used the name 'Henry' has the property of being bald. Whereas, what I say is true if and only if what I referred to by using the name 'George' has the property of being bald. The truth conditions are different because they must be stated in terms of what is referred to by different expressions, in the one case my use of the name 'George' and in the other your use of the name 'Henry'. Yet we may express the same proposition.

So with predicative statements involving proper names, given the same predicate, sameness or difference of propositions comes down to sameness or difference of the referent of the names. It seems that if we try to state the truth conditions for a particular use of such a statement, we are not going to arrive at what we should like to call the proposition expressed. But although we thus are separating truth conditions from propositions expressed, the latter notion is still a fairly clear concept. It seems, however, that we cannot in the same way preserve a clear notion of what proposition is expressed for existence statements involving proper names.

Our problem arose because we wanted on the one hand to make it possible that one child saying, 'Santa Claus does not exist' may express the same proposition as another who says 'Père Noël n'existe pas'. But, on the other hand, our explanation of the truth conditions for such statements in Rule (R) made them different for the two cases. We have seen, however, that if the historical explanation theory is correct a difference in truth conditions without a shift in proposition expressed can occur in any case with predicative statements. This can occur when there is a difference in names used without a change in referent. So that this seems to be a general feature of the theory's treatment of names. When we turn to negative existence statements and Rule (R), however, we cannot give as a criterion for propositional identity sameness of referent. For, of course, if true, the name in such a statement has no referent.

What we would like, still continuing with the example, is a reason for saying that both children express the same proposition that is at once in line with our theory and intuitively satisfying. I want to suggest that we may find such a reason once more by using the idea of an historical connection, that, in our example, it is the blocks in the historical explanation of the use respectively of the names 'Santa Claus' and 'Père Noël' that are themselves historically connected. Once again I do not have the resources to spell out a general principle for what this historical connection must be, anymore than I did with the notion of a block itself. Yet in the example before us, and others one can think of, our inclination to say that people using different names express the same negative existence proposition seems to be a matter of historical connection between the blocks involved. In our example, it seems to me that the reason we think both children express the same proposition is that the story of Santa Claus and the story of Père Noël, the stories passed on to the two children as if they were factual, have a common root. And if there were not this common history, I think we should rather hold that the two children believed similar, perhaps, but not identical falsehoods, for example, when the one attributed gifts to Santa Claus and the other to Père Noël and that they expressed different truths when one said 'Santa Claus does not exist' and the other said 'Père Noël n'existe pas'.

8. CONCLUDING REMARKS

If this discussion has been on the right track, then at least the outline of a solution to some problems concerning non-existence statements is available to the historical explanation theory. One point emerged in the course of the last sections. We can perhaps point to criteria for saying when two existence statements involving names express the same proposition, but these criteria take a different form from those for predicative statements involving names. In particular, it cannot be a matter of saneness of referent. For predicative statements we were able to suggest a way of representing propositions, as ordered *n*-tuplets, but no obvious way of representing propositions expressed by existence statements suggests itself. This does not seem to me to count against the theory, since the notion of a proposition is not, I think, a clear one that has established use outside of a theory. The fact that the representation suggested for predicative statements involving proper names has no counter-part for existence statements, however, may account in part for the fact that Russell took the alternatives for proper names to be either a Meinongian view or a concealed descriptions view. For the representation of propositions suggested is, I think, essentially Russellian and either of these views of ordinary proper names would allow him to apply it to existence statements.

University of California, Los Angeles

NOTES

* Earlier versions of this paper were read at a number of meetings and colloquia and several important changes have resulted from those discussions. I am particularly grateful for detailed comments by Tyler Burge.

[1] Reprinted in *Logic and Knowledge* (ed. by Marsh), 1956, p. 47.

[2] Why I am reluctant to use the word 'causal' may become somewhat clearer further on, but the main reason is that I want to avoid a seeming commitment to all the links in the referential chain being causal.

[3] *Translations from the Philosophical Writings of Gottlob Frege*(ed. by Geach and Black), 1952.

[4] Reprinted in *Logic and Knowledge* (ed. by Marsh), 1956.

[5] If we divide the theory into its negative aspects (see Section 3) and its positive (see Section 4), what the theory denies and the reasons for doing so have been, perhaps better delineated in the literature than the content of the positive theory. (This is certainly true of my own contributions.) My papers dealing with various parts of the theory as I see it are: 'Reference and Definite Descriptions', (*The Philosophical Review*, 1966); 'Putting Humpty Dumpty Together Again', (*The Philosophical Review*, 1968); 'Proper Names and Identifying Descriptions', (*Synthese*, 1970, reprinted in Davidson and Harman, eds., *Semantics of Natural Language,* Dordrecht: Reidel, 1972). By others, Saul Kripke 'spaper, 'Naming and Necessity' (in *Semantics of Natural Language, op. cit.*) is the most important in that it gives not only arguments for the negative aspects of the theory, but also a positive account (that, however, I do not altogether agree with).

[6] The terminology, of course, is for convenience and not supposed to reflect a pre-judgment that existence cannot be in some sense a genuine predicate.

[7] See Middleton and Adair, 'The Mystery of the Horn Papers', *William and Mary Quarterly,* 3rd series, IV (1947); reprinted in Winks, ed., *The Historian as Detective,* Harper and Row, N. Y., 1968.

[8] The denial of Snow White's existence, it should be noted, is in discourse about actuality, while the statement that she enraptured a prince is in discourse about fiction. (If the

question of existence arose in discourse about fiction alone, Snow White existed, whereas Hamlet's father's ghost, again presuming we are talking about fiction, probably did not.) This does not disturb the point: no such contrast can be made out for Jacob Horn; if Jacob Horn did not exist then there are no true predicative statements to be made about him.

⁹ E.g., Searle, J., 'Proper Names', *Mind* (1958) and *Speech Acts* (Cambridge University Press, 1968), Ch. IV.

¹⁰ See references in footnote 9.

¹¹ In 'Proper Names and Identifying Descriptions', *op. cit.*

¹² That is to say, the first use of a name to refer to some particular individual might be in an assertion about him, rather than any ceremony of *giving* the individual that name. (In fact, my own name is an example: I discovered that colleagues were pronouncing my last name differently than my parents do – so, orally, they referred to me by a different name – and I let it stand. But I was never dubbed by that new name. I am sure that the first use of it was either an assertion, question or whatever about me and not a kind of baptism. And I think it is probable that whatever audience there was knew to whom the speaker referred.)

¹³ See my 'Proper Names and Identifying Descriptions', *op. cit.*

¹⁴ Given that this a statement about reality and that proper names have no descriptive content, then how are we to represent the proposition expressed?

ZENO VENDLER

THE STRUCTURE OF EFFICACY

I.   In some recent publications[1] I argued that Austin's intuitive classification of illocutionary verbs[2] can be justified on grammatical grounds: verbs belonging to the various classes require verb objects with different structures. There is only one group, Austin's 'exercitives', that needs to be split in two on this new basis.

It seems to be clear that the following verbs in Austin's list of exercitives[3], *order*, *command*, *urge*, *direct*, *advise*, *entreat* and *beg*, share a common type of object. The surface structure of the sentences in which they characteristically occur is this:

(1) $N_1 \ V_{exerc} N_2$ to $V+$

where both *N*'s are human noun (phrase)s. As usual, the infinitive, *to V +*, replaces a verb phrase that contains a subjunctive or equivalent modal (*should*). Thus the source of (1) is

(2) $N_1 \ V_{exerc} \ (N_2 \ \text{mod} \ (V+))$

Indeed, the original form of the enclosed sentence can be resurrected with fair grammaticality. E.g.,

> I order you to go
> I advise you to remain silent

are but shorter, and more idiomatic forms of

> I order you that you should go
> I advise you that you (should) remain silent.

This structure, once recognized, picks out a considerable number of other verbs, which, according to semantic intuitions too, belong to the same class: *request*, *counsel*, *beseech*, *dare*, *challenge*, etc., then *allow* and *permit*, with their opposites, *forbid* and *prohibit*.

I claim that Austin has added another class of performatives to these real exercitives, a class which ought to be kept distinct both on structural

*Hockney et al. (eds.), Contemporary Research in Philosophical Logic
and Linguistic Semantics, 119–136. All Rights Reserved*
Copyright © 1975 by D. Reidel Publishing Company, Dordrecht-Holland

and on semantic grounds. We find, for instance, the following verbs in his
exercitive list: *appoint, nominate, degrade, demote, proclaim,* and *dedicate.*
First of all, there is a considerable semantic difference between this group
and the previous. Speech acts marked by the real exercitives call for
action (or inaction) from the part of the addressee: they try to influence
his conduct. The use of this new group, however, does not call for action,
does not try to influence the conduct of the addressee, it changes his status
instead. Their proper use is 'effective' in itself; the desired effect *ipso dicto*
takes place.

Accordingly, the typical surface forms of the sentences in which they
occur do not end with an 'action-phrase' (*to V* +), but with a noun-phrase
specifying the new status or rank. E.g.,

> I appoint you to the presidency
> I degrade you to the rank of private
> We proclaim you king.

By virtue of the appointment (etc.) the addressee *becomes* private or king.
Therefore, ignoring details, the underlying structure must be something
like

(3) N_1 V (N_2 becomes N_3)

Here it is more difficult to duplicate this on the surface. Yet the result,
when possible, is instructive:

> I appoint you *so that* you be(come) the president
> I degrade you *so that* you be(come) a private.

The *so that*, rather than *that* is typical: it expresses the efficacy of the
utterance. Compare: *I pushed him, so that he fell.*

I have called these verbs 'operatives'. They are members of a very big
class, probably the largest of the performative domain. Following semantic intuition, and syntactic analogy, we can add *name, elect, hire, admit,*
assign, consign and *relegate* on the one hand, and *dismiss, fire* and *suspend*
on the other. Then there are some special groups pertaining to one sphere
of life or another: *arrest, sentence, condemn, fine* and *appeal* operate in the
legal domain; *baptize, confirm, absolve,* and *excommunicate* occur in
religious rites, *knight* and *invest* in feudal ones; *offer, give, grant, sur-*
render, accept, refuse and *reject* govern transfers of property; in some

respects even the greeting verbs, *greet, salute* and *welcome,* seem to belong here.

As we look at this list, we feel far more confident about semantic coherence than about syntactical kinship. We recall that the role of a performative verb is to mark the illocutionary force of an utterance. Accordingly, with every group of performatives, it is not difficult to locate a sentence in the deep-structure, which, in a nominalized form, appears as the verb-object of the performative. Thus the general form of a performative utterance is this:

$$I \; V_{pf} \; nom \; (S)$$

We just saw that the genuine exercitives and the initial examples of the operative group indeed bear out this assumption. But, we have to ask, how are we to find a nominalized sentence behind the verb-object in such examples as *I arrest you, I fire you, I appeal the sentence,* or, worse, *I surrender*? This is a serious trouble, at least serious for me, who claimed that one of the necessary conditions for all performatives is the nominalized sentence in the verb-object.

But, perhaps we need not surrender yet. If our intuitions are right, and these verbs are operatives, then the operative schema, (3) above, together with the *so that* version, ought to work. Try *I arrest you*:

I arrest you, so that....

So that what? The obvious answer is... *so that you be(come) arrested.* This is not so silly as it looks. In the appropriate circumstances the sheriff's saying *I arrest you* results in the culprit's being arrested and this is quite a change in his status. The same holds true of firing, appealing, sentencing or even surrendering.

The reason why this way out looks silly is that it seems trivial, since – one might argue – any active sentence can be connected by *so that* to its passive, e.g.,

I kick you, so that you be(come) kicked.

This is not true however. **You are kicked* is not a sentence; *You are arrested* is. Now we suddenly realize that this form,

$$N \; is \; V^{en}$$

works for *all* operatives, but only for a limited class of other verbs. And that class comprises such items as *cook, bake, burn, break, shatter, tear,* and so forth, which, like the operatives, indicate actions producing a permanent change in something or other. The difference between these and the operatives is that the action producing the change is a speech act in the operative cases, and some other act with the rest. At this point we feel that we are confronted with a very general and very important linguistic move. A detailed account of these and similar causative constructions, which I shall pursue in the sequel, will not disappoint us.

II.   We may begin with the class of 'cooking' verbs we just mentioned: *cook, bake, break, grow,* etc. As it is well known to grammarians, these verbs, together with some others, enter a peculiar transformation usually referred to as the 'middle voice':

> John cooks the meat – The meat cooks
> Jane bakes the cake – The cake bakes
> Mary grows flowers – Flowers grow
> Jim walks the dog – The dog walks,

and so on. These verbs are intransitive, since they occur, on the right hand side, without a verb-object. With genuine transitives such an inversion fails. E.g.,

> John pushes the cart – *The cart pushes
> Mary eats meat – *(The) meat eats.

Yet, in some cases, even genuine transitives can be forced into the mold provided a suitable adverb is added: *The car drives easily, The horse rides smoothly.* Whatever the derivation of these sentences may be, however, the lack of the adverb-less form is sufficient to show that the verbs here involved are not really intransitives.

A related phenomenon is worth noting. There is a small group of intransitives that show a morphological change when put into the transitive frame. E.g.,

> The tree *falls* – John *fells* the tree
> Lazarus *rises* – Christ *raises* Lazarus.

The same is true of *lie (lay), bite (bait)* and *sit (set)*.

In accordance with intuition I shall assume that it is the flower that really grows and not the gardener, and that it is the cake that really bakes and not the cook. Accordingly, it is not *The cake bakes* that is, for example, a derivative of *Somebody bakes the cake*, but the other way around. This second is to be derived along the lines of *The cake bakes and somebody does it*. This is a barbaric sentence, but the idea is right. In an abstract form, what happens here may be represented as follows:

(a) $\qquad N_i\ C(N_j\ V) - N_i\ V\ N_j$

C here represents a semantically neutral 'causative' factor, best approximated by the surface verbs *make* and *cause*. Indeed, we have such sentences as

> John made the cake bake
> Jim caused the window to break.

Thus, in most cases (a) will have the alternative

$(a_2) \qquad N_i\ C(N_j\ V) - N_i\ v_c\ N_j\ (to)\ V$

where v_c represents the neutral causative surface verb. Finally, as we just saw, with certain verbs (*fall*, etc.) their causative employment is marked by an *Umlaut*. This gives us:

$(a_1) \qquad N_1\ C(N_j\ V) - N_1\ V^u\ N_j$

For the sake of simplicity, I shall consider (a) as a special case of (a_1), the *Umlaut* being zero. Thus we can represent the two ways of coding the causative factor as follows:

$$
(A) \qquad N_i\ C(N_j\ V) \Big\langle {\;N_i\ V^u\ N_j \atop \;N_i\ v_c\ N_j\ (to)\ V}
$$

I shall call the first path 'syntactic path', and the second 'lexical path'.

This way of looking at things has several advantages. First, it eliminates the need for talking about the so-called middle voice: $N_i\ V\ N_j$ is a transformational product, not $N_j\ V$, if the latter occurs at all, i.e., if V is intransitive. Second, it keeps the transitive-intransitive distinction intact.

In addition, and more importantly, (A) leads us to the recognition of a very general pattern which operates beyond the limits of *NV*-kernels.

III. What are the ways of expressing the causative situation in case the object of *C* is not *NV*, but *N is N*?

First I shall try the syntactic path. Consider the following sentences:

> The Queen knighted the hero
> Fisher queened the pawn
> Joe cuckolded the husband.

The pattern of this relatively rare move strictly parallels (a_1) above:

(b_1) $\quad$ N_i $C(N_j$ is $N_k) - N_i$ V_{Nk} N_j

The difference, of course, consists in the fact that whereas in (a_1) an intransitive verb dons the transitive paraphernalia (and occasionally acquires the *Umlaut*), in (b_1) a noun takes on verb-like fixtures (tense, etc.). Category boundaries, even major ones, are not sacrosanct.

The lexical path, however, is far more common in these cases. For one thing, even instances of (b_1) can be expressed by using the neutral causative *make*:

> The Queen made the hero a knight

i.e.,

(b_2) $\quad$ N_i $C(N_j$ is $N_k) - N_i$ v_c N_j N_k

In this category, however, we have a wider choice of causative surface verbs. E.g.,

> We *elected* him president
> They *declared* him king
> He *left* her a widow
> I *named* him Joe.

We can say that these verbs, unlike the neutral *make*, are semantically specific causative verbs. Notice, moreover, that they are no mere functions of N_k, but contain independent semantic information: after all, naming a president and electing a president are not the same thing.[4] With this possibility in mind, I add one more schema:

(b_3) $\quad$ N_i V_c $(N_j$ is $N_k) - N_i$ V_c N_j N_k

The availability of specific verbs here makes us ask the question whether (a_2) could contain specific verbs as well. The answer is in the affirmative. Take

> I helped him walk
> I forced him to give up.

The *to V* version reminds us of the genuine exercitives discussed at the beginning: *order*, *advise*, etc., and of Austins's intuition of lumping exercitives and operatives together. Yet the difference remains: the man who was helped (or forced) to walk *did* walk, but the one who was only ordered or advised to walk may not have walked. Once more: operatives are *per se* effective, exercitives are not. There are, of course, certain *perlocutionary* verbs, such as *deter*, *convince*, *seduce* and *entice*, which include the feature of compliance, but this feature is distinct from the speech-act(s) – warning, arguing, promising, etc. – performed.

In view of the relevant specific verbs, we may complete, in retrospect, our discussion of the causative situation involving NV-kernels by adding:

(a_3) $N_i \, V_c \, (N_j \, V) - N_i \, V_c \, N_j \, (to) \, V$

In any case, we have found that both the syntactic and the lexical paths work with *N is N* kernels too:

$$N_i \, V_{Nk} \, N_j$$

(B) $N_i \, C(N_j \, is \, N_k)$

$$N_i \, v_c \, N_j \, N_k$$

In addition, as we just saw, if there is a specific semantic input coloring the causal factor, then we have (b_3) to match (a_3).

IV. Continuing our explorations, the next candidate is the kernel *N is A*. In the neutral situation both paths work beautifully. The sentences

> Joe blackened the window
> Jim thinned the paint
> The city widened the street

and so forth, are clear instances of

(c₁) $N_i\ C(N_j\ \text{is}\ A) - N_i\ V_A\ N_j$

The category crossing goes from adjective to verb rather than from noun to verb as above. There is even an isolated Umlaut-phenomenon corresponding to (a₁): the adjective *full* has the verb-form *fill*.

The lexical path is available too:

> Jim made the paint thin
> The city made the street wide.

These sentences sound a bit thin. In these cases we prefer the syntactic path. Given a specific causal verb, however, the lexical path goes through smoothly:

> Joe *painted* the window black
> He *kicked* her unconscious
> He *shot* her dead.[5]

These possibilities give us the neutral

(c₂) $N_i\ C(N_j\ \text{is}\ A) - N_i\ v_c\ N_j\ A$

and the colorful

(c₃) $N_i\ V_c\ (N_j\ \text{is}\ A) - N_i\ V_c\ N_j\ A$

V.   The next type of simple sentence I shall consider in the causative frame is this: *N is PN*, e.g., *The book is on the table*. Interestingly enough, the syntactical path works well. Some examples:

> John floored his opponent
> The chairman tabled the resolution
> The workers crated the merchandise,

and so forth, i.e.,

(d₁) $N_i\ C(N_j\ \text{is}\ PN_k) - N_i\ V_{Nk}\ N_j$

This surface form is identical with the one in (b₁). We have to follow semantic clues to realize that, for instance, *The Queen knighted the hero* is to be accounted for differently from, say, *The Queen cornered the hero*. Semantic considerations are also relevant to the recovery of the lost preposition (*on* the table, *in* crates).

It is important to distinguish such causative contractions from what may be called 'instrumental' ones. Compare

> They bottled the wine
> They shipped the wine

or

> The hero cornered the Queen
> The hero axed the Queen.

The difference is obvious. They did something with the wine *so that* it is now in bottles. The hero did something with the Queen *so that* she is in a corner. These are causative situations. On the other hand, they did something with the wine (transported it) *by means of* a ship, and the hero did something to the Queen (bashed her) *with* (by means of) an axe. Here, once more, we must rely on semantic clues to find the right analysis.

The lexical path is facilitated by a wide range of verbs ranging from the pretty neutral *put* to such highly specific ones as *throw* or *push*:

> The chairman put the resolution on the table
> John threw his opponent on the floor
> He pushed her in the corner.

Compare:

> He put her on the train
> He kicked her on the train.

Obviously, in this last case, his kicking of her has occurred on the train. In the previous case, however, it does not even make sense to say that his putting of her has occurred on the train. *He put her* is not a sentence as *He made him* (from, e.g., *He made him kneel*) is not a sentence. These facts reinforce the impression that these verbs are 'purely' causal verbs: their semantics is exhausted by this aspect. This is not so with specific verbs: *He kicked the ball over the fence* entails *He kicked the ball*.

Thus the lexical path works as follows:

$$(d_2) \qquad N_i \, C(N_j \text{ is } PN_k) - N_i \, v_c \, N_j \, PN_k$$

where v_c is something like *put* or *take*, and, with a more specific verb,

$$(d_3) \qquad N_i \, V_c \, (N_j \text{ is } PN_k) - N_i \, V_c \, N_j \, PN_k$$

VI.   I round out the picture by considering the kernel type *NVN* in a causative situation. The lexical path is always open with or without a colorful causal verb. First without one:

> The lady caused the butler to ring the bell
> The king made him renounce his title,

and so forth. With a colorful verb:

> The lady helped the butler to ring the bell
> The king forced him to renounce his title.

In this case, however, the syntactic path fails. We do not have

> *The lady rang the butler the bell.

Yet the pattern of this last non-sentence is not empty. By putting *gave* for *rang* we get

> (1)   The lady gave the butler the bell.

Now, clearly, this sentence expresses a causative situation too. The lady did something *so that* the butler (came to) have the bell. This suggests:

$$N_i \; C(N_j \text{ has } N_k) - N_i \; v_c \; N_j \; N_k$$

where v_c is the appropriate neutral *give*. One might elaborate however: she *handed, sold, lent, willed*, etc., the butler the bell.

The relevant kernel, N_j *has* N_k, has a synonym: N_k *belongs to* N_j. And, behold, (1) has a corresponding synonym:

> (2)   The lady gave the bell to the butler

i.e.:

$$N_i \; C(N_k \text{ belongs to } N_j) - N_i \; v_c \; N_k \text{ to } N_j$$

The colorful verbs follow suit nicely, e.g.,

> The lady sold the bell to the butler.

VII.   Before returning to our operatives, let us sum up the results thus far achieved. They present a very broad and strikingly uniform pattern.

It appears that there are two basic ways of coding a causal structure. One is the long, full, or, as I called it before, the lexical way. If the causal factor is untainted, then, with the various kernels, it works as follows:

$$
\begin{array}{lll}
\text{C (NV)} & - v_c \text{ NV} & \text{(make) the dog walk} \\
\text{C (N is N)} & - v_c \text{ NN} & \text{(make) the hero knight} \\
\text{C (N is A)} & - v_c \text{ NA} & \text{(make) the street wide} \\
\text{C (N is PN)} & - v_c \text{ NPN} & \text{(put) the book on the table} \\
\text{C (NVN)} & - v_c \text{ NVN} & \text{(make) the butler ring the bell} \\
\text{C (N has N)} & - v_c \text{ NN} & \text{(give) the butler the bell.}
\end{array}
$$

The pattern is obvious. The causal factor is expressed by the appropriate neutral causal verb (*make, put, give*) followed by an 'emasculated' version of the sentence in question. This emasculation consists in depriving the sentence of its copula (or *has*), or, if it contains a real verb, in stripping it of its tense. The leftovers of the poor sentence then are just spilled out in sequence. This sad result reminds us of an exactly similar emasculation: the one occurring in question (and negation) transformations. Consider:

> (Did) the dog walk?
> (Is) the hero knight?
> (Is) the street wide?
> (Is) the book on the table?
> (Did) the butler ring the bell?
> (Has) the butler the bell?

We may conclude, then, that a sentence in a causal frame is the victim of the same '*do*-napping' as in the question-frame.

What happens to the *do* (*be, have*)? Obviously it gets ascribed to the agent: it gets absorbed by the causal factor, *C*, and yields *make* (*put, give*). This corresponds to the intuition that the 'action' expressed in the caused sentence is really due to the agent: although the dog walks, it is the man who *makes* him *do* it; although the hero becomes knight, it is the Queen who *makes* him *become* one, etc. The agent, as it were, 'steals the action' out of the caused sentence.

Since the same thing happens even if we operate with a colorful causal verb, it is reasonable to suppose that these verbs contain the causal factor, among other elements, in their semantic structure. Indeed, to force is to make do (under duress), to throw is to put (with a certain motion), and to sell is to give (for value received).

In the syntactic path the 'power grab' is more radical; it amounts to an amputation. Not only *do,* and its kind, are stolen, but the whole verb-phrase (suitably trimmed) gets appropriated by the agent, the subject of *C.* The instances are these:

$$C(NV) \qquad - VN \qquad \text{walk the dog}$$
$$C(N_i \text{ is } N_j) \quad - V_{N_j}N_i \quad \text{knight the hero}$$
$$C(N \text{ is } A) \quad - V_A N \quad \text{widen the street}$$
$$C(N_i \text{ is } PN_j) - V_{N_j}N_i \quad \text{bottle the wine.}$$

Accordingly, one may represent the operation of the lexical way as follows:

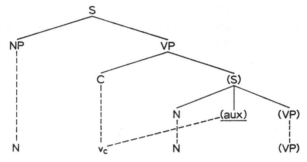

where *aux* denotes *do, be* or *have,* (*VP*) the complements of these, and v_c the neutral causal verbs: *make, put, give.* And the syntactic path may be represented in this way:

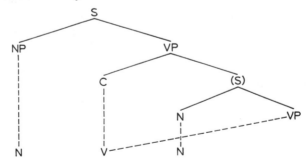

VIII.   One can take a further step to understand the 'emasculation' and 'amputation' just described more clearly. Let us assume – following the suggestion of some logicians and linguists – that a sentence can be analyzed into a function (or predicate) and its ordered arguments. E.g., the sentence *The dog bit the man* may be represented either as *Did (the dog/ bite/the man)* or *Bit (the dog/the man.)* Similarly, for *The window is black* we would get either *Is (the window/black)* or *Is black (the window)*; for *The book is on the table* either *Is (the book/on the table)* or *Is on the table (the book)*; etc.

Then the next move is obvious. Put in a causal frame, the sentence is stripped of its function (narrowly or broadly conceived), and the arguments then get spilled out in order, within the framework of a larger sentence governed by an appropriate causal function. In these terms, the general derivation of a causal construction is this:

$$C[A_1/F(A_2/A_3/.../A_n)] - F_c[A_1/A_2/A_3/.../A_n]$$

By 'appropriate causal functions' I mean the products of the following semantic constructions (omitting such trivial ones as *blacken, knight*, etc.)

C (do) →	make
C (be) →	make
C (be (located)) →	put
C (have) →	give
C (rise) →	raise
C (be full) →	fill
C (be dead) →	kill
C_{duress} (do) →	force
$C_{intent.}$ (be dead) →	murder

and so forth.

There are a couple of interesting facts to be learned from these results. The first is that the language seems to allow us to consider either the auxiliary as the function governing the sentence, or the whole verb-phrase. The second is that the function that governs an *N is PN* sentence is not *is P*, but *is*, since *via* the lexical path we get, e.g., *put the book on the table*, and not **put the book the table*.[6]

IX.   It is time to return to the subject of our original concern, the performative class I called 'operatives'. How do they operate?

We remarked at the beginning that these verbs, together with such other permanent effect verbs as *cook* and *break* enter the frame *N is V*[en],

e.g., *The criminal is arrested, The meat is cooked, The window is broken,*
which is not true of other verbs, e.g., **The cart is pulled, *The dog is
walked.* Notice, moreover, that *The meat is cooked* is not a short-passive,
since the addition of the original subject in a *by N* phrase would change
the meaning of the sentence. *The meat is cooked by the maid* is either a
report on kitchen practice, or a sloppy form of *The meat is being cooked
by the maid,* which indeed yields the genuine short passive, namely, *The
meat is being cooked.* This, however, is by no means a synonym for *The
meat is cooked.* This latter means that the meat has been cooked, i.e., it is
now cooked meat. Such 'adjectivization' does not work with verbs that
do not connote permanent effects. Even though the cart has been pulled,
and the dog has been walked, this does not mean that we now have a
pulled cart and a walked dog on hand.

If, then, *The window is broken* is not a short-passive, what is it? I shall
assume that it is a sentence of the type *N is A,* analogous to, say, *The
window is black.* This reminds us of the causative pattern (c_1), i.e.,

> NC(the window is black) – N blackened the window.

On this analogy I suggest the following:

> NC(the window is broken) – N broke the window.

We remember, of course, that *N broke the window* can also be produced
via another path (a_1), which gives us

> NC(the window broke) – N broke the window.

Combining the two paths we get the alternatives:

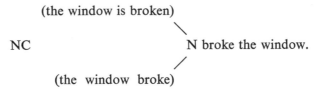

I shall call the upper derivation 'adjectival' and the lower one 'verbal'.
The equivalence of the two is supported by the intuition that tells us that
to break is to get broken. This is not so with non-permanent-effect verbs:
to walk is not to get walked, and to sleep is not to get slept. Accordingly,
such a sentence as *Joe walked the dog* cannot be accounted for by the
adjectival derivation.

X. One might object at this point that the adjectival derivation puts the cart before the horse, inasmuch as it seems to drive a verb (*break*) from its participle (*broken*). This should not surprise us, however, at this stage. As we remarked above, category boundaries are by no means sacrosanct, and the same word root may act in one or in another grammatical category, showing, of course, the appropriate paraphernalia. Think of *black* and *blacken* (adjective to verb with suffix), *rise* and *raise* (intransitive to transitive with Umlaut), *knight* and *knight* (noun to verb with no change). In all these cases we assumed that the noncausal form is the primary one morphologically. But is this always so? Consider *tame*: adjective, transitive causal, and – at least in old English – intransitive. It is academic to argue about its 'original' category; contemporary speakers cannot decide. Yet, logically, the causal sense is obviously a derivative of the noncausal (now adjectival) sense: to tame a beast is to render it tame. Thus it is not necessary that the morphological appearance reflect semantic priorities.

If this is so, then it is perfectly acceptable that, although *broken* or *arrested* are participles of *break* and *arrest*, semantically speaking the former enjoy the priority, i.e., that we understand breaking something in terms of its being broken, and arresting somebody in terms of his being arrested. If you like: the derivatives *broken* and *arrested* code more simple ideas than the roots *break* and *arrest*.[7]

Moreover, wheras in the case of *break* we have the option of the verbal and the adjectival derivations, with respect to such operatives as *arrest*, *baptize, fire, convict, discharge*, and so forth, the verbal derivation is not available. Thus we have to account for, say, *The sheriff arrested the criminal* in terms of *The sheriff (got) the criminal arrested*, i.e.,

$$N_i \ C(N_j \ \text{is} \ V^{en}) - N_i \ VN_j$$

The main difference between feats like arresting, firing and convicting somebody, and feats like breaking, raising and boiling something is the following. These latter feats are achieved by physical action; the former by simply saying something (in the appropriate circumstances). Accordingly, whereas the thing that breaks, the thing that boils, etc., itself changes in the process (shatters, bubbles, etc.), there is no change *in* the criminal as he gets arrested, or *in* the secretary as she gets fired. Their *status* changes, but they do not. This intuition may account for the fact that we have the intransitive verbs *break*, *rise* and *boil*, but not such intransitives as *arrest* or *fire*.[8] After all, unlike the breaking glass or the boiling soup, the criminal and the secretary do not *do* anything in getting arrested or fired. The effect *ipso dicto* follows: the sheriff's, or the boss's, saying so makes it so.

Their saying what, exactly? There is a very significant option here. The boss, for example, might say "I (hereby) fire you," or equivalently "You are (hereby) fired." Similarly, "You are (hereby) suspended, promoted, sentenced to...," etc., or even, "You are welcome." The reason for this alternative becomes clear as we consider the deep structure of such operative utterances. It conforms to the syntactic path, i.e., should be sketched as follows:

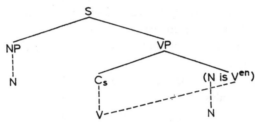

The C_s here is a special C: it represents causal efficacy by saying not by otherwise doing. Consequently the line $NC_s(N \text{ is } V^{en})$ is analogous to the general performative schema $NV_{pf} \text{ nom } (S)$. E.g. *He said that it was raining*. Now we know that in the first person present singular case the *I say* may be omitted:

It is raining

said by Joe is as good as

I say that it is raining

said by him. Since, therefore, in the case of the operatives the efficacious act consists in saying, the same possibility is available. Thus it is enough for the boss to say

You are fired

to get the secretary fired. Yet, since *he* said it, it will be true that she has been fired *by the boss*. Later on, *I* may say to the same secretary *You are fired*, and it will be true. What will not be true, however, is that she has been fired by me. My utterance was not efficacious; my 'saying' did not have the 'operative' illocutionary force, but the 'expositive' one: it was a statement (true or false).

XI.   A few concluding remarks on causality. Austin writes in 'A Plea for Excuses' that " 'Causing,' I suppose, was a notion taken from a man's own experience of doing simple actions, and by primitive man every event was construed in terms of this model: every event has a cause, that is, every event is an action done by somebody – if not a man, then by a quasi-man, a spirit," [9] We do not believe in spirits, yet we are still inclined to believe in universal causality; the 'causes', however, that we give are not persons or spirits, but facts that condition the occurrence of events.[10]

This shift is mirrored in grammar. Compare, for instance, the following sentences:

(1)   The butler rang the bell
(2)   The shaking of the earth caused the ringing of the bell
(3)   ?The butler caused the ringing of the bell
(4)   His having pulled the string caused the ringing of the bell
(5)   *His having pulled the string rang the bell.

What goes wrong in (3) and (5)? First about (5). It seems to me that the verb *ring* is attributed to a subject of the wrong type. A bell can ring (intransitively), and so can the butler (transitively). Facts, however – such as his having pulled the string – cannot ring in either way.[11] What they can do is to cause an event, e.g., the ringing of the bell (as in (4)). This, on the other hand – as (3) shows – a person cannot do.

One might object here that above we admitted such sentences as

(6)   The lady caused the butler to ring the bell.

But notice, first, that here the contrastive set of *cause* contains such verbs as *help, force, ask*, etc., which is not true of *cause* in (2) or (4). Second, whereas *cause* in (6) can be exchanged for *make* (*She made him do it*), no such substitution is possible in (2) and (4). Finally, (6) tolerates the additions *by asking him, by giving him a sign*, etc., (4) cannot be completed by phrases like *by shaking it*.

What to conclude? Simply this. The word *cause* may function either as a neutral verb of efficacy (like *make*), in which case it occurs between two nouns (e.g., *The lady caused the butler to ...*), or – and this is its prevalent use – it expresses the dependence of an event upon a fact, in which case it occurs between two nominalized sentences (e.g., *The firing of the gun caused the breaking of the window*). This hypothesis explains the three differences just mentioned. So the 'spirits' turn out to be facts.

University of California,
San Diego

NOTES

[1] 'Say What You Think', in *Studies in Thought and Language* (ed. by J. L. Cowan), University of Arizona Press, Tucson, 1970; *Res Cogitans*, Cornell University Press, Ithaca and London, 1972, Chapter II.
[2] *How to Do Things with Words*, Clarendon, Oxford, 1962, Lecture XII.
[3] *Ibid.*, pp. 154–155.
[4] The identity of N_i and N_j may account for such sentences as *Every night he (the gambler) rose a winner*, but I am not sure.
[5] Compare this sentence with? *He killed her dead.* This is redundant, since *kill* means $C (... is dead)$ in the same way as *fill* means $C (... is full)$. The verb *murder* adds something to the C, namely intentionality; thus *murder* means $C_{int} (... is dead)$.
[6] Nevertheless, since $C (... is ...)$ in this case yields *put* rather than *make*, I think that *is* here should be interpreted as an ellipsis for something like *is located*.
[7] Thus the list of causal functions given in Section VIII may be continued as follows

$$C \text{ (is broken)} \rightarrow \text{break}$$
$$C \text{ (is arrested)} \rightarrow \text{arrest}$$

and so on.
[8] We have a substitute though: *get arrested*.
[9] *Philosophical Papers*, Clarendon, Oxford, 1961, p. 150.
[10] See my 'Causal Relations', *Journal of Philosophy* **64** (1967), 704–713; and my *Linguistics in Philosophy*, Cornell University Press, Ithaca, 1967, Chapter VI.
[11] Notice, however: *The explosion broke the window*. Thus events but not facts, can be agents. Compare: *His firing of the gun broke the window* and ** His having fired the gun broke the window*.

RAY C. DOUGHERTY

HARRIS AND CHOMSKY
AT THE SYNTAX-SEMANTICS BOUNDARY*

Both Harris and Chomsky formulate questions about language structure in terms of algebraically formalizable tools of description, e.g. transformations. Harris and Chomsky differ on specifying the goals of research and in defining transformations. In Harris' system, a transformation relates one surface string with another under certain conditions of paraphrase and cooccurrence. In Chomsky's system, a generative transformation applies to abstract structures that often bear no close resemblance to actual surface strings. In Harris' system 'Does T_x change meaning?' is a focal point of research, and the question 'Which aspect of the syntactic structure correlates with which aspect of the semantic interpretation?' makes no sense. In Chomsky's system, however, the latter question is the focal point of research, while the former makes no sense. It is shown that one can impose an interpretation on the meaningless questions and force an answer, that is, one can use Harrisian ideas to formulate problems in Chomsky's system and Chomsky's ideas to formulate questions in Harris' system. The answers to the forced questions are misleading. An example of a generative grammar with a surface structure interpretive rule is presented to assign readings to sentences containing the elements *either/or* and *not*. The conclusion discusses the sense in which *Syntactic Structures* offered a new conception of *explanation* in linguistics. Evidence suggests that generative semantics developed within the Harrisian transformational taxonomic framework. Generative semantics might best be considered to be a Harrisian transformational taxonomic grammar with abstract structures; that is generative semantics is neo-taxonomy.

1. HARRIS AND CHOMSKY ON TRANSFORMATIONS

Harris' (1957, 1965) concept of a transformational rule differs considerably from that of Chomsky. Many of these differences (perhaps all of them) stem from two facts: (1) Chomsky wishes to formulate sets of rules to generate the syntactic structures which characterize the infinite number

Hockney et al. (eds.), Contemporary Research in Philosophical Logic and Linguistic Semantics, 137–193. All Rights Reserved
Copyright © 1975 by D. Reidel Publishing Company, Dordrecht-Holland

of well-formed sentences of a language, while Harris wishes to discover
sets of rules which will factor generalizations concerning distributional
similarities from a fixed corpus of data. (2) Chomsky wants to construct a
grammar of a language. In Chomsky's system, a grammar is a theory of a
language which defines the concept of grammatical sentence. It makes
sense to improve our grammar, to develop the theory comparison method
to seek more accurate grammars.[1] Hence, Chomsky (1957: 49–60) proposed a grammar evaluation procedure which must decide which of two
alternative grammars provides the most insightful explanation of the
principles of sentence construction. On the other hand, Harris feels that
linguistics is exhausted by the study and formalization of methods. There
is no 'grammar' of a language, there are, in fact, as many grammars as
your methods of analysis will give you. 'Grammar' is not a crucial notion
in Harris' system. He does not develop a grammar as a theory of a language, rather, he develops methods of text analysis. There is no 'best
grammar' or 'more explanatory grammar', rather there are as many different grammars as there are ways of looking at the data. In Harris' system
it is senseless to try to choose between grammars; the problem plays
essentially no significant role in Harris' theory. Harris states:

... Transformational analysis is of particular interest, first, because it can be described
and investigated with algebraic tools, and second, because it provides exceptionally
subtle analyses and distinctions for sentences.
   To interrelate these [various transformational] analyses, it is necessary to understand that these are not competing theories, but rather complement each other in the
description of sentences.[6] It is not that grammar is one or another of these analyses,
but that sentences exhibit simultaneously all of these properties. (1965: 365)

[6] [Footnote] The pitting of one linguistic tool against another has in it something of the
absolutist postwar temper of social institutions, but is not required by the character and
range of these tools of analysis. (*ibid*: 365)

Chomsky (personal communication) presents another way of looking
at this: Harris' methods allow the discovery of some transformational
systems but not the discovery of the grammar. In some formulations of
Harris' system, one could have a set of transformations, but not the grammar. One could not have 'the' grammar because there are as many
grammars as one's methods allow, and they are, according to Harris,
complementary and equally legitimate. Some particular set of transformational rules may be interesting for textual analysis of some sort, but
it is no more 'the' grammar than is any other set of generalizations one

might discover to characterize the regularities in the data under consideration.

Since Harris' goal is to construct from a corpus a catalog (or a factorization) of the elements which function in a language and to indicate their restrictions on distribution, he is working within the taxonomic perspective. The particular theoretical proposals he offers, however, are far richer than anything permitted by any previous taxonomic linguist.

Harris' transformational taxonomic grammar attempts to factor from a given corpus of sentences information about the structure internal to any given sentence, and further, information concerning the relation of a given sentence to other sentences in the corpus. Much information about the internal structure of a sentence would be given by surface structure diagnostic environments. Additional information about the internal structure of a sentence and also information about certain paraphrase and cooccurrence relations existing between sentences would be factored from the corpus and expressed by transformations.

Given a corpus of sentences, which is for Harris a set of surface structure strings, $(S_1, S_2, , , , S_n)$, a Harrisian transformation relates one string with another: $S_x \rightleftarrows S_y$, where both S_x and S_y are in the corpus. In theory, Harris' transformations are biconditional relations which obtain between sentences.[2] They have no directionality. They should therefore be written with the biconditionality sign: $\rightleftarrows$.

Two surface structure strings are transformationally related if certain relations of paraphrase and cooccurrence obtain between them. The specific paraphrase and cooccurrence relations significant in analyzing a given corpus are determined by informant responses and the linguist's specific interests in obtaining a set of transformations (for discourse analysis, text analysis, etc.). For example, this would be a Harrisian transformation:

(1) $(_{S_1} (_{N_1}$---$)$ V $(_{N_2}$---$)$ and $(_{N_2}$---$)$ V $(_{N_1}$---$)) \rightleftarrows (_{S_2} (_{N_1}$---$)$ and $(_{N_2}$---$)$ V *each other*$)$

Working with an informant, a linguist could find triples: (N_1, N_2, V), such that when substituted into (1), they yielded two sentences S_1 and S_2, as defined by (1), which are essentially paraphrases and have the same level of informant acceptability. For example, the triple (*John, Mary, saw*) could be substituted into (1) to yield the two sentences: *John saw Mary and Mary saw John* and *John and Mary saw each other:*

(2)   ($_{s_1}$ John saw Mary and Mary saw John) $\rightleftarrows$ ($_{s_2}$ John and Mary saw each other)

There is no sense of directionality here. It is not the case that one sentence 'derives from' another. A Harrisian transformation expresses a biconditional relation between two sentences with respect to paraphrase and cooccurrence.[3]

Transformational rules play a crucial role in Harris' view that linguistics is defined by its methods, and the goal of linguistic analysis is to formulate a discovery procedure. Harris' transformational devices represent a development of the discovery procedure in that: (1) Transformations permit a linguist to discover the interrelations of sentences in a discourse and to discover systematic relations of paraphrase and cooccurrence which exist between them. They permit a linguist to factor inductive generalizations of a specific sort, i.e. those transformationally expressible, from a given finite corpus of data. (2) Transformations can be used to get sentences into a 'normalized' form so that procedures of segmentation and classification could be used in discourse analysis. For example, suppose a linguist had these sentences in his corpus:

(3)   John drank beer.
(4)   What Mary ate was cheese.

Segmentation procedures would not reveal the similarities between these two sentences. Suppose, however, the linguist could formulate a transformation like this:

(5)   ($_{s_1}$ ($_{N_1}$---) V ($_{N_2}$---)) $\rightleftarrows$ ($_{s_2}$ what ($_{N_1}$---) V *was* ($_{N_2}$---))

Through informant testing, he could find that the triples: (*Albert, saw, water*), (*Mary, ate, cheese*), etc. could be substituted into (5) to yield:

(6)   ($_{s_1}$Albert saw water) $\rightleftarrows$ ($_{s_2}$ What Albert saw was water)
(7)   ($_{s_1}$ Mary ate cheese) $\rightleftarrows$ ($_{s_2}$What Mary ate was cheese)

Transformation (5) enables the linguist to see that (4) has an alternative – more normalized – form, (8), which has the same paraphrase and cooccurrence properties as (4):

(8)   Mary ate cheese.

The slot-filler tests could show that (3) and (8) had similar structures, and in some sense, the structural information discovered about (8) carries over to (4) in discourse analysis.[4]

Harris' transformations differ from Chomsky's in at least three ways:

(9) (a) Harris' transformations are not used to generate sentences, rather, they are used to factor generalizations concerning the distributional similarities of strings, cooccurrence, and paraphrase from a given finite corpus of surface structure strings.

   (b) Chomsky's transformations play a role in generating an infinite number of sentences from abstract underlying structures.

(10) (a) Harris' transformations relate one surface structure string with another surface structure string. They are not ordered nor are there any abstract underlying forms. Ideally all transformations should be biconditional.

   (b) Chomsky's transformations derive surface structure strings from abstract underlying structures which in no direct way correspond to surface structure strings (except of course through the transformations). Chomsky's transformational rules are ordered and require the existence of abstract underlying forms.

(11) (a) For Harris' system, the fact that certain relations of paraphrase and cooccurrence obtain between two surface structure strings is a necessary and sufficient condition to postulate a transformational relation between them.

   (b) Within Chomsky's system, it is impossible to define the ideas of paraphrase and cooccurrence in any non-circular way, i.e. in any way that does not specifically refer to the transformation which relates the strings. See Chomsky (1964: 62, fn.2). A transformation in Chomsky's system relates an abstract structure with another abstract structure. (See fn. 20). If cooccurrence and paraphrase arguments were used within the Chomskian framework to motivate a transformation, the argument would be circular, i.e. one would essentially be saying that the transformation was motivated because it related what it related.

2. HARRIS AND CHOMSKY AT THE SYNTAX-SEMANTICS BOUNDARY

For Harris, the question: 'Do transformations change meaning?' is well-defined since he relates one surface structure string with another. Harris discusses the problem:

> ... That many sentences which are transforms of each other have more or less the same meaning, except for different external grammatical status (different grammatical relations to surrounding sentence elements), is an immediate impression. This is not surprising, since meaning correlates closely with range of occurrence, and transformations maintain the same occurrence range. When we have transformations which are associated with a meaning change, it is usually possible to attribute the meaning change to the special morphemes (combiners, introducers, subclasses of the primary V) in whose environment the transformation occurs. To what extent, and in what sense, transformations hold meaning constant is a matter for investigation; but enough is known to make transformations a possible tool for reducing the complexity of sentences under semantically controlled conditions. (Harris, 1957: 209)

Harris mentions three things: (1)'... sentences which are transforms of each other...' indicates that the transformations are biconditional relations, (2) '... transformations a possible tool for reducing the complexity of a sentence...' indicates that he uses transformations like those discussed in examples (1–8), and (3) the whole paragraph indicates that the question 'Do transformations change meaning?' is important in Harris' system.

For Chomsky, the question 'Do transformations change meaning?' is hollow because Chomsky's transformations relate an abstract object with a surface structure sentence. The underlying structure is not a 'paraphrase' of the surface structure in any definable sense. The question in Chomsky's system, as he formulates the problem, is: 'What aspects of the syntactic structure correlate with what aspects of the semantic interpretation?' Let us examine Chomsky's ideas about the interrelation of syntax and semantics.

Chomsky (1968) sketches the general properties of the *Aspects* model, called here the 'standard theory':

> Observe that a standard theory specifies, for each sentence, a syntactic structure $\Sigma = (P_1,...,P_i,...,P_n)$ (where P_i is the deep and P_n the surface structure), a semantic representation S, and a phonetic representation P. It asserts, furthermore, that S is determined by P_i and P by P_n under the rules of semantic and phonological interpretation, respectively. More generally, the theory is 'syntactically-based' in the sense that it assumes the sound-meaning relation (P, S) to be determined by Σ. (Chomsky, 1968:66)

In *Aspects*, Chomsky discusses which aspects of Σ correlate with which aspects of the semantic interpretation:

Thus the syntactic component consists of a base that generates deep structures and a transformational part that maps them into surface structures. The deep structure of a sentence is submitted to the semantic component for semantic interpretation, and its surface structure enters the phonological component and undergoes phonetic interpretation. The final effect of a grammar, then, is to relate a semantic interpretation to a phonetic representation – that is, to state how a sentence is interpreted. This relation is mediated by the syntactic component of the grammar, which constitutes its sole 'creative' part.

The branching rules of the base (that is, its categorial component) define grammatical functions and grammatical relations and determine an abstract underlying order (cf. §4.4, Chapter 2); the lexicon characterizes the individual properties of particular lexical items that are inserted in specified positions in base Phrase-markers. Thus when we define 'deep structures' as 'structures generated by the base component', we are, in effect, assuming that the semantic interpretation of a sentence depends only on its lexical items and the grammatical functions and relations represented in the underlying structures in which they appear.[9] This is the basic idea that has motivated the theory of transformational grammar since its inception (cf. note 33, Chapter 2.) Its first relatively clear formulation is in Katz and Fodor (1963), and an improved version is given in Katz and Postal (1964), in terms of the modification of syntactic theory proposed there and briefly discussed earlier. The formulation just suggested [i.e. the position in the quote above, RCD] sharpens this idea still further. In fact, it permits a further simplification of the theory of semantic interpretation presented in Katz and Postal (1964), since Transformation-markers and generalized transformations, as well as 'projection rules' to deal with them, need no longer be considered at all. This formulation seems to be a natural extension and summary of the developments of the past few years that have just been summarized. (1965:135–6)

[9] Footnote: As it stands, this claim seems to me somewhat too strong, though it is true in one important sense of semantic interpretation. For example, it seems clear that the order of 'quantifiers' in surface structures sometimes plays a role in semantic interpretation. Thus for many speakers – in particular, for me – the sentences 'everyone in the room knows at least two languages' and 'at least two languages are known by everyone in the room' are not synonymous. Still, we might maintain that in such examples both interpretations are latent (as would be indicated by the identity of the deep structures of the two sentences in all respects relevant to semantic interpretation), and that the reason for the opposing interpretations is an extraneous factor – an overriding consideration involving order of quantifiers in surface structures – that filters out certain latent interpretations provided by the deep structures. In support of this view, it may be pointed out that other sentences that derive from these (e.g. 'there are two languages that everyone in the room knows') may switch interpretations indicating that these interpretations must have been latent all along. There are other examples that suggest something similar. For example, Grice has suggested that the temporal order implied in conjunction may be regarded as a feature of discourse rather than as part of the meaning of 'and', and Jakobson has also discussed 'iconic' features of discourse involving relations between temporal order in surface structure and order of importance, etc. Also relevant in this connection is the notion of Topic-Comment mentioned in note 32, Chapter 2. For some references to remarks in the Port-Royal Logic on the effect of grammatical transformations on meaning, see Chomsky (forthcoming). (*ibid.*: 224)

Chomsky refined and developed the ideas relating to the semantics-syntax boundary in two papers (1968, 1969). He presents the following picture:

> ... Let us assume given the notion 'phrase marker' and the notion 'grammatical transformation' as a mapping of phrase markers into phrase markers. We may say, then, that a grammar G generates a class K of derivations Σ, where Σ is a sequence of phrase markers:
>
> (2) $G \rightarrow K = \{\Sigma : \Sigma = (P_1, ..., P_n)\}$
> Σ is maximal, in the obvious sense
> $P_i = T(P_{i-1})$, by some transformation T of G
>
> The grammar G specifies a set of transformations and various conditions on them, for example, ordering conditions. We may assume that P_n, which we will call the 'surface structure', determines the phonetic form of the sentence generated by phonological rules. (Chomsky, 1969: 123–4)

> ... the grammatical relations represented in deep structure are those that determine semantic interpretation. However, it seems that such matters as focus and presupposition, topic and comment, reference, scope of logical elements, and perhaps other phenomena, are determined in part at least by properties of structures of K other than deep structures, in particular, by properties of surface structure. In short, these phenomena suggest that the theory of grammar should be reconstructed along the lines intuitively indicated in (113), using the notation of the earlier discussion:
>
> (113)   Base: $(P_1, ..., P_i)$ (P_1 the K-initial, P_i the post-lexical (deep) structure of the syntactic structure which is a member of K) Transformations: $(P_i, ..., P_n)$ (P_n the surface structure; $(P_1, ..., P_n) \in K$)
>   Phonology: $P_n \rightarrow$ phonetic representation
>   Semantics: $(P_i, P_n) \rightarrow$ semantic representation (the grammatical relations involved being those of P_i, that is, those represented in P_1).

> Notice, incidentally, that it is, strictly speaking, not P_n that is subject to semantic interpretation but rather the structure determined by phonological interpretation of P_n, with intonation center assigned. (Chomsky, 1968: 113–4)

Chomsky (1969) states more precisely which aspects of the semantic interpretation correlate with which aspects of the syntactic structure:

> ... semantic interpretation is held to be determined by the pair (deep structure, surface structure) of Σ, rather than by the deep structure alone; further, it is proposed that insofar as grammatical relations play a role in determining meaning, it is the grammatical relations of the deep structure that are relevant (as before), but that such matters as scope of 'logical elements' and quantifiers, coreference, focus and certain kinds of presupposition, and certain other properties, are determined by rules that take surface structure (more precisely, phonetically interpreted surface structure) into account. A number of examples were given there. [Chomsky, 1968, RCD] For a much more extensive discussion, along somewhat similar lines, see Jackendoff (1968). (Chomsky, 1969: 134)

Chomsky has always formulated the issues relating to the semantics-syntax boundary in terms of the question: 'Which aspects of Σ correlate with which aspects of the semantic interpretation?' Similarly, the issues relating to the phonetic-syntax boundary have been formulated in terms of the question: 'Which aspects of Σ correlate with which aspects of the phonetic representation?'

Consider this passage where Chomsky outlines one of his basic assumptions:

A central idea in much of structural linguistics was that the formal devices of language should be studied independently of their use. The earliest work in transformational-generative grammar took over a version of this thesis, as a working hypothesis. I think it has been a fruitful hypothesis. It seems that grammars contain a substructure of perfectly formal rules operating on phrase-markers in narrowly circumscribed ways. Not only are these rules independent of meaning or sound in their function, but it may also be that the choice of these devices by the language-learner (i.e. the choice of grammar on the basis of data) may be independent, to a significant extent, of conditions of meaning and use. If we could specify the extent precisely, the working hypothesis would become a true empirical hypothesis. Such an effort may be premature. It does, however, seem noteworthy that the extensive studies of meaning and use that have been undertaken in recent years have not – if the foregoing analysis is correct – given any serious indication that questions of meaning and use are involved in the functioning or choice of grammars in ways beyond those considered in the earliest speculations about these matters, say in Chomsky (1957). (Chomsky, 1969: 198–9)

Chomsky's position is, as far as I can see, well-defined and unambiguous. He has never developed his TGG system by asking 'Do transformations change meaning?' In many places he indicates that the question has no place in a TGG, for example, above he states: 'It seems that grammars contain a substructure of perfectly formal rules operating on phrase markers in narrowly circumscribed ways. Not only are these rules independent of meaning or sound in their function, but...' (Chomsky, 1969: 198–9). See n. 23.

Chomsky's position on the nature of the semantics-syntax boundary has changed little in basic character since 1957. Developments have taken place in two main areas. First, the syntactic structure, Σ, has been simplified by the elimination of the transformation marker, etc. which characterized the pre-*Aspects* models. This point is made in the passage quoted above from *Aspects*: 'The formulation just suggested... permits a simplification of the theory of semantic interpretation presented in Katz and Postal (1964), since Transformation-markers and generalized transformations, as well as 'projection rules' to deal with them, need no longer be con-

sidered at all.' (1965: 136) Second, the claims about the semantics-syntax
boundary made based on the *Aspects* model are far more specific than
those made previous to the *Aspects* model. For example, Chomsky (1968)
discusses *specific* relations between scope, presupposition, etc. and the
intonation center assigned to surface structure strings.

Insofar as one asks: 'Do transformations change meaning?', he is
working on a Harrisian transformational taxonomic grammar and not on
a transformational generative grammar as this has been defined by
Chomsky in any of his writings. Working on a TGG, one would be led to
a basic misconception of the interrelation between syntax and semantics if
one conceived of the deep structure, or underlying structure, as a paraphrase of the surface structure.

3. RECENT WORK ON SEMANTICS

Partee (1972), attempts to clarify the issues separating the *SS-ASPects*
position from the generative semantics position.

In the following passage, excerpted from the section in which Partee
discusses the empirical nature of the hypothesis that transformations do
not change meaning, Partee probes the meaning of *meaning-preserving
transformation* in Chomsky's TGG system. Since, in this quote, Partee uses
the word 'sentence' to mean 'surface structure string' – cf. Partee:
'surface structures, that is, sentences' (1972: 5) – I have added *surface
structure string*, or *SS string*, in brackets at each occurrence of the word
sentence. Partee states:

2.2.   The Empirical Nature of Hypothesis. The various stands taken on synonymy all
have to do with synonymy between *sentences* [surface structure strings], and in talk
about transformations preserving or changing meaning, the most common examples
are transformations which can informally be thought of as relating sentences [SS
strings] to other sentences [SS strings]. But transformations in fact operate not on
sentences [SS strings] but on abstract phrase-markers, and it is not obvious that we
have any direct semantic intuitions about these abstract structures, in particular any
notion of synonymy between them. Failure to distinguish sentences [SS strings] from
abstract P-markers is often harmless, as in discussion of very late optional 'stylistic'
transformations, where the abstract structures involved are very close to surface
structures, that is, sentences [SS strings]. But for obligatory transformations the fact
that abstract structures and not sentences [SS strings] are involved is significant. For
obligatory rules, in fact, the question of meaning-preservingness does not even make
sense, for the input to the rule is an abstract structure with which we have no independent acquaintance. This point can be illustrated by considering the affix-switching rule

that moves -*ing*, -*en*, and so forth, into their surface positions: it makes no sense to ask whether the rule preserves meaning or not, because the question presupposes that we have some independent idea of the meaning of sentences [SS strings] whose affixes are not switched. (Partee, 1972: 4–5)

Partee's second sentence, numbered here for reference, states a defining property of Chomsky's transformations, a property differentiating them from Harris':

(12)   '... transformations in fact operate not on sentences [SS strings] but on abstract phrase markers, and it is not obvious that we have any direct semantic intuitions about these abstract structures, in particular any notion of synonymy between them.' (Partee, 1972: 5)

In the notation of Chomsky (1968, 69), one could write:

(13) $PM_j = T(PM_{j-1})$

The input to the transformation, i.e. PM_{j-1}, is an abstract phrase marker. The syntactic component will yield a syntactic structure, Σ, which is a set of PM's produced by transformations like (13). In the Σ, such as (14), $PM_1, ..., PM_{ss-1}$ are abstract phrase markers which are input to a transformation.

(14) $\Sigma = PM_1, , , , PM_{j-1}, PM_j, , , , PM_{ss-1}, PM_{ss}$

To say that PM_{j-1} is synonymous to PM_j, etc., is meaningless, because, as Partee points out: 'It is not obvious that we have any direct semantic intuitions about these abstract structures, in particular any notion of synonymy between them.' (1972: 5).

On the basis of her analysis, Partee concludes:

(15)   '... for obligatory transformations the fact that abstract structures and not sentences are involved is significant. For obligatory rules, in fact, the question of meaning-preservingness does not even make sense, for the input to the rule is an abstract structure with which we have no independent acquaintance.' (Partee, 1972: 5)

Partee's statement (12) is true for all Chomsky-type transformations

like (13), obligatory and optional, so it therefore follows that (15) could
be generalized to this:

>   (16)   For any transformation like (13), obligatory or optional, the
>   question of meaning-preservingness does not even make sense,
>   for the input to the rule is an abstract structure with which we
>   have no independent acquaintance (see fn. 20).

Although (16) follows from Partee's statement (12), and is in fact the
only possible view in Chomsky's TGG, Partee continues the above quoted
passage thusly:

> The question of whether transformations change meaning can therefore be meaning-
> fully asked only of optional transformations. The clearest case is that in which two
> sentences [SS strings] are derived from the same deep structure, their derivations
> differing only in the application versus non-application of a certain optional rule. If
> the two sentences [SS strings] are synonymous, and if the same is true of all pairs re-
> lated by the given rule, the rule is meaning-preserving; otherwise it is not. A slightly
> more complicated case is that in which pairs of sentences [SS strings] differ in derivation
> by one optional rule and one or more subsequent obligatory rules; it still seems reason-
> able in such cases to attribute any change in meaning to the optional rule...
>   A case in which it would be much more difficult to assign responsibility for meaning
> change could arise in the following sort of situation...
>   ... it would be rather difficult to decide nonarbitrarily what rule or rules were
> responsible for the change of meaning...
>   To simplify the remainder of the discussion, we will ignore potential cases of the
> last-mentioned sort, and assume that the question of meaning-preservingness is mean-
> ingful for optional transformations and not for obligatory ones. (Partee, 1972: 5–6)

But in Chomsky's TGG, the question of meaning-preservingness makes
as little sense for optional transformations as for obligatory ones for the
excellent reasons Partee cites in (12).

Since the question 'Do transformations change meaning?' makes no
sense in Chomsky's TGG, Partee prepares a Procrustean bed in the above
passage.

4. HARRIS AND CHOMSKY OFFER
DIFFERENT CONCEPTUAL FRAMEWORKS

Let us examine the development of ideas in Partee's two paragraphs. In
the first, she rejects the Harrisian framework which she develops in the
second. Consider the first sentence of the earlier quote:

>   (17)   'The various stands taken on synonymy all have to do with
>   synonymy between *sentences* [SS strings], and in talk about

transformations preserving or changing meaning, the most common examples are transformations which can informally be thought of as relating sentences [SS strings] to other sentences [SS strings].' (Partee, 1972: 4–5)

This is the position Partee rejects in the earlier quote because, as she says in (12), a Chomskian transformation operates not on surface structure strings but on abstract phrase markers. Partee does not point out that a Harrisian transformation relates surface structure strings to other surface structure strings, and that the 'informal' thinking in Chomsky's generative grammar is 'formal' thinking in Harris' taxonomic system.

Partee states: 'Failure to distinguish sentences [SS strings] from abstract P-markers is often harmless...' (*ibid.*: 5). However, failure to make this distinction is to confuse the Harrisian and Chomskian ideas of transformation. To confuse transformations which relate surface structure strings, like (1) and (5), with transformations which operate on abstract phrase markers, like (13), can be extremely misleading since it can guile one into believing the question 'Do transformations change meaning' is meaningful in TGG.

In the second quote, Partee defines *meaning-preserving transformation*:

(18)   'If the two sentences [surface structure strings] are synonymous, and if the same is true of all pairs related by the given rule, the rule is meaning preserving; otherwise it is not.' (*ibid.*: 5)

Partee formulates her definition (18) in line with (17) and rejects (12). Her definition is essentially identical to Harris'. Harris' definition of meaning-preserving transformation would be something like this: If for all pairs of surface structure strings, SS_1 and SS_2, related by a transformation, SS_1 and SS_2 are synonymous, the rule is meaning-preserving; otherwise it is not.[5]

When Partee assumes the question 'Do transformations change meaning?' is significant in Chomsky's TGG system, and when she investigates constraints on transformations using definition (18), she is using conceptual tools valid in one intellectual constellation (Harris') to gain a perspective on issues in another constellation (Chomsky's) in which they are not valid. Partee's definition (18) does not hold for a Chomskian transformation like (13) but for a Harrisian transformation, like (1) and (5).

To attempt to formulate substantive problems in an intellectual framework, IF_1, while basing definitions, etc. on ideas crucial to a second intellectual framework, IF_2, may well lead one to form a distorted perspective in IF_1. Holton (1973) discusses this phenomenon at length. Consider an analogy:

Suppose Mr. X attempted to spear motionless fish in still water. He can see the fish clearly, can see their positions relative to each other, their number, their relative sizes, their colors, their species, etc., but when he throws his spear directly at one of the fish, the fish escapes unhurt. Although close enough to see its gills and fins, Mr. X cannot spear the fish because its apparent position is not its real position. Only in one case does the apparent position of a fish line up with the real position. When the fish is directly below him, Mr. X can throw at the apparent position and spear the fish. In all other cases, however, as the fish are farther and farther from the one point where real and apparent positions accord, the fish are never where they appear to be.

Partee discusses many constellations of data which suggest that there are definitely points where syntactic patterns and semantic patterns interplay in ways which could be formulated to yield substantive insights into the interaction of semantics and syntax in Chomsky's TGG. The real character of the semantics-syntax interaction is given by asking: 'Which aspects of Σ correlate with which aspects of the semantic interpretation?' The apparent character of the semantics-syntax interaction in Chomsky's TGG for someone working in Harris' system is given by asking: 'Do transformations change meaning?' The one situation in which the real character and the apparent character of the semantics-syntax interaction line up, but only if one thinks 'informally' (see 17), is the case in which two SS strings are derived from the same underlying structure and differ in that an optional transformation applies in the derivation of one SS string, but not in the derivation of the other. In all other cases, the apparent character and the real character of the semantics-syntax interaction do not line up. The interpretation to assign to Partee's second paragraph (quoted above) is that her qualifications (i.e. '... it still seems reasonable...', '... it would be rather difficult to decide non-arbitrarily...') indicate points at which Harris' and Chomsky's systems differ.[6]

In the final sentence of her paper, Partee concludes:

... In short, I would suggest that the hypothesis of meaning-preservingness of transformations has so far eluded both demonstration and refutation; that it is clearly
worth pursuing as far as possible; and that further work on the sorts of apparent counterexamples discussed above may well be the key to a deeper understanding of the
relation between semantics and syntax. (Partee, 1972: 21)

Our previous analysis explains why 'the hypothesis of meaning-preservingness has so far eluded both demonstration and refutation'. (*ibid.*: 21) In
TGG the question 'Do transformations change meaning?' is a hollow
echo of a Harrisian problem statement. If we are working in Chomsky's
TGG, the question of meaning-preservingness makes no sense and is not
worth pursuing.

On the other hand, if a linguist is working in Harris' system, the question of meaning-preservingness is a focal point of research and clearly
worth pursuing as far as possible.

5. DESCRIPTIVE SEMANTICS IN AN EXTENDED HARRIS GRAMMAR

We have only looked from Harris' scheme into Chomsky's scheme. Let
us now look from Chomsky's into Harris'.

What would it mean to ask in Harris' system: 'Which aspects of Σ
correlate with which aspects of the semantic interpretation?' This is an
ill-defined question because Harris does not discuss Σ, and it is not clear
the idea plays any role in his system. But, at the one point at which
Harris' and Chomsky's systems line up, one might make some sense out
of the question: 'Is the semantic interpretation of all of the paraphrases
related by transformations given in a "purer form" by one of the paraphrases?' Or alternatively, since Harris views transformations as a means
for simplifying or normalizing sentences, one might ask: 'Is the semantic
interpretation of the paraphrases given more clearly by the normalized
form?' This question can be sharpened and made precise in Harris'
system.

Consider a hypothetical example which illustrates how Harris' and
Chomsky's systems might appear superficially the same. Suppose Harris'
transformational taxonomic grammar were extended into the area of
descriptive semantics. This could be done by simply dropping the requirement that transformations only relate surface structure strings and by

permitting biconditional transformations to relate surface structure strings with abstract underlying structures in which the semantic relations were, in some sense, explicit. Consider an example.

Harris' system permits a transformation like (19). Working with an informant, a linguist might find cooccurring pentuples, like in (20), which, when substituted into (19), yielded sentences like (21) and (22). Work with the informant would reveal that S_1 and S_2, in (21-2), have the same level of informant acceptability and that they were paraphrases.

(19) $(_{S_1} \overline{NP_1} \ \overline{AUX} \ \overline{v} \ \overline{NP_2}$ with $\overline{NP_3}) \rightleftarrows (_{S_2} \overline{NP_2} \ \overline{AUX}$ be $\overline{v}$ en by $\overline{NP_1}$ with $\overline{NP_3})$

(20)   Cooccurring pentuples: (AUX, V, NP_1, NP_2, NP_3): (will, break, John, the window, the hammer), (will, open, John, the door, the key), etc.

(21) $(_{S_1}$ John will break the window with the hammer) $\rightleftarrows (_{S_2}$ The window will be broken by John with the hammer)

(22) $(_{S_1}$ John will open the door with the key) $\rightleftarrows (_{S_2}$ The door will be opened by John with the key)

Suppose one asks: 'Is the semantic interpretation of these two paraphrases S_1 and S_2, related by transformation (19), given more clearly by one of the two sentences S_1 or S_2?' The question is certainly meaningful in Harris' system, although it may not be clear how it could be answered when applied to the above cases.

Imagine, however, that Harris developed a system of descriptive semantics and permitted abstract structures. Suppose Harris allowed transformations of the following sorts:

(23) $(_{S_1} \overline{NP_1} \ \overline{AUX} \ \overline{v} \ \overline{NP_2}$ with $\overline{NP_3}) \rightleftarrows (_{S_{abstract}} (_{Modality} AUX)$
        $(_{Proposition} (_v \text{---}) (_{Agent} NP_1) (_{Object} NP_2) (_{Instrument} NP_3)))$

(24) $(_{S_1} \overline{NP_1} \ \overline{AUX} \ \overline{v} \ \overline{NP_2}$ with $\overline{NP_3}) \rightleftarrows (_{S_{abstract}}$ I DECLARE to you that
        $(_S$ it $(_{AUX} \text{---})$ that $(_S$ it BE that $(_S (_{NP_1} \text{---})$ DO CAUSE $(_S$ it
        COME ABOUT that $(_S$ it be $(_S (_{NP_3} \text{---}) (_v \text{---}) (_{NP_2} \text{---}))))))))$

Let us call the abstract structures developed in the extended Harris system *deep structures*. These deep structures might be developed in many different ways to represent directly, in some sense, one's introspective feelings about the meaning of sentences.

Transformations will relate surface structure strings with other surface structure strings and also with abstract deep structures. This is schematized by the following:

(25) $(SS\ string)_1 \underset{T_a}{\rightleftarrows} (SS\ string)_2 \underset{T_b}{\rightleftarrows} \underset{T_y}{\dots} \rightleftarrows (SS\ string)_n \underset{T_z}{\rightleftarrows} (deep\ structure)$

A linguist developing this system might incorporate these two principles:

(26)   All and only sentences which are paraphrases shall have the same deep structure.

(27)   Transformations do not change meaning.

The question: 'Do transformations change meaning?' is well-defined in this extended Harrisian system.

Now let us examine this system from Chomsky's perspective. The question: 'Which aspects of Σ correlate with which aspects of the semantic interpretation' is not meaningful because there is no Σ defined.

However, since Harris' and Chomsky's alternative conceptual schemes line up at one point, one can ask: 'Is semantic interpretation entirely on deep structure?' The answer is: 'Yes'.

In this extended Harris system the question 'Does information from the surface structure string play any role in the semantic interpretation of a sentence?' is meaningless. The question would have to be rephrased: 'Do transformations change meaning?'[7]

Whatever might be the merits of Harris' system or Chomsky's system, one must realize they are conceptually very different. In brief, one might say Harris offers a notation for representing information about sentences, Chomsky offers a set of rules which automatically assigns notation to sentences. This is, in essence, the difference between Harris' taxonomic grammar and Chomsky's generative grammar. It is this difference which has led Harris and Chomsky to develop the idea of *transformation* in different directions. See note 20.

6. GENERATIVE AND INTERPRETIVE SEMANTICS

As Partee points out, the question of meaning-preservingness plays a crucial role in the generative semantics perspective. McCawley, according to Partee, endorses the strong form of the meaning-preserving transformation hypothesis. Partee states:

1.3.   Current Positions. In the more recent past, Lakoff, McCawley, Postal, and others have accepted the hypothesis that transformations preserve meaning and extended it to the position that all and only sentences which are paraphrases of each other should have the same deep structures. They have shown that consistent adherence to such a principle requires much more abstract deep structures than were previously contemplated. Many of their analyses have independent support from purely syntactic arguments, and it is often not easy to determine how much of the weight of their arguments is borne by the criterion of meaning-preservingness of transformations. Chomsky and Jackendoff, on the other hand, have argued that the more abstract deep structures do not have sufficient independent syntactic motivation, and that a simpler overall grammar will be achieved by keeping a more conservative deep structure and allowing semantic interpretation to take into consideration some aspects of surface structure and perhaps of intermediate structures as well.

It would appear then that within the abstract-deep-structure or generative semantics camp, the principle of meaning-preservingness of transformations is a fundamental condition on most of the grammar, but not necessarily on those transformations which introduce lexical items. This exception would appear to be inconsistent with the strongest version of 'generative semantics', which is that the deepest level of structure is pre-lexical but is the only level relevant to semantic interpretation – in some sense *is* the semantic interpretation. I am not certain whether anyone seriously holds such a view, but it is certainly the view suggested by the term 'generative semantics'.[2] (Partee, 1972: 3-4)

[2] Footnote: McCawley in the discussion following this paper asserted that he does indeed hold the strong form of the generative semantics position; ... (*ibid.*: 4)

Insofar as the idea of a 'meaning-preserving transformation' plays a crucial role in generative semantics, generative semantics has been developed internal to Harris' transformational taxonomic system and not internal to Chomsky's transformational generative grammar.[8]

Partee (1971) discusses the issues which define these four positions: generative semantics, interpretive semantics, Montague grammar, and the Katz-Postal-*Aspects* theory. We are not here concerned with the Montague grammar. We are concerned with the fact that Partee uses the idea of a 'meaning preserving transformation' to differentiate the generative semantics and the interpretive semantics positions. In her introduction Partee outlines her objectives:

What I intend to do here is three-fold: ... Second, I'll outline the main features of three current approaches: the interpretive semantics and generative semantics variants of transformational grammar, and very briefly, Richard Montague's quite different approach. I won't attempt to choose sides, because, I think it's way too early to judge and because all three seem worth exploring as far as possible if only for negative results... (Partee, 1971: 652)

Except for the possibility of Montague grammar, Partee feels that interpretive semantics is the alternative to generative semantics. She defines the interpretive semantics position in terms of meaning-preserving and meaning-changing transformations:

A. Interpretive Semantics: *PRO* Think back to the examples where certain transformations changed meaning when quantifiers were involved, e.g. ... (1971: 657)
... the main thrust of the arguments *for* this approach seem to me to be as I've just sketched: the derivations which change meaning do not change grammaticality, so we have no syntactic basis for rejecting them; and furthermore the semantics can be done at the surface. (1971: 658)
... Against the interpretivist view that grammaticality is never affected by the meaning-changing transformations, there has been offered a considerable amount of counter-evidence. (1971: 661)

Partee indicates who support this position: 'When I talk about interpretivists, I'm really talking about Chomsky, Jackendoff, Akmajian, Emonds, Dougherty, and the like.' (1971: 680)

But 'meaning-preserving transformation' and 'meaning-changing transformation' do not make sense in Chomsky's TGG for the reason cited in (12). By defining the interpretive semantics position in terms of meaning-changing transformations, Partee has essentially defined it as an incoherent position. Partee offers no textual references to indicate that any of the interpretive semanticists she cites have ever formulated their positions in terms of meaning-preserving or meaning-changing transformations. Chomsky has never defined interpretive semantics in terms of meaning-preserving or meaning-changing transformations.[9] Insofar as I am classed as an interpretive semanticist, I accept the position defined by Chomsky (1968, 1969) (quoted in Section 2). Interpretive semantics, as defined by Partee, is an incoherent position; as defined by Chomsky (1968, 1969), it is well-defined in a TGG framework.

The key to Partee's analysis is contained in this paragraph:

In many respects, I believe that generative and interpretive semantics are in essential agreement, and jointly in opposition to the Katz-Postal-*Aspects* theory, which was more elegant than either, but unfortunately wrong. (Partee, 1971: 669)

As Partee formulates the issues, generative semantics and interpretive semantics are defined in terms of transformations which change or preserve meaning. Since meaning-preserving transformation makes no sense for a Chomskian transformation, generative semantics and interpretive semantics, as Partee defines them, are not coherent TGG proposals, as TGG is defined by any of Chomsky's writings. Generative semantics and interpretive semantics appear to Partee to be in essential agreement since they are defined in terms of Harrisian transformations, i.e. transformations which preserve or change meaning. In Partee's view, therefore, generative semantics and interpretive semantics, well-defined in Harris' transformational taxonomic grammar, are jointly in opposition to the *Aspects* theory, which is a transformational generative grammar.[10]

7. CHOMSKY (1968,69) AT THE SEMANTICS-SYNTAX BOUNDARY

This discussion is intended to illustrate, via examples, a transformational generative grammar of the type proposed by Chomsky (1968, 1969). Chomsky's proposals could be interpreted to mean that a grammar might be written incorporating these assumptions:

(28) Transformational rules function independent of sound and meaning, and relate one PM to another; symbolically: $PM_j = T(PM_{j-1})$.

(29) Many transformational rules (Question, Passive, etc.), which in earlier formulations were triggered by underlying dummy markers, are no longer triggered, but are optional.[11]

(30) The semantic interpretation, SI, correlates with information from the deep structure, PM_{DS}, and surface structure, PM_{SS}. Symbolically: $SI = F(PM_{DS}, PM_{SS})$, where F is the interpretive rule, or function, which pairs a specific aspect of the semantic interpretation with a specific aspect of the deep structure-surface structure pair.

(31) A semantic rule can block a sentence as deviant, i.e. a possible output of a rule of semantic interpretation is [*].

The grammar in Figure 1, henceforth G_{int}, although deficient in many respects, is compatible with these assumptions and shall serve to illustrate general principles.[12]

We will be concerned with one small aspect of surface structure interpretation. We will study the correlation of the order of the elements *either* and *not* in the SSPM with the semantic interpretation.

Suppose we are discussing a malfunctioning double-barreled shotgun with our local gunsmith. Sentences (32–3) differ in a crucial way:

(32) Either barrel *A* or barrel *B* will not fire.

(33) It will not fire on either barrel *A* or barrel *B*.

Fig. 1. G_{int}: A grammar of a fragment of English.

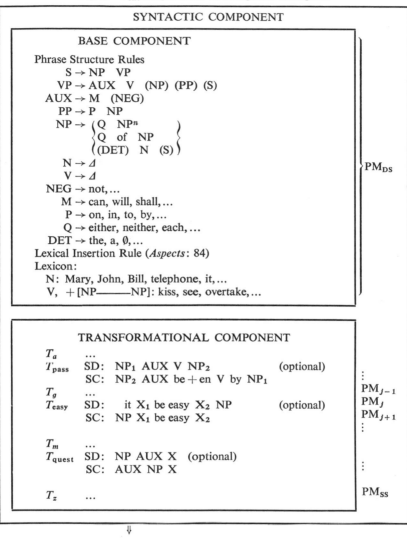

Sentence (32) asserts only that one of the two barrels is defunct; it does not assert that both barrels are defunct. Sentence (33) asserts either (a) that only one of the two barrels is defunct, or (b) that both barrels are defunct. The reading sentence (33) has, which sentence (32) does not have, will be called the *both barrels (BB) reading*. Sentence (32), lacking the BB reading, will be considered [−BB]. Sentence (33), with the BB reading, will be considered [+BB].

Our goal is to present a rule of semantic interpretation. A rule of semantic interpretation will be defined by specifying (a) its range of inputs, (b) its range of outputs, and (c) the specific ways in which a given input is paired with a particular output. In our case, the range of inputs will be sentences containing the elements *either* and *not*. The range of outputs will be the readings [+BB], [−BB], and [*] (i.e. semantic anomaly). Our objective is to provide a semantic rule which will specify on the basis of the Σ assigned to a sentence containing *either* and *not* whether the sentence has the reading [+BB], [−BB], or [*].

The following sentences will be marked by the semantic rule as indicated:

(34)	Either John or Bill cannot kiss Mary.	[−BB]
(35)	Mary cannot be kissed by either John or Bill.	[+BB]
(36)	Mary cannot kiss either John or Bill.	[+BB]
(37)	Either John or Bill cannot be kissed by Mary.	[−BB]
(38)	It will not be easy for Mary to kiss either John or Bill.	[+BB]
(39)	Either John or Bill will not be easy for Mary to kiss.	[−BB]
(40)	Can't either John or Bill be kissed by Mary?	[+BB]
(41)	Can't either John or Bill kiss Mary?	[+BB]
(42)	Won't either John or Bill be easy for Mary to kiss?	[+BB]
(43)	*Either of them cannot kiss Mary.	[*]
(44)	Mary cannot be kissed by either of them.	[+BB]
(45)	Mary cannot kiss either of them.	[+BB]
(46)	*Either of them cannot be kissed by Mary.	[*]
(47)	It will not be easy for Mary to kiss either of them.	[+BB]
(48)	*Either of them will not be easy for Mary to kiss.	[*]
(49)	Can't either of them kiss Mary?	[+BB]
(50)	Can't either of them be kissed by Mary?	[+BB]
(51)	Won't either of them be kissed by Mary?	[+BB]
(52)	We can't contact either John or Bill by telephone.	[+BB]

(53)   We can't contact either of them by telephone.   [+BB]
(54)   Either John or Bill can't be contacted by telephone. [−BB]
(55)   *Either of them can't be contacted by telephone.   [*]
(56)   Can't either John or Bill be contacted by telephone? [+BB]
(57)   Can't either of them be contacted by telephone?   [+BB]

The transformational component of G_{int} contains transformations $T_a, , , T_z$. In this section, we are only concerned with T_{pass}, T_Q, and T_{easy}, three optional transformations which rearrange the order of constituents in phrase markers. T_a, T_b, etc. represent the transformations required to describe grammatical processes we will not consider except to note they exist. These transformations affect agreement, move affixes, insert the coordinating elements (*and, or, nor*), play a role in generating complement constructions, etc.

In discussing the syntactic structure assigned to a sentence by G_{int}, only PM_{DS} and PM_{SS} will be presented. Intermediate PM's in derivations will be ignored and will be represented in the Σ by, , , PM, , , .

The base of G_{int} will generate PM(1) as a DSPM:

PM(1) $(_S(_{NP}Mary) (_{VP}(_{AUX}(_Mcan) (_{NEG}not)) (_Vkiss) (_{NP}(_Qeither) (_{NP}$ John) $(_{NP}Bill))))$

This is input to the transformational component. If only obligatory transformations apply, then a SSPM like this results:

PM(2) $(_S(_{NP}Mary) (_{VP}(_{AUX}(_Mcan) (_{NEG}not)) (_Vkiss) (_{NP}(_Qeither)$ $(_{NP}John) (_{COOR}or) (_{NP}Bill))))$

If PM(1) is input to the transformations, and T_{pass} plus only obligatory transformations apply, a SSPM like this results:

PM(3) $(_S(_{NP}(_Qeither) (_{NP}John) (_{COOR}or) (_{NP}Bill)) (_{VP}(_{AUX}(_Mcan)$ $(_{NEG}not)) (_{VP}be (_Vkissed) (_{PP}(_Pby) (_{NP}Mary)))))$

If PM(1) is input to the transformations, and T_Q plus only obligatory transformations apply, a SSPM like this will result:

PM(4) $(_S(_{AUX}(_Mcan) (_{NEG}not)) (_{NP}Mary) (_{VP}(_Vkiss) (_{NP}(_Qeither)$ $(_{NP}John) (_{COOR}or) (_{NP}Bill))))$

If PM(1) is input to the transformational component, and is operated on by T_{pass}, T_Q, and, except for these, only obligatory transformations apply, then a SSPM like this results:

PM(5) $(_S(_{AUX}(_M can)\ (_{NEG}not))\ (_{NP}(_Q either)\ (_{NP}John)\ (_{COOR}or)\ (_{NP}Bill))$
         $(_{VP}\ be\ (_V kissed)\ (_{PP}(_P by)\ (_{NP}Mary))))$

In the following, (b) is the syntactic structure assigned to the (a) surface structure string by G_{int}. The reading of the sentence is indicated with respect to $[+BB]$ and $[-BB]$:

(58) (a) Mary can't kiss either John or Bill.[13] $[+BB]$
     (b) $\Sigma = PM(1),\,,\, PM,\,,\, PM(2)$
(59) (a) Either John or Bill can't be kissed by Mary. $[-BB]$
     (b) $\Sigma = PM(1),\,,\, PM,\,,\, PM(3)$
(60) (a) Can't Mary kiss either John or Bill? $[+BB]$
     (b) $\Sigma = PM(1),\,,\, PM,\,,\, PM(4)$
(61) (a) Can't either John or Bill be kissed by Mary? $[+BB]$
     (b) $\Sigma = PM(1),\,,\, PM,\,,\, PM(5)$

The base of G_{int} will generate this DSPM:

PM(6) $(_S(_{NP}(_Q either)\ (_{NP}John)\ (_{NP}Bill))\ (_{VP}\ (_{AUX}(_M can)\ (_{NEG}not))$
         $(_V kiss)\ (_{NP}Mary)))$

If only obligatory transformations apply to PM(6), this SSPM results:

PM(7) $(_S(_{NP}(_Q either)\ (_{NP}John)\ (_{COOR}or)\ (_{NP}Bill))\ (_{VP}(_{AUX}can)\ (_{NEG}$
         $not))\ (_V kiss)\ (_{NP}Mary)))$

If only T_{pass} and obligatory transformations apply to PM (6), this SSPM results:

PM(8) $(_S(_{NP}Mary)\ (_{VP}(_{AUX}(_M can)\ (_{NEG}not))\ (_{VP}\ be\ (_V kissed)\ (_{PP}(_P by)$
         $(_{NP}(_Q either\ (_{NP}John)\ (_{COOR}or)\ (_{NP}Bill)))))$

If only T_Q and obligatory transformations apply to PM(6), this SSPM results:

PM(9) $(_S(_{AUX}(_M can)\ (_{NEG}not))\ (_{NP}(_Q either)\ (_{NP}John)\ (_{COOR}or)\ (_{NP}Bill))$
         $(_{VP}(_V kiss)\ (_{NP}Mary)))$

If T_{pass} and T_Q plus only obligatory transformations apply to PM(6), this SSPM will result:

PM(10) $(_S(_{AUX}(_M can) (_{NEG} not)) (_{NP} Mary) (_{VP} be (_V kissed) (_{PP}(_P by) (_{NP}(_Q either) (_{NP} John) (_{COOR} or) (_{NP} Bill)))))$

In the following, (b) is the syntactic structure assigned by G_{int} to the surface string in (a). The reading of the sentence with respect to [+BB] is listed:

(62) (a) Either John or Bill can't kiss Mary.   [−BB]
     (b) $\Sigma = PM(6),,, PM,,, PM(7)$
(63) (a) Mary can't be kissed by either John or Bill.   [+BB]
     (b) $\Sigma = PM(6),,, PM,,, PM(8)$
(64) (a) Can't either John or Bill kiss Mary?   [+BB]
     (b) $\Sigma = PM(6),,, PM,,, PM(9)$
(65) (a) Can't Mary be kissed by either John or Bill?   [+BB]
     (b) $\Sigma = PM(6),,, PM,,, PM(10)$

The Σ's of sentences (58–61) are such that they all have PM(1) as DSPM. But sentence (59) is not synonymous with (58, 60, and 61). The Σ's of sentences (62–65) are similar in that they all have PM(6) as DSPM. But sentence (62) is not synonymous with (63–65). The difference in reading [+BB] does not correlate with deep structure differences in Σ.

A simple rule of surface structure interpretation, like (66), will correctly correlate the readings [+BB] and [−BB] with differences in the surface structure order of quantifiers *either* and *not*.

(66)   Surface Structure Interpretation Rule for [+BB] reading:[14]
       (a) if $PM_{SS} = (_S ...$ either NP or NP... not...$) \rightarrow$ [−BB]
       (b) if $PM_{SS} = (_S...$ not... either NP or NP $) \rightarrow$ [+BB]

This rule of surface structure interpretation assigns the correct reading to sentences (58–65) on the basis of information present in the SSPM. In sentences (59) and (62), with the [−BB] reading, the order of elements in the SSPM is that in (66a). In sentences (58, 60, 61, and 63–65), with the [+BB] interpretation, the order of elements in the SSPM is that in (66b).

Rule (66) gives the correct interpretation in cases beyond those above. G_{int} might be extended to generate a DSPM like this:[15]

PM(11) $(_S it will not be easy for Mary to kiss either John Bill)$

If only obligatory transformations apply, a SSPM like this results:

PM(12) $(_S it will not be easy for Mary to kiss either John or Bill)$

162   RAY C. DOUGHERTY

If T_{easy} and only obligatory transformations apply, a SSPM like this results:

PM(13) (_seither John or Bill will not be easy for Mary to kiss)

If T_{easy}, T_Q, and only the obligatory transformations apply, a SSPM like this results:

PM(14) (_swill not either John or Bill be easy for Mary to kiss)

In the following, (b) is the syntactic structure assigned to the (a) surface structure string. The reading of the sentence with respect to [±BB] is listed:

(67) (a) It won't be easy for Mary to kiss either John or Bill.   [+BB]
     (b) $\Sigma = $PM(11), , , PM, , , PM(12)
(68) (a) Either John or Bill won't be easy for Mary to kiss.   [−BB]
     (b) $\Sigma = $PM(11), , , PM, , , PM(13)
(69) (a) Won't either John or Bill be easy for Mary to kiss?   [+BB]
     (b) $\Sigma = $PM(11), , , PM, , , PM(14)

The Σ's of (67–69) all have PM(11) as DSPM. In sentence (68), with the [−BB] interpretation, the SSPM order of constituents is that in (66a). In (67) and (68), with the [+BB] interpretation, the SSPM order of constituents is that in (66b).

G_{int} will generate a DSPM like this:

PM(15) (_seither of them can not kiss Mary)

If only obligatory transformations apply, the grammar yields a SSPM like this:

PM(16) (_seither of them can not kiss Mary)

If T_{pass} and only obligatory transformations apply, the grammar yields this SSPM:

PM(17) (_sMary can not be kissed by either of them)

If T_Q and only obligatory transformations apply, this SSPM results:

PM(18) (_scan not either of them kiss Mary)

Consider another set of derivations. The base generates a DSPM like this:

PM(19) (_sMary can not kiss either of them)

If only obligatory transformations apply, this SSPM results:

PM(20) ($_s$Mary can not kiss either of them)

If T_{pass} and only obligatory transformations apply, this SSPM is generated:

PM(21) ($_s$either of them can not be kissed by Mary)

If T_{pass}, T_Q, and only obligatory transformations apply, this SSPM results:

PM(22) ($_s$can not either of them be kissed by Mary)

In the following, (b) is the Σ assigned to the (a) surface structure string by G_{int}.

(70) (a)	*Either of them can't kiss Mary	[*]
(b)	$\Sigma = $PM(15),,, PM,,, PM(16)	
(71) (a)	Mary can't be kissed by either of them.	[+BB]
(b)	$\Sigma = $PM(15),,, PM,,, PM(17)	
(72) (a)	Can't either of them kiss Mary?	[+BB]
(b)	$\Sigma = $PM(15),,, PM,,, PM 18)	
(73) (a)	Mary can't kiss either of them.	[+BB]
(b)	$\Sigma = $PM(19),,, PM,,, PM(20)	
(74) (a)	*Either of them can't be kissed by Mary.	[*]
(b)	$\Sigma = $PM(19),,, PM,,, PM(21)	
(75) (a)	Can't either of them be kissed by Mary?	[+BB]
(b)	$\Sigma = $PM(19),,, PM,,, PM(22)	

Suppose we permit the surface structure interpretive rule to assign [*] as a possible output. We can expand rule (66) to include *either of* NP
$$[+plu]$$
in addition to *either* of NP or NP.
The new rule is this:

(76)   Rule of SS interpretation for *either/not*:[16]
(a) PM$_{SS}$ = ($_s$... either NP or NP... not...) → [−BB]
(b) PM$_{SS}$ = ($_s$... not... either...)   → [+BB]
(c) PM$_{SS}$ = ($_s$... either of   NP   ...not...) →   [*]
$$[+plu]$$

This rule will describe all of the cases presented above. The Σ's of (70–72) have PM(15) as DSPM. The Σ's of (73-75) have PM(19) as DSPM. The SSPM of (70) meets condition (76c), and therefore, the sentence is marked as deviant [*]. The SSPM's of (71) and (72) meet condition (76b) and these sentences are interpreted as [+BB]. The Σ's of (73–75) have PM(19) as DSPM. The SSPM of (74) meets condition (76c) and this sentence is marked as deviant [*]. The SSPM's of (73) and (75) meet condition (76c), and they are interpreted as [+BB].

The above analysis might be extended in many ways. It might be modified to describe these sentences:

(77) (a) *Either man can't kiss Mary.
     (b) Mary can't be kissed by either man.
     (c) Can't either man kiss Mary?

Perhaps the properties of *either* and *not* taken together follow from properties of *either/or* and *not* taken separately. For example, *either NP or NP* functions differently than *either of NP* in rule (76). It is also the $[+plu]$ case that *either* with a plural functions differently than *either* with a coordination in cases independent of *not* constructions. Sentences (80–81) are well-formed, (78–79) are not:

(78)   *Is either A or B smaller than A^2 or B^2 respectively?
(79)   *Neither A nor B is smaller than A^2 nor B^2 respectively.
(80)   Is either of the numbers smaller than its respective square?
(81)   Neither of the numbers is smaller than its respective square.

One might develop a surface structure interpretive rule for *either/or* and one for *not* and then see if rule (76) followed as a natural consequence of the interaction of the two rules.

Our above analysis, compatible with the general assumptions (28–31), is based on these specific assumptions:

(82)   Quantifiers, like *either*, are inserted freely in a DSPM into NP expansions by a rule like this:

$$NP \rightarrow \begin{cases} Q\ NP'' \\ Q\ of\ \ NP \\ \quad\quad [+plu] \end{cases}$$

(83)   *Not* is inserted freely into a DSPM AUXiliary expansion.

(84)   The rule of semantic interpretation, (76), indicates that the correct range of interpretations with respect to [+BB], [−BB], and [*] readings for a sentence containing the elements *either* and *not*, is a simple function of the relative positions of *either* and *not* in the SSPM.

Assumption (82) is motivated in Dougherty (1970, 1971). Lasnik (1972) discusses assumption (83).

An interpretive semantic rule expresses a systematic correlation between Σ and semantic interpretation. An interpretive rule is defined (a) by specifying its range of inputs, i.e. which aspects of Σ are operated on by the rule; (b) by specifying its range of outputs, i.e. the various readings possible; and (c) by indicating how a specific aspect of Σ correlates with a specific semantic interpretation. Rule (76) satisfies these three conditions.

8. Do Transformations Change Meaning?

Let us now investigate the results of the previous section in terms of the question 'Do transformations change meaning?'. We can lead into our investigation by asking the perhaps more important question: 'Do transformations change grammaticality?'

The base of G_{int} will generate a DSPM like this:

PM(23)   ($_S$either of them can not kiss Mary)

If only obligatory transformations apply, an SSPM like this results:

PM(24)   ($_S$either of them can not kiss Mary)

If T_{pass} and only obligatory transformations apply, a SSPM like this results:

PM(25)   ($_S$Mary can not be kissed by either of them)

These (a) surface structure strings have the Σ's in (b):

(85) (a)   *Either of them can't kiss Mary.
     (b) $\Sigma = PM(23), , , PM_j, PM_k, , , PM(24)$
(86) (a)   Mary can't be kissed by either of them.
     (b) $\Sigma = PM(23), , , PM_j, PM_{j+1}, , , PM(25)$

In the derivation of (86), T_{pass} applies and converts PM_j into PM_{j+1}. In the derivation of sentence (85), T_{pass} does not apply.

Does T_{pass} change grammaticality? In the derivation of (86) is there some 'deep structure ungrammaticality' which is changed by the passive transformation?

Consider a more complex case. The base will generate a DSPM like this:

PM(26) ($_s$Mary can not kiss either of them)

If only obligatory transformations apply, this SSPM results:

PM(27) ($_s$Mary can not kiss either of them)

If T_{pass} applies to PM(26), this derived structure PM results:

PM(28) ($_s$either of them can not be ed kiss by Mary)

If only obligatory transformations apply to PM(28), this SSPM results:

PM(29) ($_s$either of them can not be kissed by Mary)

If T_Q and only obligatory transformations apply to PM(28), this SSPM results:

PM(30) ($_s$can not either of them be kissed by Mary)

In the following, (b) is the Σ of the (a) surface structure string:

(87) (a)   Mary can't kiss either of them.
    (b) $\Sigma = PM(26),\,,\,PM_j,\,PM_m,\,,\,PM(27)$
(88) (a) *Either of them can't be kissed by Mary
    (b) $\Sigma = PM(26),\,,\,PM_j,\,PM_{j+1} = PM(28),\,,\,PM(29)$
(89) (a)   Can't either of them be kissed by Mary?
    (b) $\Sigma = PM(26),\,,\,PM_j,\,PM_{j+1} = PM(28),\,,\,PM_k,\,PM_{k+1},\,,\,$
      $,\,,\,PM(30)$

Assume $PM_{j+1} = T_{pass}(PM_j)$ and $PM_{k+1} = T_Q(PM_k)$.

Sentences (87–89) are derived from PM(26) as DSPM.

Sentences (87) and (88) differ in that T_{pass} applies in the derivation of (88), but not in the derivation of (87). But sentence (88) is ill-formed. In the derivation of (88) is there some 'deep structure grammaticality' which is changed by T_{pass}? Das T_{pass} introduce 'ungrammaticality'? More generally: Do transformations change grammaticality?

Sentences (88) and (89) differ in that T_Q applies in the derivation of (89) but not in the derivation of (88). Sentence (88) is ill-formed, but (89) is grammatical. T_{pass} applies in the derivation of both (88) and (89), and both Σ_{88} and Σ_{89} contain PM(28), the output of T_{pass}.

Should we assume that in the derivation of (88) and (89) T_{pass} produces PM(28) and in doing so changes some 'deep structure grammaticality' of PM(26) by introducing some 'ungrammaticality'? Should we further assume that, in the derivation of (89), T_Q removes the transformationally introduced 'ungrammaticality' and restores the 'deep structure grammaticality'?

Do both T_{pass} and T_Q change grammaticality, and further, change grammaticality in such ways that they can cancel each other's effects?

The preceding discussion has been an oblique view of the analysis in Section 7. An important fact has been overlooked:

(90)   To say that there exist surface structure conditions which can mark a sentence as anomalous, (i.e. 76c), is not equivalent to saying that transformations change grammaticality.

The simplest way to block sentences (85) and (88) is to rule them out by a surface structure condition like (76c).

If the Σ of a sentence contains a SSPM meeting condition (76c), the sentence is ill-formed regardless of what other PM's the Σ may contain or what transformations have applied in the derivation.

The *either/not* condition, (76c), is a condition defined on surface structure. In this analysis, there seems to be no meaningful sense in which one can talk about 'deep structure *either/not* ungrammaticality' which might be changed in the course of transformational derivation. The fact that PM(29), the SSPM of the ill-formed (88), and PM(28), an intermediate derived PM of the Σ of sentence (89), have essentially the same order of constituents does not mean they are equally ill-formed or equally well-formed. PM(29), a SSPM, violates the surface structure condition (76c). PM(28), not being a SSPM, cannot violate the surface structure constraint (76c) by definition.

Let us now analyze the results of section 7 by asking 'Do transformations change meaning?'

The base will generate a DSPM like this:

PM(31) ($_S$Mary can not kiss either John Bill)

If only obligatory transformations apply, this SSPM results:

PM(32) ($_s$Mary can not kiss either John or Bill)

If PM(31) is input to the transformational component, and T_{pass} applies, this intermediate PM will be produced:

PM(33) ($_s$either John or Bill can not be en kiss by Mary)

If only obligatory transformations apply to PM(33), this SSPM results:

PM(34) ($_s$either John or Bill can not be kissed by Mary)

If T_Q and only obligatory transformations apply to PM(33), this SSPM results:

PM(35) ($_s$can not either John or Bill be kissed by Mary)

In the following, (b) is the Σ of the (a) surface structure string. The reading of the sentence with respect to [$\pm$BB] is indicated:

(91) (a) Mary can't kiss either John or Bill.   [+BB]
     (b) $\Sigma = PM(31), , , PM_j, PM_m, , , PM(32)$
(92) (a) Either John or Bill can't be kissed by Mary.   [−BB]
     (b) $\Sigma = PM(31), , , PM_j, PM_{j+1} = PM(33), , , PM(34)$
(93) (a) Can't either John or Bill be kissed by Mary?   [+BB]
     (b) $\Sigma = PM(31), , , PM_j, PM_{j+1} = PM(33), , , PM_k, PM_{k+1}, , ,$
          $, , , PM(35)$

Assume $PM_{j+1} = T_{pass}(PM_j)$ and $PM_{k+1} = T_Q(PM_k)$.

All these sentences have PM(31) as DSPM.

Sentences (91) and (92) differ in that T_{pass} applies in the derivation of (92) but not (91). (91) and (92) are not synonymous. Does T_{pass} change meaning? If T_{pass} changes meaning, then in Σ_{92} the [+BB] reading of PM_j went to the [−BB] reading of $PM_{j+1} = PM(33)$.

If T_{pass} changes meaning in the derivation of sentence (92), it must change meaning in the derivation of (93). In Σ_{93}, PM(31) and PM_j are synonymous and have the [+BB] reading. T_{pass} changes meaning and yields, PM(33) with the [−BB] reading. But PM(35), the SSPM, is understood with the [+BB] reading. Since T_Q is the only optional transformation which applies in relating PM(33) to the surface structure, it must be the case that T_Q changes meaning. PM_k with the [−BB] reading is operated on by T_Q to yield PM_{k+1} with the [+BB] reading.

If we ask: 'Do transformations change meaning?', we are led to the conclusion that some of the intermediate PM's in a derivation have readings which differ from the readings of both the DSPM and the SSPM. In particular, PM (33), an intermediate PM in the derivation of sentence (93), has the [− BB] reading while the DSPM, PM (31), and the SSPM, PM (35), have the [+BB] reading.

By formulating the interpretive semantics position in terms of meaning changing transformations, one is led to assume that one has intuitions of synonymy between the abstract underlying phrase markers in a derivation. It is, however, not clear that we have any direct semantic intuitions about these abstract structures, in particular any notion of synonymy between them.[17]

The following expresses a crucial point:

(94)   To say that certain information from the SSPM correlates with the semantic interpretation of a sentence and that a surface structure rule of semantic interpretation can relate specific aspects of the SSPM to specific aspects of the semantic interpretation is *not* equivalent to saying that specific transformations (T_{pass}, T_Q, etc.) change meaning.

If '*either/not* meaning' (i.e. the reading [+BB]. [−BB], or [*]) is determined by properties of the SSPM, there is no '*either/not* meaning' in the DSPM, or in any intermediate underlying PM, such that it could be 'changed'. The fact that PM (34), the SSPM of (92), and PM (33), an intermediate derived PM in the Σ of sentence (93), have essentially the same structures and order of constituents does not imply they are synonymous. PM (34) is interpreted by the surface structure rule (76), and in this sense, one can say certain aspects of PM (34) correlate with certain aspects of meaning. But PM (33), not being a SSPM, is not interpreted by surface structure rule (76), and therefore, one cannot say that certain aspects of PM (33) correlate with meaning. By definition, only surface structure phrase markers can meet surface structure conditions.

In Chomsky's TGG, a transformation relates an abstract PM with another PM. Transformations do *not* express paraphrase relations between these abstract phrase markers. Further, a transformation does *not* relate one surface structure string with another, and so a transformation does not express paraphrase relations between sentences. The relations of synonymy, paraphrase, etc. which exist between two sentences, S_1 and S_2 with syntactic structures Σ_1 and Σ_2 respectively, are expressed in a TGG by correlating properties of synonymy, paraphrase, etc. with properties of Σ_1 and Σ_2. More specifically, relations of paraphrase, etc. are given by comparing $(PM_{DS}, PM_{SS})_1$ with $(PM_{DS}, PM_{SS})_2$.

Harris' system is very different than Chomsky's. Recall from our earlier discussion, in Harris' transformational grammar, a transformation is a descriptive tool for expressing cooccurrence and paraphrase relations between surface structure strings. The following would be Harrisian transformations:

(95) $(_{S_1} \overline{NP_1}\ \overline{AUX}\ \bar{v}\ \overline{NP_2}) \overset{T_{pass}}{\rightleftarrows} (_{S_2} \overline{NP_2}\ \overline{AUX}\ be\ \bar{v}\ en\ by\ \overline{NP_1})$

(96) $(_{S_1} \overline{NP}\ \overline{AUX}\ X) \overset{T_Q}{\rightleftarrows} (_{S_2} \overline{AUX}\ \overline{NP}\ X)\quad X = \text{variable}$

On the basis of these transformations, one could set up these relations:

(97) $P(32) \overset{T_{pass}}{\rightleftarrows} PM(34) \overset{T_Q}{\rightleftarrows} PM(35)$

In this system, since the transformations express cooccurrence relationships directly between SSPM's, it is meaningful to ask: 'Do transformations change meaning?' In fact, this question is a focal point of research. In a case like (96), where the question transformation, T_Q, changes meaning, Harris points out that frequently one can attribute the meaning change to a 'special morpheme in whose element the transformation occurs': '…meaning correlates closely with range of occurrence, and transformations maintain the same occurrence range. When we have transformations which are associated with a meaning change, it is usually possible to attribute the meaning change to the special morphemes (combiners, introducers, subclasses of the primary V) in whose element the transformation occurs. To what extent, and in what sense, transformations hold meaning constant is a matter for investigation; but enough is known to make transformations a possible tool for reducing the complexity of sentences under semantically controlled conditions.' (Harris, 1957: 209.)

In the extended Harris system of Section 6 one might postulate abstract elements to which one might attribute the meaning change caused by a transformation like the question transformation. Rather than investigate this possibility, however, let us simply illustrate some properties of the extended Harris system presented in Section 6.

One might postulate either of these deep structures as expressing more clearly the intuitive semantic relations between elements:

PM(36) ($_S$ it is NOT ($_S$ Mary DO ($_S$ |John, Bill| be EITHER ($_S$ Mary kiss | John, Bill|))))

PM(37) ($_S$($_{Modality}$AUX not) ($_{Proposition}$ ($_V$kiss) ($_{Agent}$ Mary) ($_{Object}$either John or Bill)))

Suppose some transformation or set of transformations relates the abstract deep structure with the surface structure PM's. That is:

(98)   PM(36) $\overset{T_{abst}}{\rightleftarrows}$ PM(32)

(99)   PM(37) $\overset{T_{abst}}{\rightleftarrows}$ PM(32)

In this extended Harris system we have 'derivations' like these:

(100)   PM(36) $\overset{T_{abst}}{\rightleftarrows}$ PM(32) $\overset{T_{pass}}{\rightleftarrows}$ PM(34) $\overset{T_Q}{\rightleftarrows}$ PM(35)

(101)   PM(37) $\overset{T_{abst}}{\rightleftarrows}$ PM(32) $\overset{T_{pass}}{\rightleftarrows}$ PM(34) $\overset{T_Q}{\rightleftarrows}$ PM(35)

In this extended Harris system, both of these questions are meaningful: 'Do transformations change meaning?' and 'Is the semantic interpretation entirely on deep structure?'.

9. CHOMSKY REDEFINED 'EXPLANATION' AND 'IMPORTANT DATA'

Partee offers this sketch of the current state of linguistics:

A picture of linguistic theory in 1971 is a picture of a field very much in flux. It was much easier to teach a course in syntax in 1965 or 1966 than it is now. In 1965 we had Chomsky's *Aspects* model, and if one didn't pay too much attention to disquieting things like Lakoff's thesis and Postal's underground *Linguistic anarchy notes*, one could present a pretty clear picture of syntax, with a well-understood phonological component tacked on one end and a not-yet-worked-out but imaginable semantic component tacked on the other end. There were plenty of unsolved problems to work on, but the paradigm (in Kuhn's sense) seemed clear. But now we're in a situation where there is no theory which is both worked out in a substantial and presentable form and compatible with all the data considered important. So what I find myself doing in syntax classes is first showing some of the many elegant solutions to exciting syntactic problems that have been worked out in the *Aspects* framework, and then showing them the additional data which doesn't seem to be amenable to treatment in that framework at all. (1971: 651–2)

One reason that certain data does not seem amenable to treatment in the *Aspects* (or Chomsky, 1968, 1969) framework is that Partee confuses Harris' concept of a transformation as a descriptive tool for expressing cooccurrence and paraphrase relations between surface structure strings and Chomsky's concept of a transformation as a descriptive tool which plays a role in the generation of syntactic structures.[18] In Harris' framework, one can ask 'Does T_x change meaning?' since transformations relate one surface structure string to another. In Chomsky's framework, 'meaning changing transformation' makes no sense because transformations relate abstract structures. When Partee offers the following characterization of interpretive semantics, she is viewing transformational generative grammar from a Harrisian transformational taxonomic perspective: '*A. Interpretive semantics: PRO.* Think back to the examples where certain transformations changed meaning when quantifiers were involved,... (1971: 657).' 'The main thrust of the arguments *for* this approach seem to me to be as I've just sketched: the derivations which change meaning do not change grammaticality, so we have no syntactic basis for rejecting them; and furthermore the semantics can be done at the surface.' (*ibid.*: 658) '... Against the interpretivist view that grammaticality is never affected by the meaning-changing transformations, there has been offered a considerable amount of counter-evidence.' (*ibid.*: 661) Consider these passages in the light of Section 7, and in particular, examples (90) and (94).

In the above passage, Partee states: '... now we're in a situation where there is no theory which is both worked out in a substantial and presentable form and compatible with all the data considered important'. (*ibid.*: 651) By what criteria are data to be considered important?

Data should be considered important only insofar as they resolve interesting questions of language structure.[19] Data should be unimportant insofar as they do not bear on interesting questions of language structure. Quite possibly, and in fact very probably, the unimportant data will be intrinsically far more interesting than the important data.

Interesting questions about the structure of language can be raised only internal to a well-defined set of assumptions. If we are dealing with two alternative conceptual schemes, for example, with a taxonomic grammar and with a generative grammar, the interesting questions about language structure which can be posed will differ between the two systems. The system of assumptions we make will determine what is a problem and what data are to be analyzed.

Consider a basic difference between taxonomic and generative approaches.

A taxonomic grammar is a classification of the elements that function in a language. Since the elements of a language can be classified in various ways, a taxonomist defines his problem by specifying the parameters which will be used in his classification. Grammars written in the taxonomic perspective frequently group the elements in such a way either to be interesting as a contribution towards the solution of some specific problem or to be interesting to some particular group of readers. Jespersen classified elements according to historical properties. Poutsma classified them to be of interest to Dutch and Indonesian students. Harris, perhaps owing to his interest in text analysis, formulated his taxonomic grammar to classify the elements of language according to cooccurrence and paraphrase. The problem posed by the taxonomist defines the theoretical model in that the classification will follow from his arbitrarily chosen parameters. This taxonomic approach of developing a grammar to classify data according to some arbitrarily chosen parameters contrasts sharply with the generative approach developed by Chomsky. In a sense, for taxonomic studies the problems posed by the linguist (e.g. to characterize cooccurrence and paraphrase, to illuminate the history of English, to aid Dutch and Indonesian students, etc.) define the grammatical model, while for generative studies, the theoretical model defines the problems to be posed.

The idea of writing a grammar which is not intended for any particular user or for any particular practical purpose, while perhaps not original with Chomsky, is emphasized by him. Chomsky argues that each language has an intrinsic structure which is to be described by a grammar. A grammar is a theory of a language. The study of language structure must be dissociated from the practical utility of such studies.

A generative grammar may or may not be useful to Dutch and Indonesian students, may or may not illuminate the history of English, and may or may not characterize cooccurrence and paraphrase between surface structure strings. As a historical fact, TGG has its antecedents in Harris' text analysis studies. Since Harris was concerned with cooccurrence and paraphrase, many linguists feel that a central task of transformational generative grammar should be to describe cooccurrence and paraphrase relations between surface structure strings.[20] I strongly suspect that if TGG had found its antecedents in Jespersen's studies on the history of English, and if *Syntactic Structures* had appeared in 1927 instead of 1957, then instead of asking 'Do transformations change meaning?' linguists would ask 'Do synchronic transformational generative grammars reflect diachronic processes?' And no doubt, just as there are linguists today who subscribe to the strong form of the meaning-changing hypothesis, e.g. 'Transformations do not change meaning!', there would be those subscribing to the strong form of the synchronic-diachronic hypothesis, e.g. 'Any synchronic generative grammar must reflect historical processes!'.[21]

'Do synchronic generative grammars reflect diachronic processes?' is an interesting empirical question since it bears on the process of language acquisition. It would be interesting if a synchronic generative grammar did reflect diachronic processes, but it would be equally interesting if, owing to restructuring, it did not. Consider this principle:

(102)   Synchronic generative grammars must reflect historical processes.

To assume (102) as a restriction and to write grammars under this assumption would at best only show one *could* write synchronic grammars which reflected diachronic processes. Far more important would be a study which wrote grammars compatible with assumption (102) and grammars not compatible with assumption (102). If it were the case that grammars written compatible with (102) consistently offered more explanatory insight into the principles of sentence construction than did grammars incompatible with (102), then this would be a strong argument for (102) and against restructuring. A study of this sort would show not only that grammars *could* be written under assumption (102), but that grammars *should* be written under assumption (102).

In elevating an assumption like (102) to the status of a descriptive principle used to restrict formulations, one must be very cautious not to use the principle to exclude the very data which might show its inadequacy. One can all too easily fit the data into a Procrustean bed.

Of the two questions 'Do transformations change meaning?' and 'Do synchronic grammars reflect diachronic processes?', the latter points research in a more fruitful direction. By asking the former question, there can be no choice between alternatives. Although one might make sense out of the assertion 'The passive transformation preserves meaning', the assertion 'The passive transformation changes meaning' makes no sense in a transformational generative framework.

One might well ponder the question: Are certain data considered important because of a historical accident or because these data bear on the choice between conflicting conceptions of language structure internal to a well-defined framework of assumptions?

One reason Partee might feel 'we are in a situation where there is no theory which is both worked out in a substantial and presentable form and compatible with all the data considered important' (1971: 651), is because much of the data considered important is not important in any well-defined framework of assumptions. Once one sharpens his assumptions, much data considered important initially is seen to be much less important than thought. If our goal is to construct a generative grammar, and if we are working in the set of assumptions formulated in Chomsky (1957, 1965, 1968, and 1969), then much data which is considered by many to be important is not important – although it may possess high intrinsic interest.

In a real sense, certain data relating to relations of synonymy and cooccurrence between surface structure strings, while they may be intrinsically interesting, are not at the focal point of research in the well-defined set of assumptions known as TGG. The fact that many transformational generative grammarians consider these data important reflects the fact that when Chomsky's 1957 revolution in linguistics redefined the nature of linguistics as a science by redefining the concept 'explanation in linguistics', many linguists did not realize that this meant a redefinition of what was a problem. Chomsky redefined the goals of study. Our goal is not to offer generative solutions to taxonomic problems. Our goal is to work out the new model of transformational generative grammar and apply it to appropriate data. It might be offered as a general principle that when a revolutionary new concept of explanation appears and displaces the old concept of explanation, a class of new problems will displace the old problems. Consider an example from astronomy.

Both Kepler and Newton looked for universal physical laws based on terrestrial mechanics in order to comprehend the whole universe in its quantitative details. They both attempted to apply mathematics to the study of astronomy. Since Kepler, for various reasons, never developed an adequate theory of mechanics, he frequently had to formulate his problems in this view of explanation: *the physically real world is the world of mathematically expressed harmonies which man can discover in the chaos of events*. This led him to ask these questions: Why are there exactly five planets? Why are the planets exactly the distances they are from the sun? He answered the first question by pointing out that there were five planets because there were five Platonic solids. The second question he answered by contending that the planets were spaced at harmonic intervals.

Newton, having developed an adequate theory of mechanics, formulated his questions about the solar system in this view of explanation: *the physically real world, which defines the nature of things, is the world of phenomena explainable by mechanical principles*. 'Newton's aim,' says Einstein (1927: 201), 'was to find an answer to the question: Does there exist a simple rule by which the motion of the heavenly bodies of our planetary system can be completely calculated, if the state of motions of all these bodies at a single state be known?' Einstein continues: '... Newton succeeded in explaining the motions of the planets, moon, comets, down to fine details, as well as the ebb and flow of tides and the precessional movement of the earth – this last a deductive achievement of peculiar brilliance.' (*ibid.*: 203)[22]

Newton's work is, in a sense, based on Kepler's earlier studies, but in another sense, it is quite different. By offering a new concept of explanation, Newton redefined what was to be considered a problem. He thereby redefined what was to be considered important data. For example, the problems in Kepler's system – Why are there exactly five planets? Why are the planets exactly the distances they are from the sun? – are not problems answerable in Newton's system. In fact, Newton's system would work equally well for any number of planets spaced at any distances from the sun. Newton, by offering mechanical principles which could explain the world of phenomena, redefined the nature of explanation in astronomy and physics. This new concept of explanation simultaneously redefined the class of answerable questions and the important data.

Both Harris and Chomsky formulate questions about language structure in terms of algebraically formalizable tools of description, e.g. transformations. But Harris and Chomsky differ in defining explanation in linguistics. In the transformational taxonomic framework of Harris, the nature of explanation in linguistics is to express, by formalized rules of grammar (transformations, etc.), regularities and generalizations which obtain between observable phenomena (surface structure strings). In the transformational generative framework of Chomsky, the nature of explanation in linguistics is to offer a principled account, based on mechanical principles of sentence construction (PS rules, transformations, etc.), of the ability a speaker has to recognize certain sentences as well-formed and others as ungrammatical. One main aim of TGG research is to construct a generative grammar. A generative grammar is a combination of descriptive devices (the principles of sentence construction) which provides a principled description of the patterns of grammatical and ungrammatical sentences in a language by generating all of the grammatical sentences and none of the ungrammatical ones.

For Chomsky, explanation goes beyond the classification of data (according to cooccurrence and paraphrase, according to diachronic processes, etc.) using algebraic tools like transformational rules. Chomsky uses algebraic tools to formalize the mechanical principles of sentence construction and to construct a theory (a grammar) from which one can deduce consequences (the sentences generated) which can be verified or refuted in comparison with observable data (the primary data of the language studied).

10. CONCLUSIONS

Why is Chomsky (1957) called *Syntactic Structures* and not *Generative Grammar* or *Transformational Generative Grammar? Syntactic Structures*, more clearly than either of the other two titles, captures the idea of autonomous syntax. Let us investigate the ideas underlying TGG.

A *syntactic structure*, as defined by Chomsky (1957), is a formal object generated by recursive sets of PS and transformational rules. A generative grammar generates the set of syntactic structures which characterize the well-formed sentences of a language. The syntactic structure of a sentence, an abstract object, is related to observable properties like the phonetic representation by interpretive rules which operate on aspects of the syntactic structure.

Recall that Chomsky stated:

A central idea in much of structural linguistics was that the formal devices of language should be studied independently of their use. The earliest work in transformational-generative grammar took over a version of this thesis, as a working hypothesis. I think it has been a fruitful hypothesis. It seems that grammars contain a substructure of perfectly formal rules operating on phrase-markers in narrowly circumscribed ways. Not only are these rules independent of meaning or sound in their function, but it may also be that the choice of these devices by the language-learner (i.e., the choice of grammar on the basis of data) may be independent, to a significant extent, of conditions of meaning and use. If we could specify the extent precisely, the working hypothesis would become a true empirical hypothesis. Such an effort may be premature. It does, however, seem noteworthy that the extensive studies of meaning and use that have been undertaken in recent years have not – if the foregoing analysis is correct – given any serious indication that questions of meaning and use are involved in the functioning or choice of grammars in ways beyond those considered in the earliest speculations about these matters, say in Chomsky (1957). (Chomsky, 1969: 198–9)

A basic assumption in the view introduced by Chomsky is that an essential part of any human language is an abstract formal system, largely unconscious, which specifies the internal structure of a sentence at various levels of analysis and defines classes of grammatical constructions. To an extent to be determined, this abstract formal system, characterizable by recursive sets of rules, is independent of sound, meaning, and use. One of Chomsky's main contributions to linguistics as a science is that he offered a means to characterize the abstract formal properties of a sentence in a *syntactic structure* which is generable by a recursive set of phrase structure rules and transformations.

Partee discusses the view of syntax introduced by Chomsky:

... [Consider] Chomsky's view of syntax in 1957. In *Syntactic Structures*, Chomsky expressed doubts about the possibility of *any* systematic connection between syntax and semantics. Furthermore, he believed it not only necessary, but even possible, to describe syntax in completely autonomous terms. This may seem surprising in retrospect, particularly from one who was so articulate in rejecting the idea of trying to do autonomous phonetics. I think his outlook was probably very much affected by his concurrent work on formal languages, where classes of languages could be very rigorously described in syntactic terms, and very interesting formal properties of the languages could be deduced from the form of their grammars. And these approaches *did* bear fruit in the investigation of natural languages. (Partee, 1971: 654)

This tersely summarizes the autonomous syntax position of Chomsky (1957).[23] I would agree with Chomsky 1969 that 'it is noteworthy that the extensive studies of meaning and use that have been undertaken in recent years have not... given any serious indication that questions of meaning and use are involved in the functioning or choice of grammars in ways beyond those considered in the earliest speculations about these matters, say in Chomsky (1957).' (1969: 198–9)

One reason many linguists feel that semantic information has shown Chomsky's ideas about autonomous syntax to be incorrect is that they have been asking the wrong questions and misinterpreting the answers. Questions concerning the syntax-semantics boundary in Chomsky's TGG are formulated by asking 'What aspects of Σ correlate with what aspects of meaning?' and not 'Does a particular transformation (T_{pass}, T_{Quest}, etc.) change meaning?'

Let us investigate the idea offered by Chomsky above: If we could specify the extent to which the rules which operate on phrase markers in narrowly circumscribed ways are independent of sound, meaning, and use, then we could formulate a true empirical hypothesis.

'To what extent do aspects of Σ correlate with aspects of the semantic interpretation?' is an interesting question. It would be interesting to find that aspects of Σ correlate closely with aspects of meaning, but it would be equally interesting to find that no correlation existed between Σ and the meaning of a sentence. Consider this principle:

(103)   The Σ must correlate with certain aspects of the semantic interpretation.

To assume (103) as a restriction and to write grammars under this assumption would, at best, only show one *could* write grammars in which the Σ and the semantic interpretation correlated. Far more interesting would be a study which wrote grammars compatible with assumption (103) and grammars not compatible with (103). If it were the case that grammars written compatible with (103) consistently offered more explanatory insight into the principles of sentence construction than did grammars incompatible with (103), then this would argue strongly for (103). A study of this sort would show not only that grammars *could* be written under assumption (103), but that grammars *should* be written under assumption (103).

As discussed earlier, in elevating an assumption like (103) to the status of a descriptive principle used to restrict formulations, one must be cautious not to use the principle to exclude the very data which might show its inadequacy. One can all too easily fit the data into a Procrustean bed.

There is, as far as I can see, no way to determine to what extent and in what interesting sense (103) is true, except by examining syntax and semantics as two separate phenomena. One must not employ (103) as merely a working assumption; one must reformulate (103) as an empirical question. To simply accept (103) as a working assumption may well result in studies of no clear significance. On the other hand, to determine the extent to which syntactic devices are, or are not, used systematically to express meaning would deepen our understanding of the principles of sentence construction and language use. To summarize in brief: In any empirical science, there are no shortcuts to interesting answers. It is no good, echoing Bertrand Russell's phrase, to attempt to gain by theft what can only be obtained by honest toil: Because, at least in serious science, what is gained by theft is not gained at all.

New York University

NOTES

* Material support for this research derives from several sources: This work was supported by National Endowment for the Humanities grant RO-7837-73-205. This work was initiated while working under an American Council of Learned Societies grant. Some of the research was performed through (partial) support of the National Science Foundation Institution Grant to New York University. Planet Earth, Inc. provided some clerical assistance.
    For comments on this paper thanks must go to many persons, but especially to Joan Bachenko, Roy Byrd, Noam Chomsky, Evelyne Delorme, Mike Fetta, Karen Flynn, David Halitsky, Michael Helke, Justin Lieber, Kathleen Riordan, and Virginia Sterba.
    Certain terms are abbreviated as follows: transformational generative grammar, TGG; transformational taxonomic grammar, TTG; phrase marker, PM; phrase structure rule, PS rule; deep structure, DS; surface structure, SS. Therefore, deep structure phrase marker will be DSPM, etc.
[1] Hypothesis testing, the general method by which we compare alternative grammars with each other and with the data in order to select the grammar which provides the most explanatory insight into the principles of sentence construction, is discussed in Dougherty (1973). Dougherty (forthcoming) develops hypothesis testing in a more general direction and studies the general aspect of the problem of theory justification. The Theory Comparison Method, discussed in Dougherty (to appear) is a generalization of the hypothesis testing procedure.
[2] In examining Harris' system, it is useful to think of the term 'biconditional relation' as meaning that a sequence of terms (an n-tuple) satisfies S_x if and only if an appropriate permutation of it satisfies S_y. The crucial idea is to find a set of elements, an n-tuple, which satisfies certain conditions of cooccurrence in the strings S_x and S_y. The term 'biconditional relation' seems to be the most descriptive expression to describe the essential process involved.

[3] Harris assigns a different status to paraphrase and cooccurrence. The method (and criteria for transformations) is *cooccurrence*. If the method is pursued, one gets *paraphrase*.

[4] The basic idea seems to be this. Suppose we have a discourse (corpus) which contains (3) and (4). If we normalize (4) as (8), then we can apply the methods of substitution to state that for this text (but not for the language), *beer* and *cheese* are somehow equivalent. This could not be asserted, on the basis of substitution, given the non-normalized text containing (4).

The general idea is that the structural information provided by analysis is about a text (hence, discourse analysis) based on normalizations (transformation (5), etc.) that might be justified by generalizations (arrived at inductively by fixed procedures) about the language.

[5] Consider a thought experiment which illustrates a property of Partee's definition (18). Suppose the grammar generated abstract underlying structures like (i-a) and (ii-a). Suppose further that the grammar contained a transformation, T_x, (iii), which applies optionally if the quantified NP is plural and obligatorily if the quantified NP is a coordination.

(i) (a) $(_S(_{NP}(_Q\text{all}) (_{NP}\text{the men})) (_{VP}(_{AUX}\text{will}) (_V\text{go})))$
   (b)   All the men will go.
   (c)   The men will all go.
(ii) (a) $(_S(_{NP}(_Q\text{all}) (_{NP}\text{John}) (_{NP}\text{Bill}) (_{NP}\text{Tom})) (_{VP}(_{AUX}\text{will}) (_V\text{go})))$
   (b)   *All John, Bill, and Tom will go.
   (c)   John, Bill, and Tom will all go.
(iii) T_x: optional transformation
         SD: Q NP AUX
         SC: NP AUX Q

Sentence (i-b) is derived if T_x does not apply to (i-a), (i-c) is derived if it does. Sentence (ii-c) is derived by obligatory application of T_x to (ii-a).

According to Partee, since T_x is obligatory in (ii), it makes no sense to ask if T_x is meaning-preserving. In particular, one cannot ask if (ii-a) and (ii-c) are synonymous because (ii-a) is an abstract underlying PM, and we have no intuitions of synonymy about underlying PM's. (See (12)). Appealing to definition (18). Partee might claim that T_x is meaning-preserving in case (i) since (i-b) and (i-c) are synonymous. But what meaning is preserved? If in case (ii) it makes no sense to assume that (a) and (c) are synonymous, it should make no sense to assume in case (i) that (a) and (c) are synonymous.

Consider a more general problem. Suppose we have two sentences, $S_1 = (SI_1, \Sigma_1, P_1)$ and $S_2 = (SI_2, \Sigma_2, P_2)$, where SI = semantic interpretation, Σ = syntactic structure, and P = phonetic representation. Assume that the DSPM of S_1 is identical to the DSPM of S_2. The two sentences differ in that an optional transformation, T_{opt}, applies in the derivation of S_1 but not in the derivation of S_2. S_1 and S_2 will have syntactic structures, Σ_1 and Σ_2 respectively, which are the same up to the point at which T_{opt} applies. Σ_1 and Σ_2 are represented in (iv). The sign $\|$ means that the PM in Σ_1 is identical to the PM in Σ_2. The sign ⧣ means the PM in Σ_1 is different from that in Σ_2.

(iv) $\Sigma_1 = PM_{DS}, PM_2 \ldots PM_j\; PM_{j+1} \ldots PM_k, PM_m \ldots PM_{SS_1}$
         $\qquad\quad \| \qquad \| \qquad\quad \| \qquad \text{⧣} \qquad\quad \text{⧣} \quad \text{⧣} \qquad \text{⧣}$
         $\Sigma_2 = PM_{DS}, PM_2 \ldots PM_j,\; PM_q \ldots\quad PM_y, PM_z \ldots PM_{SS_2}$
(v) $PM_{j+1} = T_{opt}(PM_j)$

182 RAY C. DOUGHERTY

What would it mean to say 'T_{opt} changes meaning'? Would this mean that PM_{SS_1} is synonymous with PM_{J+1}, and PM_{DS} is synonymous with PM_J, but PM_J and PM_{J+1} are not synonymous? In Chomsky's TGG, as defined in Chomsky (1957, 1965, 1968, and 1969), this seems to be the only interpretation of this question.

What would it mean to say 'T_{opt} preserves meaning'? Would this mean that PM_{SS_1} is synonymous with PM_{J+1}, and PM_{DS} is synonymous with PM_J, and PM_{J+1} and PM_J are synonymous? In Chomsky's TGG, this seems to be the only interpretation of the question.

The question 'Does T_{opt} change meaning or preserve meaning?' makes no sense in Chomsky's TGG since, as pointed out in (12), we can have no intuitions of synonymy between PM_J and PM_{J+1}.

Chomsky (1968, 1969) specifies the position that, for two sentences S_x and S_y, if the semantic interpretation of S_x is different than that of S_y in certain ways (e.g. grammatical relations, scope, presupposition, etc.), then $(PM_{DS}, PM_{SS})s_x \neq (PM_{DS}, PM_{SS})s_y$ in certain ways (e.g. deep structure dominance relations differ, or they differ in surface structure order of quantifiers, location of main stress, etc.).

To say that all aspects of the semantic interpretation cannot be determined from the DSPM and that certain information from the SSPM is relevant in determining the semantic interpretation is *not* to say that transformations change meaning. If scope, for example, is determined in surface structure, there is no 'scope meaning' present in the deep structure such that it could be changed. As discussed in connection with example (iv), meaning changing transformations make no sense in Chomsky's TGG.

Chomsky believes that rules like (v) function independently of sound and meaning: 'It seems that grammars contain a substructure of perfectly formal rules operating on phrase markers in narrowly circumscribed ways. Not only are these rules independent of meaning or sound in their function, ...' (Chomsky, 1969: 198–9)
6 In the following passage, Partee focuses on the one point at which the real character and the apparent character of the syntax-semantics interaction seem to line up: 'Note that as long as the notion of a syntactically defined deep structure is accepted, the claim that semantic interpretation is entirely on deep structure is indeed equivalent to the claim that transformations preserve meaning.' (Partee, 1972: 2).

The line 'the claim that semantic interpretation is entirely on deep structure' defines a coherent position on Chomsky's TGG. Now consider the line 'the claim that transformations preserve meaning'. Partee stated earlier: 'But transformations in fact operate not on sentences but on abstract phrase-markers, and it is not obvious that we have any direct semantic intuitions about these abstract structures, in particular any notion of synonymy between them.' (1972: 5). See notes 5 and 20.

The line 'the claim that transformations preserve meaning' can only be understood in terms of a Harrisian transformational system which relates surface structure strings to other surface structure strings – as Partee points out: 'The various stands taken on synonymy all have to do with synonymy between *sentences*, and in talk about transformations preserving or changing meaning, the most common examples are transformations which can informally be thought of as relating sentences to other sentences.' (Partee, 1971: 4–5).

Throughout her analysis Partee vacillates between Chomsky's and Harris' alternative transformational systems. Her equivocation on the use of the technical term *transformation* becomes clear when one juxtaposes passages in which the term *transformation* is used differently.

Section 5 discusses the point of tangency between Chomsky's and Harris' alternative conceptual schemes.

One point bears mentioning, although it can not be pursued in this limited study. Some people think that the revolution caused by *Syntactic Structures* is essentially over and that all linguists who say they are working in TGG have accepted Chomsky's theories and methods. There is some evidence against this position. Let us examine some general phenomena associated with scientific revolutions and then return to linguistics.

In studying scientific revolutions, and in general, how ideas change, many of the facts we unearth may strike us as paradoxical and contradictory. For example, Kuhn, in his interesting study of scientific revolutions, points out that it is not unusual for some of the leading protagonists of a new scientific movement to be actually protagonists only in words and not in deeds. In some cases, a protagonist of the new movement may not be a practicing adherent of the creed he champions, and in other cases, he may in his actual practice deny the basic assumptions of the new movement while using the results and formulations provided by the new movement. Discussing the development of ideas following the publication of Copernicus' *De Revolutionibus*, Kuhn points out that many of the astronomers who applauded Copernicus' work were actually ambivalent in their allegiance to the basic ideas of Ptolemy and Copernicus:

But the success of *De Revolutionibus* does not imply the success of its central thesis. The faith of most astronomers in the earth's stability was at first unshaken. Authors who applauded Copernicus' erudition, borrowed his diagrams, or quoted his determinations of the distance from the earth to the moon, usually either ignored the earth's motion or dismissed it as absurd. (Kuhn, 1957: 186)
... Many astronomers found it possible to exploit Copernicus' mathematical system and to contribute to the success of the new astronomy while denying or remaining silent about the motion of the earth. (*Ibid.*: 187)

The concept of a scientist using the results of a new movement while denying the central thesis of the new movement is not restricted to astronomy. Poincaré, in discussing the scientific revolution caused by Einstein in mathematical physics, points out that many scientists, although they professed to accept the basic assumption that space was relative, still continued in their work to think as though space were absolute. Poincaré states:

Everyone knows that space is relative, or rather everyone says so, but how many people think still as if they considered it absolute. Nevertheless, a little reflection will show to what contradictions they are exposed. (p. 10)

Apparently in astronomy and in physics there were some researchers who contended they were working in the post-revolutionary framework but who actually presented work which denied the basic assumptions of the post-revolutionary perspective. Could the linguistics revolution be similar to the revolutions in astronomy and physics? What would be a case of a linguist who, in producing a study in generative grammar, was actually denying the main theses of generative grammar? I believe that a study of such questions would shed great light on many of the current trends in linguistic research.

[7] In this modified Harrisian system, one can even ask the question: 'Does a particular transformation, T_x, change meaning?' In Chomsky's system it makes no sense to ask: 'Does a particular transformation, T_x, change meaning?' See notes 5, 6, and 20.

[8] For an analysis of generative semantics as a version of transformational taxonomic grammar, see Dougherty (forthcoming).

The above quote from Partee merits discussion beyond that offered in my text. The text develops the role of 'meaning-changingness' and 'meaning-preservingness' in the transformational systems of Harris and Chomsky, and further, discusses Partee's attempts to use these notions to clarify issues relating to the generative semantics versus interpretive semantics debate. Three issues which arise in the quoted passage and which merit discussion are: (a) 'weak' versus 'strong' hypotheses, (b) abstract generative semantic deep structures, and (c) independent syntactic motivation.

For some discussion of the meaning of the terms 'strong form' and 'weak form' of a hypothesis, see n. 21.

Partee indicates that consistent adherence to the principle of meaning-preservingness 'requires much more abstract deep structures than were previously contemplated'. (p. 4) As we shall see below, there are other reasons for the abstract structures postulated in generative semantics. For further discussion, see Dougherty (1973: 454, n. 10).

Partee indicates that many of the generative semantic analyses have 'independent syntactic motivation'. Let us examine this notion. Partee states:

... Many of their [Lakoff, Postal, McCawley, etc.] analyses have independent support from purely syntactic arguments, and it is often not easy to determine how much of the weight of their arguments is borne by the criterion of meaning-preservingness or transformations. Chomsky and Jackendoff, on the other hand, have argued that the more abstract deep structures do not have sufficient independent syntactic motivation... (1972: 3–4)

Much of the discussion in Partee (1971, 1972) concerns quantifiers and conjunction. Concerning *Conjunction Reduction*, a theory of coordination and quantifiers which forms the basis for the generative semantic claim that quantifiers and negatives are verbs in higher sentences, Partee states:

3.2.1. *Conjunction-reduction: a problem for everyone.* Another case where a rule as traditionally stated is meaning-preserving most of the time but not so when quantifiers are involved is the case of conjunction reduction, noted in Partee (1970) and discussed further in G. Lakoff (1968b)...' (Partee, 1972: 12)

What type of independently motivated syntactic arguments have generative semanticists offered for conjunction reduction? Lakoff and Ross (L & R) (1970) discuss the relative merits of two grammatical models proposed to describe sentences containing coordinate conjunctions and quantifiers: the conjunction reduction (CR) hypothesis and the phrase structure rule (PSR) hypothesis. The CR hypothesis, advocated by L & R, would transformationally derive the following (b) examples by a CR transformation from underlying structures with essentially the order of constituents in the (a) examples. The PSR hypothesis, which L & R argue against, would not transformationally relate the (a) and (b) examples. Instead, the base generates DSPM's with essentially the order of constituents in (i-a, b), (ii-a), and (iii-a, b). Sentence (ii-b) would be transformationally derived from an underlying structure with essentially the order of constituents in *Ann and John each dislike the other.* The PSR hypothesis is discussed in detail in Dougherty (1970, 1971).

(i) (a)   Ann is erudite and John is erudite. (L & R's example (2a), p. 271)
   (b)   Ann and John are erudite. (L & R's example (1a), p. 271)

(ii) (a)   Ann dislikes John and John dislikes Ann.
  (b)   Ann and John dislike each other.
(iii) (a)   Ann laughed and John cried.
  (b)   Ann and John laughed and cried respectively.

The CR hypothesis and the PSR hypothesis differ considerably in what they claim to be a DSPM, which sentences are derived by optional transformations, which sentences are grouped into which natural classes, etc. The choice between these hypotheses is an empirical question. Let us look at the type of argument and the nature of the evidence that L & R adduce to choose between these grammars:

Another interesting set of facts which supports a transformational derivation for certain coordinate phrases, but not for all, is the following. While some speakers accept (11b) (as an approximate paraphrase of (11a)), no one finds (12) grammatical, to the best of our knowledge.

(11) (a)   Who is similar to whom?
  (b)   Who and who are similar?
(12)   *Who and who are erudite?

If (2a) [(i-a)] is converted to (1a) [(i-b)], by some rule of *Conjunction Reduction*, then the ungrammaticality of (12) can be explained on the basis of the fact that (13) is ungrammatical.

(13)   *Who is erudite and who is erudite?

As might be expected, *respectively*-sentences and *each other*-sentences, which the facts of (10) suggested should be derived by some transformational process of reduction, cannot occur with *who and who* coordinate NP's.

(14) (a)   *Who and who laughed and cried, respectively?
  (b)   *Who and who dislike each other? (Lakoff and Ross: 272)

I renumber L & R's data for reference in my discussion. The derivation of (iv-b) from (iv-a) parallels the derivation of (i-b) from (i-a). Similarly, the derivation of (v-b) from (v-a) parallels the derivation of (iii-b) from (iii-a).

(iv) (a)   *Who is erudite and who is erudite? (L & R's ex. 13)
  (b)   *Who and who are erudite. (L & R's ex. 12)
(v) (a)   Who laughed and who cried?
  (b)   *Who and who laughed and cried, respectively? (L & R's ex. 14a)

L & R state: 'the ungrammaticality of (iv-b) can be explained on the basis of the fact that (iv-a) is ungrammatical'. But how will the CR hypothesis block (v-b)? If, as L & R assume, sentence (v-b) is derived by a CR transformation from (v-a) – a sentence conspicuously absent from L & R's discussion – then the logical expectation would be that (v-b) should be well-formed. I can only wonder why L & R state: 'As might be expected, *respectively*-sentences ... cannot occur with *who and who* coordinate NP's.'

Under the assumptions of L & R's grammar, which derives (iii-b) from (iii-a), the logical expectation is that (v-b) will be well-formed since (v-a) is well-formed. This expectation of the CR hypothesis is at odds with the primary data of English. Consequently, the example cited by L & R as support for their grammar, L & R's example (14a), is actually a counterexample to their grammar.

A strong case could be built that, in general, generative semantic studies of coordination, plurals, and quantifiers are empirical but not explanatory (see n. 21), and further, that the substantive material presented in generative semantics articles selects the *Aspects*-type model over the generative semantics model – despite the fact that the generative semanticists usually conclude otherwise. Consider these cases:

Lakoff and Ross (1970) wish to argue against the PSR hypothesis of coordination. At no point in their discussion do they even indicate what the PSR hypothesis claims about the data they discuss, although they contend, incorrectly, that the data provide counterevidence against the PSR hypothesis. In fact, the examples L & R produce to support their proposals are strong counterexamples against the basic assumptions of their own proposals, as we saw above. Lakoff and Ross (1970) is a case of regression since they reject the grammar which describes the data and select the grammar to which the data constitute a counterexample.

Lakoff and Peters (1966), an early harbinger of the generative semantics perspective, wish to motivate their *conjunction reduction-phrasal conjunction* analysis over the analysis of coordination offered by Gleitman (1965). But each and every distribution of data cited by Lakoff and Peters to choose their proposal over Gleitman's actually would select Gleitman's grammar over their own. The one example they offer as a counterexample to Gleitman's grammar is actually irrelevant, i.e. a neutral example (see Dougherty, 1971, 73). If our goal is to construct an explanatory theory of coordination, quantifiers, negation, etc., then Lakoff and Peters (1966) is a case of regression since their proposals are not as good as the proposals of Gleitman which they reject.

Many generative semantic coordination studies reflect a basic misunderstanding of the goals and methods of linguistic research, i.e. basic misconceptions about what constitutes an explanation in linguistics and about the process of hypothesis testing. Hypothesis testing (see n. 1), is a general method employed to choose the superior grammar from a field of alternative grammars which make conflicting claims about a given range of data. If hypothesis testing is misunderstood, and systematically misapplied to select the least explanatory grammar, then this situation must be corrected since it can lead to unfortunate consequences.

Returning to the question of independent syntactic justification for abstract semantic deep structures, it is with some justification that I feel that Chomsky's position is well-taken, i.e. that independent syntactic support is frequently lacking for generative semantic proposals. (See Dougherty, 1973: 485-7.) Partee, on the other hand, feels the contrary, at least with respect to conjunction-reduction. In the section '*Conjunction Reduction: a problem for everyone*', Partee (1972: 12) details the interactions of the *meaning-preserving hypothesis*, an idea which makes no sense in a generative framework, and the *conjunction-reduction hypothesis*, a theory which has no demonstrable descriptive or explanatory power and whose basic assumptions are at variance with the data cited in its behalf by its champions.

[9] In Chomsky's formulation of the interpretive semantics position, he concludes that the semantic interpretation of a sentence is not entirely determined by the DSPM. Partee's criticisms of interpretive semantics are in terms of meaning-changing transformations.

There seems to be some unformulated assumption by Partee of the following sort:

(i)   The claim that semantic interpretation is not entirely on deep structure is equivalent to the claim that certain specific transformations change meaning.

But these claims are not equivalent for the reasons given in notes 5 and 6. The claim that the semantic interpretation is not entirely defined by the deep structure is a meaningful statement in Chomsky's TGG. The claim that specific transformations change meaning is not a meaningful statement in Chomsky's TGG.

The claim that a specific transformation changes meaning is a meaningful statement in the extended Harrisian system of descriptive semantics presented in Section 5. See n. 7.

[10] Partee (1971: 652), quoted in the text, indicates she will 'not attempt to choose sides' between generative semantics and interpretive semantics because 'it is way to early too judge...'. In fact, since interpretive semantics, as Partee defines it, is incoherent, there should be no question about rejecting it as a possible model. The fact that Partee cannot choose between the two models might mean that they are essentially equivalent in descriptive and explanatory power, i.e. equally incoherent. See the discussion of generative semantics in n. 8.

The material presented here supports the thesis offered in Dougherty (1973) that the current dispute in linguistics between the *Syntactic Structures – Aspects* school and the generative semantics school, although often considered a theoretical dispute, is actually a dispute about the methodology and argumentation appropriate to linguistic research. The theoretical differences between generative semantic and *SS-Aspects* proposals are merely symptomatic of fundamental methodological differences. It might well be profitable to think that the major difference between the generative semantics school and the *SS-Aspects* school is that these alternative schools are based on different conceptions of 'explanation in linguistics'. The difference in definition of 'explanation in linguistics' correlates with the different research methodologies. I return to this idea in the conclusion.

[11] It is not crucial to any arguments in this paper if transformations are triggered or optional. To simplify the grammar, I assume they are optional.

[12] G_{int} is a simplified fragment of the PSR grammar presented in Dougherty (1970, 1971).

[13] Chomsky (1968: 113–4) defines P_n as the surface structure phrase marker. In discussing surface structure interpretation, he states: 'Notice, incidentally, that it is, strictly speaking, not P_n that is subject to semantic interpretation but rather the structure determined by phonological interpretation of P_n, with intonation center assigned.' (*ibid.*: 114).

In order to indicate that there is a difference between the terminal string of the SSPM and the interpreted string, all of the examples discussed will have contractions (*can't, won't*, etc.) instead of the longer forms (*can not, will not*, etc.) present in the SSPM. In our discussion this distinction makes no difference, but there are cases in which the distinction is crucial, and it should be kept in mind.

[14] In (66) there would have to be further conditions placed if one were considering not the fragment of language described, but the whole language. That is, the... in (a) could not be filled by the italicized elements in: *if* either NP or NP *leave then I will* not.

[15] Since labeled bracketing plays no role in the interpretive rules, the phrase markers will not be specified. The symbol ($_s$...) abbreviates the labeled bracketing which one should assume is present.

[16] This analysis describes the data considered but offers no explanation for them. An interesting avenue of research would be to seek an explanation for the fact that SSPM's like (76c) are marked as deviant. Perhaps a detailed analysis extending to more data might show that the deviance of (76c) follows from an independently motivated optimal

formulation of the semantic rules which interpret *either* and those which interpret *not*. That is, two (or more) independently motivated semantic rules might lead to a contradiction when applied to sentence (70).

[17] Chomsky (personal communication) points out that under the assumptions of the Extended Standard Theory (see Chomsky, 1969: 134) it is senseless to contend we have direct semantic intuitions about abstract structures because semantic intuitions will have to do with meaning and meaning is determined by the pair (DS, SS).

[18] Of course there are many distributions of data which do not seem to be, and might very well not be, amenable to treatment in the *Aspects* model or *Extended Standard Theory*. Many problems, however, which have been considered to be beyond the *Aspects* model turn out upon investigation either to be describable entirely within the *Aspects* model or to be pseudoproblems. See Dougherty (1973) for a review of case theory, the conjunction reduction analysis, and the pronouns as articles hypothesis. (See n. 8.)

[19] In any science data are considered important only insofar as they resolve interesting questions concerning the structure of the phenomena under consideration, i.e. insofar as they choose between alternative conceptions of the mechanisms postulated to underlie the phenomena. To use an example mentioned by Chomsky in lectures, physicists were much concerned a few years ago about what would happen to a photographic plate at the base of a South African coal mine, but one could hardly imagine a more 'unimportant' fact (particularly in South Africa) from a practical human point of view. The photographic plate was to provide a crucial example to choose between conflicting claims deduced from a priori equally plausible, but mutually incompatible, theories. See Dougherty (to appear) for discussion of deductive and inductive logic in the interpretation of crucial examples.

[20] Chomsky has always pointed out that great conceptual errors can result from failure to recognize the significant differences between his version of grammar and Harris'. Chomsky (1964) states: 'The notions of "co-occurrence relation" and "generative transformation" are rather different in formal properties as well as in their role in actual syntactic description, and a great deal of confusion can result from failure to distinguish them. Thus it makes no sense to arrange cooccurrence relations "in sequence", but generative transformations can (and in practice, must) be ordered and applied in sequence. The examples of Section 2 depend essentially on appropriate ordering and sequential application of transformational rules, and on appropriate choice of base versus derived forms (a distinction which is also not definable in terms of co-occurrence). Furthermore, cooccurrence is a relation defined on actual sentences, while generative transformations apply to abstract structures that often bear no close relation to actual sentences.' (p. 62, n. 2)

In *Syntactic Structures* semantics plays a little role. Partee says: '... [Consider] Chomsky's view of syntax in 1957. In *Syntactic Structures*, Chomsky expressed doubts about the possibility of *any* systematic connection between syntax and semantics. Furthermore, he believed it ... necessary ... to describe syntax in completely autonomous terms.' (1971: 654) I believe that Partee has exaggerated Chomsky's position, see n. 23.

[21] One frequently hears discussions involving 'strong forms' and 'weak forms' of hypotheses. It is worth noting that the 'strong form' of a hypothesis is not necessarily easier to refute than the 'weak form' for the simple reason that one can have a strong form or a weak form of a non-empirical, purely metaphysical hypothesis. Suppose the question is 'How many angels can dance on the head of a pin?'. A hypothesis which asserts that the number of dancers depends on the type of dance, the footgear of the

angels, and the size of the pinhead is 'weaker' than the hypothesis that claims there are always 7312 angels independent of the dance executed or the size of the pinhead. If we have a hypothesis which makes no refutable claims about empirical data (because it is a purely metaphysical hypothesis, because it is incoherent owing to internal contradictions, etc.), then a 'strong form' of that hypothesis might be no more interesting than a 'weak form'.

The ideas which arise in comparing the 'weak form' versus the 'strong form' of a hypothesis are similar to those which arise in comparing hypotheses for *simplicity*. In choosing between two alternative grammars we will prefer the 'simpler grammar', but the idea of *simplicity* must tie in with the data. A chemical theory which claims that all matter is composed of four elements, *fire*, *earth*, *air*, and *water*, is in some sense 'simpler' than a theory which postulates more than ninety two elements. The ninety two element theory is more complex than the four element theory, but is preferable because the increased complexity 'pays its way' in the sense that the ninety two element theory provides more explanatory insight into the principles underlying chemical processes than does the four element theory. Similarly, in linguistics: A theory which claims that there are only four catagories in underlying structure might be judged in some sense simpler than a theory which postulates many more categories. For example, the theory of *conjunction-reduction* (see n. 8) forms the basis for the generative semantic claim that quantifiers and negatives are verbs in higher sentences in underlying structures. The generative semantic theory, which claims that the nodes *quantifier* and *negative* are not in deep structure, has less nodes than the non-generative semantic theory, the PSR hypothesis, which claims the nodes *quantifier* and *negative* are in deep structure. In some absolute sense one might argue that the generative semantic theory is simpler. When however one turns to the empirical data, one can see that there is motivation for having deep structure nodes *quantifier*, etc., see n. 8.

Chomsky mentions in several places that the concept of *simplicity* must be tied in with explanatory power, e.g.: 'Notice that is is often a step forward, then, when a linguistic theory becomes more complex, more articulated and refined – a point that has been noted repeatedly (see, for example, Chomsky (1965: 46)). For example, it is a step forward when we complicate linguistic theory by distinguishing among all imaginable rules the two categories of "transformational rules" and "phonological rules", with their specific properties, and formulate conditions on their application and inter-relation…' (Chomsky, 1969: 126)

Both *strength* and *simplicity* must be characterized in terms of *explanatory power*. But then what is the nature of explanation in linguistics? Cohen (to appear) contributes substantive answers towards the eventual resolution of this question.

In the *Syntactic Structures – Aspects* view of linguistic research, explanation goes beyond the classification of data using algebraic tools like transformational rules. In a TGG, algebraic tools are used to formalize the mechanical principles of sentence construction into a theory (a grammar) from which one can deduce consequences (the sentences generated) which can be verified or refuted in comparison with the observable data (the primary data of the language studied). Our goal is to develop a grammatical model which will generate all and only the grammatical sentences of English by appealing to strong assumptions which narrowly constrain the notions *language* in general and *English* in particular. Explanation correlates with the narrowness with which our assumptions constrain the notions *English* and *language*, i.e. with the tightness of fit between the theory and the data. An explanatory theory derives its explanatory power from the fact that it not only indicates why the data take the form they do, but further, why the data take that form and not some other, a priori equally plausible, form. A grammar that is not only compatible with the actually occurring data, but that is also incompatible with the hypothetical non-occurring data, provides principled reasons for why the data take a certain form. Such a grammar goes beyond the question 'What is the form of the data?' and asks 'Why do the data take this one particular form and not another a priori equally plausible form?'. This is, in large measure, the essence of explanation in linguistics as linguistics is defined in the *SS-Aspects* framework. Questions of explanation arise when we speculate about the process by which a generative grammar, which makes claims about an infinite number of sentences, is selected on the basis of a finite amount of data.

In a way, one might interpret the following passage by Chomsky to mean that a hypothesis has explanatory power insofar as it contributes towards solving the problems of language acquisition:

2.2.   The general point may be worth a slight digression. The fundamental problem of linguistic theory, as I see it at least, is to account for the choice of a particular grammar, given the data available to the language-learner. To account for this inductive leap, linguistic theory must try to characterize a fairly narrow class of grammars that are available to the language learner; it must, in other words, specify the notion 'human language' in a narrow and restrictive fashion. A 'better theory', then, is one that specifies the class of possible grammars so narrowly that some procedure of choice or evaluation can select a descriptively adequate grammar for each language from this class, within reasonable conditions of time and access to data. Given alternative linguistic theories that meet this condition, we might compare them in terms of general 'simplicity' or other metatheoretic notions, but it is unlikely that such considerations will have any more significance within linguistics than they do in any other field. For the moment, the problem is to construct a general theory of language that is so richly structured and so restrictive in the conditions it imposes that, while meeting the condition of descriptive adequacy, it can sufficiently narrow the class of possible grammars so that the problem of choice of grammar (and explanation, in some serious sense) can be approached. (Chomsky, 1969: 125)

Harris offers a conception of explanation which differs considerably from that of the *SS-Aspects* system. Harris offers no rules to generate the constructions he discusses. He does not use algebraic rules (transformations) to formulate the principles of sentence construction and to construct a generative grammar; instead, he employs algebraic tools to factor generalizations from the data and to classify constructions. Harris' proposals are empirical, that is they can be verified or refuted in comparison with data, but they are not explanatory in the sense that a generative grammar is explanatory. See Dougherty (to appear) for discussion of explanation in Chomsky's TGG.

For reasons explained in Dougherty (1971, 1973) and in n. 8, the theory of conjunction-reduction developed by Lakoff and Ross is empirical but not explanatory. I return to the concept of *explanation in linguistics* in the conclusion.

[22] The above discussion of explanation in Kepler's and Newton's work is based on Holton's studies on the history of science, in particular, Holton (1973: 68–90). In my discussion I have quoted verbatim from this passage:

This is the main question, and to it Kepler has at the same time two very different answers, emerging, as it were from the two parts of his soul. We may phrase one of the two answers as follows: *the physically real world, which defines the nature of things, is the world of phenomena explainable by mechanical principles*. This can be called Kepler's first criterion of reality, and assumes the possibility of formulating a sweeping and consistent dynamics which Kepler only sensed but which was not to be given until Newton's *Principia*. Kepler's other answer to which he keeps returning again and again as he finds himself rebuffed by the deficiencies of his dynamics, and which we shall now examine in detail, is this: *the physically real world is the world of mathematically expressed harmonies which man can discover in the chaos of events*. (Holton, 1973: 78)

[23] Chomsky's 1957 attitude might be illuminated by the following analogy.

A jigsaw puzzle has two types of information aiding in its assembly: the irregularly shaped interlocking pieces which fit together in some ways but not in others, and the picture printed on its surface. Both types of information are used in assembling the puzzle. One type of information, the picture, is meaningful, it provides 'semantic' information. The other type, the particular shapes of the pieces, is structural information, or, 'syntactic' information. The semantic and syntactic information can be more or less related. In a simple puzzle, the pieces are shaped almost to match the picture, i.e. the cuts are along borders of the components of the picture. In an advanced puzzle for the jigsaw cognoscenti, there is no picture printed on the pieces, the puzzle is defined solely in terms of its syntactic information. Puzzles of varying degrees of complexity exist between these extremes. Applying this analogy to language, we might say that language has two types of structure, semantic and syntactic. Semantic structure indicates the patterns of meaning in the language; syntactic structure indicates the abstract formal system which governs the principles of sentence structure. Most human languages studied lie somewhere between the two extremes in that the syntactic structure and the semantic structure are not completely matched up, but not exactly independent. To determine the extent to which the syntactic devices of a language are used systematically to express meaning is a challenging empirical problem.

Chomsky (personal communication) points out that although *Syntactic Structures* denies that there is a systematic connection between syntax and semantics that permits the definition of the notions of syntax in terms of semantic primitives, it acknowledges that there exist striking correspondences which might be (or even, must be) studied in some more general theory of language that will include a theory of linguistic form and a theory of the use of language as subparts. At the level of linguistic theory, a systematic syntax-semantics interaction exists in the sense that we shall naturally rate more highly a theory of formal structure that leads to grammars that meet the requirement of supporting semantic descriptions.

The basic idea that a language has two types of patterns, syntactic and semantic, which might not line up, is the concept underlying Sapir's sentence 'All grammars leak'. According to Sapir, the 'leaks' occur where the syntactic patterns do not parallel the semantic ones: '... all languages have an inherent tendency to economy of expression. Were this tendency entirely inoperative, there would be no grammar. The fact of grammar, a universal trait of language, is simply a generalized expression of the feeling that analogous concepts and relations are most conveniently symbolized in analogous forms. Were a language ever completely "grammatical", it would be a perfect engine of conceptual expression. Unfortunately, or luckily, no language is tyrannically consistent. All grammars leak.' (Sapir: 38).

BIBLIOGRAPHY

Chomsky, Noam: 1957, *Syntactic Structures*, Mouton, The Hague.
Chomsky, Noam: 1964, *Current Issues in Linguistic Theory*, Mouton, The Hague.
Chomsky, Noam: 1965, *Aspects of the Theory of Syntax*, MIT Press, Cambridge, Mass.
Chomsky, Noam: 1968, 'Deep Structure, Surface Structure, and Semantic Interpretation', in Chomsky (1972), 62–119.
Chomsky, Noam: 1969, 'Some Empirical Issues in the Theory of Transformational Grammar', in Chomsky (1972), 120–203.
Chomsky, Noam: 1972, *Studies on Semantics in Generative Grammar*, Mouton, The Hague.
Cohen, David (ed.): *Explaining Linguistic Phenomena*, Hemisphere Publishing Company, Washington, D.C., to appear.
Dingwall, William (ed.): 1971, *A Survey of Linguistic Science*, University of Maryland Press, Baltimore.
Dougherty, Ray: 1970, 'A Grammar of Coordinate Conjunction, Part I', *Lg*. **46**, 850–93.
Dougherty, Ray: 1971, 'A Grammar of Coordinate Conjunction, Part II', *Lg*, **47**, 298–339.
Dougherty, Ray: 1973, 'A Survey of Linguistic Methods and Arguments', *Fol*. **10**, 423–90.
Dougherty, Ray: 'What Explanation Is and Isn't', in Cohen (ed.), to appear.
Dougherty, Ray: *Chomsky's Revolution in Linguistics*, forthcoming.
Einstein, Albert: 1927, 'Isaac Newton'. Annual report of the Smithsonian Institution, U.S. Government Printing Office.
Fillmore, Charles and D. Terence Langendoen (eds.): 1972, *Studies in Linguistic Semantics*, Holt, Rinehart, and Winston, N.Y.
Gleitman, Lila: 1965, 'Coordinating Conjunction in English', *Lg*. **41**, 260–93.
Harris, Zelig: 1957, 'Co-occurrence and Transformation in Linguistic Structure', *Lg*. **33**, 283–340; in Katz and Fodor (eds.), 1964: 155–211.
Harris, Zelig: 1965, 'Transformational Theory', *Lg*. **41**, 363–401.
Holton, Gerald: 1973, *The Thematic Origins of Scientific Thought*, Harvard University Press, Cambridge, Mass.
Jackendoff, Ray: 1968, 'Some Rules of Semantic Interpretation for English', Phd dissertation, MIT.
Jackendoff, Ray: 1972, *Semantic Interpretation in Generative Grammar*, MIT Press, Cambridge, Mass.
Jespersen, Otto: 1961, *A Modern English Grammar on Historical Principles*, in seven volumes, George Allen and Unwin, Ltd, London.
Katz, J. and Fodor, J.: 1963, 'The Structure of a Semantic Theory', *Lg*, **39**, 170–210.
Katz, J. and Fodor, J. (eds.): 1964, *The Structure of Language*, Prentice Hall, New Jersey.
Katz, J. and Postal, Paul: 1964, *An Integrated Theory of Linguistic Descriptions*, MIT Press, Cambridge, Mass.
Kuhn, Thomas: 1957, *The Copernican Revolution*, Harvard University Press, Cambridge, Mass.
Kuhn, Thomas: 1962, *The Structure of Scientific Revolutions*, The University of Chicago Press, Chicago.

Lakoff, George: 1968, 'Repartee, or a reply to 'Negation, conjunction and quantifiers' ', mimeographed. Appeared in *Fol.* (1970), 389–422.

Lakoff, George and Peters, Stanley: 1966, 'Phrasal Conjunction and Symmetric Predicates', Computation Laboratory, Harvard University, Mathematical Linguistics and Automatic Translation, Report no. NSF-17, pp. VI-1 to VI-49.

Lakoff, George and Ross, John: 1970. 'Two Kinds of *and*', *Linguistic Inquiry* 1, 271–2.

Lasnik, Howard: 1972, 'Analyses of Negation', PhD dissertation, MIT.

Maitland, Francis (trans.): 1965, *Science and Method*, by Henri Poincaré, Dover, New York.

Partee, Barbara: 1970, 'Negation, Conjunction and Quantifiers: Syntax vs Semantics', *Fol.* 6, 153–65.

Partee, Barbara: 1971, 'Linguistic Metatheory', in Dingwall (ed.), pp. 651–80.

Partee, Barbara: 1972, 'On the Requirement that Transformations Preserve Meaning', in Fillmore and Langendoen (eds.), pp. 1–21.

Poincaré, Henri: 1910, *Science and Method*. See Maitland (trans.).

Sapir, Edward: 1921, *Language*, Harcourt, Brace and World, Inc., New York.

BARBARA PARTEE

SOME TRANSFORMATIONAL EXTENSIONS
OF MONTAGUE GRAMMAR*

0. Introduction

Richard Montague's work on English, as represented in Montague (1970a), (1970b), (1972), represents the first systematic attempt to apply the logician's methods of formal syntax and semantics to natural language. With few exceptions,[1] linguists and logicians had previously been agreed, although for different reasons, that the apparatus developed by logicians for treating the syntax and semantics of artificially constructed formal languages, while obviously fruitful within its restricted domain, was not in any direct way applicable to the analysis of natural languages. Logicians seem to have felt that natural languages were too unsystematic, too full of vagueness and ambiguity, to be amenable to their rigorous methods, or if susceptible to formal treatment, only at great cost.[2] Linguists, on the other hand, emphasize their own concern for psychological reality, and the logicians' lack of it, in eschewing the logicians' approach: linguists, at least those of the Chomskyan school, are searching for a characterization of the class of possible human languages, hoping to gain thereby some insight into the structure of the mind, and the formal languages constructed by logicians appear to depart radically from the structures common to actual natural languages.

Montague's claim, as represented in the title of one of his papers, 'English as a Formal Language', is that English *can* be treated in a natural way within the logical tradition in syntax and semantics. A few remarks about that tradition are in order here. Since Tarski (see, e.g., Tarski (1944)), the concept of truth has played a key role in semantics. It is held that an essential part of the semantic interpretation of any sentence is a specification, given in a metalanguage antecedently understood, of the conditions under which the given sentence is true. Thus an essential part of semantics is the construction of a theory of truth for a language. The mechanism for doing this involves syntax in a fundamental way: first, a set of recursive syntactic rules are given defining the set of *wffs* (well-

Hockney et al. (eds.), *Contemporary Research in Philosophical Logic and Linguistic Semantics*, 195–220. *All Rights Reserved*
Copyright © 1975 *by D. Reidel Publishing Company, Dordrecht-Holland*

formed formulas), starting with the smallest, primitive elements and specifying how units of various categories can be combined to form larger units. Then the task of the semantics is to assign interpretations to the smallest units and then to give rules which determine the interpretation of larger units on the basis of the interpretation of their parts. A key feature of this approach is that the part-whole analysis should be the same in the syntax and the semantics; the syntactic analysis should build up larger units from (or equivalently, analyze them into) just those parts on the basis of which the meaning of the larger unit can be determined. (This one-one correspondence between syntactic and semantic structure is not an absolute condition on the construction of formal languages, and some treatments of the semantics of the two standard quantifiers, for instance, violate it;[3] languages constructed in accordance with it are often called 'logically perfect languages').

Note that the logical tradition involves a bottom-up view of both sentence construction and semantic interpretation. In the case of purely context-free phrase structure rules and something like a Katz-Fodor-Postal semantics of the 1963–1965 period, it is easy enough to see a close correspondence between linguistic and logical practice, since *CF*-rules can be equally well interpreted as starting at the bottom (with the lexical units) and applying to build up larger and larger phrases. Then the only gross divergence between the Katz-Fodor view of semantics and that of the logical tradition is in the nature of the output of the semantic rules (see Vermazen (1967)); the idea of a fundamental connection between the syntactic and semantic rules is preserved. But transformational grammar in general has gotten away from that, and semantics was never developed far enough within the 'standard theory' to reach the point of influencing the syntax in any systematic way. What we find now in linguistics are two main approaches which depart radically, in different ways, from the principle of a one-one correspondence between syntactic and semantic rules. One approach, generative semantics, was founded in part on the conviction that semantic and syntactic rules could not be separated in any principled way, and that 'semantic-interpretation' and 'deepest structure' could be identified.[4] The other, interpretive semantics, maintains the distinction between syntactic rules as formation rules and semantic rules as interpretive rules, but does not posit any systematic relation between them.[5]

Within the logical tradition, there are just two criteria of adequacy for syntactic rules: (i) that they define the set of *wffs* of the language (which is not an empirical constraint for constructed languages, unless some independent characterization of the set of *wffs* is already given), and (ii) most importantly, that they provide a basis for the rules of semantic interpretation. To illustrate the consequences of the second condition, consider the long-standing disputes among linguists as to the hierarchical constituency relations within noun phrases containing a determiner, a noun, and a relative clause, e.g., 'the boy who lives in the park'. There have been at least three basically different alternatives suggested in the literature, schematically represented below[6] as (1), (2), and (3).

There are syntactic arguments pro and con each of these structures[7], but semantic arguments have entered in only peripherally, because no systematic attempt was ever made in any of the linguistic treatments to

(1)

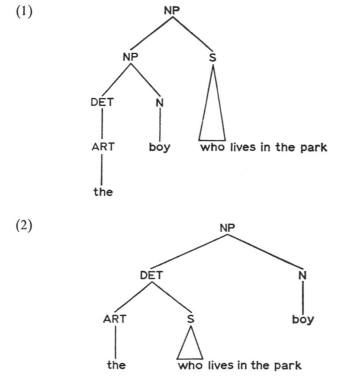

(2)

(3)

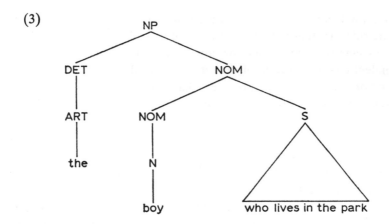

find rules to determine the interpretation of the whole *NP* on the basis
of its parts. But the following informal sketch of the relevant semantics [8]
shows that a structure like (3) can provide a direct basis for the semantic
interpretation in a way that (1) and (2) cannot. The construction has
three parts: *the*, a noun, and a relative clause. Each analysis makes two
binary subdivisions, and in fact, apart from linear order the three analyses
exhaust the possible binary sub-groupings. The semantic consequences
of the differences can be seen most clearly by focussing on the interpretation of *the*. Ignoring controversial details, the general principle for interpreting singular phrases of the form *the* α will include an assertion or presupposition that the class denoted by α has one and only one member.
The noun *boy* denotes a class (the class of boys), and so does the relative
clause *who lives in the park* (the class of entities which live in the park.[9])
Under analysis (3), the two class-denoting phrases are first combined to
form a complex class-denoting phrase, which can be interpreted as denoting the intersection of the two classes [10], namely the class of entities which
both live in the park and are boys; combining *the* with the results leads
to the correct assertion that it is that class that has one and only one
member. On analysis (1), on the other hand, *the* is first combined with
boy, which would lead to an assertion that there is one and only one boy,
and only a non-restrictive interpretation of the relative clause could
naturally be gotten by combining that assertion with the interpretation of
who lives in the park. Similarly, the first stage in the interpretation of (2)
would lead to an assertion that there is one and only one entity that lives

in the park, leaving no natural way to add the interpretation of *boy*. Put another way, the problem with trying to use structure (1) for semantic analysis is that the meaning of the phrase *the boy* is not a part of the meaning of the phrase *the boy who lives in the park*. The problem for structure (2) is analogous. Only by making the major syntactic sub-division between *the* and *boy who lives in the park* can a uniform semantic treatment of *the* be given.[11]

The example just discussed shows that the requirement that semantic interpretation rules correspond structurally to the syntactic rules can put very strong constraints on possible syntactic analyses. This point is worth emphasizing because Montague offers virtually no constraints on syntactic rules themselves; it is only in the connection between syntax and semantics that the grammar is constrained, but that constraint is strong enough that I think it is a serious open question whether natural languages can be so described.

1. MONTAGUE'S 'THE PROPER TREATMENT OF QUANTIFICATION IN ORDINARY ENGLISH'

In this section I will sketch some of the key features of the last (and to a linguist the most interesting) of Montague's three treatments of fragments of English, that in Montague (1972) (henceforth *PTQ*). Since the syntactic rules work bottom-up, I will start with the grammatical categories and the lexicon, then mention the rules most like *CF*-rules, and finally discuss the treatment of quantification. (The fragment also includes relative clauses, about which I will say no more than the few informal remarks above.)

1.0. *Categories and Lexicon*

The categories are defined as in a categorial grammar,[12] though the rules that combine them are not limited to simple concatenation (categorial grammars are a subclass of CF grammars, but Montague's syntax is not.) The two basic categories are t, the category of sentences (t for truth bearing), and e, the category of 'entity-expressions'. The category e seems quite mysterious if one looks only at the syntax, since it turns out that no words or phrases of English are assigned to that category. But it, along with the category t, is used in defining the remaining categories, and in the language of intensional logic into which the English expressions are translated, there *are* expressions of category *e*, and they are interpreted as denoting entities in a straightforward way.

The remaining categories are defined categories; for instance, the category of intransitive verb phrases, abbreviated as *IV* (the linguist's *VP*) is defined[13] as *t/e*: something that could combine with an *e*-phrase (if there were any) to form a *t*-phrase (sentence). In this case, since there are no *e*-phrases in the object language, there is no syntactic rule combining an *IV*-phrase with an *e*-phrase to make a sentence, but the definition nevertheless has consequences in the semantics. The category of common noun phrases, abbreviated *CN*, is defined as *t//e*, another category of the same categorial (henceforth CAT) type as *IV*. (The use of single vs double slashes is simply a device for distinguishing two syntactic categories of the same CAT type; a larger fragment of English might require triple slashes or more.)

The category of term-phrases, abbreviated *T* (the linguist's *NP*) is define das *t/IV*: something that combines with an IV-phrase to make a *t*-phrase (sentence). In this and all the remaining cases, since the constituent categories are non-empty, there are syntactic rules which specify just *how* the constituent categories combine. The following chart gives all the categories of the grammar.

Category	Abbreviation	*PTQ* name	Nearest linguistic equivalent
t	(primitive)	truth-value expression; or declarative sentence	sentence
e	(primitive)	entity expression; or individual expression	(noun phrase)
t/e	*IV*	intransitive verb phrase	verb phrase
t/IV	*T*	term	noun phrase
IV/T	*TV*	transitive verb phrase	transitive verb
IV/IV	*IAV*	*IV*-modifying adverb	*VP*-adverb
t//e	*CN*	common noun phrase	Noun or NOM
t/t	none	sentence-modifying adverb	same
IAV/T	none	*IAV*-making preposition	locative, etc., preposition
IV/t	none	sentence-taking verb phrase	*V* which takes that-COMP
IV/IV	none	*IV*-taking verb phrase	*V* which takes infinitive COMP

Most of the categories have both lexical members and derived phrasal members; the category t contains only derived phrases, and the categories t/t, IAV/T, IV/t, and IV/IV contain only lexical members. The complete lexicon for the fragment is presented in the listing below; B_A means 'basic expression of category A'.

$$B_t = \Lambda$$
$$B_e = \Lambda$$
$$B_{IV} = \{\text{run, walk, talk, rise, change}\}$$
$$B_T = \{\text{John, Mary, Bill, ninety, } he_0, he_1, he_2, \ldots\}$$
$$B_{TV} = \{\text{find, lose, eat, love, date, be, seek, conceive}\}$$
$$B_{IAV} = \{\text{rapidly, slowly, voluntarily, allegedly}\}$$
$$B_{CN} = \{\text{man, woman, park, fish, pen, unicorn, price,}$$
$$\text{temperature}\}$$

$$B_{t/t} = \{\text{necessarily}\}$$
$$B_{IAV/T} = \{\text{in, about}\}$$
$$B_{IV/t} = \{\text{believe that, assert that}\}$$
$$B_{IV//IV} = \{\text{try to, wish to}\}.$$

1.1. *Rules of Functional Application*

The syntactic component of the grammar is a simultaneous recursive definition of the membership of the sets of phrases P_A for each category A, with the set of sentences being the members of P_t. Each syntactic rule has the general form

'If $\alpha_1 \in P_{A_1}$, $\alpha_2 \in P_{A_2}$, ..., $\alpha_n \in P_{A_n}$, then
$$F_i(\alpha_1, \ldots, \alpha_n) \in P_B\text{'}$$

where F_i is a specification of the syntactic mode of combination of the constituent phrases and B is the category of the resulting phrase. Some of the syntactic functions F_i are simply concatenation or concatenation plus some morphological adjustments and are hence very much like CF-rules; others of the F_i bear more resemblance to transformations. All of the syntactic rules build up larger phrases from smaller ones. The semantic interpretation rules operate in two stages. First, for every syntactic rule there is a corresponding rule of translation into an expression of intensional logic; these rules also apply 'bottom-to-top', paralleling the syntactic derivation, so that the translation of any given sentence into intensional logic is built up via translations of each of its subphrases, starting from the basic expressions. (Most of the basic expressions, e.g., *John*, *walk*, *slowly*, are translated into constants of appropriate categories in the intensional logic; a few, such as *be*, *necessarily*, and he_0, he_1, etc., receive special translations reflecting their special logical roles.) The second stage of the semantic interpretation consists of a possible-worlds semantics defined for the given intensional logic. An independent syntactic characterization of the *wffs* of the intensional logic is given, and the semantic rules for the intensional logic are based on the structure given by those syntactic rules. In some of Montague's earlier work, the possible-worlds semantics was defined directly on the English syntax; the change to two-stage semantics may reflect some measure of agreement with Quine's remarks cited in note 3.

We will concentrate on the relations between the syntactic rules and the rules of translation into intensional logic; the semantics of the intensional logic is developed in a way familiar to logicians and will not be discussed here. Among the syntactic rules there is a subset which relate directly to the CAT definitions, and whose corresponding rules of translation follow a uniform pattern. For every category A/B or $A//B$ there is a syntactic rule of the form (4):[14]

(4)   If $\alpha \in P_{A/B}$ and $\beta \in P_B$, then $F_i(\alpha, \beta) \in P_A$.

For each such rule, the corresponding rule of translation into intensional logic is (5):

(5)   If $\alpha \in P_{A/B}$ and $\beta \in P_B$, and α, β translate into α', β', then $F_i(\alpha, \beta)$ translates into $\alpha'(^{\wedge}\beta')$.

The notation $^{\wedge}\beta'$ means 'the intension (or sense) of β''. Thus each member of a complex category A/B is interpreted as denoting a function which takes as argument intensions of expressions of category B; applying that function to that argument gives the interpretation of the resultant A-phrase. For example, the function corresponding to 'rapidly' applied to the sense of 'run' gives the interpretation of 'run rapidly'; the function corresponding to 'in' applied to the sense of the T-phrase 'the park' gives the interpretation of 'in the park'.

Linguists lost interest in CAT grammar when it was shown to be a subcase of *CF*-grammar, since at that time the focus was on pure syntax.

The original point of CAT grammar, however, was to connect syntactic and semantic structure in a certain way. David Lewis (1971) suggests using a pure (i.e. *CF*) CAT grammar for the base component of a transformational grammar. Montague, who has no base component *per se*, makes use of the basic CAT notions in a system of syntactic rules not restricted to *CF* rules, and keeps the close correspondence between syntactic and semantic rules as the central feature of the CAT idea. The CAT rules, which he calls rules of functional application because of their semantic interpretation, do not exhaust the grammar: however, they may be viewed roughly as those rules which define the basic grammatical relations among the parts of simple sentences; there are additional rules for conjunction, relative clauses, quantification, tenses, and negation, to which we now turn.

1.2. *Other Rules of PTQ: Quantification*

To illustrate the workings of the rest of the grammar of *PTQ*, we will describe Montague's treatment of quantification.

Probably the most novel feature of Montague's treatment is that quantifier phrases such as *every man, the unicorn, a woman* are analyzed as term phrases along with *John* and *Mary*. Although such an analysis is not linguistically novel (both sorts have been traditionally called *NP*), it goes against the treatment of quantifier expressions, first suggested by Frege, that opened up the way for the development of quantificational logic and has become standard in logic. The standard logical analysis of, say, *every man runs* would be written as (6):

(6) $(\forall x)(Mx \rightarrow Rx)$.

What looked like a term phrase in the English sentence does not appear as a constituent in the logical expression, but is rather reanalyzed into the whole frame in which '*R*' appears. A proper name, on the other hand, does show up as a simple term-expression in standard logical notation; thus *John runs* would be simply *Rj*.

The way Montague manages a uniform treatment of *every man* and *John* is to interpret both as denoting sets of properties of individual concepts. The individual concept of John is the function which picks out John at each possible world and time. The constant *j* in the intensional logic is of category *e* and simply denotes the individual John (assuming

we have fixed on a particular interpretation of the constants of the intensional logic.) The individual concept of John is denoted by $^\wedge j$, where '$^\wedge$'
means 'intension of'. The term-phrase *John* in the English fragment is not
translated simply as j or as $^\wedge j$, however; it is translated as $\widehat{P} P\{^\wedge j\}$, the set
of all properties of the individual concept of John. There is a one-one
correspondence between individuals and the set of all properties of their
individual concepts; the only reason for giving such a 'higher-order' treatment of the proper nouns is that phrases like *every man* can also be interpreted as sets or properties of individual concepts, and in this way the
desired unification of term-phrases can be achieved. The syntactic rule
which creates quantifier phrases is given below as (7):

(7)   If $\alpha \in P_{CN}$, then $F_0(\alpha)$, $F_1(\alpha)$, $F_2(\alpha) \in P_T$, where
$$F_0(\alpha) = \textit{every } \alpha$$
$$F_1(\alpha) = \textit{the } \alpha$$
$$F_2(\alpha) = a/an\ \alpha.$$

The corresponding translation rule is (8).

(8)   If α translates into α', then

$F_0(\alpha)$ translates into $\widehat{P}[(\forall x)(\alpha'(x) \rightarrow P\{x\})]$

$F_1(\alpha)$ translates into $\widehat{P}[(\exists y)((\forall x)[\alpha'(x) \leftrightarrow x = y] \land P\{y\})]$

$F_2(\alpha)$ translates into $\widehat{P}[(\exists x)(\alpha'(x) \land P\{x\})]$.

Thus *every man* is interpreted as denoting the set of all properties which
every man has; *the king* as denoting the set of all properties such that
there is a unique entity which is a king and he has those properties; *a fish*
as denoting the set of all properties which some fish has (the union of all
the properties of all the fish there are).

A related innovation of Montague's treatment is that when a term-phrase
and an *IV*-phrase are combined to form a sentence, it is the term-phrase
which is viewed as function and the *IV*-phrase as argument. Thus the
translations of *John runs* and *every man runs* come out schematically as
(9) and (10) respectively:

(9)   *John'* ($^\wedge$*run'*)
(10)   *every man'* ($^\wedge$*run'*).

What (9) says is that the property of running is in the set of properties of
(the individual concept of) John, which is logically equivalent (at least
given certain of the meaning postulates of *PTQ* regarding the extension-

ality of *run*, etc.) to saying that John has the property of running. Expression (10) says, in a parallel manner, that the property of running is in the set of properties shared by every man, which is likewise equivalent to the usual logical formulation. The ultimate logical interpretations of these sentences are thus just the standard ones; what is new is being able to get to those interpretations from a syntax that assigns proper names and quantifier phrases to the same syntactic category.

In the sentences just discussed, the term-phrases were introduced into the sentence directly by the CAT rules; but they may also be introduced via substitution for free variables, a mechanism necessary to account for ambiguities of scope. The rule for sentence-scope quantification is given in a rough form in (11):

(11)   If $\alpha \in P_T$ and $\phi \in P_t$, then $F_{10,n}(\alpha, \phi) \in P_t$, where $F_{10,n}$ is as illustrated below:

Let $\alpha = every\ unicorn$, $\phi = he_0$ *seeks a woman such that she loves him$_0$*

Then $F_{10,0}(\alpha, \phi) = every\ unicorn\ seeks\ a\ woman\ such\ that\ she$ *loves it.*

What the rule does is combine a term phrase and a sentence (an open sentence in all the non-vacuous cases) with respect to a given free variable in the sentence (the subscript n of the syntactic-operation-schema $F_{10,n}$), by substituting the term phrase for the first occurrence of the variable and appropriate pronouns for the subsequent occurrences. The corresponding translation rule is (12):

(12)   If α, ϕ translate into α', ϕ' respectively, then $F_{10,n}(\alpha, \phi)$ translates into $\alpha'(\hat{x}_n\phi')$.

This interpretation comes out just like the interpretation of *John runs* or *every man runs* described above, except that instead of the simple property of running we have whatever property of x_n (which corresponds, albeit indirectly, to *he$_n$*) is expressed by the sentence ϕ.

To illustrate the treatment of scope ambiguity we will show two *analysis trees* for sentence (13) below. An analysis tree is a graphic representation of the steps by which a sentence has been constructed (more like a *T*-marker in pre-1965 transformational theory than like a *P*-marker), with each node labelled by an expression and an index indicating the structural operation that was applied to form it, the nodes immediately beneath in-

dicating the expressions from which it was formed. The two analysis trees
(13a′) and (13b′) correspond to the interpretations given as (13a) and
(13b). The only structural operations labelled in the trees are those that
have been presented here.

(13)   A woman loves every man.
(13a) $(\exists x)\,(\text{woman}\,(x) \wedge (\forall y)\,(\text{man}\,(y) \rightarrow \text{loves}\,(x, y)))$
(13b) $(\forall y)\,(\text{man}\,(y) \rightarrow (\exists x)\,(\text{woman}\,(x) \wedge \text{loves}\,(x, y)))$
(13a′)

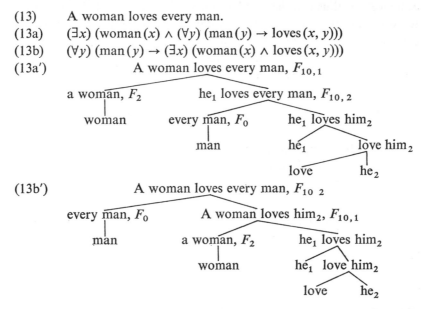

Such trees bear a striking resemblance to the abstract trees found in
generative semantic treatments of quantifiers; in particular, a higher position in the tree indicates wider scope, and the quantificational substitution rule is analogous to quantifier-lowering. On the other hand, since the
trees are not P-markers, they do not represent constituent structure, and
no grammatical relation is said to hold between a quantifier phrase and
the sentence with which it is combined. The syntactic rules generate well-
formed ('surface') expressions directly without ill-formed 'deeper' structures, with the sole exception of the occurrence of the free variables he_0,
he_1 etc. The 'abstractness' which is needed for the semantic rules to
correctly interpret the expressions is provided not by a labelled bracketing assigned to the generated expressions themselves (Montague doesn't
assign any, although it is a natural extension to make), but by the analysis
tree which is in a sense a partly temporal respresentation. For instance,
the two analyses of sentence (13) differ not in their parts or the gram-

matical relations between them, but in the order in which those parts were put together.

This point may be clarified by anticipating the first addition to the system to be proposed in the next section, namely the addition of labelled bracketing. If we assign to each generated expression a labelled bracketing, or *P*-marker, then at each node of the analysis tree there will be a *P*-marker, not simply a string. Then the analogy between an analysis tree and a *T*-marker becomes even stronger: each generated expression is given a *P*-marker which shows its internal constituent structure and to which subsequent syntactic rules may be sensitive, while the analysis tree shows its derivational history, and it is to the latter that the semantic interpretation rules correspond. Note that there is no single level corresponding to 'deep structure' in anybody's sense, since PS-like rules and transformation-like rules are not distinguished and there is no extrinsic rule ordering.

There is much more that could be said about the grammar of *PTQ*, but I want to turn now to some suggestions for extending it to include transformations.

2. TRANSFORMATIONAL EXTENSIONS

2.0. *Introduction*

The fragment Montague chose to develop was semantically a very rich one, including as it did quantification, verbs of propositional attitude, verb-phrase adverbs, *be*, and *necessarily*; but syntactically it was quite simple,[15] and the rules given provide no basis for conjecturing what Montague would have done about such classic constructions as passive sentences, reflexive pronouns,[16] or the *easy-to-please* construction. The rest of the paper is concerned with the question of whether and how such constructions can be accommodated within Montague's framework. I will suggest two additions to the framework itself, labelled bracketing and a 'starred variable convention', additions which seem to me natural and helpful although I have no proof that they are indispensable. With these two general additions and a few grammar-specific departures from the usual ways of stating certain transformations, I will sketch a way to add to Montague's grammar rules for reflexive, passive, 'tough-movement' (='easy-to-please'), subject-raising, object-raising, and derived verb phrases in general. I will also discuss some problems raised by apparent dialect differences with respect to various types of scope ambiguity.

2.1. *Labelled Bracketing*

In addition to the generally acknowledged need for labelled bracketing
in the statement of transformational rules, there is some internal evidence
in *PTQ* that the addition of labelled bracketing would be helpful, if not
indispensable.[17] One of Montague's rules adds a subject-agreement
morpheme to the first verb of a verb phrase when the verb phrase is combined with a subject to make a sentence. Thus *John* plus *walk* becomes
John walks. But *PTQ* also contains a verb-phrase conjunction rule, so the
grammar, incorrectly, generates *John walks and talk*, with *talk* instead of
talks. The problem that arises in attempting to correct the agreement rule
is with verb phrases like *try to walk and talk*, which are ambiguous. The
ambiguity shows up in the analysis tree, of course, and can be represented
by labelled bracketing as

$$_{IV}[_{IV}[\text{try to }_{IV}[\text{walk}]] \text{ and } _{IV}[\text{talk}]] \text{ vs } [\text{try to }_{IV}[_{IV}[\text{walk}] \text{ and } _{IV}[\text{talk}]]].$$

A rule sensitive to the bracketing could assign subject-agreement correctly,
giving *John tries to walk and talks* and *John tries to walk and talk*, respectively, while a rule operating only on strings could not make such a dis-
crimination.

   I will thus assume that labelled bracketing is a desirable addition to the
theory; as for implementing it, it is straightforward for all the rules which
are analogous to *PS*-rules, and I will just leave open for the time being
the details of what labelled bracketing to assign in cases where the rules
add grammatical morphemes which are not themselves assigned to any
category, or in other ways lead to indeterminacies of bracketing. I assume
that either some general principles can eventually be found to cover such
cases, or the derived structure will have to be determined for each such
rule on the basis of the requirements of subsequent rules, and explicitly
stated (as in current transformational practice, or an idealization thereof.)

2.2. *Semantic Constraint*

The constraint which Montague's theory imposes on the addition of transformational rules is that, as for all syntactic rules, there must be a single
uniform translation rule for each *T*-rule. The translation rule must be
such that the translation of the input expression(s) must occur intact in

the translation of the output; translation rules cannot change the interpretation of expressions which have already been built up by preceding rules. In the case of meaning-preserving transformations, this requirement presents no problem, since the corresponding translation rule will just be the identity mapping. So now that labelled bracketings have been added, any 'purely stylistic' transformations can be added to the grammar in essentially their usual form. (For consistency, they would be worded as follows:

'If $\phi \in P_t$ and ϕ is of the form ..., then ... $\in P_t$',

where the first '...' would be filled by the structural description and the second by the structural change.)

But the semantic constraint does pose a problem for the statement of rules that involve deletion, such as all the rules which include equi-*NP* deletion, since the translation rules must always preserve what has been built up so far, and can never delete anything. In the rules sketched below, there are two grammar-particular innovations introduced to accommodate rules which have traditionally involved deletion: in the agentless passive, what is usually called agent-deletion is expressed as a rule which syntactically deletes a free variable but semantically adds an existential quantifier over that variable; for derived verb phrases in general, a rule is introduced which syntactically deletes a free variable he_i from subject position but semantically adds an 'abstraction operator' $\hat{x}_i$ to the translation of the input expression. Thus in both cases the problem is solved by finding a way of interpreting syntactic deletion as semantic addition, and it seems to me that the resulting semantic interpretations are indeed correct. It is of course an open question whether such an approach is the best in the long run, but at least the first major obstacle to synthesizing the two theories has been overcome.

2.3. *Six Transformations*

In this section I sketch, not completely rigorously, rules for reflexivization, passivization, passive agent deletion, tough-movement, subject-raising, and object-rasising. Most of these rules can be stated in essentially their classical forms; I include them primarily to show their interaction with the derived verb-phrase rule presented in Section 2.4 below. Several of the rules are given in two forms, a 'strict form' and a 'loose form', which

I will relate to the questions of conflicting judgments of scope ambiguity.

2.3.1. *Reflexive.* If $\phi \in P_t$ and ϕ is a simplex sentence[18] of the form α $he_i\ \beta\ him_i\ \gamma$, then $F_{100}(\phi) \in P_t$, where $F_{100}(\phi) = \alpha\ he_i\ \beta\ him_i\ self\ \gamma$.[19]
  Example: he_3 sees $him_3 \rightarrow he_3$ sees him_3 self.
  Translation rule: identity mapping.

2.3.2. *Passive.* If $\phi \in P_t$ and ϕ has the form:

(a)   *strict form:* $_t[_T[\alpha]_{IV}[_{TV}[\beta]_T[him_i]\ \gamma]]$
(b)   *loose form:* $_t[_T[\alpha]_{IV}[_{TV}[\beta]_T[\delta]\ \gamma]]$
        then $F_{101}(\phi) \in P_t$, where $F_{101}(\phi)$ is:

$$_t[_T[\begin{Bmatrix}(a)\ he_i \\ (b)\ \delta\end{Bmatrix}]_{IV}[is\ EN_{TV}[\beta]\gamma\ [by_T[\alpha]]]]]$$

Example: John sees $him_2 \rightarrow he_2$ is seen by John.
Translation rule: identity mapping.

2.3.3. *Passive agent deletion.* If $\phi \in P_t$ and ϕ has the form:

  $_t[_T[he_i]_{IV}[is\ EN_{TV}[\beta]\ [by\ him_j]]]$
  then $F_{102}(\phi) \in P_t$, where $F_{102}(\phi)$ is:
  $_t[_T[he_i]_{IV}\ [is\ En_{TV}[\beta]]]$

Example: he_1 is loved by $him_3 \rightarrow he_1$ is loved.
Translation rule: If $\phi \in P_t$ and ϕ translates into ϕ', then $F_{102}(\phi)$
        translates into $(\exists x_j)\ \phi'$.

2.3.4. *Tough-movement.* (In stating this rule I have to make the contrary-to-fact assumption that the fragment already contains a syntactic category *AP* (adjective phrase), a subcategory of adjectives A_E, containing *easy, tough*, etc., and infinitive phrases in subject position.)

        If $\phi \in P_t$ and ϕ has the form:
        $_t[_{INF}[\beta\ him_i\ \gamma]_{IV}[is_{AP}[A_E\ [\alpha]]]]$
        then $F_{103}(\phi) \in P_t$, where $F_{103}(\phi)$ is:
        $_t[_T[he_i]_{IV}[is_{AP}\ [A_E[\alpha]]_{INF}\ [\beta\ \gamma]]]$.

  Example: to please him_7 is easy $\rightarrow he_7$ is easy to please.
  Translation rule: identity mapping
  N.B. The above is the strict version; the loose version would have δ in place of him_i.

2.3.5. *Subject raising.* Here I will just indicate the rule by an example. The strict version requires the moved *T*-phrase to be a variable, the loose version does not.

Example: it seems that he$_6$ is happy → he$_6$ seems to be happy
Translation rule: identity mapping.

2.3.6. *Object raising.* Same comments and translation rule as above. John believes that he$_3$ is a fool → John believes him$_3$ to be a fool.

Aside from the question of which constituents are required to be free variables, the only innovation in the rules above is in the treatment of passive agent deletion. There have been two main proposals in the previous transformational literature, one that what is deleted is the word *someone* and the other that it is an 'unspecified *NP*'. I have nothing to say about the latter because its semantic interpretation has never been made explicit, but some comparisons can be made between the treatment above and *someone*-deletion. There is a minor problem with *someone*-deletion in that the deleted agent need not always be animate, but that could be rectified. The problem I am interested in lies in the interpretation of the relative scope of the existential quantifier associated with the deleted agent and any other quantifiers that may occur in the sentence. In the rule as stated above I have only dealt with the subject and object term-phrases, but the treatment could be extended to cover all the term-phrases in the same simplex sentence, or whatever the actual restrictions should be. Consider the following sets of sentences.

(14)   (a) Someone has reviewed all of John's books.
        (b) All of John's books have been reviewed by someone.
        (c) All of John's books have been reviewed.
(15)   (a) Someone caught three fish.
        (b) Three fish were caught by someone.
        (c) Three fish were caught.

Judgments differ as to how many readings the (a) and (b) sentences have, but the (c) sentences are uniformly judged to be unambiguous, with the deleted quantifier having narrower scope than the remaining quantifier. If the (c) sentences were derived from (b) sentences, then those speakers who allow a wide-scope reading for *someone* in the (b) sentences should also do so for the (c) sentences, but they don't. The analysis presented above captures this fact by requiring deletion to occur while both term-phrases are free variables, and existentially quantifying over the deleted variable in the translation of the result. Thus the remaining variable, the derived subject, has to be quantified *after* the deleted variable, and therefore will necessarily be interpreted as having wider scope.

The other matter to be discussed before going on to the derived verb phrase rule is the question of interpretations of scope and the strict vs loose forms of the rules. The sorts of examples we are concerned with here include, for instance the (a)–(b) pairs of sentences (14) and (15) above, and sentences (16a–b) below, which were discussed in Chomsky (1957) and more extensively in Katz and Postal (1964).

(16)   (a) Everyone in this room speaks two languages.
        (b) Two languages are spoken by everyone in this room.

Now although the problem of the order of interpretation of quantifiers has many ramifications and undoubtedly involves a large number of interacting factors,[20] I want to focus on two idealized 'dialects' and their implications for whether the movement rules given above should be restricted to free variables or not. In what I will call the 'loose dialect', the (a)–(b) pairs are fully synonymous, each having two readings. (Factors such as left-right order may make one reading preferred over the other, but I am only concerned with how many readings should be generated at all.) In the 'strict dialect', each sentence has only one reading, with the subject quantifier having wider scope.

For the loose dialect, the unrestricted form of the transformations is a meaning-preserving rule; the active sentence is generated as ambiguous and can be transformed into the passive on either reading. For the strict dialect, constraints will have to be added to block one of the readings of the active sentence, which is generated as ambiguous in Montague's system. One kind of constraint might be an analog to Lakoff's derivational constraints, which could be easily added to Montague's rules (it would represent an extension of the theory, but would be no harder to formulate than for a generative semantics theory); if that were done, it would not be necessary to restrict the individual rules. But what leads me to posit the restriction of movement rules to the movement of free variables is that I suspect there may be a correlation between quantifier scope interpretation and 'dialect differences'[21] in two other phenomena. One is the breaking up of idioms, as in (17) and (18), which some but not all speakers accept:

(17)   Track was kept of the proceedings.
(18)   Little heed was paid to my warnings.

The loose form of the passive rule would permit such sentences while the tight form would not, since the superficial term-phrases *track* and *little heed* should presumably not be allowed to substitute for free variables. The other related phenomenon is opacity: sentence (19a) below has both a specific and a non-specific (or referential and non-referential, or *de re* and *de dicto*) reading, but judgments differ as to whether (19b) is likewise ambiguous or allows only the specific reading.

(19a)   John is looking for a green-eyed woman.
(19b)   A green-eyed woman is being looked for by John.

Again the two forms of the rule would make different predictions: the loose form would give (19b) both of the readings of (19a), while the strict form would predict (19a) to be ambiguous but (19b) to have only a specific reading.

Now *if* (a big if) judgments on these three phenomena were found to correlate strongly, that would suggest that there really might be a difference in people's grammars in whether moved T-phrases were restricted to variables or not. Even if matters are not this simple, as they undoubtedly are not, there still might be some psychological reality to both forms of the rules, with the strict form of the rule its fundamental form, providing the main reason why such a rule is in the grammar at all (see especially the next section, where moved free variables are crucially involved in derived verb-phrase formation), and the loose form a 'surface structure analog' of the strict rule, invoked mainly for stylistic variation. This is all much too vague to form an empirical hypothesis of any sort yet, however.

The examples above all dealt with the passive rule, but the same phenomena are to be found in connection with the other rules as well. Consider, for instance, tough-movement: since almost no one interprets (20a) and (20b) as synonymous, it might seem that only the strict form of the rule should be allowed, but the usual interpretation of (21) can be gotten only with the loose form.

(20a)   It is hard to catch every cockroach.
(20b)   Every cockroach is hard to catch.
(21)   A good man is hard to find.

In the case of subject-raising, sentences (22a, b) illustrate the quantifier scope problem and sentences (23a, b) the opacity problem. In my (un-systematic) experience, there are considerable differences of judgment here, plus plenty of 'undecided's'.

(22a)   It seems that some man loves every woman.
(22b)   Some man seems to love every woman.
(23a)   It appears that a unicorn is approaching
(23b)   A unicorn appears to be approaching.

(Montague in *PTQ* accepts (23a) and (23b) as synonymous, with two readings each, although he does not give rules to derive them.)

For object-raising, the data is particularly slippery, partly because there is a third construction whose syntactic relation to the other two is not clear.

(24a)   John believes that a woman robbed the bank.
(24b)   John believes a woman to have robbed the bank.
(24c)   John believes of a woman that she robbed the bank.

While (24a) pretty clearly allows both a specific and a non-specific read-ing, and (24c) only a specific one, (24b) seems to be hard to get clear judgments on. For the loose dialect it should be the case that not only does (24b) share the ambiguity of (24a), but so should (25), the passive of (24b).

(25)   A woman is believed by John to have robbed the bank.

If others share my intuition that it is twice as hard to get a non-refer-ential reading of *a woman* in (25) as in (24b) or a simple passive like (19b), that would be further evidence that this is not really a simple matter of dialect split nor a matter of restrictions on individual rules.

Having reached no conclusions as to the correct version of the rules given above, let us turn to the next section, for which the only crucial thing is that what gets moved *may* be a free variable, which is the case under either formulation.

2.4. *Derived Verb Phrases: Abstraction*

The rule to be given below provides a way to account for the occurrence in verb-phrase conjunction and in infinitives of verb phrases that are not built up directly in the CAT part of the grammar. It will thus allow us to provide for sentences like (26) and (27), which could not be generated in *PTQ*.

(26)   Few rules are both explicit and *easy to read.*

(27)   John wishes *to see himself.*

The rule requires the addition of a syntactic metarule, which is given below.

Derived verb phrase rule. If $\phi \in P_t$ and ϕ has the form $_t[_T[he_i]_{IV}[\alpha]]$, then $F_{104}(\phi) \in P_{IV}$, where $F_{104}(\phi) = \alpha'$, and α' comes from α by replacing each occurrence of he_i, him_i, $him_i self$ by he^*, him^*, $him^* self$ respectively.

Examples: F_{104} (he$_0$ sees him$_0$ self) = see him*self.
$\qquad$ F_{104} (he$_7$ is easy to please) = be easy to please.

Translation rule: If $\phi \in P_t$ and ϕ translates into ϕ', then $F_{104}(\phi)$ translates into $\hat{x}_i \phi'$.

Starred variable convention (syntactic metarule): Whenever any syntactic rule applies to two (or more) arguments such that one is a *T*-phrase and one contains a starred variable, replace all occurrences of the starred variable by pronouns of the appropriate gender.

Example: Mary + try to see him*self → Mary tries to see herself.

The derived verb phrase rule transforms a sentence into a verb phrase; the resulting verb phrase can then be used just like any other verb phrase in building up larger phrases. It can, for instance, enter into verb-phrase conjunction, as in (26); it can serve as a complement to verbs such as *wish* and *try*;[22] it can combine with verb-phrase adverbs. The derived verb phrase rule is incompatible with the usual transformational framework, either standard or generative semantic, since the transformationally derived verb phrase is permitted to recombine with new elements via essentially CF rules. However, it seems to offer a maximally simple way to reconcile the syntactic arguments for deriving certain phrases from whole sentences with the semantic arguments against doing so (as discussed, for instance, in Partee (1970).)

The semantic interpretation of the derived verb phrase makes use of an abstraction operator. If the translation of *he_0 sees him_0 self* is $see'(x_0, x_0)$ (a rough approximation to the *PTQ* translation), then the translation of its derivative *see him*self* will be $\hat{x}_0(see'(x_0, x_0))$, i.e. the property of seeing oneself. Since the abstraction operator binds the free variables, there is no further semantic need to keep track of the variables in the underlying sentence; but syntactically the pronouns must be made to agree with whatever term-phrase that property is eventually connected with, and that is the function of the starred variable convention.

The starred variable convention is closely analogous to Rosenbaum's minimum distance principle, except that topographical nearness is replaced by a relation which centers on the analysis tree: the term-phrase that picks up the starred variable is the first term-phrase to be combined as a constituent with the phrase containing the derived verb phrase. If *persuade to* is added to the fragment as *TV/IV*, then *persuade to* would combine with *see him*self* to form a *TV*-phrase *persuade to see him*self*; then the *TV + T-phrase → IV* rule would combine that with *Mary* and the result would be (with appropriate reordering) *persuade Mary to see herself* since the starred variable convention would apply. Richmond Thomason (personal communication) has pointed out that if *promise* is assigned to the category *(IV//IV)/T*, the difference between *promise* and *persuade* will be correctly represented with this starred variable convention; the correct predictions will be made about sentences (28) and (29) below.

(28)   John persuaded Mary to shoot $\left\{\begin{array}{c}\text{*himself}\\\text{herself}\end{array}\right\}$

(29)   John promised Mary to shoot $\left\{\begin{array}{c}\text{himself}\\\text{*herself}\end{array}\right\}$

In conclusion, I will sketch the analysis trees for some sentences whose derivations involve the derived verb phrase rule.

(30)   Every man tries to be found by a woman who loves him

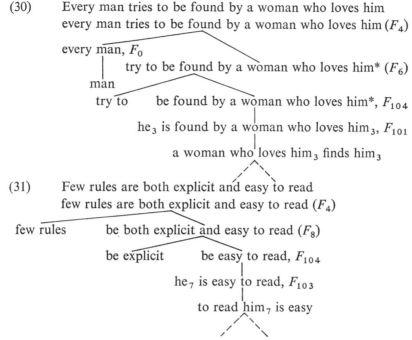

(31)   Few rules are both explicit and easy to read

University of Massachusetts at Amherst

NOTES

* This paper is a written version of a talk given in April, 1972, in the Linguistics and Semantics Workshop at the University of Western Ontario. A preliminary version was given in March at the University of Massachusetts at Amherst, and a version was also given at a colloquium at UC San Diego. The first part of the paper, like the first part of the talks, is a condensation of a talk which I gave in various forms and places in the fall and winter 1971–72. A fuller treatment of the same subject can be found in my 'Montague Grammar and Transformational Grammar'. My debts to others in this work are too numerous to list here, but I must at least mention Richmond Thomason, whose suggestions about the abstraction operator helped me get my first ideas about how to accommodate transformations in the Montague framework; Michael Bennett, whose continuing extensions of Montague's work have fertilized and challenged my own; David Kaplan, who has given me constant encouragement and taught me a great deal about philosophy and logic; and of course Richard Montague and Noam Chomsky, without whom I wouldn't have had a starting point. I am also grateful to all the students and other audiences who have given me helpful comments and criticisms, particularly the linguistics and philosophy students in my Montague seminar at UCLA, Winter-Spring, 1972.

¹ The exceptions include the work of Reichenbach (1947) and the exhortation to collaboration made by Bar-Hillel (1954), rebuffed by Chomsky (1955).

² "Simplification of theory is a central motive likewise of the sweeping artificialities of notation in modern logic. Clearly, it would be folly to burden a logical theory with quirks of usage that we can straighten. If we were to devise a logic of ordinary language for direct use on sentences as they come, we would have to complicate our rules of inference in sundry unilluminating ways." (Quine (1960), p. 158) As an example: "Our ordinary language shows a tiresome bias in its treatment of time... [*T*] he form that it takes – that of requiring that every verb form show a tense – is peculiarly productive of needless complications.... Hence in fashioning canonical notations it is usual to drop tense distinctions."

³ Tarski pointed out to me (pers. communication, 1971) that the substitutional view of quantification, as found in the work of Ruth Barcan Marcus, is an example of a departure from the scheme described above.

⁴ Actually, it appears that this principle is being abandoned, and generative semanticists are coming to view their work more as 'abstract syntax', a view that would make their approach compatible with the traditional logical approach.

⁵ Some central references for the two approaches are Lakoff (1971), (1972), Chomsky (1971), and Jackendoff (1969).

⁶ I am purposely ignoring here the question of the deep structure of the relative clause itself, although that also makes a great difference to the semantics.

⁷ For a review of a number of such arguments, see Stockwell *et al.* (1973).

⁸ The semantics here is basically from Montague; the discussion of alternatives is my own.

⁹ This view of the semantics of restrictive relative clauses is not unique to Montague; it can also be found in Quine (1960).

¹⁰ The syntactic and semantic details of such an analysis can be found in Montague (1972).

¹¹ I realize that negative arguments such as those given here against analyses (1) and (2) can never be fully conclusive; the discussion should be construed as a semantic defense of (3) plus a challenge to proponents of (1) or (2) to provide a semantic analysis that supports their syntax. The argument against (2) is weaker than that against (1), since only in (1) is the intermediate constituent called an *NP*.

¹² The originator of categorial grammar was the Polish logician Ajdukiewicz; for exposition see Lewis (1971).

¹³ Although in one sense it is correct to speak of the categories as being defined by these specifications, it should be borne in mind that in another sense the categories are defined only implicitly, by the totality of the rules of the grammar.

¹⁴ The two exceptions are *IV* and *CN*, since the set of expressions of category *e* is empty.

¹⁵ The syntactic simplicity was intentional since Montague's interest was in semantics. In the opening paragraph of *PTQ* he says, "For expository purposes the fragment has been made as simple and restricted as it can be while accommodating all the more puzzling cases of quantification and reference with which I am acquainted."

¹⁶ An earlier paper, Montague (1970a), does have a footnote suggesting a treatment of reflexive pronouns to which the one proposed here is almost identical; essentially the same treatment is found in earlier works by generative semanticists. What Montague did not have was a way to generate infinitive phrases containing reflexive pronouns.

¹⁷ The reason I am not prepared to claim that labelled bracketing is indispensable is that in Montague's system rules can, in principle, refer to the derivational history of a

string, and I have no clear cases where that would not suffice. But with labelled bracketing added, one would be free to investigate the possibility of constraining the rules so that only the bracketing, and not arbitrary aspects of the derivational history, could be used by the (syntactic) rules.

[18] This condition needs to be made precise; a first approximation would be to say ϕ contains only one verb (i.e. one basic expression of category IV, TV, IV/t, or $IV//IV$.)

[19] As presented, this rule would have to be obligatory, which would be the first such rule in the grammar. An alternative might be to build reflexivization into the rule that combines subject and verb phrase to make a sentence.

[20] These matters have been discussed extensively in the literature; see, for example, Lakoff (1971) and Jackendoff (1969). Among the factors I think are involved are not only the structural factors of dominance and left-right order, and stress, but also individual differences in 'strength' or 'precedence' among the various quantifiers, and, to complicate matters, non-linguistic judgments of absurdity vs plausibility of the different structurally possible interpretations.

[21] I am very hesitant to call any of these differences dialect differences because I have no conviction that what is going on is to be accounted for in terms of differences in grammatical rules, and I also have no evidence that these 'dialects' are related to speech communities. See Gleitman and Gleitman (1970) for a study of similar problems relating to the interpretation of noun compounds.

[22] We have several choices as to the handling of infinitival complements. The derived verb phrase rule gives appropriate inputs to the PTQ rule which combines *try to* with an *IV*-phrase; or we could add a rule forming infinitives from *IV*-phrases by systematically adding *to* and semantically taking the intension of the *IV*-phrase translation, and let *try* take an infinitive-phrase. We could also let *try* take as complement a sentence with a free variable as subject, with infinitive-formation part of the rule for combining them.

BIBLIOGRAPHY

Bar-Hillel, Yeshoshua: 1954, 'Logical Syntax and Semantics', *Language* 30, 230–237.

Chomsky, Noam: 1955, 'Logical Syntax and Semantics: Their Linguistic Relevance', *Language* 31, 36–45.

Chomsky, Noam: 1957, *Syntactic Structures,* The Hague.

Chomsky, Noam: 1971, 'Deep Structure, Surface Structure, and Semantic Interpretation', in Steinberg and Jakobovits, 1971, 183–216.

Gleitman, Lila and Gleitman, Henry: 1970, *Phrase and Paraphrase,* New York.

Harman, Gilbert and Davidson, Donald: 1971, *Semantics of Natural Languages,* Dordrecht.

Hintikka, Jaakko, Moravcsik, Julius, and Suppes, Patrick: 1972, *Approaches to Natural Language,* Dordrecht, 1973.

Jackendoff, Ray: 1969, *Some Rules of Semantic Interpretation for English,* MIT dissertation.

Katz, Jerrold: 1966, *The Philosophy of Language,* New York.

Katz, Jerrold and Postal, Paul: 1964, *An Integrated Theory of Linguistic Descriptions,* Cambridge.

Lakoff, George: 1971, 'On Generative Semantics', in Steinberg and Jakobovits, 1971, 232–296.

Lakoff, George: 1972, 'Linguistics and Natural Logic', in Harman and Davidson, 1971, 545–665.

220 BARBARA PARTEE

Lewis, David: 1971, 'General Semantics' *Synthese* **22**, 18–67.

Montague, Richard: 1970a, 'English as a Formal Language', in Visentini *et al.*, 1970, 189–224

Montague, Richard: 1970b, 'Universal Grammar', *Theoria* **36**, 373–398.

Montague, Richard: 1972, 'The Proper Treatment of Quantification in Ordinary English' in Hintikka *et al.*, 1973, 221–242.

Partee, Barbara: 1970, 'Negation, Conjunction, and Quantifiers: Syntax vs Semantics', *Foundations of Language* **6**, 153–165.

Quine, W. V.: 1960, *Word and Object,* Cambridge.

Reichenbach, Hans: 1947, *Elements of Symbolic Logic,* New York.

Steinberg, Danny and Jakobovits, Leon: 1971, *Semantics,* Cambridge, England.

Stockwell, Robert, Schachter, Paul, and Partee, Barbara: 1973, *The Major Syntactic Structures of English*, New York.

Tarski, Alfred: 1944, 'The Semantic Conception of Truth', *Philosophy and Phenomenological Research* **4**, 341–375.

Vermazen, Bruce: 1967, 'A review of Katz and Postal (1964) and Katz (1966)', *Synthese* **17**, 350–365.

Visentini, Bruno, *et al.*: 1970, *Linguaggi nella societa e nella tecnica,* Milan.

GEORGE LAKOFF

HEDGES: A STUDY IN MEANING CRITERIA AND THE LOGIC OF FUZZY CONCEPTS*

1. DEGREES OF TRUTH

Logicians have, by and large, engaged in the convenient fiction that sentences of natural languages (at least declarative sentences) are either true or false or, at worst, lack a truth value, or have a third value often interpreted as 'nonsense'. And most contemporary linguists who have thought seriously about semantics, especially formal semantics, have largely shared this fiction, primarily for lack of a sensible alternative. Yet students of language, especially psychologists and linguistic philosophers, have long been attuned to the fact that natural language concepts have vague boundaries and fuzzy edges and that, consequently, natural language sentences will very often be neither true, nor false, nor nonsensical, but rather true to a certain extent and false to a certain extent, true in certain respects and false in other respects.

It is common for logicians to give truth conditions for predicates in terms of classical set theory. 'John is tall' (or 'TALL (j)') is defined to be true just in case the individual denoted by 'John' (or 'j') is in the set of tall men. Putting aside the problem that tallness is really a relative concept (tallness for a pygmy and tallness for a basketball player are obviously different)[1], suppose we fix a population relative to which we want to define tallness. In contemporary America, how tall do you have to be to be tall? 5'8"? 5'9"? 5'10"? 5'11"? 6'? 6'2"? Obviously there is no single fixed answer. How old do you have to be to be middle-aged? 35? 37? 39? 40? 42? 45? 50? Again the concept is fuzzy. Clearly any attempt to limit truth conditions for natural language sentences to true, false and 'nonsense' will distort the natural language concepts by portraying them as having sharply defined rather than fuzzily defined boundaries.

Work dealing with such questions has been done in psychology. To take a recent example, Eleanor Rosch Heider (1971) took up the question of whether people perceive category membership as a clearcut issue or a matter of degree. For example, do people think of members of a given

*Hockney et al. (eds.), Contemporary Research in Philosophical Logic
and Linguistic Semantics*, 221–271. *All Rights Reserved*
Copyright © 1975 by D. Reidel Publishing Company, Dordrecht-Holland

species as being simply birds or nonbirds, or do people consider them birds to a certain degree? Heider's results consistently showed the latter. She asked subjects to rank birds as to the degree of their birdiness, that is, the degree to which they matched the ideal of a bird. If category membership were simply a yes-or-no matter, one would have expected the subjects either to balk at the task or to produce random results. Instead, a fairly well-defined hierarchy of 'birdiness' emerged.

(1) Birdiness hierarchy

> robins
> eagles
> chickens, ducks, geese
> penguins, pelicans
> bats

Robins are typical of birds. Eagles, being predators, are less typical. Chickens, ducks, and geese somewhat less so. Penguins and pelicans less still. Bats hardly at all. And cows not at all.

A study of vegetableness yielded a similar hierarchical result:

(2) Vegetableness hierarchy

> carrots, asparagus
> celery
> onion
> parsley
> pickle

Further experiments by Heider showed a distinction between central members of a category and peripheral members. She surmised that if subjects had to respond 'true' or 'false' to sentences of the form 'A (member) is a (category)' – for example, 'A chicken is bird' – the response time woulp be faster if the member was a central member (a good example of the category) than if it was a peripheral member (a not very good example of the category). On the assumption that central members are learned earlier than peripheral members, she surmised that children would make more errors on the peripheral members than would adults. (3) lists some of the examples of central and peripheral category members that emerged from the study:

(3)	Category	Central Members	Peripheral Members
	Toy	ball, doll	swing, skates
	bird	robin, sparrow	chicken, duck
	fruit	peaı, banana	strawberry, prune
	sickness	cancer, measles	rheumatism, rickets
	metal	copper, aluminum	magnesium, platinum
	crime	rape, robbery	treason, fraud
	sport	baseball, basketball	fishing, diving
	vehicle	car, bus	tank, carriage
	body part	arm, leg	lips, skin

I think Heider's work shows clearly that category membership is not simply a yes-or-no matter, but rather a matter of degree. Different people may have different category rankings depending on their experience or their knowledge or their beliefs, but the fact of hierarchical ranking seems to me to be indisputable. Robins simply are more typical of birds than chickens and chickens are more typical of birds than penguins, though all are birds to some extent. Suppose now that instead of asking about category membership we ask instead about the truth of sentences that assert category membership. If an X is a member of a category Y only to a certain degree, then the sentence 'An X is a Y' should be true only to that degree, rather than being clearly true or false. My feeling is that this is correct, as (4) indicates.

(4) Degree of truth (corresponding to degree of category membership)

a. A robin is a bird. (true)
b. A chicken is a bird. (less true than a)
c. A penguin is a bird. (less true than b)
d. A bat is a bird. (false, or at least very far from true)
e. A cow is a bird. (absolutely false)

Most speakers I have checked with bear out this judgement, though some seem to collapse the cases in (4a–c), and don't distinguish among them. My guess is that they in general judge the truth of sentences like those in (4) according to the truth of corresponding sentences like those in (5).

(5) a. A robin is more of a bird than anything else. (True)
b. A chicken is more of a bird than anything else. (True)

    c. A penguin is more of a bird than anything else.   (True)
    d. A bat is more of a bird than anything else.   (False)
    e. A cow is more of a bird than anything else.   (False)

That is, some speakers seem to turn relative judgments of category membership into absolute judgments by assigning the member in question to the category in which it has the highest degree of membership. As we shall see below, speakers who judge the sentences in (4) to have a pattern like those in (5) do make the distinctions shown in (4), but then collapse them to the pattern in (5).

2. Fuzzy logic

Although the phenomena discussed above are beyond the bounds of classical set theory and the logics based on it, there is a well-developed set theory capable of dealing with degrees of set membership, namely, fuzzy set theory as developed by Zadeh (1965). The central idea is basically simple: Instead of just being in the set or not, an individual is in the set to a certain degree, say some real number between zero and one.

   (1) Zadeh's Fuzzy Sets

      In a universe of discourse $X = \{x\}$, a fuzzy set A is a set of ordered pairs $\{(x, \mu_A(x))\}$, where $\mu_A(x)$ is understood as the degree of membership of x in A. $\mu_A(x)$ is usually taken to have values in the real interval $[0, 1]$, though the values can also be taken to be members of any distributive complemented lattice.

    Union: $\mu_{A \cup B} = \max(\mu_A, \mu_B)$.
    Complement: $\mu_{A'} = 1 - \mu_A$
    Intersection: $\mu_{A \cap B} = \min(\mu_A, \mu_B)$
    Subset: $A \subseteq B$ iff $\mu_A(x) \leqslant \mu_B(x)$,   for all x in X.
    A fuzzy relation R^n is a fuzzy subset of X^n.

In most of the cases of fuzzy sets that we will be interested in, the membership function is not primitive. That is, in most cases membership functions will assign values between zero and one to individuals on the basis of some property or properties of those individuals. Take tallness for example. How *tall* one is considered to be depends upon what one's *height* is (plus various contextual factors) – and height is given in terms of actual physical measurements. To see how the membership function for tallness might be given (in a fixed context) in terms of height, see Figures 1 and 2. As a subjective approximation we might say

HEIGHT	5'3"	5'5"	5'7"	5'9"	5'11"	6'1"	6'3"
DEGREE OF TALLNESS	0	0.1	0.3	0.55	0.8	0.95	1

Fig. 1.   Subjective assignment of degrees of tallness of men relative to the population of contemporary America.

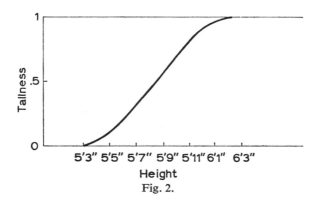

Height
Fig. 2.

that if someone is smaller than 5'3", then he is not tall to any degree. If he is 5'7", we might say that he is tall to, say, degree 0.3. If he is 5'11", we might say that he is tall to, say, degree 0.8. And if he is over 6'3", then he is tall, period. The curve plotted in Figure 2 is not to be taken with great seriousness as to its exactitude. Undoubtedly the function which maps height into tallness is itself fuzzy. However, I do think that the curve in Figure 2 is not a bad approximation to my own intuitions about degrees of tallness. The curve has about the right shape. It rises continuously, as it should. It would be wrong to have a curve that falls or has several dips. It goes up from zero at about the right place and seems to hit one at about the right place. In short, there is far more right than wrong about it, which is what makes it an interesting approximation.

We should also ask how seriously we should take the fact that the function for tallness given in Figure 2 is continuous, assigning an infinite

number of values, in fact filling the uncountable infinity of values in the
real interval between zero and one. After all, human beings cannot perceive that many distinctions. Perhaps it would be psychologically more
real not to have an infinity of degrees of set membership, but rather some
relatively small number of degrees, say the usual 7 ± 2. On the other hand,
one might consider the interesting possibility that the finiteness of human
perceptual distinctions is what might be called a surface phenomenon.
It might be the case that the perception of degrees of tallness is based on
an underlying continuous assignment of values like that given by the
curve in Figure 2. The finite number of perceived distinctions would then
result from 'low level' perceptual factors, though perhaps the number of
perceived distinctions and their distribution would depend on the shape
of the underlying curve (as indicated in Figure 3) and various contextual

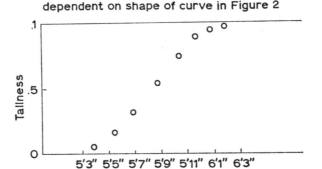

Fig. 3.

factors. I think that the latter proposal has a high degree of plausibility,
and I think that some of the facts discussed below will make it even more
plausible. For this reason, I will stick to continuous assignments of
values.

Given fuzzy sets we can, in a straightforward way extend classical
propositional and predicate logics to the corresponding fuzzy logics.
Take the syntax of a typical propositional logic with '¬', '∧', '∨', '→'
as connectives and 'P', 'Q', ... as propositional variables. Let 'P', 'Q', ...
have values in the closed interval [0, 1], and let P, Q, ... stand for the values

of the propositional variables. Valuations for the connectives are defined as follows:[2]

(2) $|\neg P| = 1 - |P|$
           $|P \wedge Q| = \min(|P|, |Q|)$
           $|P \vee Q| = \max(|P|, |Q|)$
           $|P \rightarrow Q| = 1$ iff $|P| \leqslant |Q|$.

Semantic entailment is defined as follows:

(3) $P \Vdash Q$ iff $|P| \leqslant |Q|$ in all models

As should be obvious:

           $P \Vdash Q$ iff $\Vdash P \rightarrow Q$.

To see what this means, let $P =$ 'John is tall' and $Q =$ 'Bill is rich'. Let $P = 0.7$ and $Q = 0.4$, that is, suppose John is tall to degree 0.7 and Bill is rich to degree 0.4. 'John is not tall' will be true to degree 0.3, while 'Bill is not rich' will be true to degree 0.6. 'John is tall and Bill is rich' will be true to degree 0.4, which is the minimum of 0.7 and 0.4. 'Either John is tall or Bill is rich' will be true to degree 0.7, the maximum of 0.7 and 0.4.

HEIGHT	5′3	5′5″	5′7″	5′9″	5′11″	6′1″	6′3″	6′5″
DEGREE OF 'VERY TALL'	0	0	0.1	0.2	0.5	0.8	0.9	1.0

Fig. 4.   Subjective assignment of degrees to 'very tall' relative to the population of contemporary American men.

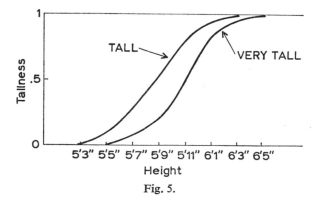

Fig. 5.

For an example of how semantic entailment works, let $P=$'John is very tall' and $Q=$'John is tall'. Clearly P semantically entails Q. Consider an assignment of values to 'very tall', as in Figure 4 and Figure 5.

If you compare the tables in Figures 1 and 4, you will find that in each case, given a height, the value for 'VERY TALL' is *LESS THAN OR EQUAL TO* the value of 'TALL'. For example, at the height of 5'11", the value for 'VERY TALL' is 0.3, while the value for 'TALL' is 0.8. This can be seen clearly in Figure 5, where both curves are given. Thus, no matter what John's height is, the value of 'John is very tall' will be less than or equal to the value of 'John is tall', and by the above definition, the former will semantically entail the latter.

'→' is the fuzzy logic correlate to material implication. '$P \rightarrow Q$' will hold in all cases where there is a real logical implication relation between P and Q, that is, where it is necessarily the case that $|P| \leqslant |Q|$. And like classical material implication, it will also hold in all cases where $|P|$ happens to be less than or equal to $|Q|$. If we restrict ourselves to propositional variables with only the values 0 and 1, '$P \rightarrow Q$' is indistinguishable from '$\neg P \vee Q$'. But when one considers the range of intermediate values between 0 and 1, '$P \rightarrow Q$' becomes very different from '$\neg P \vee Q$'. Given the above semantics, '$P \rightarrow P$' is a tautology, but '$\neg P \vee P$' is not.

Incidentally, I consider it a virtue of this system that '$\neg P \vee P$' is not a tautology. Suppose 'P' is 'This wall is red'. Suppose the wall is pretty red, say, to degree 0.6. Then 'This wall is red or not red' will be true to degree 0.6, according to the given semantics. This seems to me within the range of plausibility. Certainly one would not want to say that the sentence was true in such a situation. Similarly, '$P \wedge \neg P$' is not a contradiction in the above system. And similarly, the sentence 'This wall is red and not red' in the situation given where the wall is red to some extent seems to me not to be false, but rather to have a degree of truth.

Another fact about the fuzzy propositional logic given above is worth noting. Modus ponens is not only a valid form of inference, but it can be generalized so that it preserves degree of truth.

(4) $\vdash_\alpha P$
         $\vdash P \rightarrow Q$
         $\therefore \vdash_\alpha Q$

If we know, given our assumptions, that P is true at least to degree α, and we know that $P \to Q$ is true, then we can be sure that Q is true at least to degree α.

We can get a better idea of what fuzzy propositional logic is like if we look at the classical tautologies that are valid and not valid in FPL.

(5)

NOT VALID IN FPL	*VALID IN FPL*
$P \vee \neg P$	$P \to P$
$P \to (Q \to P)$	$(P \to (Q \to R)) \to$
	$\qquad ((P \to Q) \to (P \to R))$
$\neg P \to (P \to Q)$	$(\neg P \to \neg Q) \to (Q \to P)$
$((P \wedge Q) \to R) \leftrightarrow$	$\neg \neg P \leftrightarrow P$
$\qquad (P \to (Q \to R))$	
$(P \to (Q \wedge \neg Q)) \to \neg P$	$(P \wedge \neg P) \to P$
$(P \wedge \neg P) \to Q$	$((P \to Q) \wedge \neg Q) \to \neg P$
$Q \to (P \vee \neg P)$	$(P \to Q) \to$
	$\qquad ((Q \to R) \to (P \to R))$
The above are true in FPL in all models in which P, Q, and R are either 0 or 1.	De Morgan's Laws Associative Laws Distributive Law Commutative Laws

FPL reduces to ordinary propositional logic when the propositional variables are limited to the values 0 and 1.

Fuzzy propositional logic can be extended to fuzzy predicate logic in a straightforward way by defining valuations for predicates and for quantifiers. Let F be an n-place predicate. We define the value of $Fx_1, \ldots, x_n$ as the degree of membership of the ordered n-tuple $(x_1, \ldots, x_n)$ in the fuzzy set F, where $\bar{x}_i$ is the denotation of x_i on a given valuation. In other words,

$$|Fx_1, \ldots, x_n| = \mu_F(\bar{x}_1, \ldots, \bar{x}_n).$$

For example, suppose we have a one-place predicate TALL. The value of 'TALL(j)' is the degree to which the individual denoted by 'j' is a member of the fuzzy set TALL.

$$|\text{TALL}(j)| = \mu_{\text{TALL}}(j)$$

Valuations for quantifiers are straightforwardly defined. The value of '$\forall x Fx$' is defined as minimum of the values of Fx for all assignments of x

to elements of the universe of discourse. The value of '$\exists x Fx$' is the corresponding maximum.[3] In other words,

(6) $|\forall x Fx| = \min\{|Fx|\}$ for all assignments to x of elements of
                                           the universe of discourse
        $|\exists x Fx| = \max\{|Fx|\}$ for all assignments to x of elements of
                                           the universe of discourse.

We can get a fuzzy modal logic by adding operators '$\Box$' and '$\Diamond$' and giving the following valuations.

(7) $|\Box P|_w = \min\{|P|_{w'}\}$ for all w' such that Rww'
        $|\Diamond P|_w = \max\{|P|_{w'}\}$ for all w' such that Rww',
                          where R is the alternativeness relation.

Note that the value of '$\Box P$' will be equal to some α, $0 < \alpha < 1$, just in case the value of P never falls below α in any alternative world. If '$\Box P$' is interpreted as meaning that P is a necessary truth, then in fuzzy modal logic, we will have degrees of necessary truth, since $|\Box P|$ may fall in between zero and one. This raises the question of whether there are such things as statements which are necessarily true to a degree. The one type of possible example that comes to mind is an arithmetic statement that contains an approximation. For example, consider (8).

(8)   Approximately half of the prime numbers are of the form
                                          $4N + 1$.

Is (8) true? Well, it depends on just what you mean by 'approximately'. But if you leave 'approximately' vague, as it is in normal English, then (8) is certainly not false, though one would, I think, hesitate to say that it is absolutely true. One would, however, have to ascribe to (8) a high degree of truth. And since (8) is a statement about arithmetic, one would be ascribing to (8) a high degree of *necessary* truth. Many other similar examples can be concocted by the reader. To take just one more example:

(9)   For almost all nonnegative integers N, 2^N is much greater
        than zero.

Here there are two vague concepts, 'almost all' and 'much greater than'. But allowing their usual fuzzy meanings, I think one would want to say that (9) had a high degree of truth – necessary truth – though again I doubt than one would want to say that (9) is absolutely true.

I have no particular philosophical ax to grind here. I am merely suggesting that fuzzy modal logics might have some application in explicating the status of arithmetical statements that contain vague words. To my knowledge, the status of such statements has not been hitherto explicated.

We have been employing a many-valued logic in an attempt to provide an initial explication of fuzziness in natural language. Many-valued logics have also been used in an attempt to explicate the natural language notion of a presupposition. It seems natural to ask what happens when fuzzy logic mixes with presuppositional logic. One would not expect particularly drastic results. But something rather drastic does happen – and the results are I think surprising and interesting. Suppose that one were to try to extend *FPL* to a presuppositional logic. Recall that *FPL* is already a many-valued logic and that none of its values correspond to presupposition failure. To account for presupposition failure, we might expect to add still another value or range of values. But it is not clear just what we will be forced to.

Suppose initially that we try to extend *FPL* to a presuppositional logic, keeping the valuation: $|\neg P| = 1 - |P|$. Let us assume the usual definition of presupposition.[4]

(10)   *P* presupposes *Q*   iff $P \Vdash Q$ and $\neg P \Vdash Q$.

Taking the above definition of entailment, we find that:

(11)   *P* presupposes *Q*   iff $|P| \leqslant |Q|$ and $1 - |P| \leqslant |Q|$ in all models.

But from (11), it follows that *P* presupposes *Q* only if $|Q| \geqslant 0.5$!! This is a truly crazy result. Consider some examples.

(12)   a. The present king of France is bald.
          b. There is presently a king of France.
(13)   a. Dick Cavett regrets that he is tall.
          b. Dick Cavett is tall.

In each case, we would like to say that the (a) sentence presupposes the (b) sentence – regardless of the truth value of the (b) sentence. But if we accept (10) and we accept $|\neg P| = 1 - |P|$, then it will turn out that the

(a) sentences will presuppose the corresponding (b) sentences only if the values of the latter never fall below 0.5 in any model. Clearly this is undesirable. (12a) should presuppose (12b) even if there is no present king of France. (13a) should presuppose (13b), even though Dick Cavett happens to be tall, say, to degree 0.3.

One way to avoid this problem is by looking at standard valuations in a somewhat different way. Instead of assigning a truth value to a proposition, we can view standard valuations as assigning an ordered pair, (t, f), consisting of a truth value and a falsity value, whose sum is 1. For presuppositional logic, we propose (following an idea of Zadeh's) to extend the ordered pair to an ordered triple, (t, f, n), whose sum is 1, and whose third place would be interpreted as a nonsense value. A statement that was total nonsense would have a nonsense value of 1 and truth and falsity values of zero. The following valuation for $\neg P$ would be needed:

$$(14) \qquad |\neg P| = (\alpha, \beta, \gamma) \quad \text{iff} \quad |P| = (\beta, \alpha, \gamma), \quad \text{where} \quad \alpha + \beta + \gamma = 1$$

In other words, the truth value of $\neg P$ would be the falsity value of P and vice versa, and both P and $\neg P$ would have the same degree of nonsense.

In any presuppositional logic meeting these conditions, the above problem with the definition of presupposition does not arise. Since the value of $|\neg P|$ is not necessarily equal to $1 - |P|$, the value of $|Q|$ in (10) does not have to be 0.5 or greater. In fact, no conditions are placed on its value, as should be the case. The intuitive reason why this works is that the third place, the nonsense-value slot, provides the additional range of values to cover presupposition failure. Incidentally, given (14), the falsity value becomes redundant, since it can be computed from the truth- and nonsense-values. Consequently, we only need to assign ordered pairs, (α, γ), of truth- and nonsense-values since $\beta = 1 - (\alpha + \gamma)$.

I don't mean to suggest that the above solution is the only possible one, though it may well be the only one that permits both truth-functional negation and degrees of nonsense. Whether these are good things to have is another matter, which I will not take up here. (See Appendix II for a discussion of degrees of nonsense.)

For those interested in investigating such systems further, the connections with other presuppositional logics is worth considering with respect to the matter of how to define valuations for connectives. This will be taken up in Appendix II.

There are, of course, other issues to be considered in the study of fuzzy logic. For example, suppose we allow for fuzzy denotations. That is, suppose we generalize assignments of variables to individuals in the domain of discourse so that a variable x will denote an individual a to a degree α, $0 \leqslant \alpha \leqslant 1$. It might be useful for someone to investigate such systems, since there seem to be cases of fuzzy denotations in natural language. Consider (15).

(15)   a. The real numbers approximately equal to 5 are less than 1000.

            b. The real numbers approximately equal to 5 are less than 5.1.

These sentences contain a definite description which denotes only fuzzily. No nonfuzzy set of real numbers is picked out by 'the real numbers approximately equal to 5'. Yet we can make true statements about arithmetic using such descriptions. (15a) is one such statement. (15b) is another matter. (15b) sounds to me like a case of presupposition failure; at least it seems neither true nor false to any degree, but rather inappropriate. Such cases seem to me to be worthy of study.

Another interesting question concerns degree of entailment. We have defined '→' to have values zero and one. Suppose it were to take on intermediate values. Then one would like to generalize the notion of entailment to the notion of entailment to a degree α (written $\Vdash \alpha$), with (16) holding.

(16) $P \Vdash_\alpha Q$ iff $\Vdash_\alpha P \to Q$.

This will be discussed in Appendix I. Of course, in any such system we will want to talk about such concepts as 'degree of validity' and 'degree of theoremhood', which are natural concomitants of the notion 'degree of necessary truth'. If one wants a natural example of degree of entailment, consider (17) and (18).

(17) x is a bird.
(18) x flies.

We know that not all birds fly, but we might well want to say that once a bird has a certain degree of birdiness, say 0.7, then it flies. We might then want to say that (17) entails (18) to degree 0.7.

The purpose of this discussion of fuzzy logic has been to show that one need not throw up one's hands in despair when faced by the problems of vagueness and fuzziness. Fuzziness can be studied seriously within formal semantics, and when such a serious approach is taken, all sorts of interesting questions arise. For me, some of the most interesting questions are raised by the study of words whose meaning implicitly involves fuzziness – words whose job is to make things fuzzier or less fuzzy. I will refer to such words as 'hedges'. A small list (which is far from complete) appears on the following page.

3. HEDGES

Let us begin with a hedge that looks superficially to be simple: *sort of*. Just as *very* is an intensifier in that it shifts values to the right and steepens the curve (see Figure 5), so *sort of* is, in part at least, a deintensifier in that it shifts the curve to the left and makes it less steep. However it also drops off sharply to zero on the right. Consider the notion 'sort of tall' in Figure 9 below. The values for 'sort of tall' are greatest when you are of intermediate height. If you are of less than intermediate height, then the values for 'sort of tall' are greater than those for 'tall'. But above intermediate height the values for 'sort of tall' drop off sharply. If you're really tall, you're not sort of tall.

The same thing is true in the case of birdiness.

(1)   a. A robin is sort of a bird.   (False – it is a bird, no question, about it)

          b. A chicken is sort of a bird. (True, or very close to true)

          c. A penguin is sort of a bird. (True, or close to true)

          d. A bat is sort of a bird.   (Still pretty close to false)

          e. A cow is sort of a bird.   (False)

Sort of is a predicate modifier, but one of a type that has not been previously studied in formal semantics in that its effect can only be described in terms of membership functions for fuzzy sets. It takes values that are true or close to true and makes them false while uniformly raising values in the low to mid range of the scale, leaving the very low range of the scale constant. The effect of *sort of* cannot even be described in a two-valued system, where sentences are either true or false and individuals are either set members or not. Consider again example (4) of section I, where we saw that there were speakers who did not distinguish between the (a), (b), and (c), sentences, but rather lumped them together as all being true, as in the corresponding sentences of example (5) of section I. However, even such speakers distinguish the (a) sentence in example (1) of this section from the (b) and (c) sentences. In order for them to do this, they must have been able to make an underlying distinction in degree of birdiness between robins on the one hand and chickens and penguins on the other. The effect of the predicate modifier *sort of* depends upon just such a dis-

---

SOME HEDGES AND RELATED PHENOMENA

sort of	in a real sense
kind of	in an important sense
loosely speaking	in a way
more or less	mutatis mutandis
on the _____ side (tall, fat, etc.)	in a manner of speaking
roughly	details aside
pretty (much)	so to say
relatively	a veritable
somewhat	a true
rather	a real
mostly	a regular
technically	virtually
strictly speaking	all but technically
essentially	practically
in essence	all but a
basically	anything but a
principally	a self-styled
particularly	nominally
par excellence	he calls himself a ...
largely	in name only
for the most part	actually
very	really
especially	(he as much as ...
exceptionally	-like
quintessential(ly)	-ish
literally	can be looked upon as
often	can be viewed as
more of a _____ than anything else	pseudo-
almost	crypto-
typically/typical	(he's) another (Caruso/Lincoln/ Babe Ruth/...)
as it were	_____ is the _____ of _____
in a sense	(e.g., America is the Roman Empire of
in one sense	the modern world. Chomsky is the DeGaulle of Linguistics. etc.)

tinction. There are other types of predicate modifiers that reveal such distinctions.

(2)   a. A robin is a bird par excellence.   (true)
        b. A chicken is a bird par excellence. (false)
        c. A penguin is a bird par excellence. (false)

(3)   a. A chicken is a typical bird.   (false)
        b. In essence, a chicken is a bird. (true)

(4)   a. In a manner of speaking, a bat is a (true or close to true)
          bird.
        b. In a manner of speaking, a cow is a
          bird.   (false)
        c. In a manner of speaking, a chicken
          is a bird.   (nonsense – (c) presupposes that chickens are not really birds, which is false).

As (2) reveals, *par excellence* requires the highest degree of category membership. Robins fit, chickens and penguins don't. *Typical*, in (3), also requires a high degree of membership, which is why chickens don't fit. But a high degree of membership isn't sufficient for *typical*, as (5) shows.

(5)   a. A robin is a typical bird. (true)
        b. An eagle is a typical bird. (false, or at least far from true)

Even though eagles seem to rank high in birdiness, the fact that they are predators makes them atypical of birds. What examples (2) – (5) seem to show is that people do make the full range of distinctions in the birdiness hierarchy. Though these distinctions may be subtle, they can be thrown into clear relief by hedges.

But hedges do not merely reveal distinctions of degree of category membership. They can also reveal a great deal more about meaning. Consider (6).

(6)   a. Esther Williams is a fish.
        b. Esther Williams is a regular fish.

(6a) is false, since Esther Williams is a human being, not a fish. (6b), on the other hand, would seem to be true, since it says that Esther Williams

swims well and is at home in water. Note that (6b) does not assert that
Esther Williams has gills, scales, fins, a tail, etc. In fact, (6b) presupposes
that Esther Williams is not literally a fish and asserts that she has certain
other characteristic properties of a fish. Bolinger (1972) has suggested
that *regular* picks out certain 'metaphorical' properties. We can see what
this means in an example like (7).

(7)   a. John is bachelor.
         b. John is a regular bachelor.

(7b) would not be said of a bachelor. It might be said of a married man
who acts like a bachelor – dates a lot, feels unbound by marital respon-
sibilities, etc. In short, *regular* seems to assert the connotations of 'bachelor', while presupposing the negation of the literal meaning. (7) reveals
the same fact, though perhaps more clearly.

(8)   a. Sarah is a spinster.
         b. Sarah is a regular spinster.

(8b) asserts that Sarah has certain characteristic properties of spinsters –
presumably that she is prissy and disdains sexual activity. (8b) would not
be said of someone who was literally a spinster, but might be said either
of a married woman or a girl who was not yet past marriageable age who
acted like a spinster. What (8b) asserts is the connotation of 'spinster' –
prissiness and lack of sexual activity, while presupposing the negation of
the literal meaning.

    If this account of the meaning of *regular* is essentially correct, a rather
important conclusion follows. It is usually assumed that the connotations
of words are part of pragmatics – the wastebasket of the study of meaning.
Certainly most philosophers seem to take it for granted that connotations
and other pragmatic aspects of meaning are irrelevant to the assignment
of truth values (leaving aside sentences containing indexical expressions).
Truth is usually taken to involve literal or denotative meaning alone. Yet
in sentences with *regular*, such as (6b), (7b) and (8b), the truth value of the
sentences as a whole depends not upon the literal meaning of the predicates
involved, but strictly upon their connotations! What this indicates, I think,
is that semantics cannot be taken to be independent of pragmatics, but
but that the two are inextricably tied together.

    In the above discussion I used the terms 'literal meaning' and 'connotation' as though they were adequate to describe at least informally the types of meaning components affected by hedges and related words. But as might be expected the situation is more complex. We can see this if we try to find some hedges that are opposites of *regular*, ones which pick out literal meaning alone. Two promising candidates are *strictly speaking* and *technically*.

(9)   a. A whale is technically a mammal.
         b. Strictly speaking a whale is a mammal.

Technically and *strictly speaking* seem to have the same effect in (9a) and (b). However, in other sentences they produce radically different results.

(10)   a. Richard Nixon is technically a Quaker.   (true)
         b. Strictly speaking, Richard Nixon is a Quaker.   (false)
(11)   a. Ronald Reagan is technically a cattle rancher.   (true)
         b. Strictly speaking, Ronald Reagan is a cattle rancher.
                                                  (false)
(12)   a. Strictly speaking, George Wallace is a racist.
         b. Technically, George Wallace is a racist.

As (10) and (11) show, *technically* picks out some definitional criterion, while *strictly speaking* requires both the definitional criterion and other important criteria as well. Richard Nixon may be a Quaker in some definitional sense, but he does not have the religious and ethical views characteristic of Quakers. He meets the definitional criterion, but not other important criteria. Ronald Reagan meets the definitional criterion for being a cattle rancher since he seems to have bought cattle stocks as a tax dodge (which is reported how he avoided 1970 income taxes). However, he does not meet all of the primary criteria for being a cattle rancher. Note that, as (12) shows, *technically* seems to mean *only technically*, that is it asserts that the definitional criteria are met but that some important criterion for category membership is not met. Hence the strangeness of (12b).

Strictly speaking contrasts interestingly with *loosely speaking*.

(13)   a. Strictly speaking, a whale is a mammal.
         b. Loosely speaking, a whale is a fish.

(13) shows the need for distinguishing between important or primary properties on the one hand and secondary properties on the other hand.

(13a) says that whales classify as mammals if we take into account important criteria for distinguishing mammals from fish. For example, they give live birth and breathe air. (13b) seems to say that we can classify whales as fish if we ignore the primary properties and take into account certain secondary properties, for example, their general appearance and the fact that they live in water. Thus, we need to distinguish between primary and secondary criteria for category membership.

However, *loosely speaking* still differs sharply from *regular*, as the following examples show:

(14)   a. Harry is a regular fish.

         b. Loosely speaking, Harry is a fish.

(15)   a. Loosely speaking, a whale is a fish.

         b. A whale is a regular fish.

What is strange about (14b) is that it asserts that Harry is a member of the category fish to some degree by virtue of having some secondary property of fish. (14a) simply says that he swims well and at is home in water, while it presupposes that he is not a member of the category fish to any degree whatever. The distinction between (14a) and (14b) indicates that we must distinguish between those properties capable of conferring some degree of category membership and those properties which happen to be characteristic of category members, but do not confer category membership to any degree at all. No matter how well you swim, that won't make you a fish to any degree at all. But if you are a living being, live in the water, are shaped like a fish, and your only limbs are flippers and a tail, it would seem that, like the whale, you are loosely speaking, that is by virtue of secondary criteria, a member of the category fish to some extent. Note that (15b) is odd in that it presupposes that the whale is not a member of the category fish to any extent.

An adequate account of the functioning of characteristic-though-incidental properties should provide an understanding of at least one type of metaphor. Suppose I say 'John is a fish'. I am using a metaphor to indicate either that he swims well or that he is slimy (in the nonliteral sense). The mechanism for this is, I think, something like the following. Since it is presupposed that the subject, John, is not literally a member of the category fish, one cannot be asserting membership in that category if the sentence is to make sense. Instead, the sentence is understood in essentially the same way as 'John is a regular fish', that is, the contextually most important incidental-though-characteristic properties are asserted. (For a discussion of metaphor and fuzzy logic, see Reddy, 1972.)

By looking at just four hedges – *technically, strictly speaking, loosely speaking* and *regular* – we have seen that we must distinguish at least four types of criteria for category membership:

(16)   TYPES OF CRITERIA
         1. Definitional ⎤ – capable of conferring category member-
         2. Primary   ⎬   ship to a certain degree depending on
         3. Secondary   ⎦   various factors
         4. Characteristic though incidental – not capable of confer-
                                        ring category member-
                                        ship to any degree, but
                                        contributes to degree of
                                        category membership if
                                        some degree of member-
                                        ship is otherwise estab-
                                        lished.

These distinctions are necessary for even a primitive account of how such hedges function. Such a primitive account is given in (17).

(17)   An Informal and Inadequate Approximation to an Under-
         standing of Some Hedges
         TECHNICALLY – Truth value depends upon values of defi-
                                nitional criteria alone. Implies that at
                                least one primary criterion is below the
                                threshold value for simple category
                                membership.
         STRICTLY SPEAKING – Truth value depends on value of
                                definitional and primary criteria.
                                Values for each criterion must be
                                above certain threshold values.
         LOOSELY SPEAKING – Truth value depends primarily on
                                secondary criteria. Implies that
                                threshold values for definitional
                                and primary criteria are insuf-

ficient to confer category membership.

REGULAR – Truth value depends upon characteristic-
though-incidental criteria. It is presupposed
that the values of other criteria are insufficient
to establish any degree of category membership.

The facts in (17) cannot be handled within the framework of fuzzy logic
as developed above, since they require a distinction between types of
criteria for category membership. Nor can they, so far as I know, be
handled by any logic developed to date. Let us consider what type of
logic would be needed to handle such cases.

4. FUZZY LOGIC WITH HEDGES

Let each predicate F be assigned two values, a vector value $\|F\|$ and an
absolute value $|F|$. The absolute value will be the membership function
for a fuzzy set.

(1) $|F| = \mu_{\mathrm{L}}.$

Suppose the membership function is itself a function of a k-tuple of criteria, that is, of other membership functions:

(2)   Suppose $\mu_F = f(\mu_{G_1}, ..., \mu_{G_k}).$

For example, if μ_F is the membership function for the fuzzy set of birds,
then μ_{G_1} might be the membership function for the fuzzy set of animals
with wings, and μ_{G_2} might be the membership function for the fuzzy set
of animals with feathers, etc. We define the k-tuple $(\mu_{G_1}, ..., \mu_{G_k})$ as the
vector value of the predicate F and call each element of the k-tuple a
'meaning component'.

(3) $\|F\| = (\mu_{G_1}, ..., \mu_{G_k}).$

Corresponding to the four types of meaning components discussed above
in Section 3 – definitional, primary, secondary, and characteristic-though-
incidental – we define four functions: *def*, *prim*, *sec*, and *char*. These will,
when applied to the vector value of a predicate F, pick out the appropriate

meaning components and form a new function, which itself will be a membership function for a fuzzy set. For the sake of discussion, let us assume that *def, prim, sec* and *char* each forms the intersection of the meaning components that they pick out of the vector value of *F*. This is obviously over-simplified; various complex combinations will be needed. We are now in a position to give a first approximation to valuations for the hedges *technically* (TECH), *strictly speaking* (STR), *loosely speaking* (LOOS), and *regular* (REG).

(3)   Let TECH, STR, LOOS, and REG be predicate modifiers.
$|\text{TECH}(F)| = \text{def}(\|F\|) \cap \text{NEG}(\text{prim}(\|F\|))$ where:
$$\text{NEG}(f) = 1 - f$$
$|\text{STR}(F)| = \text{def}(\|F\|) \cap \text{prim}(\|F\|)$
$|\text{LOOS}(F)| = \text{sec}(\|F\|) \cap \text{NEG}(\text{def}(\|F\|) \cap \text{prim}(\|F\|))$
$|\text{REG}(F)| = \text{char}(\|F\|) \cap \text{NEG}(\text{def}(\|F\|) \cap \text{prim}(\|F\|) \cap$
$\cap \text{sec}(\|F\|))$.

(3) is simply a formal way of saying what is said informally in (17) in Section 3. For example, the value of *technically* is the value of the definitional criteria of the predicate modified intersected with the value of the negative of the primary criteria.

As will be seen below, the analysis given in (3) is inadequate in various ways. But inadequacies aside, (3) could not actually be applied in a fuzzy logic unless vector values were assigned to all the predicates and unless the functions *def, prim, sec* and *char* were defined in terms of those vector values. But that means that we have to seriously study the meaning of predicates in a way that has not previously been done. One thing that the study of hedges in formal terms like (3) can do is to give us a technique for doing the empirical study of meaning components. By comparing the truth conditions for predicates both unhedged and then with various hedges, we may be able to sort out the meaning components.

So far, we have looked only at hedges whose truth conditions depend on vector values. One might ask a whether there are any hedges whose valuations depend only on absolute values. Zadeh has claimed that such hedges do exist. Though I think his analyses are inadequate in certain important respects, there is also something right about them. Zadeh's basic idea is that there is a small number of basic functions that, in combination, produce a wide range of modifiers specifically, absolute value modifiers, for fuzzy predicates. Aside from the Boolean functions of inter-section, union, and complementation (which we will write NEG), Zadeh (1971a, 1972) has suggested the following:

(4)   Some Zadeh Functions
          Concentration: $\mu_{\text{CON}(F)} = \mu_F^2$
          Dilation: $\mu_{\text{DIL}(F)} = \mu_F^{1/2}$
          Contrast intensification: $\mu_{\text{INT}(F)}(x) = 2\mu_F(x),$
          $$\text{for } 0 \leqslant \mu_F(x) \leqslant 0.5.$$
          $$\mu_{\text{INT}(F)}(x) = 1 - 2(1 - \mu_F(x))^2,$$
          $$\text{for } 0.5 \leqslant \mu_F(x) \leqslant 1.$$
          Convex combination: $\mu_F = w_1\mu_{G_1} + w_1\mu_{G_2} + \cdots + w_k\mu_{G_k},$
          $$\text{where } w_i \text{ is in } (0,1) \text{ and}$$
          $$w_1 + \cdots + w_k = 1.$$

Convex combination is simply a weighted sum. Though I suggested above that functions like *prim* and *sec* were intersections of the primary and secondary criteria, respectively, for a given predicate, it seems more likely that such functions are actually weighted sums. The effects of CON, DIL, and INT are given in the following diagrams.

CON lowers the values and makes the curve steeper. If the curve is

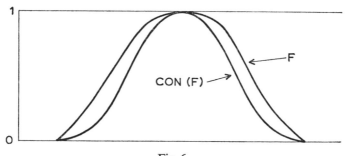

Fig. 6.

bell-shaped, CON pulls the values in toward the center as shown in Figure 6. DIL raises the values and makes the curve less steep. If the curve is bell-shaped, DIL spreads the values out as shown in Figure 7. INT raises higher values and lowers lower values, thus making for greater contrast, as shown in Figure 8. Note that the following relations hold.

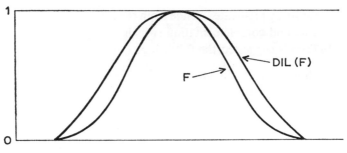

Fig. 7.

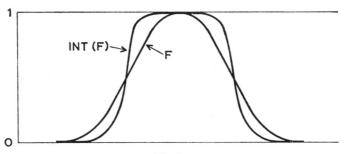

Fig. 8.

(5)   a. $\mu_{\text{DIL}}(f) = \mu_{\text{NEG(CON(NEG}(F)))}$
        b. $\mu_{\text{INT}(F)}(x) = \mu_{\text{MULT(CON}(F))}(x)$ for $0 \leqslant x \leqslant 0.5$.
        c. $\mu_{\text{INT}(F)}(x) = \mu_{\text{NEG(MULT(CON(NEG}(F))))}(x)$ for $0.5 \leqslant x \leqslant 1$,
                        where $\mu_{\text{MULT}(F)} = 2\mu_F$

In these definitions Zadeh happened to use squares, square roots, and factors of two. However, he does not intend those exact numbers to be taken seriously. What he does intend to be taken seriously is the kinds of effects these functions have on the curve. Whether 3 or 1.745 would be better numbers than 2 in such functions is irrelevant, so long as CON pulls the curve in, DIL spreads it out and INT heightens contrasts – and so long as the relations given in (5) continue to hold. In fact, all these functions may well be fuzzy themselves, so talk of an exact multiple or power in the equations may make no sense.

The point of Zadeh functions is to define valuations for modifiers using them. Zadeh has suggested the following as approximations:

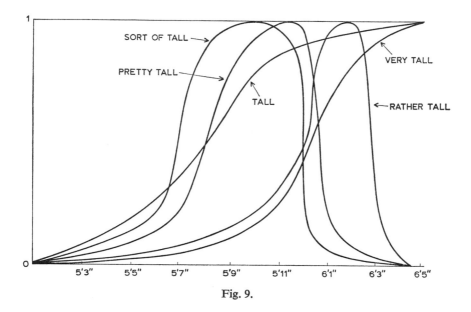

Fig. 9.

(6) Some examples of modifier valuations using Zadeh functions
$$|VERY(F)| = CON(|F|)$$
$$|SORT\ OF(F)| = INT(DIL(|F|)) \cap INT(DIL(NEG(|F|)))$$
$$|PRETTY(F)| = INT(|F|) \cap NEG(INT(CON(|F|)))$$
$$|RATHER(F)| = INT(CON(F))$$
$$\text{or } INT(CON(|F|)) \cap NEG(CON(|F|))$$
$$\text{[rather, but not very]}.$$

Figure 9 gives some idea of what the modified curves for TALL would be like. Whatever the shortcomings of the valuations in (6), I think there is something basically right about Zadeh's idea, and if there is, then there is a rather remarkable consequence: algebraic functions play a role in natural language semantics! Certainly the basic idea seems to be right – given the curve for TALL, one should be able to define derived curves for VERY TALL, RATHER TALL, PRETTY TALL and SORT OF TALL. Algebraic functions of some sort or other would seem to be necessary (though perhaps not sufficient) for the characterization of such derived curves.

Let us now return to the fact that people seem not to perceive an infinite gradation of, say, tallness, but seem rather to perceive some relatively

small finite number of discrete values for tallness. Two possible ways of
describing this were suggested above. (1) Restrict fuzzy logic to some
finite number of values. (2) Keep an infinity of values, but assume the
existence of a 'low level' perceptual apparatus that determines the number
and distribution of the perceived values depending on the shape of the
curve and various contextual factors. I think (2) is correct on a number
of grounds. First, the number of perceived values seems to be variable, to
change somewhat from concept to concept and context to context. This
means that there would be no single fixed number of values to which we
could restrict fuzzy logic. Second, the number and location of the perceived values seem to depend on the shape of the curve. Since such concepts as PRETTY TALL will be a complex function of TALL (if Zadeh
is anywhere near correct). There will be no way to guarantee, given assumption (1), that the perceived values for TALL will map directly, via
that function, onto the perceived values for PRETTY TALL, not to mention RATHER TALL, SORT OF TALL, VERY VERY TALL, etc. A
good example is a case where VERY is iterated a large number of times
with a concept where a limit will be approached, as in VERY VERY VERY
VERY CLOSE TO 1000. One could probably perceive something like the
usual 7 ± 2 values for CLOSE TO 1000, but the number seems to drop
considerably for VERY VERY VERY VERY CLOSE TO 1000, which
is not surprising on Zadeh's account of VERY, since a repeated squaring
of the values for a curve like CLOSE TO 1000 will produce a function
that approaches a vertical line. I think considerations like this force us to
reject alternative (1) in favor of (2), which is, I think, an interesting result.

5. SOME INADEQUACIES OF THE TREATMENT OF HEDGES IN SECTION 4

I don't want to give the impression that I take the proposals in section IV
to be correct in all or even most details. Hedges have barely begun to be
studied and I have discussed only a handful. I have no doubt that the apparatus needed to handle the rest of them will have to be far more
sophisticated. In fact, it is easy to show that far more sophisticated apparatus will be needed to handle merely the hedges discussed so far. Moreover I think that four types of criteria is far to few, though I have not done
further investigation.

5.1. *Dependence upon Context*

The valuations for hedges given in Section 4 were independent of context. However, it is fairly easy to show that any adequate treatment will have to take context into account. Consider (1).

(1)   Technically, this TV set is a piece of furniture.

As Eleanor Heider (personal communication) has observed, there is no generally recognized technical definition accepted throughout American culture (or any other) that will tell you whether a particular TV set is or is not a piece of furniture. The range of TV sets goes from small portable ones that can easily be carried (perhaps in one's pocket) to large consoles with fancy wooden cabinets. But whether a given TV set is technically a piece of furniture will vary with the situation. For example, insurance companies or movers may set different rates for furniture, appliances, and other personal property. In such situations, technical standards have to be set and it is doubtful that there will be much uniformity. Yet, the truth or falsity or even the appropriateness of (1) in a given context will depend on what those standards are, if there are any. Moreover, different cultures, subcultures, or even individuals may differ as to which criteria for a given predicate are primary and which are secondary. In fact, it would not be surprising to find that which criteria were considered primary and which secondary depended on context. Consider (2).

(2)   a. Strictly speaking, Christine Jorgenson is a woman.
        b. Strictly speaking, Christine Jorgenson is a man.

One can imagine contexts in which either (2a) or (2b) would be true or very close to true. Take contexts where current sex is what matters, for example, job applications, sexual encounters, examinations for venereal disease, choice of rest room, etc. In such situations, (2a) would be true and (2b) would not. Take, on the other hand, situations where former sex might matter, for example, psychological studies of early childhood, classification with respect to military benefits, etc. In such situations, one could imagine that (2b) might be true and (2a) not. That is, current sex might be primary for determining manhood vs. womanhood in some contexts and former sex primary in others.

5.2. *Modifiers that Affect the Number of Criteria Considered*

Under Zadeh's proposals for the definition of words like VERY and
SORT OF, such modifiers affect only the absolute values of the predicates
modified. However, consider cases like VERY SIMILAR and SORT OF
SIMILAR. Things are similar or dissimilar not just to degrees, but also in
various respects. In judging similarity one picks out a certain number of
contextually important criteria, and determines degree of similarity on
the basis of how closely the values match for the criteria chosen. In determining the values for VERY SIMILAR, there are two possibilities. First,
one can, for the fixed number of criteria considered in judging mere similarity, require that the values assigned to the various criteria be closer.
Secondly, one can require that more criteria be taken into account. For
example, consider (1).

(1)   a. Richard Nixon and Warren G. Harding are similar.
           b. Richard Nixon and Warren G. Harding are very similar.

In judging (1a) to be true to a certain degree, one might take into account
merely their records as president. One might then want to go on to assert
(1b) by taking into account other criteria, for instance, the personal lives,
moral values, etc.

SORT OF has the opposite effects when applied to SIMILAR.

(2)   a. George Wallace and Adolf Hitler are similar.
           b. George Wallace and Adolf Hitler are sort of similar.

(2b) can be a hedge on (2a) in two different respects. First, on the given
criteria considered, one may require less closeness of values for (2b) than
for (2a). Secondly, in judging the degree of truth of (2b) versus (2a), one
may take fewer criteria into account.

These considerations show that an adequate account of the meanings
of VERY and SORT OF cannot be given simply in terms of how they
affect the absolute values of the predicates they modify; one must take
into account the way they change the consideration of vector values. In
the case of similarity that includes both the closeness of selected vector
values and the number of them.

5.3. *Some Hedges Must Be Assigned Vector Values*

In the treatment given in Section 4, all of the hedges were assigned only absolute values. That this is inadequate can be seen by considering an expression like VERY STRICTLY SPEAKING, as in (1).

(1)   a. Strictly speaking, Sam is not the kind of person we want to hire.
          b. Very strictly speaking, Sam is just the kind of person we do not want to hire.

One can imagine a situation in which one might say (1a) and then follow it up with (1b). Suppose one were running a business and had certain criteria for filling a certain job – objective qualifications, honesty, personality traits, etc., with some criteria being more important than others. Given that Sam did not measure up according to the primary criteria, one might accurately say (1a), though perhaps nothing stronger. Suppose that, one then isolated the most important of the primary criteria and looked at how Sam ranked with respect to those. With respect to those, he might not merely be unqualified but might actually be injurious to the business. One might then be in a position to make the stronger statement (1b). One of the things that VERY does, when applied to STRICTLY SPEAKING, is further restrict the number of categories considered most important: this can be viewed as changing the weights assigned to various criteria at the upper end of the spectrum. This is, incidentally, the opposite of what it does when applied to SIMILAR – and and I have no idea why. Be that as it may, VERY seems to operate on the vector value of STRICTLY SPEAKING, not just on the absolute value. This means that we must find a way of assigning vector values to hedges like STRICTLY SPEAKING. The same is true of LOOSELY SPEAKING, as expressions like VERY LOOSELY SPEAKING show. In this case, however, one of the effects of VERY is to *increase* the number of criteria considered – or at least increase the weights assigned to the lower end of the spectrum – the opposite of what happened in the case of VERY STRICTLY SPEAKING. Any adequate description of the meaning of VERY will have to take such considerations into account. Another thing suggested by these facts is that there may not be a strict division between primary and secondary criteria; rather there may be a continuum of weighted criteria, with different hedges picking out different cut-off points in different situations.

5.4. *Perhaps Values Should Not Be Linearly Ordered, But only Partially Ordered*

So far we have discussed the concept 'true to a certain degree'; we have paid hardly any attention to the concept 'true in a certain respect'. Any serious study of hedges like IN SOME RESPECTS, IN A SENSE, IN A REAL SENSE, etc. requires it. What these hedges seem to do is say there are certain criteria which, if given great weight, would make the statement true. Consider (1).

(1)   a. In some respects, Nixon has helped the country.
         b. In a sense, J. Edgar Hoover was a great man.
         c. In a real sense, Nixon is a murderer.

But very often, sentences without such hedges are meant to be taken in the same way.

(2)   Nixon is a murderer and he's not a murderer.

The usual sense of (2) is not either a statement of a contradiction nor a statement that Nixon is a murderer to a degree. Rather it would usually be understood as saying that if you take into account certain criteria for being a murderer, Nixon qualifies, while if you give prominence to other criteria, he doesn't qualify. On a reading such as this, sentence (2) could be true. But one of the inadequacies of fuzzy logic as we have set it up is that we have no way of assigning values in such a way that (2) comes out to be true. Even though $P \wedge \neg P$ is not a contradiction in FPL, it is still constrained so that it cannot have a value greater than 0.5 – that is, it has to come out to be more false than true in FPL. The reason is, of course, that FPL does not take account of the notion 'truth in a certain respect'. Any attempt to incorporate such a notion into FPL would lead to having to give up a linear sequence of values in favor of a lattice of values. I have not investigated at all just what would have to be done to FPL to incorporate the notion of 'truth in a certain respect' – and I hope that the problem will be taken up by logicians. It is an important problem, since a great deal of ordinary discourse involves that notion. When a member of the New Left says:

(3)   Nixon is a murderer.

and the local Republican spokesman replies

(4)   Nixon is not a murderer.

the disagreement is not over the facts of the world. They may agree completely on just what Nixon has and hasn't done. The disagreement is one of values. What criteria should be considered important in conferring membership in the category of murderers? The issue is by no means trivial. Similar cases arise every day in most people's speech. Any serious account of human reasoning will require an understanding of such cases.

5.5. *More Problems With VERY*

We saw above in the discussions of VERY SIMILAR and VERY STRICTLY SPEAKING that the meaning of VERY cannot be adequately represented simply by taking a function of the absolute value of the predicate modified; vector values must be taken into consideration. There are other considerations that seem to me to indicate this. According to Zadeh's treatment of VERY, in which

$$|VERY(F)| = \mu_{CON(F)} = \mu_F^2,$$

the curve for VERY TALL hits the values 0 and 1 at exactly the same places as the curve for TALL. This seems to me to be counterintuitive. It seems to me that it can be absolutely true that someone is tall without it being absolutely true that he is very tall. The situation, of course, gets worse with VERY VERY TALL, VERY VERY VERY TALL, etc., since according to Zadeh's treatment, they all hit the value 1 at the same place as TALL. The difference between Zadeh's proposal and what seems to me to be more correct can be seen in Figures 10 and 11.

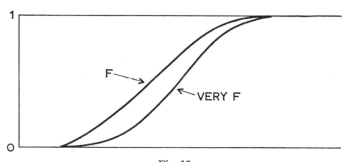

Fig. 10.

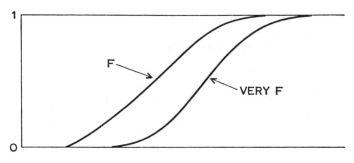

Fig. 11.

In Figure 10, the curve for TALL has been modified by the function CON to give the curve for VERY TALL. In Figure 11, the curve for VERY TALL has in addition been shifted over to the right, which seems to me to be more correct. However, there is no way to get the effect of such a shift simply by having VERY operate on the absolute value of TALL. Rather any function giving the values for VERY TALL in Figure 11 would have to range over *heights*, which would be included in the vector value for TALL. Assuming $\mu_{\text{TALL}} = f(h)$, for some function f ranging over heights, to get a shift to the right as shown in Figure 11 we would have to take some constant c and compute $f(h-c)$; then to get the curve for VERY TALL we would need apply the function CON as Zadeh suggests. Thus $\mu_{\text{VERY TALL}} = \text{CON}(f(h-c))$. How one arrives at the constants for each given predicate modified would be a serious problem. More likely, one would not be subtracting a constant but rather some function of heights, $g(h)$, which would grow smaller the more one iterated VERY. The reason for the latter suggestion is that as one iterates occurrences of VERY the curve is not shifted further and further to the right, but rather reaches a point of diminishing returns. One of the reasons for Zadeh's suggestion that VERY be represented by a function that raises the value to a power is that one gets such a result automatically. My feeling at present is that a complete understanding of VERY is very far from our grasp.

5.6. *Restrictions on the Occurrence of Modifiers*

Some modifiers can apply to other modifiers, but the combinations are quite limited. We get VERY STRICTLY SPEAKING, but not VERY RATHER. Moreover, there are firm restrictions on what modifiers can modify what predicates. We get NEARLY EQUAL TO 5, but not VERY EQUAL TO 5, though we get VERY CLOSE TO 5. A few of these restrictions follow automatically from certain of the above proposals. For example, Zadeh's suggestion for VERY accounts for the odd redundancy we find in VERY EQUAL TO 5, since squaring the graph for EQUAL TO 5 will not change any of the values, which are either 0 or 1. But most other restrictions on the occurrence of hedges seem not to follow automatically from what has been said above. Such restrictions should follow automatically from any adequate account.

Hedges raise some interesting questions:

A.   How Do Hedges Interact With Performatives?
        Take a sentence like (1).

(1)   Technically, I *said* that Harry was a bastard.

What (1) would generally be taken to mean is that I said it but I didn't mean it. That is, TECHNICALLY in (1) seems to be cancelling the implicature that if you say something, you mean it. Or suppose a sergeant says (2).

(2)   You might want to close that window, Private Snurg.

I think it would be appropriate to describe such a situation by the sentences in (3).

(3)   a. Strictly speaking, the sergeant didn't order the private to close the window.
        b. Essentially, the sergeant did order the private to close the window.

Obviously hedges interact with felicity conditions for utterances and with rules of conversation. An investigation of the subject should be revealing.
    In addition, Robin Lakoff (personal communication) has observed that certain verbs and syntactic constructions convey hedged performatives.

(4)   a. I suppose (guess/think) that Harry is coming.
        b. Won't you open the door?

(4a) is a hedged assertion. (4b) is a 'softened' request. An investigation of these would also be revealing.

B.   Are There Hedges in Lexical Items?

Robin Lakoff has suggested that one might want to describe a word like 'pink' as a hedge between red and white. This is also suggested by the metaphorical term 'pinko', which is a hedge on 'red'.

C.   What are the Primitive Fuzzy Concepts in Natural Language?

We will say that a fuzzy set is primitive if its membership function cannot be decomposed, that is, if there is no function f such that $\mu_A = =f(\mu_{B_1}, ..., \mu_{B_k})$. The question as to what such primitives are in natural language is a fundamental question about the nature of the human mind. The question has, of course, been raised innumerable times before, but to my knowledge the possibility that the primitives themselves might be fuzzy has not been discussed.

D.   What are the Possible Types of Membership Functions?

The membership function for each nonprimitive concept F is representable as a function of some finite number of other membership functions: $\mu_F = f(\mu_{G_1}, ..., \mu_{G_k})$. What are the possible f's? What constraints are there on them?

6. CONCLUSIONS

6.1. *The Logic of Fuzzy Concepts Can Be Studied Seriously*

Fuzzy concepts have had a bad press among logicians, especially in this century when the formal analysis of axiomatic and semantic systems reached a high degree of sophistication. It has been generally assumed that such concepts were not amenable to serious formal study. I believe that the development of fuzzy set theory by Zadeh and the placement of it by Scott (see Appendix I) within the general context of recent work in modal and many-valued logics makes such serious study possible.

6.2. *In Natural Language, Truth is a Matter of Degree, Not an Absolute*

Heider (1971) has shown that category membership is a matter of degree. Sentences asserting category membership of an individual or object correspondingly display a degree of truth. This is made clear by the study of

modifiers like SORT OF, PAR EXCELLENCE, TYPICAL, IN ES-
SENCE, and IN A MANNER OF SPEAKING (see Section 3 above),
whose effect on truth conditions can only be made sense of if the corresponding sentences without those modifiers admit of degrees of truth.

6.3. *Fuzzy Concepts Have Internal Structure*

The study of hedges like TECHNICALLY, STRICTLY SPEAKING,
LOOSELY SPEAKING, and REGULAR requires the assignment of
vector values to the predicates they modify. Each component is a meaning criterion, itself a membership function for a fuzzy set. There are at
least four types of meaning criteria, three of which are capable of conferring category membership to some degree, one of which is not.

6.4. *Semantics is Not Independent of Pragmatics*

The study of the hedge REGULAR by Bolinger 1972 reveals that
sentences with REGULAR assert connotations, not any aspect of literal
meaning. Connotations are considered to be part of pragmatics and, as
such, to have nothing to do with truth conditions, since semantics has been
assumed to be independent of pragmatics. However, since the truth conditions of sentences with REGULAR depend only on connotations, it
follows that if connotations are part of pragmatics, then semantics is not
independent of pragmatics. Since connotations are closely tied to the
real-world situation, it seems reasonable to maintain the traditional view
that connotations are part of pragmatic information.

6.5. *Algebraic Functions Play a Role in the Semantics of Certain Hedges*

Hedges like SORT OF, RATHER, PRETTY, and VERY change distribution curves in a regular way. Zadeh has proposed that such changes can
be described by simple combinations of a small number of algebraic functions. Whether or not Zadeh's proposals are correct in all detail, it seems
like something of the sort is necessary. (See Figure 9.)

6.6. *Perceptual Finiteness Depends on an Underlying Continuum of Values*

Since people can perceive, for each category, only a finite number of gradations in any given context, one might be tempted to suggest that fuzzy
logic be limited to a relatively small finite number of values. But the study

of hedges like SORT OF, VERY, PRETTY, and RATHER, whose effect seems to be characterizable at least in part by algebraic functions, indicates that the number and distribution of perceived values is a surface matter, determined by the shape of underlying continuous functions. For this reason, it seems best not to restrict fuzzy logic to any fixed finite number of values. Instead, it seems preferable to attempt to account for the perceptual phenomena by trying to figure out how, in a perceptual model, the shape of underlying continuous functions determines the number and distribution of perceived values.

6.7. *The Logic of Hedges Requires Serious Semantic Analysis for All Predicates*

In a fuzzy predicate logic *with hedges, (FPrLH)* the notion of a valuation is fundamentally more complex than the corresponding notion in other logics developed to date. The reason is that each predicate must be assigned a vector value as well as an absolute value and the models for each *FPrLH* must contain functions mapping vector values into absolute values, as well as the functions *prim, sec, def*, and *char*. What this amounts to is that the assignment of truth values in an *FPrLH* requires a much deeper analysis of meaning than in a classical predicate logic. In fact, by comparison, the assignment of values to predicates in a classical predicate logic is a triviality. For each n-place predicate we set up in a model a corresponding (classical) set of n-tuples of individuals. Thus, an expression like 'BIRD(x)' is true on an assignment of individuals to variables just in case the individual denoted by x is in the set of birds. Nothing is said about whether it has to have wings or a beak, whether it typically flies, what its body structure is, how it reproduces, whether it has feathers, etc. Nor is anything said in classical predicate logic about what type of criteria these are and how they contribute to degree of category membership. In a fuzzy predicate logic with hedges, *all* these matters must be taken into account in every valuation for the predicate BIRD. The reason is that all of these matters enter into the assignment of truth values when BIRD is modified by one or another of the set of hedges. Simply saying that an individual is or is not in the set of birds will tell you next to nothing about how to evaluate sentences where BIRD is modified by a hedge. In short, fuzzy predicate logic with hedges requires serious semantic analysis for all predicates.

6.8. *Claim: Hedges Show That Formal Semantics is the Right Approach to the Logic of Natural Language and That Axiomatic Theories Will Be Inadequate*

Considering the cleverness of logicians in devising axiomatizations, this claim should be hedged considerably. However, I think it will turn out to be correct. Suppose Zadeh is right in suggesting that hedges like SORT OF, PRETTY, VERY, etc. require algebraic functions such as those discussed above to account for their meaning, at least in part. It seems to me unlikely that one is going to be able to get complete axiomatizations for fuzzy predicate logics containing such hedges. At least, the question should be raised as a challenge to logicians. If my guess is correct, then we will have learned something very deep and important about natural languages and how they differ from artificial languages.

6.9. *In Addition to Degrees of Truth, Degrees of Nonsense are Needed to Account for Certain Hedges*

Suppose P presupposes Q and Q has some intermediate degree of truth. Does P make sense? Is it complete nonsense? Or does it have an intermediate degree of nonsense? A study of the hedge TO THE EXTENT THAT IT MAKES SENSE TO SAY THAT ... indicates that intermediate degrees of nonsense are necessary. Moreover, Fuzzy Presuppositional Logics with intermediate degrees of nonsense cannot be handled by Van Fraassen's supervaluations. (For discussion, see Appendix II.)

APPENDIX I: A SUGGESTION OF SCOTT'S

Dana Scott (personal communication) has suggested a method for setting up fuzzy propositional logic in a way that shows its relation to modal and many-valued logics in general. The Kripke semantics for modal logics is based on the notion of a 'possible world', that is, a complete and consistent assignment of truth values to every proposition, in other words, a classical (two-valued) valuation. A model for a classical modal logic contains a set of possible worlds (that is, a set of classical valuations) and a two-place alternativeness relation between worlds (that is, a relation between classical valuations). Scott has suggested a semantics for propositional fuzzy logic that looks like a modal semantics, though as we will see below, it differs from classical modal semantics.

Take a set of (two-valued) valuations – one for each number in the real interval [0, 1]. Let the alternativeness relation be '$\leq$'. Let '$V_i(P)$' stand for 'P is true in valuation i'. Constrain the set of valuations as in (1).

(1)   If $V_i(P)$, then for all j, $i \leq j$, $V_j(P)$.

We can represent this diagrammatically as in (2).

(2)   Error Scale

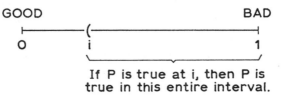

We will say that P deviates from absolute truth to degree i iff i is the greatest lower bound of the valuations in which P is true.

Scott has set this up in the reverse of the way we set up the semantics for *FPL*. We spoke of degree of truth. In Scott's treatment, we have what might be called degree of error or degree of deviation from absolute truth. To get Zadeh values, take $1 -$ Scott's values.

Scott defines valuations for $\neg$, $\wedge$, $\vee$, and $\rightarrow$ as follows.

(3) $V_i(\neg P)$ iff not $V_{1-i}(P)$
          $V_i(P \wedge Q)$ iff $V_i(P)$ and $V_i(Q)$
          $V_i(P \vee Q)$ iff $V_i(P)$ or $V_i(Q)$
          $V_i(P \rightarrow Q)$ iff $(\forall j)$ $V_j(P)$ implies $V_j(Q)$

The words 'not', 'and', 'or', and 'implies' in (3) stand for the corresponding connectives in classical propositional calculus, as used in the metalanguage. The point is to show how the connectives of fuzzy propositional logic can be defined in terms of the connectives of classical propositional logic and sequences of two-valued valuations.

Truth (absolute truth) turns out to be truth in all valuations, like necessity in an S5 modal system. If one wants, one can define an operator '$\boxdot$' so that '$\boxdot P$' is interpreted as 'P is true' then,

(4) $V_i(\Box P)$ iff $V_0(P)$, that is, iff $(\forall j) V_j(P)$.

In *FPL* we defined '$\to$' as taking only the values 0 and 1. However, it might be interesting to investigate fuzzy propositional logics where '$\to$' takes on intermediate values as well. I have not thought about any systems that might be motivated by empirical considerations taken from the study of natural language. However, the literature on many-valued logics contains extensions of our '$\to$' to intermediate values, which are motivated on purely formal grounds. One such case is a many-valued system of Gödel's (see Rescher, 1969, p. 44), which contains the same definitions of '$\neg$', '$\wedge$' and '$\vee$' as *FPL* and the following definition of '$\to$'.

(5) Gödel's '$\to$'

$$|P \to Q| = \begin{cases} 1 & \text{iff} \quad |P| \leqslant |Q| \\ |Q| & \text{iff} \quad |P| > |Q|. \end{cases}$$

Translated into Scott's treatment of fuzzy logic, we get:

(6) Scott's Version of Gödel's '$\to$'

$$V_i(P \to Q) \quad \text{iff} \quad \forall j, i \leqslant j, [V_j(P) \text{ implies } V_j(Q)].$$

As Scott observed (personal communication), (6) is an intuitionistic-style implication. As McKinsey and Tarski (1948) showed, intuitionistic logic has an S4 semantics; i.e., a modal semantics in which the alternativeness relation is reflexive and transitive, but not symmetric. In (6), '$\leqslant$' serves as an alternativeness relation, relating valuations i and j. '$\leqslant$' is, of course, reflexive and transitive, but not symmetric. The *FPL* '$\to$' is the S5 counterpart of Gödel's S4 '$\to$'.

Another interesting extension of the *FPL* '$\to$' to intermediate values is that found in the many-valued generalizations of the 3-valued system of Łukasiewicz (see Rescher, 1969, p. 36).

(7) Łukasiewicz' '$\to$'

$$|P \to Q| = \begin{cases} 1 & \text{iff} \quad |P| \leqslant |Q| \\ 1 - |P| + |Q|, & \text{iff} \quad |P| > |Q|. \end{cases}$$

Translated into Scott's treatment, we get:

(8) Scott's Version of Łukasiewicz' '$\to$'

$V_i(P \to Q)$ iff $\forall j, k$ such that
$$i + j \leqslant k \, [V_j(P) \text{ implies } V_k(Q)].$$

Intuitively, Łukasiewicz' implication in a fuzzy logic can be thought of as putting a constraint on the amount of error (or deviation from absolute truth) accumulated by an application of modus ponens. Suppose we assume P and $P \to Q$, and we deduce Q. If P has degree of deviation from truth j, and $P \to Q$ has degree of deviation from truth i, then the degree of deviation from truth of Q, namely k, must be less than or equal to the sum of i and j. Note that if $i=0$, we get the *FPL* '→'.

To me, the most interesting thing about (8) is that it is reminiscent of definitions of relevant entailment. '$i+j \leqslant k$' can be viewed as a 3-place alternativeness relation. If one replaces '$i+j \leqslant k$' with '$R(i, j, k)$' in (8) we get the general form of the definition or relevant entailment (see Meyer and Routley). This suggests a method for studying the relation between fuzzy logics and relevant entailment systems.

Given an extension of *FPL* '→' to intermediate values, we automatically get a notion of degree of entailment via the definition:

(9) $P \Vdash_\alpha Q$ iff $\Vdash_\alpha P \to Q$
        P entails Q to degree α iff the value of '$P \to Q$' never falls below α in any valuation.

Naturally, each different extension of *FPL* '→' gives us a different notion of degree of entailment.

If propositional fuzzy logic has a modal semantics, as we have just seen, then what kind of semantics does fuzzy modal logic have? The answer is straightforward. Instead of having a possible world w being a single valuation, V_w, think of a possible world as a sequence of valuations: $V_{0w}, \ldots, V_{iw}, \ldots, V_{1w}$. The value of '$\Box P$' is then characterized by:

(10) $V_{iw}(\Box P)$ iff $\forall_{w'}$ such that Rww' $[V_{iw'}(P)]$.

The beauty of Scott's suggestion is that it would allow us to treat modal and many-valued logics in a single framework, one in which they can be understood in terms of two-valued valuations and classical connectives in the metalanguage. I have, of course, considered only a special case, one where the set of valuations is linearly ordered by the relation $\leqslant$ and corresponds $1-1$ with the real interval $[0, 1]$. In the case of a 3-valued logic, there would be only 3 linearly ordered valuations. In the case of a Boolean-valued logic, the valuations would form a Boolean algebra. In a modal logic, the valuations would be structured by an alternativeness relation.

Contra Zadeh (1971, p. 33), fuzzy sets cannot be represented as sequences of classical sets, since complementation would not work correctly. This remarkable fact follows directly from the fact that negation cannot be classical in Scott's system, as we are about to see.

In an earlier version of this paper, published in the *Proceedings of the Eighth Regional Meeting of the Chicago Linguistics Society*, there was an important misprint. The definition of negation was mistakenly given as (A) instead of (B), which was Scott's suggested definition.

(A) $V_i(\neg P)$ iff not $V_i(P)$

(B) $V_i(\neg P)$ iff not $V_{1-i}(P)$.

We can see why Scott wanted (B) rather than (A) by looking at his definition of conjunction. Let us begin with a simple case.

(11) Suppose the value of P is 0.3 and the value of Q is 0.6:

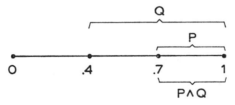

In this situation, '$P \wedge Q$' will be true in just those valuations in which 'P' is true and so it will have the value 0.3, just as in *FPL*. But now what would the value of '$P \wedge \neg Q$' be in such a situation? The answer will depend on which definition of negation we choose. Let us consider both possibilities.

(12) The value of 'P' is 0.3. the value of 'Q' is 0.6, and the value of '$\neg Q$' is 0.4.

(a) Definition (A) yields:

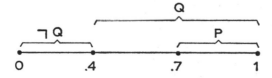

There is no valuation in which 'P' is true and '$\neg Q$' is true.

Therefore, the value of '$P \wedge \neg Q$' is zero, which does not accord with *FPL*.

(b) Definition (B) yields:

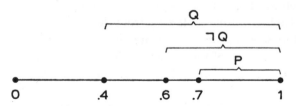

'$P \wedge \neg Q$' is true in every valuation in which 'P' is true.

Therefore the value of '$P \wedge \neg Q$' is 0.3, which accords with *FPL*.

The effect of the '$1-i$' in definition (B) is to make sure that the evaluations take place at the same end of the scale, so that the definitions of conjunction and disjunction will work correctly. Definition (B) gives the right answer, while (A) gives the wrong answer. But not without cost. Note that in (2b), 'Q' and '$\neg Q$' are both true in every valuation between 0.6 and 1, while in the valuations between 0 and 0.4, neither 'Q' nor '$\neg Q$' is true. In short, the two-valued valuations represented in (12b) are anything but classical. One may or may not want to consider this a flaw. Perhaps the appropriate way to look at many-valued logic is as a modal logic in which the individual two-valued valuations are nonclassical in this way. Note that they are not completely nonclassical however. The classical definitions of conjunction and disjunction will still hold; but negation becomes a modal operator under definition (B).[5] For many logicians, much of the appeal of Scott's system may be lost if the valuations are not classical. I think this would be a pity. Such systems are beautiful and interesting regardless of whether the valuations are classical.

APPENDIX II: FUZZY PRESUPPOSITIONAL LOGIC

In Section 2, we observed that there was an inconsistency between defining negation as $|\neg P| = 1 - |P|$ and defining presuppositions so that P presupposes Q iff $P \Vdash Q$ and $\neg P \Vdash Q$. We observed that we could get around the inconsistency if we let the values assigned be triples (α, β, γ) consisting of a truth-value, a falsity-value, and a nonsense-value, such that $\alpha + \beta + \gamma = 1$. Negation would then be defined by:

(1) $|\neg P| = (\alpha, \beta, \gamma)$ iff $|P| = (\beta, \alpha, \gamma)$.

As in all presuppositional logics, the negation in (1) interchanges the truth and falsity values and preserves the nonsense value.

Given (1), there are two possible variations one can consider. One can permit degrees of nonsense, letting γ range over the real interval $[0, 1]$. Or one can consider systems where every proposition either makes sense or it doesn't, restricting γ to the values 0 and 1. If one makes the latter decision, presuppositional fuzzy logic can be handled by a system of supervaluations of the sort developed by Van Fraassen. Suppose P contains a presupposition failure. Then in a system where negation is defined as in (1), the value of P would be $(0, 0, 1)$, and the value of $\neg P$ would also be $(0, 0, 1)$. In a supervaluation treatment, we would assign as values not triples but simply ordinary truth-values, except that in the case of presupposition failure, a value would not be assigned. We could then define negation so that $|\neg P|$ would be $1 - |P|$ just in case P was assigned a value. If P was not assigned a value, then $\neg P$ would not be assigned a value.

In a technical sense, the supervaluation approach could get around the problem without having triples assigned as values, provided it was assumed that every sentence either made complete sense or was complete nonsense. However, if we allow intermediate degrees of nonsense, no supervaluation approach will work. But even if we restrict every sentence either to making complete sense or being complete nonsense, the supervaluation approach has a serious defect. As we said, supervaluations would not assign a value *in the case of presupposition failure*. In nonfuzzy logics, it is clear what constitutes a presupposition failure, namely, if one or more of the presupposed sentences is false. But in fuzzy logic it is not clear what constitutes a presupposition failure, since the presupposed sentences can have values intermediate between 0 and 1. Thus, in the supervaluation approach, we would have to make an arbitrary decision as to what constitutes a presupposition failure, so that we would know when not to assign a truth value. We could, for example, decide that if a presupposed sentence had any value less than 1, that is, if it deviated from absolute truth at all, that would constitute a presupposition failure. Or we could decide that there was a presupposition failure only when the value of some presupposed sentence was 0, that is, when it was absolutely false. Or we could pick 0.5 as a designated value and say that we had a presupposition failure only when the value of P fell below 0.5, that is, when P was more false than true. Or we could arbitrarily designate any

other value. The point is that in the supervaluation approach the choice
is arbitrary. This, I think, is a irremediable weakness in that approach.

What provides troubles for the supervaluation approach is that a presupposed sentence may be fuzzy, that is, that it may take on a truth value
intermediate between 0 and 1. My feeling about this is that when P presupposes Q and Q has the intermediate truth value α, then P should have
the intermediate nonsense value $1-\alpha$. In other words, P lacks sense to
the degree that its presuppositions lack truth. The truer its presuppositions get, the more P makes sense. I think that there are examples that
justify this intuition.

(2)   a. Dick Cavett regrets that he is tall.
       b. Dick Cavett is tall.
(3)   a. Sam was surprised that he had approximately $10000 in
          his savings account.
       b. Sam had approximately $10000 in his savings account.
       c. Sam had $9992 in his savings account.
       d. Sam had $9950 in his savings account.
       e. Sam had $9500 in his savings account.
       f. Sam had $9200 in his savings account.
          etc.

(2a) presupposes (2b). As it happens, Dick Cavett happens to be 5'7" tall,
which is tall to about degree 0.3. Consequently (2) doesn't make much
sense. But suppose Cavett were 5'9". Then (2a) would start making more
sense. Or suppose he were 5'11". (2a) would make even more sense. And
if Cavett were 6'4", then (2a), whether true or false, would make perfect
sense in most situations.

(3a) is a similar example. (3a) presupposes (3b). But (3b) is fuzzy – it
depends on what counts as an approximation to having $10000 in ones
savings account. Suppose (3c) were the case. Then I think (3b) would be
true no matter what, and (3a) would make perfect sense. If (3d) were the
case, I think most people in most situations would still want to say that
(3b) was true and that (3a) made sense. If (3e) were true, the truth of (3b)
would become questionable. In many situations (3b) would have a high
degree of truth given the truth of (3e), and (3a) would pretty much make
sense. When we get down to (3f), however, the degree of truth of (3b) gets
lower, and it makes less sense to say (a). And so on.

Interestingly enough, there is a hedge in English which depends upon there being intermediate degrees of nonsense. In fact, its function is to remove intermediate degrees of nonsense, while not changing complete nonsense. The expression is: TO THE EXTENT THAT IT MAKES SENSE TO SAY THAT .... Consider the following example.

(4)   a. J. L. Austin was a *good* linguist. [main stress on *good*]
       b. J. L. Austin was a linguist.
       c. To the extent that it makes sense to say that J. L. Austin was a linguist, he was a *good* linguist.

J. L. Austin was primarily a philosopher, not a linguist. Yet his analyses of various natural language phenomena could certainly be considered linguistics, in fact, excellent linguistics. Thus, though (4b) is not strictly true, I don't think it would be correct to say that it was strictly false. I would say that it had some intermediate value. (4a) presupposes (4b). Thus, (4a) has an intermediate nonsense value. To some extent, (4a) seems to make sense and to some extent it seems not to. However, (4c) makes perfect sense. The effect of the *to*-phrase in (4c) has been to remove the intermediate nonsense value of (4a). Note incidentally that the *to*-phrase of (4c) presupposes (4d).

(4d)   To some extent it makes sense to say that J. L. Austin was a linguist.

Given that (4c) makes perfect sense, (4d) must be true, which seems intuitively correct. Note that (4d) asserts (truth-fully!) that there is some intermediate degree to which a proposition of (4b) makes sense.
Compare (4) with (5).

(5)   a. J. L. Austin was a *good* king of France.
       b. J. L. Austin was the king of France.
       c. To the extent to which it makes sense to say that J. L. Austin was the king of France, he was a *good* king of France.[6]
       d. To some extent it makes sense to say that J. L. Austin was the king of France.

(5b) is utterly false – it is not true to any degree. (5a), which presupposes (5b), is complete nonsense (given the facts of this world). (5d) is false.

And (5c) is complete nonsense, just like (5a). I think that the disparity between the sentences in (4) and those in (5) shows that sentences of English can take on intermediate nonsense values when their presuppositions take on intermediate truth values. Thus, I think there is real motivation for investigating fuzzy presuppositional logics that can take on intermediate nonsense values.

Let us return then to the investigation of systems where the values assigned are ordered triples whose sum is 1 and where negation is defined as in (1) above. How do we go about defining conjunction and disjunction? To get some idea of how this can be done, let us look at the corresponding definitions in the classic 3-valued systems of Bochvar and Łukasiewicz (See Rescher, 1969).

(6) Bochvar's Conjunction and Disjunction

$\wedge$	N	F	T		$\vee$	N	T	F
N	N	N	N		N	N	N	N
F	N	F	F		T	N	T	T
T	N	F	T		F	N	T	F

(7) Łukasiewicz' Conjunction and Disjunction

$\wedge$	F	N	T		$\vee$	T	N	F
F	F	F	F		T	T	T	T
N	F	N	N		N	T	N	N
T	F	N	T		F	T	N	F

There are certain general principles governing the determination of values in these systems. They are as follows:

I. The value of the conjunction (disjunction) is the same as the value of one of the component sentences (both, if they have the same value).
II. In each csse there is a hierarchy of values that determines the component sentence whose value will be assigned to the entire sentence. The hierarchies are given in (8).

(8) The Value Hierarchies

> Bochvar Conjunction: N, F, T
> Bochvar Disjunction: N, T, F
> Łukasiewicz Conjunction: F, N, T
> Łukasiewicz Disjunction: T, N, F

III. General Principles Determining the Hierarchies

    a. In conjunctions, T occupies the lowest place in the hierarchy. In disjunctions, F occupies the lowest place in the hierarchy.

    b. In the Bochvar system, N occupies the highest place in the hierarchies.

    In the Łukasiewicz system, N occupies the intermediate place in the hierarchies.

Given I, II, and III and the hierarchies in (8), we can give general directions for computing the tables in (6) and (7).

(9) How to Compute (6) and (7)

    a. If one (or both) of the component sentences has the highest value in the hierarchy, the conjunction (disjunction) has that value.

    b. If not, then if one (or both of the component sentences) has the next highest value, then the entire conjunction (disjunction) has that value.

    c. Otherwise the conjunction (disjunction) has the lowest value in the hierarchy.

Given this characterization of the Bochvar and Łukasiewicz connectives for 3-valued logic, we can get Bochvar-style and Łukasiewicz-style connectives for fuzzy presuppositional logics. We keep principles I, II, and III and the hierarchies in (8). However, in fuzzy presuppositional logics, the values assigned to propositions are not merely T, F, and N. Instead we have ordered triples of numerical values (α, β, γ). We will refer to T, F, and N as 'value-types' and α, β, and γ will be the numerical values of those types. The hierarchies in (8) now are hierarchies of value-types rather than values. We can now give directions for computing the values for Bochvar-style and Łukasiewicz-style conjunctions and disjunctions in fuzzy presuppositional logics.

(10) How to Compute Bochvar-style and Łukasiewicz-style Connectives

    a. If one of the component sentences has the highest numerical value for the highest value-type in the hierarchy, then the conjunction (disjunction) has the same triple of numerical values as that component sentence.

b. If the numerical values for the highest value-type are the same, then if one of the component sentences has the highest numerical value for the next-highest value-type in the hierarchy, then the conjunction (disjunction) has the same triple of numerical values as that component sentence.
c. Otherwise, both component sentences have the same triple of values and the conjunction (disjunction) has that triple.

An example of how these systems work is given in the chart in (10). On the right hand side we have listed whether the entire conjunction or disjunction gets the value for component sentence P or component sentence Q.

(10)

	P	Q	$P \wedge_B Q$	$P \wedge_B Q$	$P \wedge_L Q$	$P \wedge_L Q$
a.	(0.2,0.1,0.7)	(0.3,0.5,0.2)	P	P	Q	Q
b.	(0.2,0.5,0.3)	(0.4,0.3,0.3)	P	Q	P	Q
c.	(0.4,0.2,0.4)	(0.3,0.2,0.5)	Q	Q	Q	P
d.	(0.5,0.3,0.2)	(0.5,0.2,0.3)	Q	Q	P	Q

In (10a): For both Bochvar connectives, N is highest in the hierarchy. P has the highest N-value, namely, 0.7. So both connectives are assigned the triple for P. F is highest in the Łukasiewicz conjunction hierarchy. Q has the highest F-value, namely, 0.5. T is the highest in the Łukasiewicz disjunction hierarchy. Q has the highest T-value, namely, 0.3. So both Łukasiewicz connectives are assigned the triple for Q.

In (10b): For Bochvar conjunction, N is highest in the hierarchy. But P and Q have the same N-value, namely, 0.3. F is next highest in the Bochvar conjunction hierarchy. P has the highest F-value, 0.5; so the Bochvar conjunction is assigned the triple for P. For Bochvar disjunction, N is again highest in the hierarchy and again the N-values are the same for P and Q. T is next highest in the Bochvar disjunction hierarchy. Q has the highest T-value, so the Bochvar disjunction is assigned the triple for Q. The rest of the examples are obvious.

So far as implication is concerned, my feeling is that the degree of nonsense for '$P \rightarrow Q$' should always be 0. I feel that it always makes sense to ask whether or to what degree P implies Q. Moreover, I feel that implication is based solely on truth values, not on nonsense values. Therefore one can incorporate into fuzzy presuppositional logics the same definitions of implication used in fuzzy propositional logics.

I should make clear that the above definitions of Bochvar-style and Łukasiewicz-style connectives are purely a technical exercise. I certainly do not believe that any of them accurately represents the meaning of natural language *and* or *or*. In fact, these connectives are incredibly simple-minded compared to the complexities of natural language conjunction (see Robin Lakoff, 1971). My purpose here is simply to get the study of fuzzy presuppositional logics off the ground in the hope that others will carry it further. One interesting question to consider is whether the Bochvar-style and Łukasiewicz-style systems described above can be translated into the format suggested by Scott (see Appendix I). So far, I have not been able to do it.

APPENDIX III: FUZZY THEOREMS

The following is a well-known theorem of Euclidean geometry.

(1)   The three lines each of which bisect one side of a given triangle and go through the opposite angle, meet in a point.

Zadeh (personal communication) has observed that this theorem can be 'fuzzified' to a sentence which is also true in the Euclidean plane.

(2)   Three lines, each of which *approximately* bisects one side of a given triangle and goes through the opposite angle, form a triangle inside the given triangle and *much* smaller than it.

Though (2) is true in the Euclidean plane, it cannot be deduced from Euclid's postulates, since they provide no way of dealing with hedges like *approximately* and *much* (as in *much larger than*). (2) is an example of a sentence which is true in a model of Euclid's postulates but which is not deduceable from the postulates. Though Gödel showed that such cases must exist for arithmetic, his examples were of a very much different sort. (2) is an interesting curiosity, an intuitively obvious truth of Euclidean geometry which cannot be deduced from Euclid's postulates.

University of California

NOTES

* This work was supported by grant GS-2939 from the National Science Foundation of the University of Michigan and by a grant from the American Council of Learned Societies. It was written while I was in residence at the Center for Advanced Study in the Behavioral Sciences at Stanford, to whom I would like to express thanks for the use of their facilities.
The original impetus for the study of hedges came from the work of Heider (1971), Alston (1964), Ross (1970), and Bolinger (1972). The formal parts are based on the development of fuzzy set theory by Lofti Zadeh, Dept. of Electrical Engineering, U. of California, Berkeley. Professor Zadeh has been kind enough to discuss this paper with me often and at great length and many of the ideas in it have come from those discussions. In addition I would like to thank the following people whose discussed these ideas with me and who contributed to what little understanding I have of the subject: Ann Borkin, Herb Clark, Alan Dershowitz, Hubert Dryfus, Charles Fillmore, Jim Fox, Dov Gabbay, Richard Grandy, Charles Guignon, Eleanor Heider, Peter Kenen, Robin Lakoff, John Lawler, Robert LeVine, David Lewis, Ruth Barcan Marcus, James Matisoff, Jim McCawley, Robert Nozick, Michael Reddy, Haj Ross, Dana Scott, and Bas van Fraassen.

[1] Tallness is also relative to point of view. In a given population, someone who is 5'5" may consider someone who is 5'10" to be relatively tall, while someone who is 6'4" might not. We will ignore such factors at present, noting that they will have to be taken into account.

[2] Another system of fuzzy propositional logic can be found in Goguen (1971). Goguen, however, chose a different semantics for conjunction and disjunction. The system given here is identical to the system $S_{\aleph}$ discussed in Rescher, 1969, p. 47.

[3] Actually we should have least upper bound for max and greatest lower bound for min, since we are dealing with the real numbers and so may have sequences which approach a limit but do not reach it.

[4] Lauri Karttunen (1971) has shown that (10) is inadequate and must be revised to include modalities as in (10').

(10') P presupposes Q iff $\Diamond P \Vdash Q$ and $\Diamond \neg P \Vdash Q$.

However, he has not yet figured out which $\Diamond$ will work. (See the discussion in Herzberger (1971).) But whichever $\Diamond$ turns out to be adequate, (10)) will at least be a necessary if not sufficient condition for logical presuppositions. Therefore, everything we have to say will hold for Karttunen's notion of presupposition.

[5] From here it is a small step to a demonstration that fuzzy sets cannot be represented as sequences of classical sets. Suppose we try to represent a fuzzy set P with degrees of membership in the interval [0, 1] as a sequence of classical sets $P_0, ..., P_i, ..., P_1, ...,$ with one set corresponding to each point in the interval. For each P_i, we assume that $x \in P_i$ or $x \notin P_i$, and if $x \in P_i$, then for all j, $j > i$, $x \in P_j$. We then say that $\mu_P(x) = k$ iff P_k is the greatest lower bound of $\{P_i / x \in P_i\}$. Classical intersection and union can easily be defined as follows: Intersection: $x \in P_i \cap Q_i$ iff $x \in P_i$ and $x \in Q_i$. Union: $x \in P_i \cup Q_i$ iff $x \in P_i$ or $x \in Q_i$. But complementation is a problem. Consider definitions (A) and (B). (A) Classical complementation: $x \in \bar{Q}_i$ iff $x \notin Q_i$. (B) 'Modal' complementation: $x \in \bar{Q}_i$ iff $x \notin Q_{1-i}$.
Now suppose that $\mu_P(x) = 0.3$ and $\mu_Q(x) = 0.6$. According to Zadeh's fuzzy set theory, $\mu_{\bar{Q}}(x) = 0.4$ and $\mu_{P \cap \bar{Q}}(x)$ should equal 0.3. (A) gives us a situation like that

pictured in figure (12a) in the text; in other words, we will get the wrong answer that $\mu_{P \cap \bar{Q}}(x) = 0$. With definition (B), we will get a situation like that pictured in figure (12b), and will get the right answer for fuzzy set theory. Unfortunately, (B) is not the definition of complementation in classical set theory. (B) gives rise to a nonstandard set theory, what might be called a 'modal' set theory.

⁶ Note that it is also nonsensical to say (i), though not as bad as (5).

(i)   To the extent to which it makes sense to say that J. L. Austin was a philosopher, he was a *good* philosopher.

(i)   is nonsense to some degree unless there is some reason to doubt that Austin was a philosopher.

BIBLIOGRAPHY

Alston, William: 1964, *Philosophy of Language*. Prentice-Hall, Chapter 5.

Bolinger, Dwight: 1972, *Degree Words,* Mouton.

Goguen, J. A.: 1971, 'The Logic of Inexact Concepts', *Synthese*.

Heider, Eleanor Rosch: 1971, 'On the Internal Structure of Perceptual and Semantic Categories', unpublished paper, Pyschology Dept., U. of California, Berkeley.

Herzberger, Hans: 1971, 'Remarks on Karttunen's Notion of Presupposition', unpublished paper, Philosophy Dept., U. of Toronto.

Karttunen, Lauri: 1971, 'Some Observations on Factivity', *Papers in Linguistics* **4**, 55–70.

Keenan, Edward: 1969, 'A Logical Base for English', U. of Pennsylvania Dissertation. Distributed by Transformation and Discourse Analysis Project, Linguistics Dept., U. of Pennsylvania, Philadelphia, Pa.

Lakoff, Robin: 1971, 'If's, And's, and But's About Conjunction', in *Studies in Linguistic Semantics* (ed. by Fillmore and Langendoen), Holt.

McKinsey, J. C. C. and Tarki, A.: 1948, 'Some Theorems About the Sentential Calculi of Lewis and Heyting', *Journal of Symbolic Logic*.

Meyer, Robert and Routley, Richard: 1971, 'Semantics of Entailment I', in *Truth, Syntax, Modality* (ed. by H. Leblanc), North-Holland Publ. Co., Amsterdam, forthcoming.

Reddy, Michael: 1972, 'Reference and Metaphor in Human Language', Unpublished U. of Chicago Dissertation, English Dept.

Rescher, Nicholas: 1969, *Many-Valued Logics,* McGraw-Hill.

Ross, John Robert: 1970, 'A Note on Implicit Comparatives', *Linguistic Inquiry* **1**. 36–63.

Slote, Michael: 1966, 'The Theory of Important Criteria', *Journal of Philosophy*.

van Fraassen, Bas: 1971, *Formal Semantics and Logic,* Macmillan.

Zadeh, Lofti: 1965, 'Fuzzy Sets', *Information and Control* **8**, 338–53.

Zadeh, Lofti: 1971a, 'Quantitative Fuzzy Semantics', *Information Sciences* **3**, 159–76.

Zadeh, Lofti: 1971b, 'Fuzzy Languages and Their Relation to Human Intelligence', Memorandum No. ERL-M302, Electronic Research Laboratory, of California, Berkeley.

Zadeh, Lofti: 1972, 'Fuzzy Set-Theoretic Interpretation of Hedges', Unpublished paper, Dept. of Electrical Engineering, U. of California, Berkeley.

BAS C. VAN FRAASSEN

COMMENTS: LAKOFF'S
FUZZY PROPOSITIONAL LOGIC

I. INTRODUCTORY REMARKS

I wish to comment only on a small aspect of Lakoff's paper[1], namely the axiomatization of the propositional logic he introduces. Lakoff states that

(1)   Each sentence has a value in the interval [0, 1] of real numbers
(2) $(A \rightarrow B)$ has value 1 exactly if the value of A is less than or equal to that of B
(3) A semantically entails B – in symbols, $A \Vdash B$ – exactly if, for all valuations, A receives a value less than or equal to that of B.

In addition, in answer to a question, Lakoff stated

(4) $(A \rightarrow B)$ has value 0 if the value of A is greater than that of B

which completes his characterization of valuations.

The axiomatization of his logic is a bit round-about. Let me introduce as subsidiary notion

(5) $X \Vdash^+ B$ exactly if all valuations that assign a value $\geqslant \frac{1}{2}$ to all members of the premise set X; also assign a value $\geqslant \frac{1}{2}$ to B.

Then we have the following easy result:

(6) $A \Vdash B$ iff $\Vdash A \rightarrow B$ iff $\Vdash^+ A \rightarrow B$

Hence, Lakoff's logic can be axiomatized by concentrating on the $\Vdash^+$ relation. (This does not mean that I advocate replacing $\Vdash$ by $\Vdash^+$.)

II. THE LANGUAGE FUZ

There is a countable set of atomic sentences, unary connective $\neg$, binary

Hockney et al. (eds.), Contemporary Research in Philosophical Logic and Linguistic Semantics, 273–277. All Rights Reserved
Copyright © 1975 by D. Reidel Publishing Company, Dordrecht-Holland

connectives $\wedge$ and $\vee$ and $\rightarrow$. The admissible valuations of FUZ are the maps V of all sentences into $[0, 1]$ such that

$$V(\neg A) = 1 - V(A)$$
$$V(A \wedge B) = \min\{V(A), V(B)\}$$
$$V(A \vee B) = \max\{V(A), V(B)\}$$
$$V(A \rightarrow B) = 1 \text{ if } V(A) \leqslant V(B)$$
$$\qquad\qquad = 0 \text{ otherwise}$$

and $X \Vdash^+ A$ in FUZ is defined by statement (5) above. (This is equivalent to the usual definition of semantic entailment plus the stipulation that 'is true' means 'has a value $\geqslant \frac{1}{2}$'.)

Before turning to the logic proper, let us look at a valuation V. This valuation gives 1 to the sentence t (which is $A \rightarrow A$, where A is the first atomic sentence), zero to f (which is $\neg t$), and a value greater than or equal to $\frac{1}{2}$ to one of P or $\neg P$, and also to one of $P \rightarrow Q$ or $Q \rightarrow P$. Indeed, the ordering of its values is entirely reflected in what the valuation *satisfies* (gives a value greater than or equal to $\frac{1}{2}$ to). For $V(A) \leqslant V(B)$ exactly if V satisfies $A \rightarrow B$. So *a fortiori*, V satisfies $A \leftrightarrow \neg A$ exactly if $V(A) = \frac{1}{2}$, and V will satisfy $A \leftrightarrow B$ if it satisfies both $A \leftrightarrow \neg A$ and $B \leftrightarrow \neg A$. But t could never be such a sentence.

Negation is order-inverting and idempotent; modus ponens holds; but nothing like the deduction theorem holds:

$$t \Vdash^+ A \vee \neg A \quad \text{but not} \quad \Vdash^+ t \rightarrow (A \vee \neg A)$$

also, $A \wedge \neg A$ can never be true, but does not semantically entail f. Finally, if A and B are any two propositions, then $A \rightarrow B$ or $B \rightarrow A$ must be in V^*, the set of all sentences which V satisfies.

III. THE LOGIC FUZL

The usual structural rules will hold for the single turnstile $\vdash$; equivalently, Cn: $\mathrm{Cn}(X) = \{A: X \vdash A\}$ is a logical closure operator. In addition, I call a set inconsistent in case it contains all sentences; equivalently, iff it contains f. Finally, FUZL – pronounced on the model of 'fizzle' – has the following special axioms and rules.

Group A

A1	$\vdash P \to t$
A2	$\vdash (P \to Q) \lor (Q \to P)$
A3	$\vdash t \to (P \to Q) \lor t \to \neg (P \to Q)$
A4	$P, P \to Q \vdash Q$
A5	$P \to Q, Q \to R \vdash P \to R$

Group B

B1	$\vdash \neg \neg P \leftrightarrow P$ ('$A \leftrightarrow B$', short for '$A \to B \land B \to A$')
B2	$P \to Q \vdash \neg Q \to \neg P$
B3	$P, \neg P \vdash P \leftrightarrow \neg P$

Group C

C1	$\vdash P \land Q \to P; \vdash P \land Q \to Q$
C2	$R \to P, R \to Q \vdash R \to (P \land Q)$
C3	$\vdash P \to (P \lor Q); \vdash Q \to (P \lor Q)$
C4	$P \to R, Q \to R \vdash P \lor Q \to R$
C5	If $X, P \vdash R$ and $X, Q \vdash R$ then $X, P \lor Q \vdash R$
C6	$\vdash P \lor [\neg (P \leftrightarrow \neg P) \land \neg P]$

Theorems

T1	$f \vdash P$	By A1, B2, A4, B1
T2	$P \to Q \vdash t \to (P \to Q)$	By B2, B1, A4, C5, T1, A3
T3	$\neg (P \to Q) \vdash t \to \neg (P \to Q)$	As for T2, *mutatis mutandis*
T4	$\vdash P \to P$	By A2, C5
T5	$\vdash P \lor \neg P$	By C6, C1, C3, C5
T6	$P \leftrightarrow \neg P \vdash P$	By T5, A4, C1, C2, C5
T7	$P \leftrightarrow \neg P, Q \leftrightarrow \neg Q \vdash P \leftrightarrow Q.$	By A2, C1, C2, A5; C5, C2
T8	$P, Q \vdash P \land Q$	By A2, T4, C2, A4, C5
T9	$\vdash (P \lor Q) \leftrightarrow P. \lor . (P \lor Q) \leftrightarrow Q.$	By A2, C4, T4, C3, T8, C3, A4; C5
T10.	$\vdash (P \land Q) \leftrightarrow P. \lor . (P \land Q) \to Q.$	As for T9, *mutatis mutandis*
T11.	If $A \vdash f$ then $\vdash \neg A$	By T5, T1, C5
T12.	$\vdash (t \leftrightarrow \neg t)$	By C1, C2, T6, T11

IV. SOUNDNESS AND COMPLETENESS

Soundness of the axioms (if $X \vdash A$ then $X \Vdash^+ A$) follows easily from the preliminary semantic discussion. Also, by familiar reasoning, any consistent set of FUZL can be extended to a maximal consistent set. Just because $\Vdash^+$, unlike $\Vdash$, has a kind of excluded middle principle, the following lemma will help.

LEMMA. Every maximal consistent set is satisfiable.

For let X be a maximal consistent set. For each sentence A let $[A] = = \{B: A \leftrightarrow B \in X\}$, and define $[A] \leqslant [B]$ iff $A \to B \in X$. In view of T8, $[A] = [B]$ if $[A] \leqslant [B]$ and $[B] \leqslant [A]$. In view of A2, A5, and T4, the ordering is linear. Assign values by a countable series of steps: $[A \leftrightarrow A]$ gets 1; the set $\{P: \neg P \leftrightarrow P \in X\} = \Phi$ gets $\frac{1}{2}$ if it is one of the sets $[A]$ at all. Then go through the remaining members $A_1, A_2, \ldots$ of X as follows:

$[A_1]$ gets a value half-way between $\frac{1}{2}$ and 1; $[A_{n+1}]$ gets a value half-way between the two of Φ, $[A_1], \ldots, [A_n]$, $[A \leftrightarrow A]$ that it lies directly between in the $\leqslant$ ordering.

Now define the map V as follows: if $A \in X$, then $V(A)$ is the value $[A]$ received above. If A is not in X, but $\neg A$ is then $V(A) = 1 - V(\neg A)$.

Now I assert that V is a valuation. In view of T5, C3–C5, each sentence has received a value. If A and $\neg A$ are both in X, then so is $A \leftrightarrow \neg A$ by B3, so $V(A) = V(\neg A) = \frac{1}{2}$ in that case; hence each sentence received a unique value.

We note that in view of T9 and C5, $[P \vee Q]$ must equal either $[P]$ or $[Q]$, namely $[P]$ if $[Q] \leqslant [P]$ and $[Q]$ otherwise. Hence $V(P \vee Q)$ is indeed max $\{V(P), V(Q)\}$. Via T10 and C5, we see similarly that $V(P \wedge Q) = \min \{V(P), V(Q)\}$.

Finally, in view of T2 and T3, and A1, we see that whichever of $(P \to Q)$ and $\neg(P \to Q)$ happens to be in X will get the value of $[A \to A]$ and the other will get zero. But of course $P \to Q$ is in X exactly if $[P] \leqslant [Q]$.

So V is indeed a valuation.

THEOREM. If $X \Vdash^+ A$ then $X \vdash A$

Suppose not $X \vdash A$. In that case $X^* = [X \cup \{\neg(A \leftrightarrow \neg A) \wedge \neg A\}]$ is consistent in view of C5 and C6. (For if X^* were inconsistent then

$X * \vdash f$, so $X * \vdash A$; but then X, $A \vdash A$ and X, $[\neg (A \leftrightarrow \neg A) \wedge A] \vdash A$, so X, $A \vee [\neg (A \leftrightarrow \neg A) \wedge A] \vdash A$ by C5. But then, by C6, $X \vdash A$.) So by the preceding lemma, $X *$ can be satisfied. However, a valuation which satisfies $X *$, satisfies X but gives a value strictly less than $\frac{1}{2}$ to A. Hence not $(X \Vdash^+ A)$.

University of Toronto

NOTES

[1] In this volume, pp. 221–271; first published in *Journal of Philosophical Logic* 2 (1973), pp. 458–508. The author wishes to acknowledge gratefully the support of Canada Council grants S72-0849 and S73-0849.

HOWARD LASNIK

ON THE SEMANTICS OF NEGATION

It will be my purpose in this paper to examine some aspects of the meaning of negative sentences, in particular, those containing the morpheme *not*. Although the analysis will be presented within the framework of an 'interpretive theory' similar to those of Chomsky (1970) and Jackendoff (1972), I do not intend to concentrate my attention here on defending any particular theory.[1] Rather, I wish to illustrate some ways in which negative sentences differ from corresponding non-negative sentences, and to examine structural and phonetic properties of sentences that seem to correlate with the particular meaning properties discussed.

I will first consider some semantic properties of items in the 'scope of negation' (i.e., under the influence of a negative morpheme). In this regard, compare sentences (1) and (2).

(1)   Many people saw the movie
(2)   Not many people saw the movie

One striking difference between (1) and (2) is that the quantifier in (1) can be used to make specific reference while the one in (2) cannot. Thus, (1') is a possible extension of (1), but (2') is ill-formed.

(1')   Many people (namely, John, Bill, Mary, etc.) saw the movie
(2')   *Not many people (namely ...) saw the movie

Similarly, definite pronominalization produces odd sentences, when the antecedent is a negated quantifier phrase. (2") seems bad in the same way that (2') is.

(1")   Many people saw the movie. They enjoyed it.
(2")   Not many people saw the movie. *They enjoyed it.

Now notice that on one reading, in fact on the primary reading, (3) is synonymous with (2).

(3)   The movie wasn't seen by many people

Semantically, (3) can have the same unit, *not many*, that is present in (2). Apparently, it is not necessary, then, that *not* and *many* be in the same constituent in order for them to be related thus creating the semantic unit *not many*.

When *not* is not immediately contiguous to *many*, however, it is possible for *many* to escape the negating influence of *not*. Both (5) and (6) are possible paraphrases of (4), but in (6) it is evident that *many* is outside the scope of negation.

(4)   I couldn't solve many of the problems
(5)   I could solve few of the problems
(6)   There were many of the problems that I couldn't solve

(5) is a direct contradiction of (4′).

(4′)   I could solve many of the problems

But (6) and (4′) can be simultaneously true, if, for example, half of the problems were solved.

The normal reading of (4) is (5), but with a special intonation in which 'I couldn't solve' is a phonetic phrase, and 'many of the problems' is an independent phrase, the latter is isolated from the negation.[2] I will give a more precise description of that phenomenon below. That there is the potential for isolating object position from the scope of negation is made clear by the existence of sentences like (7).

(7)   I couldn't solve $\begin{Bmatrix} \text{several} \\ \text{certain} \end{Bmatrix}$ of the problems

Several in sentence (7) can always make reference in the sense discussed above. This suggests that *several* must be outside the scope of negation. A quantifier immediately following *not* can never be isolated from the latter's scope. That is, sentence (8) must be synonymous to (9); it can never have the type of ambiguity that (4) above displays.

(8)   Not many of the problems were solved
(9)   Few of the problems were solved

Since certain quantifiers, for example *several* and *some*, will always be non-negated in object position, one would predict that they cannot occur at all immediately following *not*, since in that position a quantifier will apparently always be negated. That prediction is correct, as example (10) demonstrates.[3]

(10)   *Not $\begin{Bmatrix} several \\ some \end{Bmatrix}$ of the problems were solved

The following two generalizations describe the data I have thus far presented:

(11a)   A quantifier immediately following *not* is obligatorily negated, and consequently the NP it quantifies can never be referential.

(11b)   In general, a quantifier following *not*, but not immediately, can be non-negated (if the sentence has a special intonation contour).

The scope of negation is not symmetric. If a quantifier occurs to the left of *not*, it will be outside the scope of negation[4]. Sentence (12), for example, will never be synonymous to sentence (8) above.

(12)   Many of the problems weren't solved

Another basic limitation on the scope of negation is that an element can only be in the scope of negation if it is commanded[5] by a negative morpheme. In sentences (13) and (14), *many* is outside the scope of negation even though *not* precedes it.

(13)   The man who didn't eat dinner saw many people
(14)   That John didn't leave surprised many people

There is no reading of either of those sentences in which *not* is semantically associated with *many*. These facts are incorporated with (11) above in (15).

(15a)   Only if *not* commands a quantifier and precedes it can that quantifier be within the scope of negation

(15b)   If *not* immediately precedes a quantifier, that quantifier must be within the scope of negation

It is usually the case that the distribution of *any* and *some* parallels the respective distribution of negated and non-negated quantifiers. Thus, *some* cannot occur immediately following *not*, as in example (10) above, since that position is always in the scope of negation. Likewise, a large subset of the possible positions of *any* can be described as positions that can be in the scope. If *many* is replaced by *any* in (12), (13), and (14) – examples in which *many* is non-negated – the results are all ungrammatical.

(12')   *Any of the problems weren't solved
(13')   *The man who didn't eat dinner saw any people
(14')   *That John didn't leave surprised any people

In a later section, I will explore the semantic implications of that distribution and show that it is an instance of a more general phenomenon. At present, it may be helpful simply to note the superficial parallel between negated *many* and *any*.

Quantificational adverbs display scope behavior very similar to that I have been discussing. In sentence (17), but not in (16), *not* is semantically associated with *often*, creating a semantic unit synonymous with *seldom*.

(16)   Often, demonstrators are not arrested
(17)   Not often are demonstrators arrested

As Jackendoff (1971) has observed, in sentences like (16) *often* can be used to refer to particular instances. *Not often* cannot be so used. When *not* commands and precedes *often* but is separated from it by intervening material, the latter can escape from the scope of the negation. Again, a special intonation in which the remainder of the sentence constitutes an intonational phrase from which the quantifier is isolated is often associated with such an 'escape'. Usually, a comma is the orthographic indication of that intonation in the case of adverbs. In example (18), the comma indicates that *often* is non-negated.

(18)   I don't attend class(,) often

The same quantifiers that must be non-negated in object position will also be non-negated in adverbials. In the following examples, I will use the notation [−neg] to indicate that a quantifier is outside the scope of negation, and consequently that the phrase it contains can be 'referential' (i.e., used as a referring expression); [+neg] will indicate that a quantifier is within the scope and consequently that its phrase cannot be referential.

(19)   I didn't attend several of the scheduled lectures
                        −neg
(19′)   I didn't attend the scheduled lectures on several occasions
                                                   −neg
(20)   I didn't attend many of the scheduled lectures
                        ±neg
(20′)   I didn't attend the scheduled lectures on many occasions
                                                   ±neg

The parallel between quantifiers in those two positions suggests that the scope facts are part of the same phenomenon and should be treated in the same way.

Motivational adverbials, e.g., *because* classes, interact with negation in the same structural way that the frequency adverbials I have discussed do. In Lakoff (1970a), and more extensively in Lasnik (1970), the ambiguity of sentence (21) is discussed.

(21)   George doesn't beat his wife because he loves her

(21) has two readings: in one reading, corresponding to sentence (22), the adverbial (i.e., the causal connection) is negated while the remainder of the sentence is presupposed; in the alternative reading, the matrix sentence is denied, as in (23).

(22)   Not because he loves her does George beat his wife
(23)   Because he loves her, George doesn't beat his wife

One could extend the notion of scope of negation to account for that ambiguity. In (22), the *because* clause is necessarily within the scope of negation, while in (23), it is outside the scope. This is parallel to (16) and (17) above and falls under principle (15) above. Similarly, the adverbial in (21) will not necessarily be in the scope, since it is not immediately preceded by *not*. Sentence (21) is disambiguated by intonation just as (4) and (18) were. When the negatable item is made an independent intonational phrase, it will be outside the scope of negation. As was the case in (18), a comma is the orthographic indication of such an intonation, which disambiguates (21) towards (23).

Another example of the same phenomenon is sentence (24).

(24)   Senator Eastland doesn't grow cotton(,) to make money

Without a comma, (24) could be continued, "Rather, he grows cotton out of a love for the soil." In that case, (24) is synonymous with (25).

(25)   Not (in order) to make money does Eastland grow cotton

The alternative possibility, in which (24) has an intonation pattern in which the sentence independent of the adverbial has a full sentence contour, is synonymous with (26).

(26)   (In order) to make money, Eastland doesn't grow cotton

That is, he is paid for not growing cotton.

Though the scope facts are parallel, the semantic correlation between (21) and the previous cases is not very clear. In the case of quantified NP's, and even in the case of frequency adverbials, it makes some sense to think of the non-negated phrase as being potentially referential, as Jackendoff (1971) suggested. I can think of no correlate of referentiality that would be relevant for motivational clauses. Hence, I will not exclude the possibility that negation of such clauses is an independent semantic process involving the same structural properties.

One significant factor about the scope of *not*, which I will return to later, is that it is constrained by the possessivized NP island.[6] (I discussed this phenomenon in Lasnik (1971).) To illustrate this point, I first present sentence (27), which has an ambiguous scope of negation.

(27)   I couldn't understand the proofs of many of the theorems

If 'many of the theorems' is inside the scope of negation, (27) will be synonymous with (28). If it is outside, (29) will be the correct paraphrase.

(28)   I could understand the proofs of few of the theorems
(29)   There are many of the theorems whose proofs I couldn't understand

In general, it will be possible to relate *not* occurring in auxiliary position to a quantifier on the direct object. If the direct object has a 'subject', i.e., a possessive determiner, however, it is no longer possible for a quantifier in the object to be associated with the negation. Consider sentence (30).

(30)   I couldn't understand Euclid's proofs of many of the theorems

(30) has no reading analogous to (28). It does have a reading correspond-

ing to (29), in which the quantifier is non-negated; sentence (31) is a paraphrase of (30).

(31)   There are many of the theorems whose proofs by Euclid I couldn't understand

The following two sentences are a further example:

(32)   You didn't understand the proofs of enough of the theorems for me to be justified in giving you an A
(33)   *You didn't understand Euclid's proofs of enough of the theorems for me to be justified in giving you an A

An examination of the meaning of (32) shows that *enough* has to be understood as negated for the sentence to make sense. The content is something like "You understand the proofs of some theorems, but not enough...". (32), then, has no reading in which *enough* is outside the scope of negation. As would be expected, (33) is anomalous, since the required linking of *not* and *enough* is prohibited, as in the analogous sentence (30). At this point, I will briefly summarize the results thus far. First, when a quantifier is within the scope of *not*, the NP quantified by it cannot be referential; one illustration of that is the fact that such an NP cannot be the antecedent of a definite pronoun. Second, the scope of *not* depends crucially upon precede and command relationships. Only if *not* commands a quantifier (or adverbial) can that quantifier (or adverbial) be in *not*'s scope; and even then only if *not* precedes it. When *not* does not immediately precede an element, in general it will be possible for that element to be outside the scope of *not*. Finally, at least one island constraint, namely the possessivized NP constraint, is relevant to the determination of scope. A quantifier within that island will not be subject to the influence of *not* outside of it. How these generalizations can be most naturally captured will be the major concern of the following section.

It should be evident from the preceding discussion that there is no natural way that the scope of *not* can be determined solely on the basis of p_1, i.e. deep structure configurations[7]. For example, even if (34) and (35) can be assigned deep structures differing in the relevant ways, there must be devices available to insure derived structure correspondence (assuming that there are at least some optional transformations affecting the relative order of *not* and NP's or adverbials).[8]

(34)   The students didn't solve many of the problems
(35)   Many of the problems weren't solved by the students

As I noted earlier, in (35) *many* will be non-negated, while in (34) *many* can be negated. In fact, the 'unmarked' reading for (34) is synonymous with (36), in which *many* is overtly negated.

(36)   Not many of the problems were solved by the students

The same phenomenon is evident in the behavior of adverbials.

(37)   Often, I don't attend class
(38)   I don't often attend class
(39)   I don't attend class often

Those three sentences all have different scope characteristics. In (37) *often* is necessarily non-negated; in (38) it is necessarily negated; and in (39), *often* can be negated or non-negated depending on intonation. In this case, as well as in the previous one, if scope is determined in underlying structure, movement transformations would have to be constrained in several ways.

These examples suggest that, minimally, the rule involved in assigning the scope of *not* must involve a level following the application of transformations repositioning NP's and adverbials on each cycle. An ordering consistent with this fact might include post-cyclic application of the interpretive rule,[9] as was suggested in Jackendoff (1969) and Lasnik (1970). Certain meta-theoretical considerations, however, indicate that such an ordering might be inappropriate. The first relevant consideration is the notion of the 'strict cycle' discussed by Chomsky (forthcoming) and Kean (1972). Briefly, strict cyclicity requires (1) that no cyclic transformation apply so as to involve only material entirely within a previously cycled domain; and (2) that a transformation only involving material in an embedded cyclic domain be cyclic. Requirement 2 is simply a way of saying that whether or not a rule is cyclic should depend solely on its domain of operation. It excludes the possibility of calling *passive*, for example, a post-cyclic transformation, thereby allowing it to escape from requirement 1 by a notational trick. This convention (which would be stated in the meta-theory and would not appear in particular grammars) refines the notion of the cycle, and as a result limits the class of possible grammars. If the principle is extended to interpretive rules, it would require that a rule assigning *not* a scope be S cyclic, since in the examples I have discussed scope relations would be the same even if the sentences were deeply embedded. For example, the scope of *not* is unchanged when sentence (40) is embedded as in (40').

(40)   Not many of the problems were solved by the students
(40')   John observed that Mary claimed that Bill realized that not many of the problems were solved by the students

The second argument for cyclic ordering involves simplicity of stating the semantic rule. In (15) above I summarized some of the generalizations relating syntactic distribution and scope of *not*. One generalization was that a quantifier can be within *not*'s scope only if it is commanded by *not*. If S cyclic ordering is adopted, the command condition becomes superfluous and can be dispensed with. If *not* is assigned a scope on the first sentence cycle including it, there is no way that a quantifier not commanded by *not* can be negated by it. Both arguments for cyclic ordering of the interpretive rule are basically meta-theoretical, and, in fact, I know of no data that distinguish between cyclic and post-cyclic ordering of the rule on empirical grounds. On the other hand, in Fiengo and Lasnik (1973) several empirical arguments are presented that reciprocal constructions are related to their meanings via a cyclic rule of semantic interpretation. Hence, there is both meta-theoretical and empirical support for the postulation of cyclic interpretive rules.

Earlier, I suggested some aspects of the meaning of an NP with a negated quantifier in its determiner. Here I will explore the operation of the rule producing such readings, and in particular, the information that the rule refers to. I have already given examples indicating that derived linear order is relevant. In the analysis under discussion, (41) and (42) (which I reproduce immediately below) differ only by selection of the particular location to which the adverb *often* is moved. Yet the two sentences clearly differ in meaning.

(41)   Often, I don't attend class
(42)   I don't often attend class

Particularly significant about (42) is the fact that there is no way to induce a scope ambiguity. The sequence *n't often* behaves exactly like sentence initial *not often* or *not many* in this respect. To account for this fact, the scope rule must include some statement equivalent to 43.

(43)   Quant → [+negated]/not _____

Here I am using *Quant* as a cover term for quantifiers, quantificational adverbs of frequency, and motivational adverbials such as *because-* and *in order to-* clauses. The observations at the beginning of this paper suggest that the following redundancy rule is required, as well.

(44)   [+negated] → [−referential]

In (43), and in the remainder of this paper, I will be using phonological feature notation in a rather special way, quite similar to the usage in Jackendoff (1971). In particular, the 'rules' I introduce will not be used to change features. Rather, they will be used (1) as filters to mark as ungrammatical a sentence in which a rule must assign a feature in contradiction to an inherent feature of some item in the sentence; and (2) to add information where a feature is not inherently specified. In the immediately following discussion, both uses will be illustrated.

Rule (44), which I will return to below, will be relevant in the case of quantifiers and frequency adverbials but not, apparently, in the case of motivational adverbials. If such determiners as *some, several, a number of*, which I will call [+some] quantifiers,[10] are regarded as markers of reference, that is if they are inherently referential, the ungrammaticality of example (10) can be explained.

(10)   *Not $\left\{ \begin{array}{l} \text{several} \\ \text{some} \end{array} \right\}$ of the problems were solved

Rule (43) will make the quantifiers in (10) [+negated]; by (44), they will therefore be specified as non-referential. Since the redundancy rule gives them a feature inconsistent with one of their inherent features, a contradiction results. (10)'s ungrammaticality, then, will be an instance of semantic anomaly. Here, and elsewhere in this paper, I am using 'referential' to mean "having the linguistic form of a referring expression". This notion is similar to Karttunen's (1971) 'discourse referent', particularly in that both notions are purely linguistic and independent of ontological questions. Thus, in my terminology, *several unicorns* is necessarily [+referential], even though the phrase is lacking in a real world referent.

Further, even noun phrases lacking in reference in any possible world, can be [+ referential] in the present sense: *several square circles* is an example.

When *not* is in the Aux and the Quant (i.e., negatable item) is to the right of the Aux, the scope possibilities are rather more complex than in cases subsumed by rule (43). Earlier, I commented on the difference between the two readings of sentence (18).

(18)   I don't attend class often

With comma intonation, *often* in (18) is understood as non-negated; otherwise it is generally understood as negated. These two readings are synonymous, respectively, with (45) and (46).

(45)   Often, I don't attend class
(46)   I don't often attend class

Sentence (4) was a similar example.

(4)   I couldn't solve many of the problems

Again, depending on intonation, the quantifier can be either inside or outside the scope or *not*. When *many* is within the same intonational phrase as *not*, it will usually be negated. When (4) is given an abnormal intonation in which *I couldn't solve* has the contour of an independent sentence, *many* will be non-negated. The two possibilities are informally illustrated below.

(4a)   I couldn't solve many of the problems =
         I was able to solve few of the problems

(4b)   I couldn't solve many of the problems =
         Many of the problems, I was unable to solve cf.
         I couldn't sleep

(4b) shows that the 'intonational phrase' is to a significant extent independent of constituent structure, since *solve* and *many* are dominated by the same syntactic phrase node, VP. The independence is not absolute, however, since the contour of (4b) is felt as unusual.

Motivational adverbial clauses pattern in a similar, though not identical, fashion. Sentence (24), repeated here, is a case in point.

(24)   Senator Eastland doesn't grow cotton to make money

With comma intonation, where the adverbial is separated from the intonational phrase including *not*, the adverbial is non-negated. (24a) illustrates
this situation.

(24a)   Senator Eastland doesn't grow cotton, to make money =
          The purpose of his not growing cotton is making money

Where the main intonational phrase includes the adverbial, the latter will
be negated. To this extent, (24) is parallel to (4) and (18), and it will fall
under the same generalizations. The difference between them is that (24)
does not have the usual sentence contour even when the adverbial is
negated: there will be one intonational phrase, but it will have a constantly
rising contour, lacking the characteristic sentence final drop. Since that
difference is not directly relevant to the facts under discussion, I do not
intend to discuss it here, although it deserves further investigation. The
single intonational phrase version of (24) is illustrated in (24b).

(24b)   Senator Eastland doesn't grow cotton to make money =
          His purpose in growing cotton is something other than mak-
          ing money

These facts indicate that the intonational contour of a sentence is
relevant to the determination of the scope of *not*, consequently, that the
semantic rule follows the rules assigning stress and intonation contour.
Superficially, this conclusion seems at odds with the arguments presented
above that the scope rule is cyclic, since the prosodic rules are generally
assumed to follow the last cycle of syntactic rules. However, Bresnan
(1971) persuasively argues that sentence stress is assigned by a cyclic rule
which follows the syntactic rules on each syntactic cycle. Bresnan's analysis indicates that the semantic rule can be cyclic and still refer to the
phonetic information I have shown to be relevant, assuming that the
intonational rules can be ordered to apply with the stress rules. On each
cycle, then, the rules will apply in the order given in (47).

(47)   1 syntactic transformations
          2 stress and intonation contour rules
          3 *not* scope rules

Thus, forms are generated by the syntax, and in each cyclic stage of
derivation interpreted by two components in sequence: the stress and

intonation rules from the phonology, and the scope rules from the semantics.

In its effect, the abnormal intonation contour under discussion is similar to the syntactic rule of topicalization. In both cases, an item is separated from the remainder of the sentence by a 'marked' construction. I suggest that the intonational rules can optionally generate the contours of (4b) and (24a), but that at the output the optionality is not completely free. By that, I mean that the marked construction can be generated, but that if it ultimately serves no function, the sentence will be abnormal. It seems to me that the primary function of the marked intonation is similar to that of topicalization – it signals that the remainder of the sentence is about the particular item separated.

The scope rule for *not* will consist of two sub-rules. The first of these concerns *not* contiguous to Quant: this rule was given in (43) above, and I repeat it here. The second, (48) below, concerns *not* separated from Quant, as in the cases just discussed.

(43)   Quant → [+negated]/not _____

(48)   Quant → [+negated]/not X _____
        where ⌣ indicates that *not* and *Quant* are in the same intonational phrase.

As they are presented here, (43) and (48) could be collapsed into one rule. In fact, (48) includes (43) as a sub-case, since there is no possible intonational phrase including *not* while excluding an immediately contiguous item. However, consideration of a wider range of cases shows that (43) and (48) are distinct in terms of possible inputs. (43) could reasonably be extended so as to include not just Quants but all NP's as well. The examples in (49) can all be explained if that is the case.

(49a)   Not many people showed up (non-referential)
(49b)   *Not several people showed up
(49c)   *Not John showed up

By redundancy rule (44), a negated item is necessarily non-referential. Above, I argued that such a mechanism would account for the ungrammaticality of (49b), if *several* is regarded as inherently potentially referential. Similarly, if (43) is extended to all NP's, (49c) will be explained since *John* is necessarily referential. In (49b) and (49c) the operation of the semantic rule results in semantic anomaly because of the contradiction produced. Again, it should be kept in mind that 'referential' is being used as a purely linguistic concept. *'Not square circles are here' is just as bad as (49c).

Rule (48) cannot be extended to all NP's: (50) is grammatical even though *not* and *John* are included in the same intonational phrase.

(50)   I didn't see John

Further, even as it was stated Rule (48) is too strong since it would incorrectly predict that (51) is ungrammatical when it has a normal intonation contour.

(51)   I couldn't solve $\begin{Bmatrix} \text{some} \\ \text{several} \end{Bmatrix}$ of the problems

I suggest that (48) should be restricted so that it only applies to Quant's, and only to Quant's that are not of the class I have arbitrarily labelled [+some]. One could alternatively allow (48) to apply to the full range of Adverbials and NP's, but make the rule optional. That is, the domain of the scope rule would still be the intonational phrase, but the rule would not have to apply. These proposals make distinct predictions in some instances, but more research into the interpretation of spoken sentences is required before a choice can be made. (43) on the other hand, should be extended to include all NP's and adverbials, even those that are not Quant's and do not have Quant's in their determiners. In (52a), revisions of the two rules are given: (52a) is (48) revised, and (52b) is (43) revised.

(52)   NOT SCOPE RULE
(52a)   Quant → [+negated]/not X____
          [−some]
(52b) $\begin{Bmatrix} \text{Adverbial} \\ \text{NP} \end{Bmatrix}$ → [+negated]/not____

As represented here, the *not* scope rule has the form of a feature changing rule. If, as suggested by Ross (1967), feature changing rules are subject to island constraints, the non-ambiguity of sentence (30) discussed above is easily explained. Rule (52a) will be unable to penetrate the possessivized NP. Alternatively, one could assume that a variety of rule types are subject to the same conditions, since nothing in the meta-theory *requires* that the scope rule be in the form presented.

(30)   I couldn't understand Euclid's proofs of many of the theorems

At this point, I feel that a brief digression is in order. The strongest and most general arguments presented by those linguists I will refer to as generative semanticists in support of analyses in which quantifiers originate outside of the clauses they wind up in, have depended on alleged interaction with island constraints. (See Lakoff, 1970, for example.) In Lasnik (1972), I present an extensive discussion of the shortcomings of such arguments. I will discuss two particular problems here. First, note that sentence (30) is well-formed. For most speakers, one particular reading – that in which *not* is associated with *many* – is unavailable. But to my knowledge, all speakers find for (30) a reading in which *many* is not related to *not* (and consequently, in which *many of the theorems* is referential in the sense discussed earlier). But the object NP in that sentence is an island – an NP with a genitive determiner – and the grammatical reading of (30) would have a generative semantics deep structure in which *many* is outside of the NP, and above *not* as well. In (52′) I give the structure just prior to the 'lowering' of *many*

(52′)

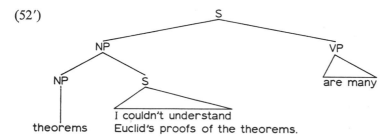

[Note that the unavailable reading would be associated with a deep structure in which *many* is outside of the NP and below *not*.] Thus in this framework, the fact the possessivized NP's are islands could not provide an explanation for the lack of one expected reading, without incorrectly predicting that the alternate reading is likewise unavailable.

The preceding discussion involved a situation in which an island phenomenon is apparently amenable to an interpretive semantics, but not to a generative semantics, analysis. I turn now to the paradigm case of claimed generative semantics superiority in dealing with similar phenomena. Lakoff (1970) discusses sentences such as (53):[11]

(53)   Abdul claims that many men and many women like baba ganouze

Lakoff correctly points out that although (54) and (55) each have the two
paraphrases indicated, (53) is only two ways ambiguous, rather than four.
That is, both quantifiers are understood as outside *believe*, or both are
inside.

(54)   Abdul believes that many men like baba ganouze
         1 Abdul believes that there are many men such that they like
           baba ganouze
         2 There are many men (namely...) such that Abdul believes
           they like baba ganouze
(55)   Abdul believes that many women like baba ganouze
         1 Abdul believes that there are many women such that they
           like baba ganouze
         2 There are many women (namely...) such that Abdul be-
           lieves they like baba ganouze

He goes on to argue that if quantifiers originate outside their final positions, Ross' co-ordinate structure constraint can explain the absence of
two ambiguities.[12] The reading where both quantifiers are understood as
'inside' *believe* would be associated with a deep structure like the
following.[13]

(56)

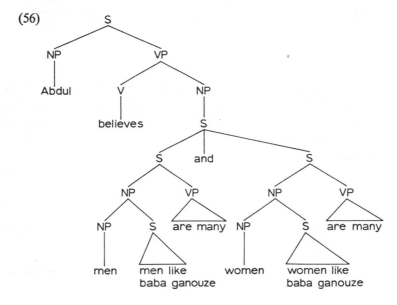

In this derivation all (cyclic) occurrences of quantifier lowering take place internal to the co-ordinate S's. The deep structure for the alternative reading would be as follows:

(57)

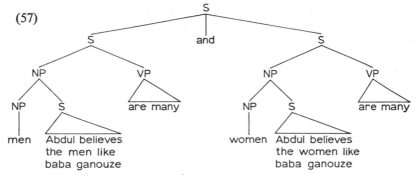

Here again quantifier lowering takes place internal to each co-ordinate S independently. [Lakoff did not discuss either derivation, but he must have had in mind what I have just presented.] Lakoff assumes that the absent readings (where one quantifier is outside *believe* and the other is inside) would not be associated with any successful derivation; i.e., the co-ordinate structure constraint would prevent the necessary deep structure from being realized as a sentence. Thus, to take one of the two cases:

(58)

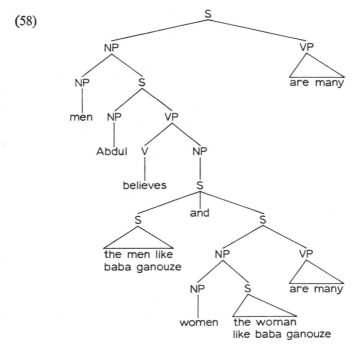

The quantifier above *believe* would then have to be inserted into a co-ordinate structure. Lakoff failed to notice an alternative derivation from another deep structure having the same relative heights. Consider the following:

(59)

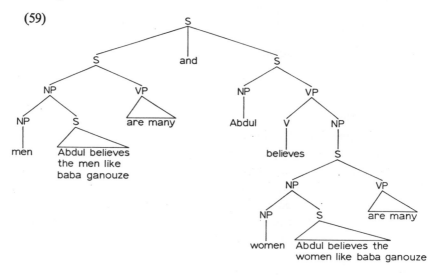

Here, exactly as in (57) above, all occurrences of quantifier lowering take place completely internal to each co-ordinate S. By the time the highest S is reached, the co-ordinate S's look exactly like those from the successful derivation discussed above, and consequently conjunction reduction will take place. The result will be a successful derivation associating sentence (53) with one of the impossible readings. Hence the generative semantics analysis of quantifiers provides *no* explanation for the missing ambiguities. In Lasnik (1972), Chapter 3, I suggest an account of these facts based upon necessary parallelism in co-ordinate structures.

In the preceding few paragraphs, I have tried to demonstrate that a particular syntactic argument cannot be maintained. It is more important to scrutinize the larger claims that the argument was intended to support. Throughout the current linguistic literature, one finds variations on this theme of McCawley's (1972): "[the generative semantics] line of development... rejects any distinction between 'transformations' and 'rules of semantic interpretation'." (In line with current usage, I have been referring to this general position as 'generative semantics'.) I will suggest that such claims may indicate a rather fundamental misunderstanding of the nature of semantics, to the extent that they are concerned with more than just arbitrary labels. Repeatedly we find it stated that there is no syntactic deep structure (in the sense of Chomsky (1965)). Rather, the deepest level of structure is the 'semantic representation'. But what is 'semantic representation'? The term is often used without definition; but if there really are no uniquely semantic phenomena or rules, 'semantic representation' must be intended as synonymous with 'meaning'. To elaborate, it is the goal of linguistic description to characterize the mapping between sound and meaning. Since generative semantics explicitly denies the existence of any interpretive semantic processes, it must be assumed that meaning is somehow present in P_1. But, of course, an examination of particular proposals reveals that generative semantics 'semantic representations' are formal objects, of exactly the same formal type as surface structures. In fact, this is often regarded as one of the fundamental claims and basic insights of the theory, as in Lakoff (1970b) (though in Lakoff (1971), this claim is true by definition). Now whatever meaning is, it is clear that it is not simply a well-formed formula in a formal language. Minimally, one would expect a semantic description of a declarative sentence, for example, to indicate under what circumstances the sentence could have a truth value, could be true, etc., but generative semantics so-called 'semantic representations' are nothing like that; rather they resemble statements in first order predicate calculus or in one of a number of modal logics. That is, *generative semantics deep structures require interpretation.*

Another way of saying this is that such deep structures are, like *Aspects* deep structures, syntactic entities. They could be the input, but not the output, of a 'semantic component'. To my knowledge, Heny (1970) has been one of the few linguists to take this problem seriously. Heny observes that

McCawley's (1969) proposed base structure is in effect an extension of the predicate calculus.... At the same time it is claimed by McCawley that the syntactic base structures are semantically primitive, embodying all aspects of the meaning of a sentence in its simplest form. From one point of view these two claims are incompatible A quantified formula of the predicate calculus... has itself no meaning. The most generally accepted way of giving meaning to such a sentence in the calculus is by interpreting it.

p. 10

and again,

... since the 'abstract' base structures of generative semantics would have to be interpreted in any case, they would not themselves be semantic.   p. 260

Perhaps when generative semanticists hint that their deep structures are
'meanings', they are really saying in shorthand that their deep structures
can be interpreted (while, by implication, *Aspects* type deep structures
cannot). If this is what they intend, we could wish that the point had been
expressed more directly, but one could not accuse them of the fundamental
mistake I have discussed. Still, they would not be entirely guilt free. On the
one hand, they would be correct in assuming with Tarski (1944) that

The problem of the definition of truth obtains a precise meaning and can be solved in a
rigorous way only for those languages whose structure has been exactly specified.

On the other hand, they would be repeating Tarski's apparent error of
assuming that natural languages could not be of this type. Tarski writes

... for all natural 'spoken' languages the meaning of the problem [i.e., of defining truth]
is more or less vague, and its solution can have only an approximate character. Roughly
speaking, the approximation consists in replacing a natural language (or a portion of it
in which we are interested) by one whose structure is exactly specified, and which
diverges from the given language 'as little as possible'.

Tarski's comments appear to be a good description of the alternative view
of generative semantics. That is, generative semantics might perhaps be
understood as an attempt to relate sentences in natural languages with
sentences in some formal language. But notice that as soon as we allow the
possibility that natural languages have (as linguists since 1957 have
usually assumed) a completely specifiable structure, this translation becomes superfluous.[14] The definition of truth for natural language sentences
can be given in terms of a complete syntactic specification (i.e., derivation)
of those sentences.[15]

The general suggestions of the preceding digression should be kept in
mind in considering the more mundane matters under discussion here.

I return now to the consideration of the interaction between *not* and
other elements of sentences. When *not* is present in the Aux but (52) is
inapplicable, either because of the pause intonation discussed, or the
absence of a Quant, or the presence of an island boundary between *not* and
the Quant, the negation apparently associates with the verb. Consider the
two readings of (60).

(60)   I didn't accept many of John's results

When (60) has normal intonation, rule (52) applies and (60) is synonymous with (60′).

(60′)   I accepted few of John's results

When the marked intonation contour isolates *many* from *not, accept* is negated and the reading produced is roughly synonymous with (60″).

(60″)   I rejected many of John's results

Similarly, the absence of an alternative possibility will force the association of *not* and the verb, as in sentence (60‴).

(60‴)   I didn't accept the proposal = I rejected it

Notice here that the reading of (60) synonymous with (60″) represents an instance of a second kind of 'internal' negation. Thus far, we have seen examples of *not* amalgamating with a quantifier, and of *not* amalgamating with a verb. [The two readings of (60) under discussion illustrate these two respective negation types.] Of course there is yet another type of negation that I haven't explicitly discussed. In particular, when *not* (or an auxiliary verb carrying it) is given emphatic stress, the resulting sentence is generally used as a flat denial (an 'external' negation) of someone else's statement. It is of some interest that verbs divide into types with respect to negation possibilities. For example, (61) can be used to introduce new information, or as a denial of a statement.

(61)   John doesn't like Mary

In the former case, there is a very strong tendency for *not* to combine with *like* into a semantic unit synonymous with *dislike* [to the general exclusion of a reading like 'John has no feeling about Mary']. (61′) on the other hand, seems very strange unless it is a direct denial.

(61′)   John doesn't love Mary

Very often, in just those cases where *not-V* corresponds to a lexical item the amalgamation reading is prominent, and where there is no corresponding lexical item such a reading is unavailable.

For an interesting and useful discussion of the negation of predicates, the reader is referred to Kiparsky (1970). Kiparsky discusses the kind of polar negation evidenced in the above examples by means of which *not like* and *not good* are equivalent to *dislike* and *bad* respectively, for example. Kiparsky observes that,

"I don't like it" normally means "I dislike it", and the logically available meaning "I'm indifferent to it" is not intended although as usual it can be forced out by explicitly excluding the normal meaning, as in "I didn't particularly like it or dislike it."

In the course of his discussion, Kiparsky suggests that the near synonymies usually accounted for by Not Hopping (or Negative Transportation or Neg Raising), a transformation first proposed by Fillmore (1963), are actually instances of this same sort of polar interpretation of negation. Kiparsky considers the following pair of sentences.

(62)   I don't believe he's here
(62')   I believe he's not here

He states that,

... since the gradable predicates like *believe* are subject to the rule that their negation is understood as polar opposition, "I don't believe he's here" comes to mean "I disbelieve he's here" (just as "I'm not happy" comes to mean "I'm unhappy"). And now a fact about the logic of belief enters the picture. "I disbelieve he's here" means logically (by projection rules) the same as "I believe he's not here" (whereas, for example, "I'm unhappy he's here" and "I'm happy he's not here" are two quite different propositions). What seemed due to a special and restricted transformational rule is, therefore, in reality the interaction of two general semantic principles: a semantic extension rule applicable to graded antonyms, and a rule of logical equivalence applicable to words denoting belief.

Kiparsky's suggestions indicate a very promising line of investigation, and they are supported by other facts about the relevant verbs. Consider, for example, the following question.

(63)   Do you think John is here?

Generally, the object of such a question will not be to find out whether the askee has thoughts about the matter, but rather to find out whether John is here. That is, the question is about the complement, just as the negation, in the earlier examples, is on the complement. But in example (63), it is not obvious how a transformation could predict these facts; on the other hand, a semantic principle very like the one suggested by Kiparsky could be operative in this case, as well. A similar situation arises in the case of sentences like (64).

(64)   I don't believe in hard work as an end in itself

Sentence (64) does not indicate that the speaker has no opinion about hard work, but rather that he believes that hard work is not *a priori* desirable. Thus, the interpretation of the sentence is parallel to that of (62) above. But in this case, there is no readily apparent underlying source in the complement of believe for the negation, and hence, the interpretation is apparently produced by some semantic principle like that under discussion. Consequently, some version of the principle Kiparsky proposes must be available to the grammar, and therefore it is also available for the interpretation of (62), making Not Hopping unnecessary in that case.

In addition to the semantic rules for negation I have already discussed, the language has a process like that described by Jackendoff (1969) as attraction to focus. Attraction to focus (AtF) is responsible for the interpretation of the negation in example (65).

(65)   I didn't see Jóhn. I saw Bíll.

AtF 'zeroes in' on an item with extra heavy stress, and semantically erases it. That is, the stressed item is labelled incorrect, and its slot is designated to be correctly refilled. The most striking aspect of the operation of AtF is that anything in the sentence can be focused and denied. This is in sharp contrast to rule (52a) which has a restricted number of possible inputs. The examples in (66) illustrate the operation of AtF with respect to various lexical classes.

(66a)   I didn't write a lóng thesis. It is shórt.
(66b)   John didn't get thé result, but he got á result
(66c)   Bill didn't play a véry good game. It was just a faírly good game. cf. Bill didn't play a very good gáme = In fact, he played a pretty bad one.
(66d)   I didn't descríbe the data. I expláined it.

Note that even 'positive polarity items' in the sense of Baker (1970) can be negated by AtF, as in (67).

(67)   John isn't somewhát smarter than Bill. He's múch smarter.
(68)   He didn't discuss a goód deal of data. He discussed a greát deal of data.

Another difference between rule (52) and AtF is that the former appears to be subject to island constraints, as I showed above, while the

latter is not. Example (69) is parallel to (30) above, but in (69) the negation is oblivious to the island boundary.

(69)   I didn't understand Euclid's proofs of mány of the theorems;
          I understood his proofs of only a féw of them.

Co-ordinate structures are similarly penetrable by AtF:

(70)   I didn't talk to Chomsky and áll of his colleagues;
          I talked to Chomsky and móst of his colleagues.

A more fundamental difference between Rule (52) and AtF is that only
the former constructs semantic entities by amalgamating *not* with another
item. AtF only provides the information that the focused item is incorrect
and will be replaced. As an example of this difference, contrast (71) with
(72).

(71)   I didn't solve many of the problems
(72)   I didn't solve mány of the problems...

By rule (52), (71) is given a reading incorporating negation into *many*.
Semantically, a new unit is created with a well-defined meaning: one of
the aspects of this meaning is the non-reference already discussed; a
second is the proportional relationship between not many ($=$few) and the
set. The semantic unit created has entailments, for example, that *all* is
false where *not many* is true. Thus, when (71) is true (73) is false.

(73)   I solved all of the problems

The negation in (72), on the other hand, is not of this type. When a focus
is negated, no such entailments result, as shown by (74).

(74)   I didn't solve mány of the problems. I solved áll of them.

The negation involved in a class of truncated sentences seems to be
closely related to attraction to focus. (75a) and (75b), for example, receive
the same interpretation.

(75a)   I didn't see Jóhn; I saw Bíll.
(75b)   I saw Bíll, not Jóhn.

In (75a), *Bill* is the focus by virtue of its heavy stress; in (75b), it is focus
since nothing else is present. Both processes can negate more than one
item simultaneously, as in (76).

(76a) Jóhn didn't see Bíll; Máry saw Súsan.
(76b) Máry saw Súsan, not Jóhn, Bíll.

In addition, reduced sentences parallel to (72) above also produce no entailments.

(72′) I solved áll of the problems, not mány of them

Attraction to focus thus represents yet another type of negation. It is applicable in two types of situations: (1) sentences where some particular item or items have heavy stress as in (75a) and (76a); (2) truncated sentences such as (75b) and (76b). Interestingly, there do not seem to be sentences analogous to (75a) in which *not* is somewhere other than in the Aux. (77) is bad in isolation, and is also bad when contrasted in (78)

(77) *Not John came
(78) *Not Jóhn came. Bíll came.

(78) is only acceptable, it seems to me, when a recitation is being taught by rote, and that sentence is used to correct someone who failed to remember a passage precisely.[16] (78) cannot be used in the way (75) can – to convey information with the purpose of changing someone's beliefs. I suggest an explanation for this in Lasnik (1972), Ch. 2.

Since Klima's monumental work on negation (Klima, 1964), it has been customary to deal with the apparent *some-any* suppletion in a discussion of negation. Indeed, some analyses have been based on such a discussion. Some may find it surprising that I have ignored this problem. In the following paragraphs, however, I will suggest that the distribution of *any* has nothing to do with negation *per se*.[17]

Jackendoff (1971), in discussing some observations made by Vendler (1967), argues that *any* cannot be a form of the universal quantifier. Before considering Jackendoff's argument, I will present a number of examples consistent with the position he opposes. First, consider the difference in meaning between the following two sentences.

(79) I didn't solve all of the problems
(80) I didn't solve any of the problems

As observed by Quine (1960), either sentence can be quite plausibly paraphrased using the universal quantifier, with the only difference being the

relative order of negation and the quantifier. (79) and (80) are informally
paraphrased by (79') and (80') respectively.

(79')   Not for all X (X is a problem → I solved X)
(80')   For all X (X is a problem → I didn't solve X)

In Quine's terms, *all* is the universal quantifier with narrow scope and
any is the universal quantifier with wide scope. Conditional sentences can
be described in similar terms.

(81)   If everyone passes the test, I'm quitting
(81')   If (for all x, x passes the test) I'm quitting
(82)   If anyone passes the test, I'm quitting
(82')   For all x (if x passes the test, I'm quitting)

A third pair, less strikingly divergent in meaning, are (83) and (84) below.

(83)   Everyone might be elected
(84)   Anyone might be elected

The primary interpretation of (83) is that there is a chance that everyone
will be elected, i.e., there are so many positions open that there might be
a position for everyone running. The only interpretation for (84), on the
other hand, is that every individual has some chance to be elected, even
though there could conceivably be many more candidates than positions.

Jackendoff discusses the sentences in (85). (Jackendoff's ex. (44), paraphrased from Vendler)

(85)   I have here some apples: you may take $\begin{Bmatrix} \text{every one} \\ \text{all} \\ \text{any one} \\ \text{any} \end{Bmatrix}$ of them

Jackendoff claims that, "Here [in (85), HL] *any* clearly is not synonymous with the universal quantifiers." Since Jackendoff neither paraphrases the sentences of (85) nor provides a definition of the universal
quantifier, I am not clear about exactly what he has in mind. Certainly,
the four sentences are not synonymous, but neither are the pairs of
sentences I discussed immediately above. Yet I showed that in those
sentences, *any* can be plausibly described as the universal quantifier. The
same analysis I used in those cases can be extended to handle most of the

facts in (85). First, compare an offer to take all of the apples, with one to take any of them. In the former case, Vendler observes,

If you started to pick them one by one, I should be surprised. My offer was sweeping: you should take the apples, if possible, "en bloc."

Further, to extend Vendler's suggestion, it seems to me that an offer to take all can generally be construed as allowing the hearer to take all or none, but not some intermediate number. Such an offer can be analyzed as having the universal quantifier within the permission modal:

(86)   You have permission (for all x, you take x)

'You may take any' is much freer; it allows a choice in every individual case. That is, the hearer may elect to take anything from zero apples up to all the apples. In this case, *any* can be analyzed as the universal quantifier with wide scope:

(87)   For all x (you have permission to take [or not take] x)

The other two cases in (85) are more complex. Superficially, *any one* and *every one* are parallel, but a closer examination reveals basic differences between them. In the former case, *one* is a numeral, and other numerals can be substituted for it: *any two*, *any three*, etc. In *every one*, *one* appears to be not a numeral but a pronoun: the substitution of numerals is impossible – *every three of them*. If this is correct, then *every one* will be expected to behave like *every* or *all* in (85), in its scope relations. Since the sentence with *every one* can reasonably be paraphrased by (86), the prediction is borne out. Assuming that *one* is a numeral in *any one*, (85) with that phrase can be represented as (88).

(88)   For all x (you have permission you take x); condition:
$\forall x \forall y$ (you take $x \wedge$ you take $y \rightarrow x = y$)

(88) like (87) gives permission to choose from the entire set of apples, but the numeral (represented in the condition) requires that only one apple can be taken. A similar representation could be given for *any two*, in which only the condition would differ. Thus, there are indeed differences between *any* and *every*, for example, but in the cases Jackendoff discusses, as in the cases I considered earlier, the basic difference is a scope difference. It can still be maintained, then, that *any* is a form of the universal quantifier.

Probably the most interesting problem about *any*, and unfortunately, one that I have no developed theory for, is why it exists, that is, why an alternate form of the universal quantifier is needed. I suspect that its primary function is the resolution of potential scope ambiguities. In all of the examples in the preceding section, I showed that plausible representations for each pair would make both *any* and *every* universal quantifiers: *any* the one with wide scope, and *every* the one with narrow scope. If *every* (and presumably *all*) is regarded as the unmarked form of the universal quantifier, then it will be possible in all contexts, as seems to be the case. Consider now the case of sentences involving negation, such as (79) above, which I repeat here.

(79)   I didn't solve all of the problems

In (79), *all* is commanded and preceded by *not*; it is also negated, the unmarked situation for its context. *Any* in (80) is analyzable as the universal quantifier outside the scope of the negation.

(80)   I didn't solve any of the problems

But *any* occupies the same position as *all* did. Hence, its semantic form represents the marked condition. I suggest that in general, *any* is possible only in positions where *all* would be both possible and logically within the scope of some operator. Thus, *any*, which is clearly the marked and more restricted form, will be possible only when its presence indicates the marked logical form.[18] I showed that in (82), (84), and (85), plausible paraphrases can be given that conform to this generalization. Further, it it correctly predicted that *any* will be ungrammatical in such sentences as (89), in which no scope ambiguity could exist.

(89)   *I spoke with anyone yesterday

My hypothesis receives some support from the fact that not all modals condition the occurrence of *any*. *Must* and *should*, for example, are incompatible with it.

(90)   *You must solve any of the problems
(91)   *You should solve any of the problems

But as far as I can tell, no meaning difference depends on whether ∀ is analyzed as inside or outside of those modals.

(91)   You must solve all of those problems
(91′)   For all x (you must solve x)
(91″)   You must (for all x, you solve x)

Note that the environments falling under this generalization seem to be just those environments for which reference to specificity alone makes incorrect predictions. *Must* and *should*, for example, both allow a non-specific reading of *some*, as in (92).

(92)   I must talk to someone, but I don't know who

Similarly, *want* permits a non-specific reading for *some*, but excludes *any*. This may fall under the same generalization, since (93) and (93′) seem to be synonymous.

(93)   For all x (I want to solve x)
(93′)   I want (for all x, I solve x)

That is, a 'trigger' for *any* is an operator capable of inducing a meaning-affecting scope ambiguity in relation to the universal quantifier. Obviously, I have left much unexplained in this description of the behavior of *any*. In particular, it is not clear what formal mechanisms can be used to capture the generalization. However, the proposals I have made seem to be a reasonable point of departure for further investigation, and whether or not they turn out to be correct, the generalizations behind them will have to be taken into account by any theory of scope.

In this paper, I have dealt in a programmatic way with a number of phenomena involving negative sentences. I say 'programmatic' since there are undeniably relevant phenomena which I have ignored here, and because I have been primarily concerned with presenting a framework for investigation rather than a fully articulated analysis. In particular, I have argued that linguistic theories cannot differ with respect to the need for 'interpretation', since a formal object such as a sentence or a phrase structure tree requires interpretation to connect it with a 'meaning'. A prerequisite to interpretation is complete syntactic specification, and I have suggested that a derivation (in the now customary sense) is precisely the syntactic specification needed. For the two kinds of 'internal' negation considered, the relevant syntactic property appears, to be the phrase structure specification at the end of each syntactic cycle. If we regard the first syntactic cycle as the sequence $P_{11}, P_{12}, \ldots P_{1n}$, and the second as $P_{21}, \ldots$ $\ldots P_{2n}$, and so forth, the input to the semantic operations linking sentences containing *not* with the relevant truth conditions is the set P_{in} for all i. This meshes particularly neatly with Bresnan's analysis of English sentence stress: the input to the stress rules is P_{in}; and if I am correct, the input to the 'scope' rules is P_{in} plus the phonetic specification of P_{in}.

University of Connecticut

NOTES

[1] The reader interested in a rather lengthy discussion of this issue is referred to Lasnik (1972).

[2] It is not completely clear that there is a *necessary* phonetic difference between the two situations; it *is* definitely easier to understand *many* as outside the scope of negation when such a phonetic indication is present.

[3] Also, compare 'not a single problem was solved' with *'not a certain problem was solved'.

[4] The quantifiers *all* and *every* constitute exceptions to two of the above three generalizations. If either of them is substituted for *many* in (7) above, object position will obligatorily be negated, as far as I can tell.

(7′)   I couldn't solve all of the problems

(7′) cannot mean 'It is true of all of the problems that I couldn't solve them'. Further those two totality quantifiers can be negated even when they precede *not*, as illustrated by (7″)

(7″)   All that glitters isn't gold

I have no clear idea why this should be the case. For some interesting speculations on this problem, see Horn (1972).

[5] The structural relation 'command' was first introduced by Langacker (1969). In his words, "... a node *A* 'commands' another node *B* if (1) neither *A* nor *B* dominates the other; and (2) the S-node that most immediately dominates *A* also dominates *B*."

[6] See Ross (1967) for an extremely important discussion of 'islands' (basically, structures prohibiting items from being extracted from them).

[7] For a more extensive discussion of this issue, see Lasnik (1972).

[8] Even if all transformations are obligatory and triggered by deep structure markers, one would have to explain why these markers should be involved with scope interpretation. Further, there are cases where *not* and a quantifier 'cross' and then re-cross, producing a sentence synonymous with the original uncrossed sentence. See Lasnik (1972), Chapter 3, Section 2.1 for discussion.

[9] That is, truth conditions, for example, related to scope phenomena would be defined on a late derived level of representation.

[10] This feature is to be regarded solely as an expository device. In a complete analysis, the properties of these particular quantifiers would be expected to follow from more general phenomena.

[11] Lakoff had "many men and few women." This conjunction seems at best marginal. I have therefore taken the liberty of altering the example in a way irrelevant to the problem at hand.

[12] Lakoff doesn't point out that Ross' version of the constraint won't be relevant here. Ross limited his description to extraction rules, and feature changing rules.

[13] Deep structures like that in (56) are central to the 'classical' generative semantics model: that explicated in Lakoff (1969, 1970, and 1971). Within this framework, quantifiers and negation had a deep structure distribution completely parallel to that of main sentence verbs; the surface main sentences in the relevant structures are derived from deep structure relative clauses. One very real problem with such structures which, to my knowledge, has only been discussed in Lasnik, (1972), is that it seems to be the case (as Lakoff, 1971 explicitly states) that "restrictive relative clauses are presupposed." For example, the following sentence is very strange – most linguists would say 'without truth value' – if no men left.

(a)   The men who left were very rude

Analogously, if quantifiers were 'higher verbs', we would expect the following sentence to be similarly strange if no men left.

(b)   Many men left

The fact that (b) is impeccable, and clearly false, casts doubt on the whole analysis. It should be noted that the strict parallelism between quantifiers and verbs is abandoned in later work such as McCawley (1972), where quantifiers appear in deep structures in positions analogous to those in standard logical languages.

[14] I am ignoring here the problem of the logical paradoxes, principally because it seems to have no direct relevance to the issues under discussion. If the problem can't be solved within the natural language itself, translation into a logical language won't improve matters, since the set of self-referring expressions will have to be translated into a higher order logical language. But this amounts to the claim that natural languages operate on two levels, one of them a meta-level. Hence, we can dispense with the translation, and bifurcate the natural language itself, and treat the two parts in separate ways.

[15] I do not mean to imply, however, that there is no 'decomposition' of individual lexical items by means of projection rules, for example. See Katz (1972), Chapter 3 for some discussion. I assume that truth conditions would be defined, then, on the syntactic specification of a sentence, where each noun phrase, verb, etc. is represented perhaps in terms of semantic primitives.

[16] Notice that in this situation, what follows *not* need not even be linguistic: a gesture, for example, would be appropriate.

[17] I have profited from several discussions of *any* with Larry Horn. For some further relevant facts, see Horn (1972).

[18] In general, *any* represents the universal quantifier immediately outside of a 'trigger' in scope.

BIBLIOGRAPHY

Bresnan, J.: 1971, 'Sentence Stress and Syntactic Transformations', *Language* **47**, 251.
Chomsky, N.: 1965, *Aspects of the Theory of Syntax*, MIT Press, Cambridge, Mass.
Chomsky, N.: 1970, 'Deep Structure, Surface Structure, and Semantic Interpretation', in *Studies in General and Oriental Linguistics* (ed. by R. Jakobson and S. Kawamoto), Tokyo.
Chomsky, N.: (forthcoming), 'Conditions on Transformations', to appear in *A Festschrift for Morris Halle* (ed. by P. Kiparsky and S. Anderson).
Fiengo, R. and Lasnik, H.: 1973, 'The Logical Structure of Reciprocal Sentences in English', *Foundations of Language*, IX, 447.
Fillmore, C.: 1963, 'The Position of Embedding Transformations in a Grammar', *Word* **19**, 208.
Heny, F.: 1970, 'Semantic Operations on Base Structures', unpublished UCLA Ph.D. dissertation.
Horn, L.: 1972, 'On the Semantic Properties of Logical Operators in English', unpublished UCLA Ph.D. dissertation.
Jackendoff, R.: 1969, 'Some Rules of Semantic Interpretation for English', unpublished MIT Ph.D. dissertation.
Jackendoff, R.: 1971, 'Modal Structure in Semantic Representation', *Linguistic Inquiry* II, 479.
Jackendoff, R.: 1972, *Semantic Interpretation in Generative Grammar*, MIT Press, Cambridge, Mass.
Karttunen, L.: 1971, 'Discourse Referents', Indiana University Linguistics Club.
Katz, J. J.: 1972, *Semantic Theory*, Harper and Row, New York.
Kean, M.-L.: 1972, 'Strict Cyclicity in Phonology', ms.
Kiparsky, P.: 1970, 'Semantic Rules in Grammar', in *The Nordic Languages and Modern Linguistics* (ed. by H. Benedikktson) Reikyavik.
Klima, E.: 1964, 'Negation in English', in *The Structure of Language* (ed. by J. Fodor and J. Katz), Prentice-Hall, Englewood Cliffs, N.J.
Lakoff, G.: 1969, 'On Derivational Constraints', in *Papers from the Fifth Regional Meeting of the Chicago Linguistic Society* (ed. by R. Binnick *et al.*).
Lakoff, G.: 1970, 'Repartee', *Foundations of Language* VI, 389.
Lakoff, G,: 1970a, *Irregularity in Syntax*, Holt, Rinehart & Winston, New York.
Lakoff, G,: 1970b, 'An Example of a Descriptively Inadequate Interpretive Theory', *Linguistic Inquiry* **1**, 539.
Lakoff, G,: 1971, 'On Generative Semantics', in *Semantics* (ed. by D. Steinberg and J. Jakobovits), Cambridge U. Press, Cambridge.
Lakoff, G.: 1972, 'Linguistics and Natural Logic', in *Semantics of Natural Language* (ed. by D. Davidson and G. Harman) Reidel, Dordrecht, p. 545.
Langacker, R.: 1969, 'On Pronominalization and the Chain of Command', in *Modern Studies in English* (ed. by D. Reibel and S. Schane), Prentice-Hall, Englewood Cliffs, N.J.
Lasnik, H.: 1970, 'The Scope of Negation', ms.
Lasnik, H.: 1971, 'A General Constraint: Some Evidence from Negation', *Quarterly Progress Report of the Research Laboratory of Electronics*, p. 101.
Lasnik, H.: 1972, 'Analyses of Negation in English', unpublished MIT Ph.D. dissertation.

McCawley, J.: 1969, 'Semantic Representation', in *Cognition: a Multiple View* (ed. by Garvin), Spartan Books, New York.

McCawley, J.: 1972, 'A Program for Logic', in *Semantics of Natural Language* (ed. by D. Davidson and G. Harman), Reidel, Dordrecht, p. 498.

Quine, W.: 1960, *Word and Object*, MIT Press, Cambridge, Mass.

Ross, J.: 1967, 'Constraints on Variables in Syntax', unpublished MIT Ph.D. dissertation.

Tarski, A.: 1944, 'The Semantic Conception of Truth', *Philosophy and Phenomenological Research* **4**.

Vendler, Z.: 1967, *Linguistics in Philosophy*, Cornell University Press, Ithaca.

JAMES D. MCCAWLEY

VERBS OF BITCHING

Fillmore's 'Verbs of judging' is subtitled 'an exercise in semantic description'. It is only to avoid compounding the chutzpah that I have not added
the same subtitle to this paper. I will be concerned here with the semantic
structure of the verbs that Fillmore investigated, roughly those that relate
to guilt and virtue, and will operate within a descriptive framework not
much different from Fillmore's. Fillmore presents his analyses in the form
of a list of atomic formulas, segregated into a 'meaning' part and a
'presupposition' part, e.g.

(1)   ACCUSE [Judge, Defendant, Situation (*of*)]
       Meaning: SAY [Judge, '*X*', Addressee]
       X=RESPONSIBLE [Defendant, Situation][1]
       Presupposition: BAD [Situation]

Each atomic formula consists of a predicate followed by a sequence of
arguments, each of which is either the name of a 'role' (Judge, Defendant,
Affected,...) or the name of a lower formula. Since each named formula
is referred to in exactly one higher formula, Fillmore's analyses are
mechanically convertible into diagrams such as (2), in which the meaning
(in the narrow sense) and the presuppositions are represented as trees and
presupposed material is connected by dotted lines to the constituent that
it is presupposed by:

(2)

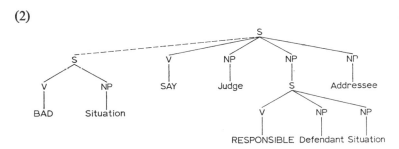

*Hockney et al. (eds.), Contemporary Research in Philosophical Logic
and Linguistic Semantics, 313–332. All Rights Reserved
Copyright © 1975 by D. Reidel Publishing Company, Dordrecht-Holland*

I will henceforth use this latter format for the presentation of Fillmore's analyses and alternative analyses. I will also assume that the analyses are to function as the logical structures of corresponding sentences (i.e. they are what can appear in the input and output of rules of inference) and that they constitute the deepest level of a syntactic derivation.[2]

This paper is concerned particularly with (i) whether the items that Fillmore treats as presuppositions really are presuppositions, (ii) whether the various roles in his analyses can be filled by the same kinds of things for the various verbs under consideration, and especially whether the role Fillmore calls 'Situation' is always filled by the same kinds of things, and (iii) the extent to which syntactic characteristics of these verbs are idiosyncratic, as opposed to being related in a systematic way to their meanings.

Let me begin by playing around a little with the first verb that Fillmore discusses, namely *accuse*. Consider the sentence

(3)   Nixon accused Agnew of wanting to end the war.

It is not clear whether Fillmore would take the 'Situation' in (3) to be the proposition that Agnew wants to end the war or the propositional function 'x wants to end the war', to mention the two most obvious possibilities. Neither of those possibilities works if 'presuppose' is understood in the usual way, since to say (3) felicitously it is not necessary that the speaker believe that is would be bad for Agnew to want to end the war nor that he believe that it is bad to want to end the war. For example, Fulbright could perfectly well use (3) in the middle of an anti-war speech. One possible correction in Fillmore's analysis to bring it into conformity with this observation would be to change the presupposition from BAD [Situation] to THINK [Judge, BAD [Situation]], i.e. the presupposition of (3) would not be that it is bad to want to end the war but that Nixon thinks it is bad to want to end the war. However, that doesn't work either, as evidenced by the fact that saying

(4)   Officer O'Reilly accused me of not offering him a bribe and threatened to take me to the police station and accuse me of offering him a bribe.

does not commit the speaker to the proposition that it is bad to offer Officer O'Reilly a bribe and bad not to offer him a bribe, nor to the proposition that Officer O'Reilly thinks both that it is bad to offer him a bribe and bad not to offer him a bribe. Indeed, one could utter (4) in good faith even under the belief that Officer O'Reilly considers the offering of bribes morally neutral. His belief that offering him a bribe is bad is certainly a condition for his being sincere in accusing you of offering him a bribe, but an insincere accusation is still an accusation.

Example (4) brings into prominence an important characteristic of accusations which is not mentioned in Fillmore's analysis, namely that an accusation creates some kind of 'jeopardy' (using that word fairly loosely). When someone is accused of something, he must successfully defend himself against the accusation or suffer the consequences. The consequences may be quite trivial, for example, the accuser being annoyed at the accused; but unless there are some such undesirable consequences, a statement cannot constitute an accusation. This is illustrated by the difference in normalness between[3]

(5)   Officer O'Reilly$_i$ took Susan $\left\{ \begin{array}{l} \text{before the judge} \\ \text{?to Tiny Tim} \end{array} \right\}$ and accused her of offering him$_i$ a bribe.

If Susan is a normal person, she would care about the possibility of the judge fining or jailing her, but she shouldn't care a hoot whether Tiny Tim shakes his finger at her and says 'Naughty, naughty'.

As Fillmore's formulas would predict, saying that a person did some foul act may constitute an accusation, i.e. it is possible for an occurrence of the sentence *Last night while you were drunk, you stabbed your mother to death* to be correctly reported by saying *Mary accused Bill of stabbing his mother to death while he was drunk the previous night*. However, such a report is not always correct. An occurrence of the sentence *Last night while you were drunk you stabbed your mother to death* is an accusation if uttered by a policeman who is going to cart you off to jail unless you come up with a good alibi quick, or if uttered by your mother's lover, who wants vengeance, but is not an accusation if uttered by a friend who is informing you of the danger of your being arrested and wants to help you escape. Note also that in a trial the prosecutor accuses the defendant of the crime, but the foreman of the jury, in reporting a guilty verdict, is saying that the defendant committed the crime but is not accusing him. The prosecutor's action creates the situation of jeopardy, whereas the foreman's action brings an existing situation of jeopardy to culmination. I thus conclude that the meaning of *accuse* includes the information that the linguistic act which it reports creates a situation of jeopardy, i.e. that the logical structure of (6a) is along the lines of (6b):

(6a)   John accused Sam of breaking the window.

(6b)   John said that Sam broke the window and thereby put Sam in jeopardy.

This actually is inadequate, since an accusation has to be made with the intention of creating jeopardy. Thus, if someone in a group which includes an FBI undercover agent discusses the group's plans to bomb the Treasury Building, he hasn't accused his friends of planning to bomb the Treasury Building, even though he has (inadvertantly) put them into some kind of jeopardy. The logical structure of (6a) must indicate not merely that jeopardy results from the act, but that the creation of jeopardy is indeed part of the act. It is evidently this characteristic of the meaning of *accuse* which is responsible for the possibility of using it as a performative verb: its logical structure is in this respect like the large subset of Austin's 'exercitives' (Austin, 1962) which Vendler (1972) calls 'operatives': verbs such as *appoint, decree* and *excommunicate* which refer to an act of making something the case by saying that it is to be the case (under appropriate circumstances).

Let me now bring up *criticize*, which Fillmore has claimed contrasts almost minimally with *accuse* with respect to the assignment of various parts of its content to 'presupposition' and 'meaning' in the narrow sense:

(7)

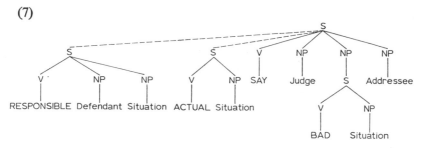

Since in this structure and the one for *accuse* the same predicates are predicated of 'Situation' (save for the additional occurrence of ACTUAL [Situation]) in (7), and likewise the same predicate is predicated of

'Defendant', there is nothing in the two structures which would imply any difference between what can fill these two roles in sentences with *accuse* and what can fill them in sentences with *criticize*, other than what can be attributed to the presence of ACTUAL [Situation] in (7). It turns out, however, that there are differences which cannot be ascribed to 'ACTUAL [Situation]'. It appears as if *accuse* but not *criticize* requires the 'Defendant' to be a person:

(8a)   Mencken criticized act 2 of *Lohengrin* for being too long.
(8b)   *Mencken accused act 2 of *Lohengrin* of being too long.
(9a)   The principal criticized Rocky's hair for being untidy.
(9b)   *The principal accused Rocky's hair of being untidy.

Here 'person' must be taken in the extended sense which includes corporate persons:

(10)   Nader accused General Motors of dumping mercury in the Detroit River.
         Nixon accused Tanzania of endangering American interests in Antarctica.

Not quite anything is possible as the 'Defendant' with *criticize*[4]:

(11a)   *John criticized wisdom for being hard to achieve.
(11b)   *Arthur criticized 17 for being an unlucky number.
(11c)   *Sam criticized the Mississippi River for being too wide.

To get a better idea of what 'Defendant' *criticize* allows, consider the following sentences, which differ only slightly from (11c) but are much more normal:

(12)   Sam criticized the Cuyahoga River for being too filthy.
         Sam criticized the Erie Canal for being too narrow.

What appears to make these sentences better than (11c) is that the filthiness of the Cuyahoga River and the narrowness of the Erie Canal are the result of the decisions and actions of people, whereas the length of the Mississippi is not. Where the object of *criticize* is not a person, it is something for which a person or persons are responsible, and the criticism of the object is at least by implication a criticism of the person(s) responsible.

Actually, (11c) is perfectly good if taken as a criticism of God for a lousy job of creation.

Let us now take a look at some differences in what *accuse* and *criticize* allow in the role of 'Situation'.

(13a)   McGovern criticized Nixon for
$\begin{cases} \text{*irresponsibility.} \\ \text{his irresponsibility.} \\ \text{?Mitchell's irresponsibility.} \end{cases}$

(13b)   McGovern criticized Nixon for the fact that he puts ketchup on his cottage cheese.

(13c)   McGovern criticized Nixon for
$\begin{cases} \text{what he said to the Knights of Columbus.} \\ \text{the basis on which he fills court vacancies.} \\ \text{the way in which his economic policy has failed.} \end{cases}$

(14a)   McGovern accused Nixon of
$\begin{cases} \text{irresponsibility.} \\ \text{*his irresponsibility.} \\ \text{*Mitchell's irresponsibility.} \end{cases}$

(14b)   *McGovern accused Nixon of the fact that he puts ketchup on his cottage cheese.

(14c)   McGovern accused Nixon of
$\begin{cases} \text{*what he said to the Knights of Columbus.} \\ \text{*the basis on which he fills court vacancies.} \\ \text{*the way in which his economic policy has failed.} \end{cases}$

Certain of the above facts are accounted for by the presence of ACTUAL [Situation] in Fillmore's analysis of *criticize*. For example, *his irresponsibility* involves a presupposition that he is irresponsible (e.g. neither *McGovern discussed Nixon's irresponsibility* nor *McGovern didn't discuss Nixon's irresponsibility* is appropriate unless the speaker believes that Nixon is/was irresponsible). It may be used with *criticize*, which for Fillmore has a presupposition that the 'Situation' is 'actual'. Similarly with the expression *the fact that he puts ketchup on his cottage cheese*, which involves the presupposition that he puts ketchup on his cottage

cheese. It is not completely clear to me why *accuse* not only allows NP's which do not carry a presupposition that the situation is actual, but indeed excludes NP's which do carry such a presupposition. One possible answer would bring in the idea that 'jeopardy' is a situation which one can get out of by defending himself successfully against the accusation, and that if you presuppose the truth of the charge, as opposed to asserting it, you are ruling out the possibility of defense.

The items in (13c) have peculiar properties that will have to be discussed before the significance of those examples can be determined. Note that the inferences in (15) are valid and those in (16) invalid:

(15a)   The length of the Bible exceeds the length of *Tropic of Cancer*.
        The length of the *Tropic of Cancer* is 287 pages.
        Therefore, the length of the Bible exceeds 287 pages.

(15b)   Many people believe what Nixon said to the Knights of
        Columbus.
        What Nixon said to the Knights of Columbus is that Mao is a
        yellow aryan.
        Therefore, many people believe that Mao is a yellow aryan.

(16a)   Schwartz criticized *Tropic of Cancer* for its length.
        The length of *Tropic of Cancer* is 287 pages.
        *Therefore, Schwartz criticized *Tropic of Cancer* for 287 pages.
        (grammatical only in an irrelevant sense)

(16b)   McGovern criticized Nixon for what he said to the Knights of
        Columbus.
        What Nixon said to the Knights of Columbus is that Mao is a
        yellow aryan.

Therefore, McGovern criticized Nixon { *for that Mao is a yellow aryan. *that Mao is a yellow aryan. *for the proposition that Mao is a yellow aryan.

The only appropriate inferences from the premises of (16) involve an expansion of the first premise:

(17a)   Schwartz criticized *Tropic of Cancer* for $\left\{\begin{array}{l}\text{having a length of} \\ \text{287 pages.} \\ \text{being 287 pages} \\ \text{long.}\end{array}\right.$

(17b)   McGovern criticized Nixon for saying to the Knights of
Columbus that Mao is a yellow aryan.

I suggest that the difference between (15) and (16) is the result of the first
premises of the inferences in (16) being abbreviated forms, i.e. that the
extra material which appears in (17) is present in the logical structure of
the first premises of the inferences of (16). Rules of inference, of course,
apply to the logical structures of sentences and not to their surface forms.
I thus maintain that the sentences in (13c) have the same logical structure
as the following sentences and have undergone an optional deletion:[5]

(18)   McGovern criticized Nixon for saying to the Knights of
Columbus what he said to them.
McGovern criticized Nixon for filling court vacancies on the
basis on which he fills them.
McGovern criticized Nixon for his economic policies failing
in the way in which they have failed.

I am not in a position to state exactly what this deletion rule does. The
rule, which I will refer to as TELESCOPING, applies to certain structures
in which a clause contains, roughly speaking, a nominalization of itself,
and deletes all of that clause but the nominalization. Telescoping has also
been noted in Elliott (1971), who observes that it is involved in exclamatory sentences such as

(19a)   It's amazing the books that John has read. (=... that John
has read the books that he has read)
(19b)   It's absurd the kind of things that I'm forced to put up with.
(=... that I'm forced to put up with the kind of things that
I'm forced to put up with).[6]

It is important to note that the possibility of Telescoping depends on the
linguistic context in which the clause in question is embedded:

(20)   I'm angry at Nixon because he said what he said.
I'm angry at Nixon despite his saying what he said.

I'm angry at Nixon as a result of his saying what he said.

I got angry at Nixon before/after he said what he said.

I was angry at Nixon until he said what he said.

I will be angry at Nixon as long as he makes appointments on the basis on which he makes them.

(21)   I'm angry at Nixon because of what he said.

I'm angry at Nixon despite what he said.

I'm angry at Nixon as a result of what he said.

*I got angry at Nixon before/after what he said.

*I was angry at Nixon until what he said.

*I will be angry at Nixon as long as the basis on which he makes appointments.

Since both *criticize* and *accuse* allow complements such as *Nixon said what he said*:

(22a)   McGovern accused Nixon$_i$ of saying what he$_i$ said.

(22b)   McGovern criticized Nixon$_i$ for saying what he$_i$ said.,

the problem which sentences (13c) and (14c) present is that of why only one of the two verbs allows Telescoping. Examples (20)–(21) suggest a conjecture: that Telescoping is permissible in a reason clause and that the complement of *criticize* (but not that of *accuse*) is a reason clause in logical structure, i.e. that the logical structure of (22b) is along the lines of 'McGovern said that Nixon is bad because Nixon said what Nixon said'.[7] I have at the moment no really strong support for this conjecture, but I note that Telescoping is possible in other complements which require an analysis as reason clauses[8], e.g.

(23)   I'm happy about what Nixon did. (=... about Nixon's doing what he did)

I'm annoyed at the attention you pay her. (=... at your paying her the attention that you pay her)

I'm distressed at the amount of time Harry spends in the pool hall. (=... at Harry's spending the amount of time in the pool hall that he does).

I thus have arrived at conjectures about the logical structures of clauses with *criticize* and *accuse* which appear to explain certain differences between those verbs which are not explained by Fillmore's analyses:

(24a) x criticize y for $S = x$ say (y is bad because S)
(24b) x accuse$_z$ y of $S = (x$ say$_z$ $S)$ and (become$_z$ (y in jeopardy))

(the subscript denotes the event in question; the double occurrence of z on the right side of (24b) means that the event of x's saying S is the same as (or includes) the event of y's coming to be in jeopardy). I do not mean to suggest that these formulas constitute a decomposition of the meanings of *accuse* and *criticize* into semantic primes; 'jeopardy', at least, is surely further decomposable. The fact that 'in jeopardy' is predicated of y in the decomposition of *accuse* but not that of *criticize* accounts for the restriction that the 'Defendant' of *accuse* but not of *criticize* must be a person: only a person (in the extended sense noted above) can be in jeopardy. One respect in which the above formulas may be inadequate is that they do not in themselves impose any restriction on the S. For example, there is nothing in (24b) which would rule out such non-sentences as

(25)   *McGovern accused the Republican Party that Nixon is irresponsible.
       *McGovern accused the Republican Party of Nixon's being irresponsible.

However, I am not sure that the ungrammaticality of (25) is due to characteristics of the meaning of *accuse* rather than to purely grammatical restrictions on what *accuse* may appear in combination with in surface structure. Note that *accusation* does not combine with the same material as does *accuse*, the verb that it apparently is a nominalization of:

(26a)   McGovern's accusation that Nixon is irresponsible (is well-founded).
(26a')   *McGovern accused that Nixon is irresponsible.
(26b)   McGovern accused Nixon of being irresponsible.
(26b')   *McGovern's accusation of Nixon of being irresponsible (is well-founded).

Note also that the accusation reported in (26a) need not be directed at Nixon but can perfectly well be directed at the Republican Party (which McGovern is accusing of nominating someone irresponsible). The discrepancy between what can appear in combination with *accuse* and what can appear in combination with its action nominalization, *accusation*, evidently involves an idiosyncratic restriction on one or the other or both of *accuse* and *accusation*, and the ground covered by the two of them appears to correspond to (24b) without any restriction such as that y be the subject of S.

I turn now to some of the other verbs that Fillmore discussed. Fillmore states that *credit* and *praise* are positive counterparts of *accuse* and *criticize* respectively, i.e. that they have the same semantic structure as *accuse* and *criticize* except for having 'GOOD' where *accuse* and *criticize* have 'BAD'[9]. If that is the case, then to the extent that syntactic properties of words are predictable from their semantic structure plus general rules of grammar, *credit* and *praise* should behave syntactically like *accuse* and *criticize*. It in fact is the case that much of what I said above about *accuse* and *criticize* is also true of *credit* and *praise* respectively. For example,

(27)   Nixon praised Agnew$_i$ for
- *wisdom
- his$_i$ wisdom
- ?Laird's wisdom
- the fact that he$_i$ has threatened reporters
- what he$_i$ said to Queen Elizabeth
- the basis on which he$_i$ picks his speech writers.

(28)   Nixon credited Agnew$_i$ with
- wisdom
- *his$_i$ wisdom
- *Laird's wisdom[10]
- *the fact that he$_i$ has threatened reporters
- *what he$_i$ said to Queen Elizabeth
- *the basis on which he$_i$ picks his speech writers.

Also, *praise* is like *criticize* and *credit* like *accuse* with respect to the interpretation of a sentence lacking an overtly expressed 'Situation'. Fillmore has noted that (29a) is normal even in a context which does not specify any grounds for the criticism, but (29b) is normal only when it refers to a specific offense already under discussion:

JAMES D. MCCAWLEY

(29a)   Max criticized Arthur. (=Max criticized Arthur for some-
                thing.
                ≠Max criticized Arthur for it.)
(29b)   Max accused Arthur. (=Max accused Arthur of it.
                ≠Max accused Arthur of something.)

The same is true, mutatis mutandis, of (30a) and (30b):

(30a)   Max praised Arthur. (=Max praised Arthur for something.
                ≠Max praised Arthur for it.)
(30b)   Max credited Arthur.(=Max credited Arthur with it.
                ≠Max credited Arthur with some-
                thing.)

If the conjectures I made above about the semantic structure of *criticize*
and *accuse* are to be consistent with the claim that they are the negative
counterparts of *praise* and *credit*, then 'BAD' must appear in the semantic
structure of 'jeopardy' and the logical structure of clauses with *praise* and
credit must be roughly

(31a) x praise y for S=x say (y is good because of S).
(31b) x credit$_z$ y with S=(x say$_z$ S) and (become$_z$ (y in schmeo-
                pardy)),

where 'schmeopardy' is what results from replacing 'BAD' by 'GOOD'
in the logical structure of 'jeopardy'. I find this highly implausible. The
closest thing to a positive counterpart to 'being in jeopardy' that I can
think of is a situation where you are assured of receiving some blessing if
you don't screw up, e.g. you will get tenure if you don't offend any
administrators. However, crediting you with something does not normally
put you in that sort of situation.

    I am accordingly led to inquire whether *credit* behaves like a positive
counterpart to *accuse* with respect to the examples which were supposed
to show that the notion of 'jeopardy' had to be part of the analysis of
accuse. Here the two verbs turn out to differ. *Credit*, unlike *accuse*, does
not require that the 'Defendant' be a person:

(32a)   *Mencken accused *Lohengrin* of being too long.
           Shaw credited *Lohengrin* with having beautiful choruses.

(32b)   *Tom accused the number 17 of having brought him bad luck.
        Tom credited the number 38 with having brought him good
        luck.

(32c)   *Max accused his belief in Taoism of breaking up his marriage.
        Max credited his belief in Jainism with improving his golf score.

This means that *credit* isn't quite a positive counterpart to my analysis of
accuse.[11] However, it isn't quite a positive counterpart to Fillmore's
analysis of *accuse* either, since it can be shown not to have a presupposition that the 'Situation' is good, in just the same way that *accuse* was
shows not to have a presupposition that the 'Situation' is bad:

(33)   Mayor Daley$_i$ credited me with saving his$_i$ life and promised
        to reward me by taking me to Mike Royko and crediting me
        with refusing to save his$_i$ life.

I have not as yet isolated the respect in which the meaning of *credit* fails to
be a positive counterpart to the meaning of *accuse*. I have a gut feeling
that the answer is intimately connected with the analysis of the notion of
'jeopardy', but I have not yet got any concrete results out of that gut
feeling.

I now turn to the three senses of *blame* which Fillmore discusses,
namely *blame*$_1$ 'shift the blame onto', *blame*$_2$ 'hold culpable', and *blame*$_3$
'think guilty', as illustrated by

(34a)   Phil put a bomb in the governor's office and then blamed$_1$ it
        on mé.

(34b)   Jack blámed$_2$ me for writing that letter.
        I don't bláme$_2$ you.

(34c)   Bert blamed$_3$ mé for what had happened.

I will henceforth ignore *blame*$_1$ and concentrate on *blame*$_2$ and *blame*$_3$.
Fillmore's analyses of *blame*$_2$ and *blame*$_3$ are as follows:

(35a)

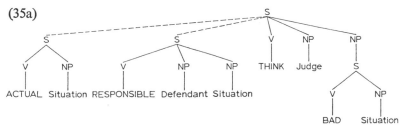

(35b)

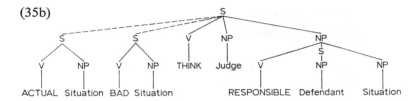

For Fillmore *blame₂* and *blame₃* thus differ only with respect to which clauses are assigned to 'presupposition' and which to 'meaning' in the narrow sense. There is thus nothing in these analyses which would imply any difference between *blame₂* and *blame₃* as to what can function as the 'Situation'. It turns out, however, that there is considerable difference as to what they allow as 'Situation':

(36)   Do you $\left\{\begin{array}{l}\text{bláme}_2\text{ me}\\ \text{*blame}_3\text{ mé}\end{array}\right\}$ for $\left\{\begin{array}{l}\text{killing/murdering Sally?}\\ \text{drinking all the beer?}\\ \text{saying something nasty to}\\ \text{Kissinger?}\\ \text{getting angry at Spiro?}\\ \text{being angry/disappointed?}\\ \text{wanting to kill Nixon?}\end{array}\right.$

(37)   Do you $\left\{\begin{array}{l}\text{blame}_3\text{ mé}\\ \text{*bláme}_2\text{ me}\end{array}\right\}$ for $\left\{\begin{array}{l}\text{the/Sally's murder?}\\ \text{Sally's death?}\\ \text{the predicament that we're in?}\\ \text{Cuba's going communist?}\\ \text{the fact that Cuba went com-}\\ \text{munist?}\\ \text{John's killing Sally?}\end{array}\right.$

Blame₃ is indeed the only verb I have discussed so far whose 'Situation' really has to be a situation (as opposed to e.g. an action), and indeed allows a NP whose head is the word *situation*:

(38) $\left\{\begin{array}{l}\text{I don't blame}_3\text{ yóu for}\\ \text{*I don't bláme}_2\text{ you for}\\ \text{*I accused him of}\\ \text{?*I criticized him for}\\ \text{?*I praised him for}\\ \text{*I credited him with}\end{array}\right\}$ the situation that we're in.

Also, *blame₂* but not *blame₃* requires that 'Defendant' be a person:

(39a)   I blăme₃ the high cost of líving for Max's suicide.

       *I bláme₂ the high cost of living for $\begin{cases} \text{causing Max to commit} \\ \text{suicide.} \\ \text{driving many shops out} \\ \text{of business.} \end{cases}$

(39b)   Nixon blămes₃ the lack of support from the Démocrats for the failure of his fiscal policy.
    *Nixon blámes₂ the lack of support from the Democrats for causing his fiscal policy to fail.

The facts given so far are perfectly consistent with Fillmore's analysis of *blame₃*, provided 'RESPONSIBLE' is taken in the sense of *responsible for* which is the converse of *attributable to*. Note that sentences with *blame₃* appear to have exact paraphrases with *responsible for*:

(40a)   Janet blames₃ the high cost of living for Phil's suicide.
    Janet thinks that the high cost living is responsible for Phil's suicide.

(40b)   Sam blames₃ the steel plant for the dirt on his windows.
    Sam thinks that the steel plant is responsible for the dirt on his windows.

With *blame₂*, there is a restriction which does not follow from Fillmore's analysis, namely that the 'Situation' must be an act or a controllable state on the part of the 'Defendant'. One revision in Fillmore's analysis which would account for that restriction is to replace BAD [Situation] with the semantic material that corresponds to a sentence like *It was bad of you to drink all the beer* or *You were bad to drink all the beer*. Note that the *bad* of *bad of* or *bad*+Infinitive allows the kinds of items that appear with *blame₂* in (36) and excludes items corresponding to those which *blame₂* excludes in (37):

(41a)   It was bad of Tom $\begin{cases} \text{to drink all the beer.} \\ \text{to get angry at Spiro.} \\ \text{to want to kill Nixon.} \\ \text{*for Sally to die.} \\ \text{*for us to be in this predicament.} \\ \text{*for Cuba to go communist.} \end{cases}$

(41b)   Tom was bad
$$\begin{cases} \text{to drink all the beer.} \\ \text{to get angry at Spiro.} \\ \text{to want to kill Nixon.} \\ \text{*for Sally to die.} \\ \text{*for us to be in this predicament.} \\ \text{*for Cuba to go communist.} \end{cases}$$

Furthermore, sentences with *blame*₂ appear to be paraphrasable by sentences with *bad of* but not by sentences in which *bad* is predicated of a 'Situation', e.g. (42a) is paraphrased by (42b), but is not even implied by, let alone paraphrased by, (42c):

(42a)   Sheila blámes₂ Tom for drinking all the beer.
(42b)   Sheila thinks it was bad of Tom to drink all the beer.
        Sheila thinks Tom was bad to drink all the beer.
(42c)   Sheila thinks it is/was bad that Tom drank all the beer.

She can think *it* was bad without thinking that *he* was bad. I thus maintain that (43) is a closer approximation than (35a) to the meaning of a clause with *blame*₂, where BAD' is the binary relation between a person and an act or controllable state of his which is expressed by *bad of* or by *bad +* Infinitive:

(43)

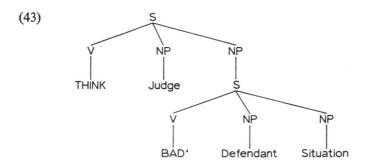

BAD' is of course surely decomposable into more basic elements, but I do not yet have a decomposition that I am happy with. Since it is BAD' that is responsible for the presuppositions that the 'Situation' is actual and that the 'Defendant' is responsible for the 'Situation', the omission of those presuppositions from (43) is justified, though they may well have to appear explicitly in the decomposition of BAD': until I have a viabel analysis of BAD', I cannot tell whether those presuppositions are predictable from the 'meaning' in the narrow sense or are idiosyncratic additions to the latter.

Since I have little in the way of conclusions, let me conclude this paper with a pep talk instead. The most widely quoted point in Fillmore's paper is the claim that verbs can differ as to whether semantic material that they contain is a presupposition or part of the 'meaning' in the narrow sense. I have shown above that the supposed examples of such differences given in Fillmore's paper really differ in some respect(s) other than that of which parts of their content are assigned to presupposition. They thus do not show presuppositions to be as idiosyncratic a part of meaning as they had initially appeared to, but they still leave quite open the important question of the extent to which presuppositions can constitute differences among words of a language. Certain presuppositions are predictable from other parts of the meanings of sentences in which they are involved; this, for example, is the case with those presuppositions whose violation constitutes a 'category mistake', e.g.

(44a)   *I poured sesame oil over August 13. [presupposition that locus of pouring is a physical object]
(44b)   *Gödel has proved the universal quantifier. [presupposition that what is proved is a proposition]

On the other hand, it is clear that some presuppositions are distinctive parts of the meaning. For example, the difference between blame₃, the mental-state sense of credit mentioned in note 9, and attribute seems to be the presence of a presupposition that the thing in question is bad, a presupposition that it is good, or neither of those presuppositions; Similarly, German schwanger and trächtig appear to have the same meaning ('pregnant') and to differ in that schwanger carries a presupposition that the subject is human and trächtig a presupposition that the subject is not human. However, I am willing to wager that a huge range of conceivable presuppositions cannot function distinctively in lexical items, e.g. that no language can have word meaning 'pregnant' which carries a presupposition that the subject is dark-haired or a word meaning 'praise' which carries a presupposition that the subject is of the same sex as the speaker. I thus am fairly convinced that the possibility of words in a language having distinctive presuppositions exists but is fairly heavily restricted. I have looked in sufficient depth at so few words that I have no hint to offer as to what those restrictions are. Finding out something about them will be an important step towards understanding the role which presuppositions can play in the lexicon of a language and in logical structure in general.

University of Chicago

NOTES

[1] I have put 'Defendant' before 'Situation' in accordance with the other occurrences of RESPONSIBLE in Fillmore's formulas. I take it that the reverse order of 'Defendant' and 'Situation' in the formula that he gave for *accuse* is a mistake.

[2] See McCawley (1972) and Lakoff (1972) for elaboration of the conception of grammar and logic to which this sentence refers.

[3] When necessary I will use paired subscripts to indicate the intended antecedent of a pronoun.

[4] There actually is a case in which (11a–c) could be used in normal discourse, though one which is irrelevant to the question under discussion, namely that they could be used to report criticisms of the choice of wisdom, 17, etc. for some purpose, e.g. criticizing the choice of 17 hexagons as part of the design of a flag on the grounds that 17 is an unlucky number. In this case it is the act of choosing 17 rather than the number 17 itself which is the 'Defendant'.

[5] (18) are ambiguous as to the scope of the definite description. The interpretation of (18) which is relevant here is that in which the definite description has the whole sentence as its scope, i.e. roughly 'the x for which Nixon said x to the Knights of Columbus is such that McGovern criticized Nixon for saying x to the Knights of Columbus'.

[6] Telescoping is also relevant to a current controversy about the syntax of nominalizations. Chomsky (1970: 217) finds implausible any derivation of *Einstein's intelligence* from a source containing the sentence *Einstein is/was intelligent*. He does not state his objections explicitly, but what he says suggests the objection that the most obvious sources, namely *the fact that S* and *the extent to which S*, are not synonymous with the nominalization under discussion, i.e.

(i)   The fact that Einstein was intelligent was his most remarkable property.
(ii)   The extent to which Einstein was intelligent was his most remarkable property.

are not paraphrases of

(iii)   Einstein's intelligence was his most remarkable property.

The following, however, appear to be exact paraphrases of (iii):

(iv)   The fact that Einstein was as intelligent as he was was his most remarkable property.
         The fact that Einstein was intelligent to the extent that he was was his most remarkable property.

Actually, (ii) can be used with this sense. Chomsky's discussion assumes a really literal reading of (ii), in which it is the extent or degree of intelligence possessed by Einstein (e.g. 210 IQ points, if you accept that as an extent of intelligence) of which 'his most remarkable property' is being predicated, and he accordingly marks it as ungrammatical. I see no objection to deriving (iii) from a structure which combines factive nominalization and extent nominalization, as in (iv), by steps one of which is Telescoping.

[7] This proposal obliterates the distinction between *criticize* and *denounce*. Since *denounce* and *criticize* are syntactically identical as far as I can determine, I conjecture that the difference between their meanings is simply the kind or degree of 'badness' that is attributed to the 'Defendant'.

[8] See Akatsuka (1972) for reasons why the complement of *happy*, etc. must be analysed as an underlying reason clause.

[9] *Credit* is ambiguous between a sense referring to a linguistic act and a sense referring to a mental state:

> Every time Nixon makes a speech, he credits Agnew with being a great statesman.
> I have always credited Agnew with being a great statesman, but this is the first time I have admitted that I feel that way about him.

That these are two distinct senses (as opposed to two stituations in which a single sense of *credit* is applicable) is shown by the fact that syntactic phenomena such as pronominalization with *so* or deletion of repeated verb phrases respect this difference:

> *Secretly I have always credited Agnew with being a great statesman, and I am delighted that Nixon did so in his speech last night.

In what follows, I have restricted my attention to the 'linguistic act' sense of *credit*.

[10] The asterisk refers only to the intended interpretation, in which the NP can be paraphrased '(the fact) that Laird is wise'. It is grammatical with another interpretation, namely 'Nixon credited Agnew with having the (degree/kind of) wisdom that Laird has'. This last fact brings out a difference between *credit* and *accuse* for which I have no explanation, namely that *credit* much more easily allows the deletion of *have* before objects like *Laird's wisdom* than *accuse* does, i.e. only marginally can I admit a sentence like

> *Chomsky accused Nixon of Hitler's inhumanity.

with the interpretation 'Chomsky accused Nixon of having the (kind/degree of) inhumanity that Hitler had'.

[11] In addition, there is no nominalization of *credit* which works anything like *accusation*:

> *Nixon's credit that Agnew is a great statesman is well-founded.

BIBLIOGRAPHY

Akatsuka, Noriko: 1972, 'Emotive Verbs in English and Japanese', *Studies in the Linguistic Sciences* **2**, No. 1, 1–16.
Austin, J. L.: 1962, *How to Do Things with Words*, Oxford University Press, New York and London.

Chomsky, Noam A.: 1970, 'Remarks on Nominalization', In Jacobs and Rosenbaum (eds.), *Readings in English Transformational Grammar*, Ginn-Blaisdell, Boston, pp. 184–221.

Elliott, Dale: 1971, 'The Grammar of Emotive and Exclamatory Sentences in English', *Ohio State Working Papers in Linguistics* 8, 1–110.

Fillmore, Charles J.: 1971, 'Verbs of Judging: an Exercise in Semantic Description', In Fillmore and Langendoen (eds.), *Studies in Linguistic Semantics*, Holt, Rinehart and Winston, New York, pp. 272–89.

Lakoff, George: 1972, 'Linguistics and Natural Logic', In Davidson and Harman (eds.), *Semantics of Natural Language*, Reidel, Dordrecht, pp. 545–665.

McCawley, James D.: 1972, 'A Program for Logic', in Davidson and Harman (*op. cit.*), 498–544.

Vendler, Zeno: 1972, *Res Cogitans*, Cornell University Press, Ithaca.

THE UNIVERSITY OF WESTERN ONTARIO
SERIES IN PHILOSOPHY OF SCIENCE

A Series of Books on Philosophy of Science, Methodology, and Epistemology
published in connection with
the University of Western Ontario Philosophy of Science Programme

1. J. LEACH, R. BUTTS, and G. PEARCE (eds.), *Science, Decision and Value*. Proceedings of the Fifth University of Western Ontario Philosophy Colloquium, 1969, 1973, vii+213 pp.
2. C. A. HOOKER (ed.), *Contemporary Research in the Foundations and Philosophy of Quantum Theory*. Proceedings of a Conference held at the University of Western Ontario, London, Canada, 1973. xx+385 pp.
3. J. BUB, *The Interpretation of Quantum Mechanics*. 1974, ix+155 pp.